BEYOND THE FRACKING WARS

A Guide for Lawyers, Public Officials, Planners, and Citizens

ERICA LEVINE POWERS AND
BETH E. KINNE, EDITORS

Section of State and
Local Government Law

AMERICAN BAR ASSOCIATION

Cover by Monica Alejo/ABA Publishing.

The materials contained herein represent the views of each chapter author in his or her individual capacity and should not be construed as the views of the author's firm, employer, or clients, or of the editors or other chapter authors, or of the American Bar Association or the Section of State and Local Government Law unless adopted pursuant to the bylaws of the Association.

Printed in the United States of America

17 16 15 14   5 4 3 2

Library of Congress Cataloging-in-Publication Data

Beyond the fracking wars / edited by Erica Levine Powers and Beth E. Kinne. — First edition.
    pages cm
Includes bibliographical references and index.
    ISBN 978-1-62722-163-4 (print : alk. paper)
    1. Hydraulic fracturing—Law and legislation—United States. I. Powers, Erica Levine, editor of compilation. II. Kinne, Beth, editor of compilation. III. American Bar Association. Section of State and Local Government Law, sponsoring body.
    KF1849.A2B49 2013
    343.7307'72—dc23

                                                                        2013036889

Discounts are available for books ordered in bulk. Special consideration is given to state bars, CLE programs, and other bar-related organizations. Inquire at ABA Publishing, American Bar Association, 321 North Clark Street, Chicago, Illinois 60654-7598.

www.ShopABA.org

For Llew
E.L.P.

For Rowan, Linnea, and Calla
B.E.K.

Summary of Contents

Contents

Foreword

The publication of *Beyond the Fracking Wars* by the American Bar Association will add to the dialogue about whether the United States should embrace the development of hydrocarbons that have been trapped within underground shale formations. The publication coincides with the recent death of George Mitchell, the owner and founder of Mitchell Oil & Gas Co., who is widely regarded as one of the most important, if not the most important, "father" of the development of unconventional shale oil and gas deposits in the United States. Through his vision and the commitment of the resources of his production company, Mr. Mitchell showed the world that unconventional shale oil and gas deposits could be technologically and economically developed. His efforts to produce shale gas in the Barnett Shale reservoir in North Texas opened the way for widespread shale development in the United States as well as in the rest of the world.

The development of unconventional shale oil and gas is the product of the refinement of technologies that have been widely used in the oil and gas industry for nearly 80 years. Hydraulic fracturing has been regularly employed in conventional oil and gas fields since the 1940s. Injecting fluids, and/or gases in order to increase the productivity of oil and gas wells is an even older technology, dating back to the use of nitroglycerin in the oil fields of the Appalachian Basin in the early part of the 20th century. Likewise, the refinement of horizontal drilling techniques that have been around for decades has allowed oil and gas producers to extend horizontal laterals for several miles, thus allowing greater production from the shale formation. All of these technological developments were harnessed by Mr. Mitchell to prove to the skeptical oil and gas community that unconventional shale oil and gas deposits could be developed. In the 8 or 9 years following the successes of Mitchell Oil & Gas in the Barnett Shale, unconventional shale oil and gas production is fast becoming the predominant source of hydrocarbon production in the United States.

A look at the widely disseminated Energy Information Administration's map of shale plays in the United States is illustrative of the public policy issues that will face us in the coming decades. Many states that did not have an active and vibrant oil and gas industry are now contemplating such development, with its attendant externalities, both positive and negative. Given our well-deserved attention to the issue of global warming, carbon footprints, and continued dependence on fossil fuels to provide much of the world's energy needs, the development of shale oil and gas resources is not a risk-free alternative. Furthermore, unconventional shale oil and gas development, as with any other industrial or extractive activity, has environmental impacts that need to be addressed. *Beyond the Fracking Wars* attempts to educate the reader about such choices and how both governmental and nongovernmental organizations, as well as the industry, are trying to resolve these critically important public policy concerns.

The understanding of basic oil and gas law principles is a necessary starting point to understand shale oil and gas development in the United States. In contrast with most of the rest of the world, the United States recognizes private ownership of mineral resources and further allows that the mineral estate may be "severed" from the surface estate into two coequal estates. This creates a basic tension between surface and mineral owners where the surface owner is receiving no financial benefits from the exploitation of the mineral estate, yet is burdened by an easement that allows the mineral owner or its lessee to use the surface estate to access the minerals. Because of the private ownership of the mineral estate, development or nondevelopment decisions are made by individuals who need to balance the benefits and harms of such development on a micro and not a macro basis. Additionally since both the United States and state constitutions protect private property interests from being taken without the payment of just compensation, regulatory programs seeking to achieve macro public-policy objectives must consider the potential for constitutional limits on such programs.

Where the government owns the minerals, as it does over a significant portion of the western United States and throughout the rest of the world, the decisions to control or limit development are made by the appropriate governmental authority and are more likely to consider broader public-policy factors than when such decisions are made by private property owners. Nonetheless, given the experience of the Bureau of Land Management's (BLM) lengthy rulemaking process relating to the use of hydraulic fracturing on public lands in the United States, it is not clear that governmental ownership of the minerals will necessarily lead to a "rational" decision-making process. BLM is the principal federal agency dealing with oil and gas development on public lands, including the national forests. BLM management of both the surface and mineral estates over the past 100 years is marked by inconsistent and changing policy decisions, off-again and on-again mandates from Congress, and distrust from all of the stakeholders in public land management decisions.

Unconventional shale oil and gas resource development creates a number of conflicts, including the one mentioned above regarding the interests of severed surface and mineral owners. One basic issue is whether or not such resources should be exploited at all. France and Vermont as well as a number of sub-state governmental units have opted for the no-development choice. New York has prohibited hydraulic fracturing operations for nearly 5 years as it explores the benefits and costs of such development. In the United States where private ownership of minerals is the norm, the rule of capture essentially deprives a mineral owner of the no-develop option because that owner's minerals may be drained into a neighbor's wellbore without liability. By contrast, where you have national ownership of mineral resources, including oil and gas, development of the resources, at least in theory, can be planned so as to maximize the total amount of recovered hydrocarbons in the most economically efficient manner while also taking into account other public policy considerations, such as environmental protection, impact on indigenous peoples, and lack of appropriate infrastructure.

Due to the negative externalities associated with a rule of capture ownership regime, states began to regulate oil and gas activities starting in the latter part of the 19th century. By the early part of the 20th century, most states had adopted minimum well-spacing requirements and compulsory pooling and unitization statutes in order to prevent the over-drilling and loss of reservoir pressure that accompanied the rule of capture ownership regime. These statutes were designed to prevent waste, protect correlative rights, and conserve natural resources. As applied to conventional vertical wells that drained substantial acreage typically in a circular pattern from the wellbore, such conservation programs led to more efficient development even in the face of a nonconsenting mineral owner's choice not to have its minerals developed. With the widespread use of horizontal wells, however, the existence of nonconsenting owners creates more difficult technological and/or economic problems with development since it is very expensive and inefficient for horizontal wellbores to make turns in order to avoid encroaching upon the lands of the nonconsenting owner. State regulatory schemes have been slow to change from a vertical well mindset to the horizontal well reality of unconventional shale oil and gas development that can, in turn, make such development less efficient.

Unconventional shale oil and gas development has also created or exacerbated conflicts between different levels of government in the United States. Other than lands owned by the federal government, the United States has been a minor player in the regulation of the exploration and production of oil and gas. Through the Natural Gas Act and various subsequent statutory enactments, the United States has been the principal regulator of downstream activities including transportation and storage of natural gas. Preemption issues have arisen over time relating to state regulation that invades the province of federal regulation. With unconventional shale oil and gas development, the principal conflict point appears to be with the Federal Energy Regulatory Commission's power to license the import and export of liquefied natural gas (LNG) as well as its licensing power to authorize the construction of LNG import or export facilities. Those debates are just now starting but they are likely to become more intense in the future since there is no consensus on the impact of allowing LNG exports on the domestic natural gas market. Additionally, other federal statutes have created exemptions from federal regulatory programs, such as the Safe Drinking Water Act, and they come into play when you are engaged in unconventional shale oil and gas development. Whether these exemptions get repealed, modified, or continued will undoubtedly impact state and sub-state regulation of such development.

Historically, state oil and gas conservation agencies have been the principal regulator of upstream oil and gas operations that include the exploration for, and production of, oil and gas. Nonetheless, sub-state governmental units have, for nearly 100 years, also been involved in regulating oil and gas operations. The first statutory pooling regulation was adopted by a pair of municipalities in Kansas in the 1910s to deal with the surface impact of the development of oil and gas on residential lots. Communities in Oklahoma and Texas have been applying their zoning regulations to oil and gas operations for more than 50 years. However, with the shale oil and gas development boom of the past several years, sub-state units have been much more actively engaged in regulating oil and gas operations, including having both temporary and permanent moratoria placed on such operations. Sub-state governmental units can also attempt to regulate through the imposition of performance standards, the most prevalent being setback requirements for wells and/or well pads. These types of regulatory programs usually entail a permit requirement that may be discretionary in nature. Thus merely because an oil and gas operator has a drilling permit issued by the state oil and gas conservation agency does not necessarily mean that the operator can drill at the permitted location. This tension between state and sub-state units is often resolved through the courts by the application of the three principal preemption doctrines—express preemption, implied preemption by occupation of the field, and implied preemption by conflict.

State legislatures historically have enacted legislation that expressly preempts sub-state units from regulating. This power is a subset of the generally accepted view that—subject to state constitutional limitations, such as prohibitions against the enactment of local laws, and home rule provisions—sub-state units are the "creatures" of the state. Exercise of this express preemption power, however, has been reasonably rare and when so exercised has often been limited as to specific units of local government or as to certain types of regulation. Only Louisiana and Ohio appear to have broad express preemption provisions while Kansas and Wyoming have more limited express preemption provisions. The Pennsylvania Legislature, which recently attempted to more clearly define the preemptive powers of the Commonwealth, has been thwarted by an opinion of the Pennsylvania Commonwealth Court invalidating the key provisions of the statute. At the time of the publication of this foreword, the Pennsylvania Supreme Court has not issued an opinion on the validity of that statute.

Even though all of the other oil and gas producing states do not have express preemption provisions, courts may still find preemption through two judicially-crafted doctrines. The first is the implied preemption by occupation of the field doctrine and the second is the implied preemption by conflict doctrine. Both require judicial determinations of the "implied" intent of the legislature to preempt sub-state unit powers in the absence of an express provision. The results of the application of these two doctrines to oil and gas operations have been inconsistent at best, depending on ad hoc analyses of ordinances, statutes, and regulations.

Beyond the Fracking Wars tries to inform the readers of many, but not all, of the potential issues, conflicts, and processes involved in the development of unconventional shale oil and gas resources. It is an invaluable resource for anyone who is concerned about such development. The editors, the contributors, and the ABA Section of State and Local Government Law are to be applauded for their efforts to educate lawyers, public officials, planners, and the public about the myriad issues that surround unconventional shale oil and gas development.

Bruce M. Kramer
Maddox Professor of Law Emeritus
Texas Tech University School of Law
Thompson Visiting Professor
University of Colorado Law School

About the Editors

Erica Levine Powers is a land use and environmental lawyer with a strong interest in transitional and alternative energy. She first became involved in land use and environmental law in 1980 as an appointed volunteer member of the Concord (MA) Natural Resources Commission and incorporated this interest into her law practice.

A *cum laude* graduate of Harvard College in Modern European History and Literature (1965), she holds J.D. (1971) and LL.M. in Taxation (1976) degrees from Boston University School of Law. Initially counsel to the Massachusetts Commissioner of Banks and then a corporate transactional lawyer at Gaston Snow & Ely Bartlett, Boston (MA), she served as counsel to the Deputy Mayor/Collector Treasurer of the City of Boston and as General Counsel to the Massachusetts Department of Food & Agriculture. She is admitted in Massachusetts, Maryland, and New York, and resides in Albany, New York.

Her university-level teaching, including sabbatical coverage at the University of Iowa, Iowa State University, Cornell University, and Massey University in New Zealand, reflects and draws on the depth and breadth of her law practice. As a lecturer at the University at Albany (SUNY) for five years, she taught law and environmental planning courses in the Master in Regional Planning program in the Department of Geography and Planning, where she developed an environmental planning seminar on hydraulic fracturing in the Marcellus Shale. On a national level, she has participated in panels and webinars on natural gas exploration and hydraulic fracturing for the American Bar Association, the American Planning Association, and the Institute for Energy Law. She writes on land use and transportation, as well as natural gas exploration and development.

In the ABA's Section of State and Local Government Law, she is editor of the quarterly *State and Local Law News* and serves on the Publications Oversight Board and the Land Use Committee. In the New York State Bar Association, she co-chairs the Committee on Coastal and Wetland Resources of the Environmental Law Section.

Beth E. Kinne is an Assistant Professor of Environmental Studies at Hobart and William Smith Colleges, in Geneva, New York, where she teaches environmental law, natural resource law, global water issues, and business law. She also teaches the senior capstone course for majors in environmental studies, with a recent focus on understanding and communicating the complex issues surrounding the development of the Marcellus Shale in New York State. In July 2011, she co-chaired a conference, *Proactive Approaches to Mitigating Impacts of Marcellus Shale Development*, at the Finger Lakes Institute, Hobart and William Smith Colleges. She is currently guest-editing a special issue, on the Marcellus Shale, of the *Journal of Environmental Studies and Science*.

Before joining the Hobart and William Smith faculty, she worked as a municipal and water rights attorney in Garfield County, Colorado from 2005 to 2008. She is admitted to practice in Washington State, Colorado, and New York. She serves on the Board of Trustees of the National Youth Science Foundation.

She holds a bachelor's degree in biology from the University of Virginia, a master of science degree in resource management and environmental studies from the University of British Columbia, and a J.D. and LL.M. in Asian and comparative law from the University of Washington, where she served as Development Director for the Pacific Rim Law and Policy Review. While completing her LL.M., she spent a year in China studying Chinese on a Blakemore-Freeman fellowship and researching the development of water rights law in China.

About the Contributors

Jill D. Cantway is an attorney with Bjork Lindley Little PC, a Denver, Colorado, law firm where, since 2005, she has specialized in oil and gas title law, oil and gas conveyances, and other property matters. She is a member of the Bar in Colorado and Wyoming and holds a Bachelor of Arts in International Relations from Colgate University. She received her J.D., *cum laude*, along with a Certificate in Environmental and Natural Resources Law, from Lewis & Clark Law School in Portland, Oregon, where she was also a member of the editorial board of *Environmental Law*.

Christopher Denton practices oil and gas law in upstate New York with extensive experience in New York State's Compulsory Integration law. He is the co-creator of the Atlantic States Legal Foundation. As the co-founder of the landowner coalition movement in upstate New York, he represents over 5000 families who own over 250,000 acres of land. He was the first attorney in New York State to employ an interdisciplinary approach when representing landowners by teaming with a geologist, a pipeline specialist, an environmental scientist, a CPA, and a field operations specialist. He has given seminars and lectures on oil and gas leasing around New York State since 1999 to educate landowners and farmers about the benefits and pitfalls of leasing mineral rights. He also teaches New York CLE courses concerning pipeline rights of way and oil and gas leasing in New York State, and serves as an adjunct instructor of oil and gas law at Elmira College. He earned his B.A. from Dartmouth College in 1972, and his J.D., with honors, from Syracuse College of Law in 1977.

R. Kinnan Golemon is the founder and President of KG Strategies, LLC, in Austin, Texas. He has provided professional advice, counsel, strategic planning, and public advocacy on complex environmental, energy, and natural resources issues for more than 45 years, including 15 years of service as General Counsel for the Texas Chemical Council. He represents the largest shale oil and gas producer in the Barnett Shale Play, Devon Energy, and Shell Oil Company, another significant shale oil and gas producer. He has held numerous leadership positions in the American Bar Association Section of Environment, Energy, and Resources Law (SEER), including Section Chair 1994–95. He was a SEER delegate to the ABA House of Delegates from 2000 to 2009 and the SEER representative to the ABA Board of Governors from 2009 to 2012. He was inducted as an Initial Fellow in American College of Environmental Lawyers (ACOEL) in 2008. He serves on the Advisory Board of the Center for Global Energy, International Arbitration and Environment at the University of Texas School of Law and also as a member of Constellation's Public Sector Energy Advisory Board. He earned a B.S. in Industrial Management Engineering from the University of Oklahoma in 1961 and an LL.B. from the University of Texas School of Law in 1967.

Benjamin E. Griffith is a partner in the Cleveland, Mississippi, firm of Griffith & Griffith. He earned a B.A. in English and German from the University of Mississippi in 1973 and his J.D. in 1975 from the University of Mississippi School of Law. His practice concentrates on federal and state civil litigation, voting rights and election law, public sector insurance coverage, and environmental law. He is a Section Delegate to the ABA House of Delegates, Chair of the ABA Standing Committee on Election Law, and Chair of the International Steering Committee of the International Municipal Lawyers Association. He served as Chair of ABA Section of State & Local Government Law, World Jurist Association's National President for the United States, President of the National Association of County Civil Attorneys, and Chair of the Government Law Section of Mississippi Bar. He has contributed chapters to numerous publications in his field of practice, and was recognized by his peers for inclusion in Best Lawyers In America® from 2007 through 2013 in the field of Municipal Law and in Mid-South Super Lawyers® from 2007 through 2013 in Government/Municipalities.

Charles C. Grubb recently retired as Parish Attorney for Caddo Parish, Louisiana, where he served from 2002 until August 2013. Caddo Parish includes the largest urban area impacted by the Haynesville Shale, one of the world's most prolific sources of natural gas. During his tenure as Parish Attorney, the parish was proactive in crafting regulations enabling the developers of the Haynesville Shale and private citizens to co-exist peacefully. He served as City Attorney for Shreveport, Louisiana, from 1978 through 1982 and again from 1986 until

1990. He currently maintains a law practice limited to state and local government law in Shreveport. A graduate of Tulane Law School (1971), he earned a B.S. degree in government from Centenary College of Louisiana. He has served as President of both the Louisiana City Attorneys Association and Louisiana Parish Attorneys Association. In 2010, he received the International Municipal Lawyers Association's Joseph I. Mulligan, Jr., Distinguished Public Service Award.

Suedeen Kelly is a partner with Akin Gump Strauss Hauer & Feld, where she co-chairs the Energy Regulatory, Enforcement and Markets Practice. She is an internationally recognized energy industry expert and two-term Commissioner with the Federal Energy Regulatory Commission (FERC). Ms. Kelly's knowledge of the national electricity and natural gas industries includes significant experience in infrastructure development and operation, market structures, and financial products. In addition to her time at FERC, Ms. Kelly served as regulatory counsel for the California Independent System Operator; as a law professor at the University of New Mexico School of Law; as legislative aide to Sen. Jeff Bingaman (D-NM), when he was the ranking member of the Senate Energy & Natural Resources Committee; and as chairwoman and commissioner for the New Mexico Public Service Commission. She has worked in the private practice of law in New Mexico and Washington, D.C., law firms, and as an attorney for the Natural Resources Defense Council. She earned a B.A., with distinction, from the University of Rochester in 1973 and a J.D., *cum laude*, from Cornell Law School in 1976.

Chad J. Lee is an attorney with Balcomb & Green, P.C., in Glenwood Springs, Colorado, where, since 2008, he has specialized in oil and gas, business, water, and real estate matters. From 2005 to 2008 he practiced law with another Colorado firm. He holds a B.S. in Wildlife Biology from the University of Nebraska and received his J.D., *cum laude*, from Lewis & Clark Law School in Portland, Oregon. While at Lewis & Clark, Chad was a member of the editorial board of *Environmental Law*. He is licensed to practice in Colorado and Wyoming.

Richard A. Liroff is founder and Executive Director of the Investor Environmental Health Network, a group of investment advisors and managers working to reduce the "toxic footprint" of businesses—their production and use of toxic chemicals. With Green Century Capital

Management in Boston, Massachusetts, he leads investor efforts to promote increased disclosure by energy companies so as to reduce the environmental and business risks of hydraulic fracturing operations for unconventional reserves. He is principal author of *Extracting the Facts: An Investor Guide to Disclosing Risks from Hydraulic Fracturing Operations*. It identifies 12 core management goals, practices to implement them, and indicators for reporting progress. It provides guidance for equity analysts and private equity firms for evaluating/benchmarking company management. It also provides companies with a framework for benchmarking themselves. He is author/editor of half a dozen books and numerous articles, reports, and blogs on environmental policy, corporate social responsibility, and sustainability. He holds a Ph.D. in Political Science from Northwestern University and a B.A. in Politics from Brandeis University.

Sorell E. Negro is a lawyer with Robinson & Cole LLP in Hartford, Connecticut, and focuses on land use, real estate, and environmental law. She earned her J.D. from Cornell Law School, where she served on the law review, and her B.S. from Georgetown University. She is active in the American Planning Association, Connecticut Bar Association, and ABA. She was one of six young lawyers selected nationally to be a fellow of the ABA's Section of Real Property, Trust and Estate Law for 2012–14. She is a vice-chair of the ABA's Water Resources Committee and the liaison between the ABA's Section of State and Local Government Law and the Young Lawyers Division. She regularly writes and presents on issues related to land use, energy, and natural resources, including regulation of shale development, and is co-editing a book on urban agriculture. She received the 2013 Jefferson B. Fordham Up & Comers Award and is a 2013 Rising Star on Connecticut's *Super Lawyers*® list for land use and zoning.

Vera Callahan Neinast is Senior Counsel with Akin Gump Strauss Hauer & Feld in Austin, Texas. She has represented a broad range of industry participants before the Federal Energy Regulatory Commission (FERC), including interstate and intrastate natural gas pipelines; oil pipelines; midstream companies (gatherers and processors); gas storage companies; and pipeline customers, including producers, marketers, and end users. She has extensive experience in administrative litigation, including initial case strategy, preparation of applications and testimony, discovery, and settlement negotiations. She has represented interstate pipelines and marketers in natural gas import and export proceedings before the U.S. Department of Energy; has broad experience before the Texas Railroad Commission on intrastate pipeline rate- and service-related issues; and has represented LNG terminal developers. Before joining Akin Gump, she spent 12 years practicing energy regulatory law in another law firm, where she was a shareholder, in Washington, D.C. Her previous legal experience includes two years as a staff attorney at FERC in Washington, D.C., and two years as a law clerk for the U.S. Tax Court. She received her B.A. in English, *summa cum laude*, from Wright State University in 1977 and her J.D. from the Ohio State College of Law in 1980. She is admitted in Texas and the District of Columbia.

Kevin Patrick is a shareholder at WATERLAW-Patrick, Miller, Kropf, Noto. The firm confines its practice to water rights, water transfers, water and waste water planning and development, basin mediation, and tribal water. He holds a J.D. from the University of Tulsa School of Law, National Energy Law & Policy Institute, and a B.A. from Virginia Tech. He is licensed in Colorado, Oklahoma, and Texas, as well as a number of U.S. District Courts, the 10th Circuit Court of Appeals, and the U.S. Supreme Court. He is a member of the Board of Visitors of the Sustainable Energy Resources Law Institute of the University of Tulsa and the Board of Advisors of the Bloomberg Water Law & Policy Monitor. He has been qualified as an expert witness on water law, and is a frequent speaker, at conferences on water planning- and water rights-related topics, throughout the United States, Latin America, South America, and Europe.

Jacque Rose is a paralegal who has specialized in civil litigation in Michigan for 27 years. She first became interested in fracking-related issues, especially in connection with potential threats to water resources, when land-leasing agents arrived in the tri-county area of the AuGres-Rifle Watershed in Northeast Michigan, where she resides. She co-founded the Friends of the AuGres-Rifle Watershed, a volunteer group dedicated to educating the public and government officials responsibly about the potential risks associated with deep-shale, high-volume hydraulic fracturing. The group gives presentations, holds public meeting forums, and provides research materials and information to other groups, throughout Michigan, concerned with fracking issues.

Laurie Stern is an attorney with Lubing & Corrigan, LLC, in Jackson, Wyoming. After completing internships with the Western Environmental Law Center and the Department of Justice, she earned her J.D., *cum laude*, and a Masters of Environmental Law & Policy from Vermont Law School in 2011. Upon graduation, she worked as a water rights attorney for Patrick, Miller, Kropf & Noto in Aspen, Colorado. Having grown up in the water-abundant northeast, working on Colorado's west slope gave her new insight into the complex and rapidly changing set of factors that shape and influence western water law. Laurie has written for the *Western Water Law & Policy Reporter* and various water symposia, and maintains a particular interest in the evolution of water law and policy in the face of increased demand for limited water resources.

Heather M. Urwiller is a nationally certified planner (AICP) with nine years of local government planning experience in Florida, Massachusetts, and New York, including service as Town Planner for the Town of Princetown, New York; former Planning Director for the Town of Randolph, Massachusetts; and Senior Planner for Citrus County, Florida. She is a 2001 graduate of Clarion University of Pennsylvania, with a B.A. in Anthropology. She is currently completing dual master's degrees in the Department of Geography and Planning at the University at Albany (SUNY): a Master in Regional Planning, concentrating in environmental and land-use planning, and an M.A. in geography, concentrating in geographic information systems. A former Citrus County representative to the Suncoast section of the Florida Chapter of the American Planning Association (APA), she currently is the University at Albany Graduate Planning Students Association representative to the APA Upstate New York Chapter.

Kenneth J. Warren is a founding partner of Warren Glass LLP, a firm concentrating in the fields of environmental and water resources law. He has been representing businesses in environmental regulatory, transactional, and litigation matters for more than 30 years. He also serves as outside general counsel to the Delaware River Basin Commission, a federal interstate agency managing the water resources of the Delaware River Basin. He is a member of the American College of Environmental Lawyers. He served as chair of the American Bar Association Section of Environment, Energy, and Resources (SEER) in 2003–04 during which he led the Section's 10,000 lawyers.

He participated as an industry stakeholder representative on EPA's National Environmental Justice Advisory Council from 2000 to 2006. He received his B.A., *magna cum laude*, from Brown University in 1975 and his J.D., *magna cum laude*, from the University of Pennsylvania School of Law in 1979, where he served on the law review.

Terrence S. Welch, who began his legal career in 1981 in the Dallas City Attorney's Office, is one of the founding partners of Brown & Hofmeister, LLP. He received his B.A. from the University of Illinois at Urbana-Champaign in 1976, his law degree in 1979 from the University of Houston College of Law, and an M.P.A. in 1981 from the Lyndon Baines Johnson School of Public Affairs at The University of Texas at Austin. He represents and advises local governments on a variety of issues, including land use and natural gas drilling. Since 1991, he has served as the Town Attorney for the Town of Flower Mound, Texas, and he also represents other growing communities in North Texas. He served as the 2004–05 Chair of the State and Local Government Law Section of the American Bar Association and is Immediate Past Section Chair of the State and Local Government Relations Section of the Federal Bar Association. He has published articles in law reviews and the Zoning and Planning Law Report and has presented more than 200 papers to professional organizations including the ABA, the APA, and municipal attorney organizations in Texas.

Lisa Wozniak serves as the Executive Director for the Michigan League of Conservation Voters (Michigan LCV), headquartered in Ann Arbor, Michigan; her career spans over two decades of environmental and conservation advocacy in the political arena. She is a three-time graduate of the University of Michigan, with a bachelor's degree and two ensuing master's degrees in social work and education. From her first campaign experience in 1994, through her work across the Midwest for the League of Conservation Voters, to the founding of the Michigan LCV in 1999, Wozniak is a nationally recognized expert in non-profit growth and management and a leader in Great Lakes protections.

Adam J. Yagelski is a land use planner and land surveyor. He holds a master's degree in urban and regional planning from the University at Albany, State University of New York, where he received the

AICP Outstanding Planning Student Award. As a planning student, he was honored by the Association of Collegiate Schools of Planning with the Ed McClure Award for Best Masters Student Paper, and he presented his work at the Finger Lakes Institute Marcellus Shale conference in 2011. Most recently he worked as associate planner with the Schoharie County, New York–based planning firm Community Planning and Environmental Associates, assisting rural communities and small towns across upstate New York with all aspects of comprehensive, farmland protection, and disaster recovery planning processes. He earned his B.A. in government *summa cum laude* from St. Lawrence University.

Drew YoungDyke is currently the Grassroots Manager at Michigan United Conservation Clubs, where he manages the citizen advocacy program, organizes volunteer fish and wildlife habitat improvement projects in coordination with the Michigan Department of Natural Resources, and writes the "On the Ground" column for *Michigan Out-of-Doors Magazine*. He is a graduate of Michigan State University College of Law, where his article on Asian carp litigation was published by the Animal Legal and Historical Center. As the recent Policy & Communications Specialist for the Michigan League of Conservation Voters, he coordinated the "Green Gavels" accountability project with the University of Michigan Law School, which analyzed Michigan Supreme Court environmental rulings. He is a member of the Environmental Law section of the State Bar Association of Michigan.

Preface

This book was designed to meet a need, nationwide, for information about unconventional hydrocarbon development that lawyers, public officials, planners, and citizens can use as a reference and starting point for further research.

It grew out of a number of conferences, beginning with *Proactive Approaches to Mitigating Impacts of Marcellus Shale Development*, at the Finger Lakes Institute, Hobart and William Smith Colleges, Geneva, New York, in July 2011, where speakers offered perspectives on the rapid development of unconventional shale gas around the United States, and particularly in areas in the Northeast where this technology had not previously been applied. This conference was followed by in-person and online presentations hosted by the ABA and the American Planning Association. The ABA's Section of State and Local Government Law presented two CLE sessions, *When Fracking Comes to a Community Near You: An Ounce of Land Use Planning Is Worth a Pound of Cure*, in New Orleans, Louisiana, in February 2012; and *Beyond the Fracking Wars*, in Dallas, Texas, in February 2013. Three ABA Sections—Energy, Environment, and Resources; Public Contract Law; and Public Utility, Communications, and Transportation Law—hosted a CLE webinar, *The Natural Gas Boom: What Lawyers Should Know*, in May 2012. And the APA presented three continuing education programs and webinars: *Marcellus Shale Development: Planning for Environmental, Community and Economic Impacts* in New York City in October 2012; *Planning for Shale Development: Booms, Busts and Beyond*, also in October 2012; and *Fracking and Resource Extraction and Community Planning*, in February 2013.

A significant number of our authors were panelists, and we solicited their views. We seek to expand on the perspectives offered in these presentations while focusing on issues of primary concern to state and municipal governments. With respect to terminology, the "fracking wars" of the title was chosen to address several angles of the controversy around unconventional hydrocarbon exploration and development. It represents the polarized debate that has developed between those in favor of this development and those opposed to or highly skeptical of it—irrespective of whether or not high-volume, long-lateral slick water hydraulic fracturing ("frac . . . ing," "fracing," "fraccing" or "fracking") or some other technique, such as acidizing, is the completion process of choice.

Within the oil and gas industry, "frac . . . ing" has long been used as shorthand for the actual completion process of fracturing a geological formation, most often using high volumes of water, mixed with silica and chemicals, and pumped at high pressure into perforated pipe run through the target rock layer; however, a number of other techniques may be employed depending on the type of formation in which the hydrocarbons are found. Hydraulic fracturing has long been used to enhance recovery of hydrocarbons in vertical wells, and has also been used to enhance production from water wells. In the case of oil and gas wells, technologies substituting liquefied propane, liquid nitrogen, or cold compressed natural gas (which is pressurized, but not cooled to the extent of liquefied natural gas) for water have recently been introduced.

Recently, in the media and among opponents of the technology as applied, "fracking" has become shorthand for the entire process of unconventional hydrocarbon exploration and development, from site selection to final capping of the well, which may cover a period of forty years, and may impact community dynamics, land use and traffic patterns, and air and water quality, among other things.

Throughout the book, as editors we have attempted to use the term "fracturing" to refer to the technical process, unless there is a direct quote; and to use the term "unconventional shale (and/or oil and/or hydrocarbon) development" to refer to the long-term life-cycle impacts of resource development, which give rise to the issues that are the main focus of this book.

These impacts—both positive and negative—have fueled debate in many states over the last decade. However, with the onset of large-scale development of the Marcellus Shale, many of them became the subject of a national discourse for the first time. Starting in 2009, when the New York Department of Environmental Conservation (DEC) first issued its draft Supplemental Generic Environmental Impact Statement (dSGEIS) for Oil, Gas, and Solution Mining, we found ourselves in the midst of a public discourse that could aptly be described as "fracking wars," a polarized and often acrimonious debate where partisans appeared to choose their facts—totally "pro" or totally "con"—and argue past one another in public, in private, in the media, in signs on front lawns and by the roadside, in legislative hearings, in supermarket parking lots, and frequently, unfortunately, *ad hominem*.

The reality is likely somewhere between two extremes: rosy visions of economic benefit and national energy independence without any health or environmental impacts on the one hand, versus the dark specter of total environmental and public health disasters on the other. As lawyers and professors, we were concerned. Many of our colleagues in the public sector, the nonprofit sector, the private bar, and the land use planning community were being asked to take positions on the issue of unconventional hydrocarbon development, primarily through hydraulic fracturing, and were grappling with conflicting sources of rapidly changing information.

While unconventional oil and gas development is an industrial activity with a potentially large footprint, and as such has the capacity to have significant environmental, health, and social consequences, the equation has more than one variable. The questions of "how," "when," "where," "by whom," "using what technology," and "under what regulatory supervision and public scrutiny does this development takes place" all have the power to influence the extent to which the positives of this development outweigh the negatives, or vice versa. The existence—or lack thereof—of sound scientific data and the ability of industry and regulators alike to incorporate scientific knowledge into their practices may also have profound consequences for the impact of shale gas and oil development on the economy, environment, and community character.

Beyond the Fracking Wars as a whole does not take a "pro-" or "anti-" position. It provides case studies pulled from various parts of the United States where unconventional oil and gas development is occurring. (As illustrated on the inside cover of this book, shale plays—productive or prospective—underlie large areas of the United States.) Additional case studies provide an international perspective on the impact this technology will likely have on relationships among nation states. *Beyond the Fracking Wars* offers a window into the basics of the technology, regulatory framework, and potential hurdles and pitfalls of unconventional oil and gas exploration and development that will be useful to a reader unfamiliar with the topic. It then discusses these topics in detail. Finally, the chapter endnotes enable a reader to pursue further information and education on any of the subjects presented. Our goal is to create an accessible and credible reference useful to seasoned legal practitioners, land owners, public officials, land use planners, and concerned citizens—and even managers and engineers in the oil and gas industry.

Unconventional oil and gas exploration and development is here. Many, if not most, of the authors point out in great detail the potential drawbacks of being unprepared for these activities. But all of them offer extensive coverage of the approaches that state and local governments have used in various situations, often in collaboration with industry, to mitigate or avoid the negative aspects of rapid development of this resource. The case studies in this volume offer particularly important insights, given that the lion's share of regulation of impacts of oil and gas development is within the purview of state and local governments.

The book is organized into four parts. Part 1 provides a detailed yet accessible overview of the technology of shale oil and gas development over the life cycle of a well and the multifaceted structure of the industry engaged in this exploration and development in the United States, and its relationships with regulators, including a discussion of best practices.

Part 2 provides the legal foundations of the oil and gas lease and the impact of forced pooling statutes, the federal regime governing pipeline infrastructure, and local approaches to mitigate inevitable impacts on road infrastructure. In addition, this part provides coverage of the federal and state legal frameworks applicable to impacts that can be more readily classified as "environmental," such as air pollution, water sourcing, and water pollution.

Part 3 offers a series of case studies, documenting real challenges faced by municipalities where unconventional shale gas development is occurring. The combination should provide the reader with a basic understanding of the regulatory backdrop and a view of how real people in real places have navigated the challenges that this type of intensive industrial development brings.

Part 4 focuses on some of the less frequently addressed issues in this debate: those of long-range planning, stakeholder participation, shareholder involvement, and the need for international standards. These chapters challenge the reader to think more broadly and deeply about the implications of the current legal relationships and common practices that govern the oil and gas industry.

Beyond the Fracking Wars is not exhaustive. In fact, due to the rapidly changing technology and regulatory environment, it is not possible to keep up with the current status of the many applicable statutes and regulations across the United States. Rather, our intention is for this book to serve as a useful resource on common issues associated with unconventional oil and gas exploration and development, and to open up progressive topics of discussion for all stakeholders dealing with the high level of uncertainty associated with the intensive development of this resource.

Acknowledgments

Our first acknowledgment is to one another, as editors. This book is the product of a remarkable collaboration, with mutual respect and trust, writing and editing so seamlessly that it is hard to recognize who wrote which words. We thank our authors, who provided original material and took part in multiple revisions; our peer reviewers; Hannah Jacobs Wiseman, Bruce Kramer, and Mark Lapping, who read the entire manuscript; Darrin Magee, Kinnan Golemon, and "Thyag" Thyagarajan, who read and critiqued specific chapters; and Scott Anderson, Mark Boling, and Rene Ruiz, for their assistance in shaping the book. We particularly appreciate the assistance of Adam Yagelski for additional research and editorial assistance on multiple chapters. We also thank all of the panelists of the various conferences and webinars listed in the Preface, many of whom became chapter authors and all of whom influenced our thinking.

Each of us thanks our respective academic institutions and departments: the Department of Geography and Planning and the College of Arts and Sciences at the University at Albany (SUNY); and the Department of Environmental Studies and the Finger Lakes Institute at Hobart and William Smith Colleges. We thank our students, from whom we continually learn.

At the American Bar Association, we thank our superb editor, Leslie Keros; the members of the Publications Oversight Board of the Section of State and Local Government Law, especially Martha Chumbler, Chair, and David Callies, our liaison; Richard Paszkiet, who originally suggested this book; and Tamara Edmonds-Askew and Marsha Boone, who are the professional backbone of the Section.

And of course we thank our families, for their love and support, and powerful intellectual curiosity.

E.L.P. and B.E.K.

PART
1

Technology and Industry Overview

1

The Technology of Oil and Gas Shale Development

Beth E. Kinne

This chapter provides an overview of many steps in the development of unconventional oil and gas resources from shale via hydraulic fracturing.[1] It is designed to walk the reader through a series of commonly occurring events. These include the identification of a promising drilling location to the negotiation of the lease(s) with landowners; pad site preparation; placement of the drilling rig, ancillary equipment, and temporary structures; drilling; movement of sand, water, and chemicals; well completion (including hydraulic fracturing); pipeline installation; capture and separation of gas and other hydrocarbons; periodic reworking of the well; and reclamation of the pad site. It does not address other unconventional methods of harvesting hydrocarbons, such as acidizing of tight formations or harvesting coalbed methane or methane hydrates, nor does it cover all of the legal requirements or technical considerations involved with hydrocarbon development via hydraulic fracturing. However, by providing the reader with an overarching understanding of key processes and key terms involved in unconventional oil and gas development using hydraulic fracturing, we hope to enhance the utility of the other chapters in the book.

Unconventional oil and gas development targets hydrocarbons not accessible through traditional technologies. As with "conventional" hydrocarbon sources, silt, mud, and organic material laid down millennia ago were converted by pressure, heat, and time to the hydrocarbons that make up gas and oil and the geologic strata that contain them. In conventional drilling, the oil or gas has pooled in pockets within sand formations or between layers of rock. Hydraulic fracturing has been employed for decades as part of the completion stage of vertical wells (described below) in these formations to enhance the hydrocarbon recovery. However, in "tight" formations, (e.g., shale and sandstone), effective hydraulic fracturing (or other means of well completion, such as acidizing) becomes essential to produce oil or gas. Employment of this technology enables hydrocarbons to be released from low-permeability, dense formations and to flow to an area of low pressure (i.e., the wellbore) for capture and recovery. In many of the tight oil and gas shales in the United States, the rock formations have natural vertical fractures. These natural vertical fractures led industry and government geologists to correctly suspect that further fractures could be induced in the rock to release the hydrocarbons sequestered there.[2]

IDENTIFYING AND MAPPING THE TARGET FORMATION

Many places have multiple layers of potentially profitable rock, such as shales, limestones, and sandstones, containing varying concentrations of valuable hydrocarbons.[3] For example, in the eastern United States, the Marcellus Shale is currently being developed at a rapid pace, mainly for natural gas and natural gas liquids (NGLs). However, below the Marcellus Shale is the much older Utica Shale, which is proving in Ohio to be a source of oil. Deeper still are the Orinsky Sandstone[4] and the Trenton Black River Limestone formations, layers that have been a target for conventional gas development in southwestern New York for decades.[5] Other states with shale gas and oil reserves have similar histories, although the formations have different names and origins. The amount of hydrocarbons recoverable over the life of any well varies with type of formation (e.g., shale, coalbed methane, and tight sands), and from formation to formation (e.g., Marcellus Shale versus Barnett Shale). Moreover, the U.S. Geological

Survey (USGS) reports that the total expected production of wells in the same formation may differ by up to two orders of magnitude.[6]

The oil and gas industry uses seismic testing to map underground rock layers, and then drills test wells to confirm the presence of a productive layer and delineate the boundaries of the target formation. Seismic testing may be conducted from public roadways or on private land. In the latter case, the testing company usually executes a written agreement with the landowner that defines the scope of the testing. Seismic mapping involves sending a vibration into the earth from a large, specially equipped truck—often dubbed a "thumper truck" and sometimes referred to by the trade name Vibroseis—and "listening for" and recording the refracted vibration waves at other places.[7] Various layers of the earth refract and absorb the vibrations differently, and computer analysis of refraction data allows for construction of 3-D maps of the underground geology.[8] The geophones, remote sensor recorders, and associated infrastructure remain on the ground for several weeks during the mapping process and are then removed.[9]

Merely locating a mineral resource does not give the oil and gas company the right to produce it. Under common law, a real property owner owns his land "to the center of the earth," unless he has relinquished rights to some portion of it.[10] However, it is possible to sever mineral rights from rights in the surface property. Particularly in regions of the country with a long history of extraction of oil, gas, or coal from at least one formation, many mineral rights were long ago severed from the surface estate and conveyed in separate deeds. The industry subcontracts "landmen" to search the public records and identify the owners of mineral interests their companies hope to acquire. The landmen then set out to negotiate with the owners for the purchase, or more commonly, the lease, of the rights to those interests. Chapter 3 explains in more detail the legal norms involved in acquiring rights to develop oil and gas resources.

SUPPORTING INFRASTRUCTURE: PAD SITES, ROADS, PROCESSING PLANTS, PIPELINES, AND STORAGE

Acquisition of mineral rights generally conveys to the lessee an implied easement to use the surface estate for the many "upstream production activities" necessary to bring the gas to the surface, including locating and constructing a pad site.[11] However, state law[12] or the terms of a surface use agreement may limit or preclude access to the surface estate under certain circumstances. The pad site must be large enough to accommodate numerous tanker trucks and store a variety of equipment and chemicals used during production operations. Access roads are typically constructed to the pad, which may also be connected to water supply pipelines in areas where pipelines have been constructed. Once the gas flows to the surface, it must be collected and transported to the point of sale. To varying degrees, it may also be further processed or refined before it is sold. These "post-production activities" can include a mix of gathering, dehydrating, processing, and compressing the gas once it is produced.[13] The associated infrastructure, such as compressor stations and gathering lines, may occupy additional space on the lessor's property and are often the subject of agreements outside of the original lease. The construction and operation of the well and other infrastructure associated with these production and post-production activities can subject landowners and their neighbors to noise, lights, viewscape impacts, and truck traffic inherent in the construction and operation of the pad site, wells, and pipelines that transport the hydrocarbons to market. This can cause significant conflict between drillers, landowners, and neighbors.

Pad Sites

Pad sites can vary in size depending on the number of wells to be drilled from a given location, but are commonly two to five acres. A 2013 study by Resources for the Future, which analyzed regulation in thirty-one states that have existing or potential for shale gas development, found that 65 percent of those states imposed setback requirements.[14] There is high variability in setback requirements among these states. Some examples include the separation of wells, supporting infrastructure, or both from buildings in general; certain types of buildings, such as schools or residences; public roadways; places where people are known to congregate; and from certain water resources.[15] In some cases, the setback is a default around which the parties are free to contract.[16] In addition, some municipalities impose their own restrictions on pad site or well locations.

The area for the pad site is first cleared of vegetation and topsoil, leveled, and often lined with an impervious material, which is intended to prevent migration of any chemical or water spills onto the surrounding property. In some states, the entire pad site must be lined with an impervious liner and surrounded by a berm to help contain any potential spills. Liner accidents, such as tears or seams giving way, are difficult to prevent and can result in contamination of surrounding soils or water sources.

On or adjacent to the pad site there may be various pits for fresh water, drilling cuttings, drilling muds, and flowback water. In areas where multiple pad sites are in close proximity, state law may allow the use of centralized freshwater or flowback pits.[17] The pad site also needs to provide room for multiple tanker trucks. Some may hold fresh water and some may be pump trucks containing fluids used in fracturing the well. Others may collect and transport flowback water to a treatment or recycling center or for disposal. State regulations usually require that pad sites be reclaimed to a fraction of their original size after the completion of drilling. Topsoil must be replaced, and any compacted soil must be decompacted before being reseeded.[18] In some states, flowback pits may be dewatered and the resultant salts or sludge wrapped up in the impervious pad liner and buried on site.[19] After reclamation, certain minimal infrastructure remains on the now smaller pad site, including the well head and containment vessels for produced water.

Roads

Trucks bring in fresh water, chemicals, pipe, equipment and other supplies. They also remove flowback and produced water and equipment. Drilling a horizontal well can take between 65,000 and 600,000 gallons of water, much of which is incorporated into the drilling muds. An additional four to five million gallons of water is needed to fracture a typical horizontal well.[20] Transporting five million gallons of water and the necessary chemicals, pipe, and other supplies by truck requires approximately 1,800 loaded (one-way) heavy truck trips and about 800 loaded (one-way) light truck trips per well.[21] Depending on the formation and the site, one pad site can have up to eight wells (although some may have as many as sixteen). Re-fracturing of the wells after the initial decline in production requires additional water, chemicals, and the associated truck trips.

Access roads, which are usually made of gravel or chip and seal, are often constructed across private property to access the pad site. Proper maintenance is necessary to ensure that erosion from these roads is not problematic. Impact on local secondary roads is also significant. Municipal governments need to plan for and/or require the industry to pay for the replacement and maintenance of local roads. A related issue is the challenge of maintaining road safety in the face of increased traffic combined with road surface deterioration. As detailed in chapter 11, which covers municipal navigation of the boom-and-bust cycle of gas development, and chapter 6 on road agreements, bonding, and enforcement, municipalities can employ multiple strategies to ensure they are not left without the funding necessary to repair and replace damaged public infrastructure.

DRILLING AND CASING THE WELL

The drilling rig is a temporary fixture at the well site. The floor of the drilling rig usually is at an elevation of somewhere between 25 to 45 feet above the pad surface. The rig mast, mounted atop the rig floor, may extend upward as much as 140 feet. The newer onshore drilling rigs also use a box-on-box design that allows the entire rig to "walk" in multiple directions in order to drill from multiple locations at the pad site without rigging down. Thus, the rig may be at a pad site for weeks or months, depending on how quickly drilling progresses and the number of wells to be drilled. At Benbrook, Texas, for instance, Devon Energy has a single site that contains thirty-four completed wells and a waste disposal well.[22] The rig is lighted twenty-four hours a day, and during drilling, it is quite noisy. Chapter 12 provides examples of municipal noise and light ordinances to minimize the negative impacts.

In drilling a well, the drill moves through the top layers of soil and rock, through the saturated aquifer layer, and down through numerous layers of rock until the target formation is reached. Specially formulated drilling muds lubricate the drill bit and minimize disruption to the aquifer and other layers the drill bit goes through. Drilling is completed in stages. The first stage creates a space for the conductor casing, the outermost string of steel casing in the well. Regulations of conductor casing vary considerably by state, but the conductor casing is generally between 16 and 20 inches in diameter and extends from the surface of the ground to between 30 and 75 feet below the surface.[23] The conductor casing protects the well from caving in and reduces the risk of contamination of aquifers from the surface.[24] Inside the conductor casing is the surface casing. The surface casing normally extends from 500 to 1,500 feet below the surface.[25] It must extend below the water table and is intended to protect the aquifer from any oil, gas, or other fluid contamination that might migrate along the annulus of the well. Inside the surface casing is either production casing or intermediate casing. In a well with four layers of casing (the current standard in Pennsylvania),[26] intermediate casing is installed outside the production casing. The production casing is the steel pipe through which the oil or gas is removed from the formation. It can run to a depth of up to 10,000 feet before turning horizontally at the "kickoff" point and running up to a mile or more through the target formation. The horizontal portion of the well allows contact with an extensive area of the formation, which is what makes unconventional oil and gas development so attractive for producing hydrocarbons.

Cement is used to affix each string of casing to the surrounding rock and soil so that it is stable and will not shift. In regions of the well where one casing is inside another, cement is also used to bond the steel casing pipes to each other. The cement for the conductor and surface casings runs all the way to the surface. Improper cementing—using too little cement, or using an inappropriate mix so that curing time is not optimal—can result in the formation of channels within the cement or along the casing through which fluids or gases from the surrounding rock can migrate up the casing to the surface or to aquifers.[27] For example, ineffective cementing could allow gas from a shallower, non-target layer to migrate along the outside of the casing into an overlying aquifer. Most states require cementing of the entire length of the surface casing and also require the surface casing to run below the deepest groundwater aquifer.[28] In addition, many states require drillers to conduct tests to ensure proper bonding of the cement and to keep a cement bond log.[29]

Once a well is drilled, it may be completed (described below), or it may be shut in (temporarily capped) for completion at a future time. Factors that influence if and when wells are drilled and completed include market price of natural gas and the availability of completion equipment in the region. As an example of the elasticity of demand for natural gas, rates of drilling and completion of wells in the Marcellus Shale in eastern Pennsylvania slowed in 2012, as drilling equipment, which is expensive and in limited supply, moved to the western part of the state and to Ohio, where Utica formation wells are producing mixes of hydrocarbons that are more valuable than the dry gas produced from the Marcellus formation in the eastern part of the state.[30]

FRACTURING THE FORMATION

Once the production casing is installed, the horizontal sections of the casing are perforated in preparation for hydraulic fracturing of the target rock formation. Perforation is achieved by sending small charges into the wellbore using perforating guns. These charges create holes in the casing into the formation.[31] After perforation, an acid solution may be used to clean debris out of the well.[32] Then the hydraulic fracturing slurry (i.e., "gel")—a mixture of water, sand (or other proppant, such as ceramic beads), and some other chemicals, such as friction reducers, biocides, and corrosion inhibitors—is pumped at high pressure into the well and out through the perforations, creating microscopic cracks in the formation. The proppant in the hydraulic fracturing fluid holds open the cracks, creating channels through which the hydrocarbons can flow into the wellbore. Wells are usually fractured in segments of several hundred feet at a time, starting at the farthest end of the horizontal section. Once a segment is fractured, a plug is inserted to prevent premature hydrocarbon flow and the next segment is fractured. When the entire horizontal length of the well has been fractured, the plugs are drilled out so that the gas can flow back up the wellbore.

While the well is being fractured, the drilling technicians monitor the pressure in the annulus of the well and the wellbore.[33] Sudden changes in either of these pressures can indicate unintended results. For example, a sudden drop in pressure in the wellbore with no associated increase in pressure in the well annulus could indicate that the induced fractures have gone outside of the target formation, while a sudden increase in the pressure in the well annulus combined with loss of pressure in the wellbore can indicate loss of casing integrity.[34] Using specialized equipment, some operators also monitor the growth/propagation of induced fractures. Once hydraulic fracturing is completed, the well is shut in for a time to allow redistribution of the water and gas molecules in the formation.[35]

MANAGING WASTEWATER

Water returning from a well changes over time. "Flowback" is defined as the initial returns of water from a well during the first days or weeks after fracturing. It is similar in makeup to the fracturing fluids that went into the well. "Produced water" is defined as the later returns, which gradually flows to the surface after the well has been brought online and is simultaneously producing hydrocarbons. Produced water has been in contact with the target formation for a prolonged period of time and therefore contains high concentrations of salts. In some formations, such as the Marcellus Shale, produced water may also contain naturally occurring radioactive materials (NORMS).

Currently there are several approaches to managing flowback and produced water. In some states, flowback can be stored temporarily in open pits on the pad site, but eventually it must be trucked to treatment, recycling, or disposal facilities. In other states, it must be collected in tanks.[36] While a portion of the flowback water can often be reused to fracture another well, eventually the residual must be disposed of either in a wastewater treatment plant equipped to handle industrial wastes, or in Class II deep injection wells.[37] Deep injection disposal wells are often old oil and gas wells that are no longer productive, and they must be located in geological formations that allow for effective isolation of the waste. Pennsylvania has eight deep injection wells that are permitted to take oil and gas waste, and only five of these are active.[38] New York has very few wells.[39] The management of flowback and produced water waste is an area where technological advances are desirable to minimize cost of disposal and potential for spills and contamination.[40]

Treatment of wastewater may include simple de-watering and burial of the remaining material on site, treatment in industrial wastewater treatment plants and disposal of the solids or sludge in a landfill, or injection of the brine in a Class II deep well licensed under the Underground Injection Control program of the Clean Water Act.[41] Chapter 14 provides additional details on wastewater content and recycling and disposal processes being developed from the perspective of the industry. Chapter 10 discusses the importance of state regulations in mitigating impacts of unconventional oil and gas development on water resources.

BRINGING A NATURAL GAS WELL ONLINE

Once the formation is fractured, the pressure is released and fluids and gas flow back out of the well. After the first few days or weeks, the ratio of water to hydrocarbons coming out of the well decreases significantly. Once the percentage of water is small compared to the percentage of gas, the well can be hooked up to a sales line after final water separation at or near the pad site. Smaller amounts of water will continue to come out of the well alongside the hydrocarbons for the life of the well.[42]

Processing Plants

Natural gas must be purified before it enters the transmission pipeline so that it does not cause problems with pipeline safety.[43] Processing plants separate the various hydrocarbons that can come from the production and gathering lines from each other by removing impurities, such as water and oil; separating natural gas liquids, such as ethane, natural gasoline, propane, butane, and iso-butane; and removing non-hydrocarbon gases, such as carbon dioxide and sulfur.[44] The purified streams of hydrocarbons are then routed to the appropriate transportation lines.

Pipelines and Compressor Stations

The gas well is attached to a production line, which connects to a gathering line. Gathering lines in turn connect to larger transmission lines to carry gas long distances. Pipelines vary in diameter and operating pressure. As discussed in detail in chapter 5, the location and size of a given pipeline determines whether it comes under state or federal regulatory jurisdiction. Installation of pipelines can create disturbances to farmland, ecosystems, and habitats, and gas lines running through inhabited areas can create human safety risks if not properly operated and maintained.

In addition, gas must periodically be compressed and recompressed as it moves along the network of pipelines; therefore, compressor stations are located periodically along the pipeline route. Gas must be recompressed to compensate for loss of pressure due to friction between the pipeline and the gas, new gas entering the pipeline, and gas leaving the pipeline. As gas is pressurized it heats up and requires cooling before being returned to the pipeline.[45] Transmission lines, or "trunklines," have the largest diameter and the highest pressure. At the user interface, the size and pressure of the gas lines must be stepped down again before entering municipal distribution systems and homes.

Storage

Storage of natural gas is important because gas use peaks during the winter months—particularly in the Midwest and Northeast—and is much lower during summer months. Therefore, provider companies often store oil and gas in depleted oil and gas reservoirs, depleted aquifers, or retired salt caverns to enable guaranteed flows during the peak winter months. The Energy Information Administration provides a map of underground natural gas storage facilities in the United States on its website.[46] The majority of these storage sites are exhausted oil and gas reservoirs, with a smaller percentage being depleted aquifers or salt caverns. The Federal Energy Regulatory Commission website contains records of storage facilities permitted, pending, "on the horizon," and in the prefiling stage.[47]

REWORKING UNCONVENTIONAL WELLS

In formations like the Marcellus Shale, gas production from horizontal wells, which initially is very high, declines significantly over time.[48] It is not uncommon for the daily production volume at the first anniversary to be half of what it was during the first month the well was in production.[49] Analysis of several mature shale plays indicated that this steep, linear decline profile lasts ten to fifteen months. Rates of production thereafter continue to decline, but at a shallower—though still linear—rate.[50] Maintaining steady production rates from a shale play like the Marcellus, therefore, requires continued drilling of new wells or restimulation (a repeat of the hydraulic fracturing treatment) of existing wells to increase production. At the time of writing, restimulation of wells is not a common practice, and oil and gas companies primarily depend on continued drilling of new wells to maintain production volumes.

RECLAMATION

The Bureau of Land Management, which manages the federal public land upon which many oil and gas wells have been drilled, states, "[t]he ultimate objective of reclamation is ecosystem restoration, including restoration of the natural vegetation community, hydrology, and wildlife habitats."[51] Drilling permits may limit the maximum area disturbed at any one time. This necessitates interim reclamation, which may also include revegetation and recontouring of the land. Final reclamation involves removal of almost all of the equipment, save the "Christmas tree" well head and a small condensate tank to collect the small amounts of water that will continue to be produced with the gas. In some instances a separator or compressor station may also be installed on the pad site. The pad site is usually reclaimed from the original five acres to an area of about one-half acre (although larger pad sites might not be reclaimed to such a small area). Access roads may be removed and the area under them that was compacted by thousands of truck trips tilled and reseeded to promote the return to close to normal hydrological flow and vegetation patterns. Reclamation standards are typically set by individual states and determination of reclaimed status dependent on approval by state inspectors. Industry best practices also set standards for reclamation.[52] In many states where high-volume hydraulic fracturing techniques are being used, such as Pennsylvania and West Virginia, few of the horizontal wells are old enough for the pad sites to have been fully reclaimed.

CONCLUSION

For attorneys, mineral rights owners, or regulating bodies entering into or enforcing the legal relationships involved, a basic understanding of the technical processes promotes informed decision making. The steps in producing oil and gas using hydraulic fracturing technologies are manifold and complex as are the legal relationships involved. As technologies for accessing hydrocarbon resources develop further, the list of technologies qualifying as "unconventional" will also likely change. Although they are addressed here with respect to a specific set of technologies used to extract oil and gas, many of the issues addressed by the authors in this book are inherent in many types of extractive resource development, and therefore will likely continue to require creative management and evolving regulatory strategies.

NOTES

1. Hydraulic fracturing is one completion method used in development of unconventional oil and gas resources such as tight sands and shales. The category "unconventional" is somewhat fluid, and is used to describe formations

in which newer technologies are necessary to exploit hydrocarbons histori-cally inaccessible via vertical drilling technology, as well as those technologies themselves (directional drilling, hydraulic fracturing, acidizing, and collec-tion of coalbed methane, for example). For an explanation of unconventional gas resource types, see http://www.naturalgas.org/overview/unconvent_ng _resource.asp.

2. *See, e.g.*, T. Engelder, G.G. Lash & R. Uzcategui, *Joint Sets That Enhance Production from Middle and Upper Devonian Gas Shales of the Appalachian Basin*, 93 Am. Ass'n Petroleum Geologists Bull. 857 (2009).

3. For current productive formations in New York State, see, e.g., New York State Geological Survey Reservoir Characterization Group, *available at* http://www.nysm.nysed.gov/nysgs/research/oil-gas/rcg.html.

4. John A. Harper, *The Marcellus Shale: An Old "New" Gas Reservoir in Penn-sylvania*, 38 Pa. Geology, no. 1, 2008 at 2.

5. For a stratigraphic diagram of the geology of southwest New York State showing the relationship among these three formations, see NY DEC, *Stratigraphic Section, SW New York State*, *available at* http://www.dec.ny .gov/energy/33893.html.

6. R.R. Charpentier & T.A. Cook, U.S. Geological Surv. Open-File Rep. 2013–1001, Variability of Oil and Gas Well Productivities for Con-tinuous (Unconventional) Petroleum Accumulations (2013), *avail-able at* http://pubs.usgs.gov/of/2013/1001/.

7. M. Landefeld & C. Hogan, *Seismic Testing and Oil & Gas Production*, Oil and Gas, Ohio State University Extension, Oil and Gas Development Fact Sheet Series, *available at* http://serc.osu.edu/sites/drupal-serc.web /files/2012%20seismic%20testing%20Fact%20Sheet(1).pdf.

8. U.S. Dep't of Transp., Pipeline & Hazardous Materials Safety Admin., *Technologies of Oil and Gas Exploration*, http://primis.phmsa.dot.gov/comm /Technologies.htm (last visited Sept. 20, 2013).

9. Information in this paragraph was taken from Chesapeake Energy, Seis-mic Exploration, *available at* http://www.askchesapeake.com/Barnett-Shale /Natural-Gas/Pages/Seismic-Exploration.aspx.

10. There is some evidence that the further underground the rights are, the less secure ownership by the owner of the surface estate. J. Sprankling, *Owning the Earth*, 55 UCLA L. Rev. 979 (2008).

11. George A. Bibikos & Jeffrey C. King, *A Primer on Oil and Gas Law in the Marcellus Shale States*, 4 Tex. J. Oil Gas & Energy L. 156 (2009).

12. For example, New York State's compulsory integration law (New York Envi-ronmental Conservation Law, Title 9, Art. 23) precludes the well operator from trespassing on the property of a landowner that has been subject to compulsory integration. *Land Owner Option Guide*, N.Y. Department of Environmental Conservation, http://www.dec.ny.gov/energy/1590.html (last visited Sept. 20, 2013).

13. *Id.*

14. Nathan Richardson et al., Resources for the Future, The State of State Shale Gas Regulation (June 2013), *available at* http://www.rff.org /rff/documents/RFF-Rpt-StateofStateRegs_Report.pdf.
15. *Id.*
16. *Id.*
17. *E.g.*, W.Va. Code § 22-6A-9; Pa. Dep't of Envtl. Prot., form 5500-PM-OG0084 Rev. 12/2010, Application Instructions for a Dam Permit for a Centralized Impoundment Dam for Oil and Gas Wells (2010), *available at* http://www.elibrary.dep.state.pa.us/dsweb/Get/Document-82541 /5500-PM-OG0084%20Instructions.pdf; and N.Y. Dep't of Envtl. Conservation, Preliminary Revised Draft Supplemental Generic Environmental Impact Statement on the Oil, Gas and Solution Mining Regulatory Program chs. 1.1.1 and 5.7.2 (2009), *available at* http://www .dec.ny.gov/data/dmn/ogprdsgeisfull.pdf.
18. *See* N.Y. State Dept. of Agric. and Mkts., Guidelines for Construction and Restoration at Natural Gas Well Drilling Sites in Agricultural Areas, *available at* http://www.agriculture.ny.gov/AP/agservices /Well_Pad_Guidelines.pdf; *see also* Colorado Oil and Gas Conservation Commission, Reclamation Regulations, sections 1003 and 1004, *available at* http://cogcc.state.co.us/RR_Docs_new/rules/1000Series .pdf (last visited Sept. 20, 2013).
19. *E.g.*, Mich. Admin. Code r. 324.407(9).
20. Chesapeake Energy, *Water Usage in Hydraulic Fracturing*, Hydraulic Fracturing Facts, http://www.hydraulicfracturing.com/Water-Usage/Pages /Information.aspx (last visited Sept. 20, 2013). For water usage data by shale play, see individual fact sheets at *Water*, Chesapeake Energy, http://www .naturalgaswaterusage.com/Pages/information.aspx (last visited Sept. 20, 2013).
21. N.Y. Dep't of Envtl. Conservation, Revised Draft Supplementary General Environmental Impact Statement, at 6-603 tbl.6.60 (2011).
22. Author's correspondence with Kinnan Golemon, Esq., Contract Governmental Affairs Representative for Devon Energy (Apr. 2013) (on file with author).
23. Harvey Consulting, LLC, New York State Casing Recommendations for Regulation: report to NRDC (Sept. 16, 2009), *available at* http:// docs.nrdc.org/energy/files/ene_10092901e.pdf.
24. *Id.*
25. *See Texas Oil and Gas Industry, Oil and Gas in Texas: A Joint Association Communication from the Texas Oil and Gas Industry*, Oil and Natural Gas in Texas, http://www.oilandnaturalgasintexas.com/flipbook/#/4 (last visited Sept. 20, 2013).
26. *See* 25 Pa. Code § 78.83 (2011).
27. U.S. Dep't. of Energy, State Oil and Natural Gas Regulations Designed to Protect Water Resources (2009), *available at* http://

energy.wilkes.edu/PDFFiles/Library/State%20Oil%20and%20Gas%20
Regulations%20Designed%20to%20Protect%20Water%20Resources.pdf.
28. *Id.*
29. *Id.*
30. Andrew McGill, *Low Gas Prices Drive Drillers West*, Pittsburgh Post-Gazette (July 30, 2012, 12:07 AM), http://www.post-gazette.com
/stories/local/marcellusshale/low-gas-prices-drive-drillers-west-in-search-of
-profit-646802/ (includes rig count graphic based on US EIA gas price data
and Baker Hughs rig count).
31. Rick von Flatern, *Defining Completion: The Science of Oil and Gas Well
Construction*, Oilfield Rev., Winter 2011, at 50, *available at* http://www
.slb.com/resources/publications/oilfield_review/~/media/Files/resources/oil
field_review/ors11/win11/defining_completion.ashx.
32. *Id.*
33. YCELP, *Balancing Environmental, Social and Economic Impacts of Shale Gas
Development Activities*, Vimeo (Jan. 23, 2013), http://vimeo.com/58162903
(video of webinar with Mark K. Boling, *Emerging Issues in Shale Gas Development Series*, Yale Law School).
34. *Id.*
35. Terry Engelder, Fracking: A Conversation with the Public about Risk, Public Lecture at Hobart & William Smith Colleges (Dec. 7, 2012).
36. Nathan Richardson et al., Resources for the Future, The State of
State Shale Gas Regulation (June 2013), *available at* http://www.rff.org
/rff/documents/RFF-Rpt-StateofStateRegs_Report.pdf.
37. EPA, *Natural Gas Extraction, Hydraulic Fracturing*, http://www2.epa.gov
/hydraulicfracturing#wastewater (last visited Sept. 20, 2013).
38. Susan Philips, *Deep Injection Wells in Pennsylvania*, StateImpact (June 26,
2012, 11:52 AM), http://stateimpact.npr.org/pennsylvania/maps/location-of
-deep-injection-wells-in-pennsylvania/.
39. Ohio Dep't of Natural Res., Preliminary Report on the Northstar 1
Class II Injection Well and the Seismic Events in the Youngstown,
Ohio, Area, (2012), *available at* http://ohiodnr.com/downloads/northstar
/UICreport.pdf.
40. According to the Produced Water Society, approaches to treatment can be
categorized into removal of total suspended solids (TSS); removal of hard-
ness (salts) and oil and grease; removal of total dissolved solids; and centralized treatment (used with water with a specified re-use or that is destined to
be discharged). *See* Mark Kidder et al., *Treatment Options for Reuse of Frac
Flowback and Produced Water from Shale*, World Oil, July 2011, *available
at* http://www.worldoil.com/July-2011-Treatment-options-for-reuse-of-frac
-flowback-and-produced-water-from-shale.html.
41. *Class II Wells—Oil and Gas Related Injection Wells*, Envtl. Prot. Agency,
http://water.epa.gov/type/groundwater/uic/class2/index.cfm (last visited
Sept. 20, 2013).

42. The process described here is somewhat different from what is required to bring a crude oil or crude oil and liquids well on line.

43. ENERGY INFO. ADMIN., NATURAL GAS PROCESSING: THE CRUCIAL LINK BETWEEN NATURAL GAS PRODUCTION AND ITS TRANSFER TO MARKET (2006), *available at* http://www.eia.gov/pub/oil_gas/natural_gas/feature _articles/2006/ngprocess/ngprocess.pdf.

44. U.S. Dep't of Transp., Pipeline & Hazardous Materials Safety Admin., *Fact Sheet: Natural Gas Processing Plants*, PIPELINE & HAZARDOUS MATERIALS SAFETY ADMIN., http://primis.phmsa.dot.gov/comm/factsheets/fsnatural gasprocessingplants.htm (last updated Dec. 1, 2011).

45. ENERGY INFO. ADMIN., NATURAL GAS COMPRESSOR STATIONS ON THE INTERSTATE PIPELINE NETWORK: DEVELOPMENTS SINCE 1996 (2007), *available at* http://www.eia.gov/pub/oil_gas/natural_gas/analysis_publications /ngcompressor/ngcompressor.pdf.

46. *About U.S. Natural Gas Pipelines*, ENERGY INFO. ADMIN, http://www.eia .gov/pub/oil_gas/natural_gas/analysis_publications/ngpipeline/undrgrndstor _map.html (last visited Sept. 20, 2013).

47. *Natural Gas Storage*, FED. ENERGY REGULATORY COMM'N, http://www.ferc .gov/industries/gas/indus-act/storage.asp (last updated June 10, 2013).

48. Matt Kelso, *Marcellus Shale Production Decline over Time in Pennsylvania*, FRACTRACKER (Sept. 5, 2011), http://www.fractracker.org/2011/09 /marcellus-shale-production-decline-in-pennsylvania/.

49. Jason Baihly, et al., *Study Assesses Shale Decline Rates*, AM. OIL AND GAS REP., May 2011, *available at* http://www.slb.com/~/media/Files/dcs/industry _articles/201105_aogr_shale_baihly.ashx.

50. Arthur E. Berman & Lynn F. Pittinger, *U.S. Shale Gas: Lower Abundance, Higher Cost*, THE OIL DRUM (Aug. 5, 2011, 10:15 AM), http://www.theoil drum.com/node/8212.

51. U.S. Dept. of Interior, Bureau of Land Management, *Reclamation and Abandonment*, BUREAU OF LAND MGMT., http://www.blm.gov/wo/st/en/prog /energy/oil_and_gas/leasing_of_onshore/og_reclamation.html (last updated Oct. 20, 2009).

52. *See Reclamation Resources Guide for Oil and Gas Development*, INTERMOUNTAIN OIL AND GAS BMP PROJECT, http://www.oilandgasbmps.org/resources /reclamation.php (last visited Sept. 20, 2013). This site includes links to reclamation regulations for Utah, New Mexico, and Wyoming.

2

The Oil and Gas Industry
Operations and Best Practices

Erica Levine Powers and Adam J. Yagelski

INTRODUCTION

This chapter provides an overview of the structure of the industry for oil and gas shale exploration and development in the United States. Specifically, it outlines how companies are organized during the exploration and production phase and how contractual relationships among operators and oilfield service companies are structured and how they have changed. This chapter also discusses industry best practices in anticipating and preventing accidents in high-risk technologies, including industry-proposed collaboration with stakeholders for baseline scientific research, model disclosure statutes, and regulatory oversight. Although this chapter does not address recent tort cases, it references related articles.[1] For a technical overview of the process of exploration, drilling, and bringing a well online, see chapter 1.

The authors acknowledge the research assistance of Heather Urwiller, AICP.

19

What Comprises the Shale Oil and Gas Industry?

Far from being monolithic, this industry is comprised of oil and gas companies that range from some of the largest companies in the world—both privately and publicly held—to small players active in one region of the United States. In addition to these "operators," which are essentially companies responsible for oilfield management and day-to-day operation, there are manifold companies providing services of all types, from specialized downhole operations to logistics and trucking. Bringing such a diverse set of companies together on a given well pad necessitates establishing some key operational and contractual relationships, including agency and insurance, to address responsibility, risk, and liability.

What is known as the U.S. "oil and shale gas industry" actually includes entities active in each of three sectors: upstream, midstream, and downstream. The upstream sector, also known as exploration and production (E&P), includes entities engaged in one or more of the following activities: finding, developing, or producing oil or gas. The midstream sector encompasses activities related to processing, transportation, storage, and marketing of both raw hydrocarbons and refined products. Downstream sector activities include refining and processing as well as marketing and distribution. Some companies may have investments or operations in more than one sector. The figure below provides an overview of the activities necessary to bring oil and gas products from underground deposits to consumers and how the activities are structured. As this diagram indicates, there is some overlap in function among the three sectors.

Operators

Oil and gas companies are probably the best-known component of the E&P sector. Also known as "operators," they decide where to drill; specify well depth, diameter, and direction; obtain drilling permits; and secure the right to access the well site.[2]

To access the hydrocarbon reserves, operators usually lease the mineral rights from landowners. For a more extended treatment of mineral estate and surface access and other issues involved in leasing, see chapter 3.

Among operators, there is a basic distinction between "fully integrated" companies, which are active in all three sectors, and

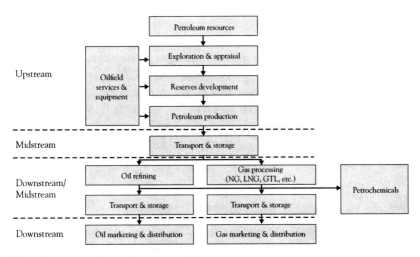

Overview of petroleum industry activities

Source: Adapted from Silvana Tordo, Brandon S. Tracy & Noora Arfaa, *National Oil Companies and Value Creation 2* (World Bank, Working Paper No. 218, 2011), *available at* http://siteresources.worldbank.org /INTOGMC/Resources/9780821388310.pdf. Reprinted by permission of the World Bank.

"independent producers", which typically are active in the upstream and midstream sectors but do not have refining capacity. Fully integrated companies include the so-called oil majors, such as Exxon-Mobil, BP, ChevronTexaco, and Shell Oil. These companies—some of the largest in the world—are engaged in all aspects of the oil industry, from E&P to refining and marketing of refined products. Independent producers explore and/or produce crude oil and natural gas, and they may also own pipeline infrastructure or otherwise be active in the midstream sector. These include companies like Devon Energy, Anadarko, Apache Corporation, Range Resources, Southwestern Energy, Chesapeake Energy, and some 8,000 other entities varying in number of employees from a handful to thousands.[3]

Many fully integrated and independent producers also have midstream operations in the areas where they have extensive shale oil and gas E&P operations. However, these entities, including most independent producers, may also rely on some third-party midstream operators in many of the shale oil and gas plays. This is particularly true in regions with new plays that lack gathering and transmission infrastructure, or where the pipeline and processing infrastructure requires upgrades to handle the increased pressures associated with unconventional wells and to carry liquids.

There is not a direct correlation between the size of an operator and the number of sectors in which it operates. A common way to measure the size of operators is natural gas produced per day. In the third quarter of 2012, both fully integrated and independent companies were listed among the top 10 producers of natural gas in the United States. ExxonMobil topped this list with 3,847 MMcf/day produced and was followed by independent Chesapeake Energy with 3,095 MMcf/day. Hess Corporation, a large integrated company, ranked near the bottom with daily production of 112 MMcf.[4]

Private vs. Nationally Controlled Oil Companies

Not all companies operating in U.S. plays of unconventional hydrocarbons are U.S. companies. In addition, it is also important to distinguish between privately held operators and those that are state-owned. To varying degrees, government-controlled national oil companies (NOC) like PDVSA, Venezuela's state oil company, operate with state-mandated, non-market objectives, such as wealth re-distribution and jobs creation. This is in contrast to the private international oil companies (IOC), which are responsive to shareholders. A further distinction between many IOCs and NOCs is that the degree of vertical integration among NOCs is typically lower, though it appears to be growing. Much like their counterparts in the private sector, some state-controlled oil companies have refining and sales operations, which oil companies—especially IOCs—have long used to capture the value-added of downstream products, create demand security, and hedge risk in volatile, changing oil markets. Other NOCs are less integrated and have activities concentrated primarily in the upstream sector.[5] In contrast, IOCs appear to be concentrating on the more profitable upstream sector. An example of this trend is a steady decrease of retail sales (e.g., gasoline at gas stations) as a percentage of total sales of U.S. refiners.[6]

Some large NOCs also are conducting business in the United States as operators. In some instances, they have taken positions in U.S. unconventional plays to replace declining reserves at home.[7] Foreign investment in U.S. shale gas plays—whether by NOCs or other private investors—has generally increased. Since 2008, there have been at least 21 joint ventures between U.S. acreage holders or operators and foreign companies.[8] For example, Statoil, which is majority-controlled by the Norwegian government, has become an active operator in several U.S. unconventional plays, including the Marcellus, Eagle Ford, and Bakken formations.[9]

Chinese oil companies, many of which are now stock corporations whose assets remain majority-controlled by the central government, also have a significant presence in U.S. shale plays. Since 2010, there have been several joint ventures between U.S. operators and Chinese firms. These deals allow U.S. companies to access capital while Chinese and other foreign firms benefit from exposure to unconventional drilling technology. Some transactions have involved purchase of drilling rights as well. For example, Sinopec recently purchased from Chesapeake Energy rights to drill in Oklahoma, and state-owned China National Petroleum Corp. (Cnooc), China's largest oil company, has purchased Canadian company Nexen Inc.

The Cnooc-Nexen deal is instructive in terms of the degree of control U.S. regulators exercise over access to mineral resources: Cnooc was blocked from access to Nexen's Gulf of Mexico operations in U.S. waters.[10] Indeed, legislation passed in the wake of a controversial attempt by a company ultimately owned by the United Arab Emirates to acquire operating leases to six major U.S. ports led to a broadening of oversight of "major energy assets." This has caused increased scrutiny for transactions involving U.S. energy resources.[11]

Oilfield Services Companies

The E&P sector also includes oilfield services companies (OFS)—the "unsung workhorses"[12] of the oil and gas industry. Entities providing a very wide range of services constitute OFS. While they were much smaller in the 1980s when operators performed more of their own drilling work, OFS have since grown as operators have outsourced a number of these functions. Recent growth has been driven by both higher oil and gas prices and investment in new technology (e.g., 4D seismic and directional drilling).[13]

The activities of OFS companies can be divided into at least three categories: manufacturing and supply of drilling equipment and materials; owning and leasing of drilling equipment; and carrying out tasks associated with finding and extracting oil and natural gas.[14] Some analysts also include seismic and oil/gasfield analysis as a fourth category.[15] Drilling companies provide equipment (e.g., a drill rig), personnel, and expertise to drill the well according to specifications provided by well operators. These entities can be large companies with global operations and many rigs, subsidiaries of the oil companies operating gas wells, or small companies with a few rigs and operations limited to one play.

OFS also includes a host of companies of all sizes that provide various services, such as pipe and equipment suppliers; trucking firms; sand, chemical and drilling additive producers; general construction and excavation contractors; water and waste water hauling, treating, and disposal firms; consulting engineers, geologists, land surveyors, landmen and right-of-way agents; tubing and downhole equipment manufacturers; well testing and completion entities; drilling mud engineers; and a multitude of other enterprises.

Some OFS companies that provide an array of sophisticated technologies, services, and other products to support well drilling and completion are, by some measures, larger than the oil companies they serve. For example, the market capitalization of Schlumberger, at $91 billion, exceeds that of Statoil and Conoco-Philips by over 20 percent. One thing that differentiates the largest OFS companies, such as Schlumberger, Halliburton, and Baker Hughes, from operators is that OFS companies spend higher percentages of revenue on research and development.[16]

Putting It Together

The process of drilling a well can involve a complex relationship between an operator, OFS companies, and companies involved in the midstream sector. With some exceptions, operators do not own drilling equipment but perform management and interpretive functions, such as using geophysical data provided by OFS companies to locate drilling activities.[17] Typically, once the location of a well is determined, the principal contractual relationship during the drilling phase is between an operator, which has the legal right to drill in a particular place, and a drilling contractor, which supplies the drill rig and labor.[18] Under this standard model, the operator is responsible for well designs and supervision of well construction activities, and the drilling contractor is responsible for implementing this design. Yet operators, as well as drilling contractors in turn, can utilize many sub-contractors to perform a range of functions.[19] Thus, a number of additional OFS companies become third parties providing a variety of essential services, such as site preparation, equipment supply, logging and testing, well completion, well servicing, etc.

Due in part to the intensity of drilling and completion activity involved with the development of shale hydrocarbon resources and in part to a long-term trend in which operators contract more "noncore activities" to the service sector,[20] the contractual terms and requirements insisted upon by many operators for OFS services have recently undergone rapid change so that the drilling and completion more resembles a continuous manufacturing setting compared to the more or less "one off" deal terms of the past.[21] What is broadly changing is a move toward the packaging of services within incentive-based relationships focused on "the well" as a product and a move away from proliferating individual contracts that sometimes placed the interests of operators and OFS at odds.

A good example of this is the integrated services drilling process model used by Schlumberger.[22] In traditional drilling processes, operators might supervise, coordinate, and manage many discrete tasks. For instance, during well construction, tasks treated separately might include directional drilling, cementing, and testing functions—sometimes under individual contracts. Each task would be treated separately, and each contractor would have a narrowly defined scope of work. Operators, responsible largely for well design, would be required to supervise the implementation program.

Under integration, defined as "the packaging of various services or products under a single contract,"[23] these tasks are grouped, or "bundled," as an integrated drilling services contract, potentially involving several OFS company product lines as well as third-party contracts. Separate integrated contracts might then be issued for other bundled services under the broader heading of "well construction." These could include drilling rig operations (e.g., logistics and casing running) and data acquisition (e.g., geophysical data, drilling reports, and completion drawings). Among the variables influencing how these relationships will play out are the size of the operator, the extent of an operator's presence in a particular play, the specific geologic conditions, and any changes in well conditions.[24]

Market conditions for supply of OFS are also important. For example, a scarcity of available OFS providers, along with the dynamic changes in downhole equipment and diagnostic technologies, can mean rapid evolution of relationships between operators and suppliers. In some cases, this has resulted in the use, in long-term contracts between operators and rig contractors, of rates indexed to commodity and labor prices, thus maintaining a degree of certainty for both parties and allowing each to share in market pricing risks.[25]

Market conditions may also have an impact on the availability of skilled OFS providers. These in turn may be a factor in the incidence of accidents or system failures, such as blowouts or cement casing failures.[26]

Cross-Indemnification and Risk Apportionment

In the oil and gas industry, the contractual relationships commonly governing these multiple interlocking operations are "relatively uniform in how the risks are allocated."[27] Under contracts known as "knock-for-knock" indemnities, or KK indemnities, parties (e.g., operators and drilling contractors) indemnify each other for claims arising out of death or personal injury of their personnel, loss or damage to their property, and pollution emanating from their property— regardless whether any negligence, breach of contract, or violation of statutory duty exists.

In addition, so-called pass-through indemnification may extend these indemnities to cover members of a named party's group— subcontractors and third parties, for example—whether named in the agreement or not. Although there may be no privity of contract between the operator, including its agents and assigns, and the landowners or mineral rights owners ("landowners") who granted exploration and development rights to the operator, some leases now provide such indemnifications to landowners. See, for example, this model lease language from the state of Ohio:

Indemnity:
Lessee agrees to defend, indemnify, and hold harmless Lessor and Lessor's heirs, successors, representatives, agents, and assigns ("Indemnitees"), from and against any and all claims, demands, and causes of action for injury (including death) or damage to persons, property and/or natural resources and fines or penalties, or environmental matters arising out of, incidental to, or resulting from the operations of or for Lessee or Lessee's servants, agents, employees, guests, licensees, invitees, or independent contractors, and from and against all costs and expenses incurred by Indemnitees by reason of any such claim or claims, including attorneys' fees; and each assignee of Lessee of this Lease, or an interest therein, agrees to indemnify and hold harmless Indemnitees in the same manner provided above. Such indemnity shall apply to any claim arising out of operations conducted under or pursuant to this Lease, however caused.[28]

Although indemnification clauses in leases are increasingly common,[29] absent such provisions the landowners may be limited to compensation provided by tort law.

The justification for widespread use of KK indemnities in the oil and gas industry rests on the following conditions: the difficulty of proving fault where complex, inherently hazardous operations are taking place; the complex structure of relationships and numerous parties involved in developing any single well; and the possibility that contractors and third parties would each require insurance for the manifold potential risks due to exposure created by these many relationships.[30]

Indeed, the BP Macondo well blowout in 2010 (BP Macondo incident), even though offshore, has functioned as something of a test of the use of KK indemnities in the onshore oil and gas industry.[31] Some states, notably Louisiana, Texas, New Mexico, and Wyoming have in place Oilfield Anti-Indemnity Acts that impose limitations on KK indemnities.[32] Insurance industry commentators suggest that certain jurisdictions may have public policy objections to these indemnities.[33] Protection of local firms is one example. The Texas and Louisiana statutes limiting indemnities appear to have been driven by some oil companies' attempts to contractually transfer all liability to local providers of materials and services.[34] Many states, including Texas and Louisiana, have statutes that limit the ability of parties to indemnify themselves against their own negligence. In fact, Texas and Louisiana take different and conflicting approaches to that problem.[35]

Cross-indemnification agreements attempt to apportion risk, which is then backed by several types of insurance. Perhaps the most common form of coverage is commercial general liability (CGL), yet there are more specialized insurance products available. These are predominantly carried by operators, which assume control of a drilling site, although additional coverage might also be purchased by some large drilling contractors.[36] Among these are operators extra expense (or OEE, which is also known as "control of well") coverage, which covers blowouts, as well as coverage designed specifically to cover environmental risks, broadly called environmental impairment liability (EIL) coverage, which covers gradual release from a well site—"latent hazards," like groundwater contamination.[37] This form of coverage is used to supplement GCL policy extensions, most of which limit coverage to "abrupt and instantaneous" releases.

Although unconventional operations entail new risks, EIL-type coverage is less commonly carried by onshore operators compared to GCL and OEE coverage.[38] While its use is growing, only a subset—about 30 percent to 40 percent of oil and gas companies "with significant fracturing operations" currently carry it.[39] There are concerns that fewer insurers will be willing to provide EIL coverage for fracking operations and that EIL coverage prices may make this coverage prohibitively expensive for operators.[40] Lack of regulatory clarity and high profile announcements by insurers like Nationwide that they will not insure against fracking-related risks are part of the reason for insurers' trepidation.[41] The potential for coverage disputes are another, with some observers likening the issues raised by fracking to asbestos litigation.[42] The potential for widespread contamination presents a particular problem in light of how KK indemnities relate to insurance risk transfer and the incentives these contracts create to reduce pollution risk.[43]

Regional Diversity

Underlying these and other variables influencing the nature of production activities are "the realities of regional diversity" as articulated in 2011 by the Shale Gas Production Subcommittee of the Secretary of Energy Advisory Board (Subcommittee Report),[44] which highlights the fact that the nature of operations can be highly variable within and between individual plays. Much variation is attributable to differences in underlying geologic conditions. Moreover, the rapid integration of regions across the United States into the "supply mix," particularly those areas without a recent history of drilling and production activity but now experiencing significant development pressure, has led to the evolution of drilling and completion technology, field practices, and regulation.[45]

BEST PRACTICES

The evolution in technology and practice, the geological diversity in shale oil and gas exploration, and the increased potential for—and awareness of—environmental contamination risks posed by shale exploration and development[46] have each brought new attention to best practices within the industry.[47] The Subcommittee Report defined best practices as "industry techniques or methods that have proven over time to accomplish given tasks and objectives in a manner that most acceptably balances desired outcomes and avoids undesirable consequences."[48] The drilling technology is rapidly evolving, so there is understandable concern[49] lest a specific technology become a regulatory requirement.

Best Practices and Regional Variation

How closely regulations governing industry practices are tailored to local conditions and the needs of industry remains a potent issue. According to the Subcommittee Report, "A single best engineering practice cannot [be] set for all locations and for all time."[50] Local variation in regulation can be beneficial because it results in regulatory controls more responsive to region-specific variables, such as geology and history of hydrocarbon development, and is less "removed from field operations."[51]

The idea that best practices can serve as a basis for environmental protection is not a new one.[52] For example, a well-known analogy from the water quality arena is the National Pollutant Discharge Elimination System (NPDES) Phase II requirements, which place primacy upon decisions taken at the municipal level. The oil and gas industry also has a history of using best management practices (BMPs).[53]

One recent example in the oil and gas industry is a collaboration between independent producer Southwestern Energy and the Environmental Defense Fund (EDF) to develop a set of model regulations for hydraulically fractured wells. The effort focuses on well integrity because it was found to be common to all reported cases of water well contamination linked to fracking.[54] Still in draft form, this document is an outgrowth of a review of state regulatory programs as well as industry standards. It sets out standards for all phases of well construction, from well planning and permitting, to predrilling water sampling, casing and cementing, well completion and fracturing, and plugging and abandonment. The document also contains disclosure provisions.[55]

A related effort is the set of fifteen performance standards developed by the Center for Sustainable Shale Development (CSSD) tailored to shale gas development in the Appalachian Basin, which includes the Marcellus formation. The performance standards include the following provisions: 90 percent recycling of flowback and produced water; use of closed loop containment in place of open pits for handling of flowback; analysis of stratigraphic confinement adequacy to prevent migration of frac fluids from the target formation; implementation of a sourcewater (surface and groundwater) monitoring program; and frac fluid disclosure, among others.[56] In addition, these standards will be linked to a certification process, which is currently under development.

At the time of writing, the CSSD partnership includes operators like Shell, Chevron, and Consol Energy as well as environmental groups like EDF and the Pennsylvania Environmental Council.[57] As some observers have commented, strategic collaborations like these are "lonely in the middle," where the pressure of pro-industry groups, opposition of environmental interests, and primacy of state regulation have created a challenging and polarized environment.[58]

The Subcommittee Report concludes that "a more systematic commitment to a process of *continuous improvement* to identify and implement best practices is needed, and should be embraced by all companies in the shale gas industry."[59] This includes a public health and protection element. The Subcommittee Report states, "Many companies already demonstrate their commitment to the kind of process we describe here, but the public should be confident that this is the practice across the industry."[60] For example, FracFocus, the industry-supported disclosure mechanism increasingly required by states such as Pennsylvania, is intended to satisfy the public's need to know what chemicals are used locally in frac fluids.

Beyond Best Practices

The specification of best practices is not a guarantee that oil and gas operations will always be safer from an environmental or a health perspective.[61] Organizational theorists dealing with socio-technical systems that involve high-risk technologies and high catastrophic potential have recognized that certain features of these systems, including deepwater drilling, are inherently risky and that accidents can be considered "normal." That is, a degree of unpredictability, complexity, and tight coupling of system elements makes accidents intrinsically likely—even under proper management and even after careful design.[62] This may be applicable to mineral resource recovery technologies, such as hydraulic fracturing and underground injection wells, and to dam construction and failure, where interactions between an industrial activity and the natural environment may as one system generate highly unpredictable consequences causing what Perrow calls an "eco-system accident."[63] An example might be increased seismic activity at certain wastewater injection wells.

Although the theory of "normal" accidents is based upon on high-risk enterprises and the organizations responsible for their operation, such as nuclear power, aircraft and airways, and marine shipping accidents—where the likelihood of an accident may be relatively small, but the consequences can be drastic—arguably, certain aspects of shale oil and gas exploration carry many of the same risks. While the "interactive complexity" of common high-volume hydraulic fracturing operations may be relatively low and the possibility for failure to cascade unpredictably through the system may, therefore, be limited, certain identified risks do carry the potential to cause an eco-system accident, as defined by Perrow. Such accidents might include induced seismicity (i.e. earthquakes) and the potential for "fracture intersection" with abandoned or "orphaned" wells, which is "a rare, but known occurrence."[64]

Normal accident theory rests on the relationship between high-risk systems and organizational structure, finding that failures occur even when operators are doing their best. Other research on accidents highlights certain high reliability organizations, such as aircraft carriers, in which accidents are extremely uncommon when everyone involved is aware, knowledgeable, and attuned to the ramifications of what everyone else is doing. This includes the ability of an organization to manage surprises through an understanding of detail and capacity for action.[65]

Transposing this more optimistic view of organizations to the development of an unconventional gas well, there are risks inherent in how OFS and operators work together and understand one another's jobs and how responsibility for safety is distributed and managed. In short, accident risk is not just a function of equipment failure. Organizational form and performance are also important. Attentiveness to safety underlies every aspect of the shale exploration and development process, such as ensuring the integrity of cement casings—not just fracturing.[66]

This also means that to be effective, regulators—and regulations—need to proactively emphasize training, process, and understanding, rather than merely being prescriptive. To the extent that the BP Macondo incident raises awareness of the possibility of similar accidents in onshore shale exploration, it is important for stakeholders to learn from the BP Macondo failures, including miscommunications, economic pressures, inadequate training, undue reliance upon engineering, and issues of organizational culture, as underscored in the Chief Counsel's Report.[67]

In addition, there are lessons from the BP Macondo incident about reliance on regulation and regulatory enforcement that may be pertinent in unconventional shale development.[68] A number of questions emerged about the relationship between the offshore drilling industry and regulators, particularly the Minerals Management Service (MMS), which was reorganized and renamed following the blowout and spill.[69] As analysts have noted, the approach of MMS to regulating the novel challenges posed by offshore oil and gas developments was premised upon collaboration with major oil companies and equipment vendors in the development of standards, highlighted by the DeepStar Research Project. While MMS cooperated with large, integrated oil companies, it focused its limited resources on the smaller independents launching deep sea operations.[70]

Thus, MMS was primed to accept these well design changes—however risky. Further, MMS was known to have suffered from a lack of technical capacity due to gaps in employee skills and experience. The agency has consistently had difficulty hiring, training, and retaining experienced staff, which may have compromised its oversight and management responsibilities.[71] These challenges have affected the agency's ability to measure and verify production in particular.[72] As the Government Accountability Office recently found, these challenges remain in spite of the reorganization of activities previously overseen by MMS.[73]

Whether a similar capacity gap will affect state-level agencies charged with oversight of unconventional oil and gas operations is an ongoing issue, and there have been suggestions of developing new regulatory paradigms. Meehan, for example, has suggested the creation of a new regulatory agency for transitional and clean energy technologies to separate the promotion and regulatory roles of the Department of Energy. Osofsky and Wiseman suggest a range of paradigms to address the current fragmented, yet overlapping, jurisdictions.[74] A shale play rarely is located beneath a single state. For example, the Haynesville shale lies beneath the states of Texas, Arkansas, and Louisiana. Well sites may be located beneath more than one state, as well as beneath overlapping local jurisdictions with their separate road regulations, noise, light ordinances, and zoning requirements.

As Wiseman notes, industry often has an important claim to technical knowledge associated with unconventional shale oil and gas development and should, therefore, be among the key voices influencing how the process of exploiting these resources unfolds.[75] Still, there are pitfalls. In an analysis of industry disclosure of frac fluid chemical composition, Wiseman notes that best practices and other voluntary industry initiatives have several drawbacks. These include the fact that industry itself may not know the full range of risks; the potential that agencies and the public can be "boxed in" by precedents set using industry-derived voluntary standards and agreements; the squelching of voices of non-industry actors; and the fact that they are potentially weighted toward industry needs.[76]

> In the substantive realm, efforts by state regulators and industry to work together to identify risks, write guidelines, and propose regulatory changes have been impressive, although not comprehensive. . . . More consistent efforts to compare gaps among states and regulatory change in response to suggestions from STRONGER [The State Review of Oil and Natural Gas Environmental Regulations], industry groups, scientists and other stakeholders will be needed.[77]

CONCLUSION

This chapter has described broadly the form and organization of companies involved in the upstream segment of unconventional resource development. It has described the entities involved, including fully integrated oil majors, national oil companies, independent operators, and oilfield services companies; shown how relationships among each are structured and risk is apportioned; and introduced some of the actors behind the increasing focus on best management practices. As the ongoing push for use of best practices illustrates, it is increasingly necessary to have a basic understanding of the industry in order to gauge its impacts and effects.

NOTES

1. See, e.g., Joe Schremmer, Comment, Avoidable "Fraccident": An Argument Against Strict Liability for Hydraulic Fracturing, 60 KAN. L. REV. 1215 (2012); Jesica Rivero Gilbert, Assessing the Risks and Benefits of Hydraulic Fracturing, 18 Mo. ENVTL. L. & POL'Y REV. 170–208 (2011).
2. Owen Anderson, The Anatomy of an Oil and Gas Drilling Contract, 25 TULSA L. REV., 359, 382–95 (1989).
3. For a quarterly list of the Top Forty natural gas producers, see Analyses & Studies, NATURAL GAS SUPPLY ASSOC., http://www.ngsa.org/analyses -studies/ (follow "Top 40 Producers: 2012 3rd Quarter" hyperlink) (last visited Mar. 27, 2013).
4. Analyses & Studies, NATURAL GAS SUPPLY ASSOC., http://www.ngsa.org /analyses-studies/ (follow "Top 40 Producers: 2012 3rd Quarter" hyperlink) (last visited Mar. 27, 2013).
5. ROBERT PIROG, CONGRESSIONAL RESEARCH SERVICE, THE ROLE OF NATIONAL OIL COMPANIES IN THE INTERNATIONAL OIL MARKET (Aug. 21, 2007), available at http://www.fas.org/sgp/crs/misc/RL34137.pdf.
6. ERNST & YOUNG, THE OIL DOWNSTREAM: VERTICALLY CHALLENGED? (2012), available at http://www.ey.com/Publication/vwLUAssets/The_oil_down stream:_vertically_challenged/$FILE/The_oil_downstream_vertically _challenged.pdf.
7. For Norway's Statoil, investments abroad, including in U.S. unconventional plays, helped push its 2011 fourth quarter reserve replacement ratio over 100% for the first time in six years. Kari Lundgren, Statoil Net Rises as Reserves Replaced for First Year in Six, BLOOMBERG (Feb. 8, 2012, 11:38 AM), http://www.bloomberg.com/news/2012-02-08/statoil-profit-more-than -doubles-on-assets-sales-oil-prices.html).
8. Foreign Investors Play Large Role in U.S. Shale Industry, U.S. ENERGY INFO. AGENCY TODAY IN ENERGY (Apr. 8, 2013), http://www.eia.gov/todayinenergy /detail.cfm?id=10711.
9. See, e.g., Our Shale Resources, STATOIL, http://www.statoil.com/en/our operations/explorationprod/shalegas/pages/where.aspx (last updated July 4, 2013).
10. Bloomberg News, China Joining U.S. Shale Renaissance with $40 Billion, BLOOM- BERG (Mar. 6, 2013, 6:13 AM), http://www.bloomberg.com/news/2013-03 -05/china-joining-u-s-shale-renaissance-with-40-billion.html.
11. Joshua Zive, Unreasonable delays: CFIUS Reviews of Energy Transactions, 3 HARV. BUS. L. REV. 169 (2013), available at http://www.hblr.org/wp-content /uploads/2013/04/Zive_Unreasonable-Delays.pdf.
12. Oilfield Services: The Unsung Masters of the Oil Industry, ECONOMIST, July 21, 2012.
13. Id.

14. *Id.*
15. ERNST & YOUNG, REVIEW OF THE UK OILFIELD SERVICES INDUSTRY 2012 (2013), *available at* http://www.ey.com/publication/vwLUAssets/Review _of_the_UK_oilfield_services_Industry_2012/$FILE/EY_Review_of_the _UK_oilfield_services_Industry_2012.pdf.
16. *Oilfield Services, supra* note 12.
17. *Oilfield Services, supra* note 12.
18. Anderson, *Anatomy of an Oil and Gas Drilling Contract, supra* note 2, at 364–65.
19. AM. PETROL. INST., CONTRACTOR SAFETY MANAGEMENT FOR OIL AND GAS DRILLING AND PRODUCTION OPERATIONS: API RECOMMENDED PRACTICE 76 (2d ed., 2007), *available at* http://xa.yimg.com/kq/groups/17553945/12829 49026/name/API+Contractor+Safety+Management+Sys+OilandGas+Drill ing_76_e2.pdf.
20. Jacques Bourque, et al., *Business Solutions for E&P Through Integrated Project Management,* OILFIELD REV., Autumn 1997, at 35.
21. Authors' interview with Kinnan Golemon, Esq. (Apr. 7, 2013).
22. This section is adapted from Stephane Chafcouloff et al., *Integrated Services,* OILFIELD REV., Summer 1995, at 11–25, *available at* http://www.slb .com/~/media/Files/resources/oilfield_review/ors95/sum95/06951125.pdf.
23. *Id.* at 11.
24. *See, e.g.,* YCELP, *Balancing Environmental, Social and Economic Impacts of Shale Gas Development Activities,* VIMEO (Jan. 23, 2013), http://vimeo .com/58162903 (video of webinar with Mark K. Boling, *Emerging Issues in Shale Gas Development Series,* Yale Law School) [hereinafter *Boling*]. *See generally* SEC'Y OF ENERGY'S ADVISORY BOARD, SHALE GAS PRODUCTION SUB-COMMITTEE: NINETY-DAY REPORT (Aug. 18, 2011) [hereinafter *Subcommittee Report*].
25. C. Newton, P. Cody, & R. Carr, *Sourcing Critical Oilfield Services for Shale Plays in a Tightening Supply Market,* 231 WORLD OIL, no. 8, Aug. 2010, at 63–66.
26. *Boling, supra* note 24.
27. The quote is from Thomas Swartz, *Hydraulic fracturing: risks and risk management,* 26 NAT. RESOURCES & ENV'T, Fall 2011, at 30, *available at* http://usa .marsh.com/NewsInsights/ThoughtLeadership/Articles/ID/12717/Hydraulic -Fracturing-Risks-and-Risk-Management.aspx. This section draws upon Chidi Egbochue, *Reviewing 'Knock for Knock' Indemnities Following the Macondo Well Blowout,* 7 Construction L. Int'l, Jan. 2013, at 7–14.
28. HARVARD LAW SCH., EMMETT ENVTL. LAW AND POLICY CLINIC, AN OHIO LAND OWNER'S GUIDE TO HYDRAULIC FRACTURING: ADDRESSING ENVIRONMENTAL AND HEALTH ISSUES IN NATURAL GAS LEASES 56–57 (June 16, 2011), *available at* http://blogs.law.harvard.edu/environmentallawprogram /files/2013/01/elpc-ohio-leasing-guide-v2-june-2011-web.pdf.

29. *See, e.g.*, Thomas West and Cindy M. Monaco, Presentation at the 3rd Law of Shale Plays Conference: Do Conventional Leases Work for Unconventional Plays in Unconventional Times? 18 (June 6–7, 2012) (unpublished manuscript) (discussing the fact that it is increasingly common for leases to include indemnifications between landowners and operators in favor of landowners).

30. Egbochue, *supra* note 27, at 9–10.

31. LeRoy Lambert, *Knock-for-knock contracts are enforceable in the US*, STANDARD OFFSHORE BULL., Oct. 2011, at 10.

32. Egobuchue, *supra* note 27, at 10–11 and n.18.

33. Egobuchue, *supra* note 27, at 10, 14.

34. Lambert, *supra* note 31, 10.

35. Authors' communication with Bruce Kramer, Esq. (July 28, 2013).

36. Swartz, *supra* note 27.

37. M. Jokajtys, *Insuring Fracking Risk: Can Conventional Insurance Tools Manage Unconventional Risk?*, 27 NAT. RESOURCES & ENV'T, Winter 2013, at 1–4.

38. See Swartz, *supra* note 27, for a discussion of the additional risks to insurers posed by shale gas fracking operations.

39. Douglas McLeod, *Fracking Risk Coverage Limited*, BUSINESS INSURANCE (Feb. 25, 2013), *available at* Academic OneFile, File No. 0014.

40. Jokajtys, *supra* note 37.

41. Jokajtys, *supra* note 37, at 4.

42. Douglas McLeod, *The Coming Conflicts*, RISK AND INSURANCE ONLINE (Oct. 1, 2012), http://www.riskandinsurance.com/printstory.jsp?storyId=533351196.

43. *See, e.g.*, Swartz, *supra* note 27, discussing involvement of "nonoperating" owners, who may be required under operating agreements to purchase their own insurance programs.

44. *Subcommittee Report, supra* note 24, at 10.

45. *Subcommittee Report, supra* note 24, at 6, 10.

46. Swartz, *supra* note 27, at 31.

47. Boling, *supra* note 24.

48. *Subcommittee Report, supra* note 24, at 26.

49. Boling, *supra* note 24.

50. *Subcommittee Report, supra* note 24, at 26.

51. U.S. DEP'T ENERGY, STATE OIL AND NATURAL GAS REGULATIONS DESIGNED TO PROTECT WATER RESOURCES 37 (May 2009).

52. This section draws heavily upon a 2012 presentation by Kathryn Mutz and Bruce Kramer. *See* Kathryn Mutz and Bruce M. Kramer, Presentation at the 3d Law of Shale Plays Conference: Should Best Management Practices Be Defined By Regulation? (June 6–7, 2012).

53. For instance, the Intermountain Oil and Gas BMP Project (IOGP) maintains a database of both required and recommended BMPs (see http://www

.oilandgasbmps.org/). The federal Bureau of Land Management uses BMPs as part of its drilling permit program (see http://www.blm.gov/wo/st/en /prog/energy/oil_and_gas/best_management_practices.html). And in the eastern United States, the Marcellus Shale Coalition has identified "recommended practices" that provide guidance on a range of issues, such as water pipelines, motor vehicle safety, pre-drilling water supply surveys, and supply chain management, among others (recommended practice documents are available for download at http://marcelluscoalition.org/category/library /recommended-practices/).

54. Boling, *supra* note 24.

55. A copy of the draft can be accessed here: http://portal.ncdenr.org/c/document _library/get_file?uuid=8356eb89-9c9f-4f8e-bb4d-4bb51b605575&group Id=8198095.

56. CENTER FOR SUSTAINABLE SHALE DEVELOPMENT, PERFORMANCE STANDARDS (Mar. 2013), *available at* http://037186e.netsolhost.com/site/wp-content /uploads/2013/03/CSSD-Performance-Standards-3-13R.pdf.

57. Kevin Begos, *Both Sides Agree on Tough New Fracking Standards*, ASSOCIATED PRESS (March 20, 2013, 4:50 PM), http://bigstory.ap.org/article /both-sides-agree-tough-new-fracking-standards.

58. Peter Behr, Authors of Model Fracking Regulation Find that it's Lonely in the Middle, MIDWEST ENERGY NEWS (Oct. 4, 2012), http:// www.midwestenergynews.com/2012/10/04/authors-of-model-fracking -regulation-find-its-lonely-in-the-middle/.

59. *Subcommittee Report*, *supra* note 24, at 9–10 (emphasis in original).

60. *Subcommittee Report*, *supra* note 24, at 10.

61. Hannah J. Wiseman, *The Private Role in Public Fracturing Disclosure and Regulation*, 3 HARV. BUS. L. REV. ONLINE 49, 66 (2013), http://www.hblr .org/wp-content/uploads/2013/02/Wiseman_The-Private-Role-in-Public -Fracturing-Disclosure-and-Regulation.pdf.

62. CHARLES PERROW, NORMAL ACCIDENTS: LIVING WITH HIGH-RISK TECHNOLOGIES (1999) (for systems analysis, see ch. 3: *Complexity, Coupling, and Catastrophe*, 62–100).

63. *Id.* at 14.

64. *See* George E. King, Society of Petrol. Eng'rs, *Hydraulic Fracturing 101: What Every Representative, Environmentalist, Regulator, Reporter, Investor, University Researcher, Neighbor and Engineer Should Know About Estimating Frac Risk and Improving Frac Performance in Unconventional Gas and Oil Wells* (Report No. 152596, 2012), *available at* http://fracfocus.org/sites /default/files/publications/hydraulic_fracturing_101.pdf; *See also* Boling, *supra* note 24 (for further discussion of earthquake and abandoned gas well risks).

65. Karl E. Weick, Kathleen M. Sutcliffe & David Obstfeld, *Organizing for High Reliability: Processes of Collective Mindfulness*, *in* 1 RESEARCH IN ORGANIZATIONAL BEHAVIOR 81–123 (R.S. Sutton & B.M. Staw eds., 1999).

66. Boling, *supra* note 24.
67. National Commission on the BP Deepwater Horizon Oil Spill and Offshore Drilling, Chief Counsel's Report, Macondo: The Gulf Oil Disaster, at x–xi, 225–50 (2011), *available at* http://www.oilspillcommission.gov/sites/default/files/documents/C21462-220_CCR_Chp_5_Overarching_Failures_of_Management.pdf [hereinafter *Chief Counsel's Report*].
68. *See id.* at 251, summarizing Chapter 3 of the Full Final Report of the National Commission on the BP Deepwater Horizon Oil Spill and Offshore Drilling (available in full at http://www.oilspillcommission.gov/sites/default/files/documents/4_OSC_CH_3.pdf).
69. While official reports found that BP allowed a number of risky decisions to take place, some of which violated industry best practices, only one—an unusual temporary abandonment design—required MMS approval. *Id.* at 246.
70. Christopher Carrigan, *Captured by Disaster? Reinterpreting Regulatory Behavior in the Shadow of the Gulf Oil Spill*, at 40–43 (forthcoming chapter in Daniel Carpenter & David Moss, Preventing Regulatory Capture: Special Interest Influence and How to Limit It (Cambridge University Press, 2013)), *available at* http://www.tobinproject.org/sites/tobinproject.org/files/assets/Carrigan%20Captured%20by%20Disaster%20%281.16.13%29.pdf.
71. *See* U.S. Gov't Accountability Office, GAO-11-487T, Oil and Gas Leasing: Past Work Identifies Numerous Challenges with Interior's Oversight 5 (2011), *available at* http://www.gao.gov/assets/130/125795.pdf.
72. *See* U.S. Gov't Accountability Office, GAO-10-313, Oil and Gas Management: Interior's Oil and Gas Production Verification Efforts Do Not Provide Reasonable Assurance of Accurate Measurement of Production Volumes 68–72 (2010), *available at* http://www.gao.gov/assets/310/301947.pdf.
73. *See generally id.* at 3 (discussing failure at Interior to incorporate recommendations of GAO during reorganization intended to address "numerous weaknesses and challenges").
74. Taylor Meehan, Note, *Lessons from the Price-Anderson Nuclear Industry Indemnity Act for Future Clean Energy Compensatory Models*, 18 Conn. Ins. L.J. 339 (2011). *See also* Hari M. Osofsky & Hannah Jacobs Wiseman, *Dynamic Energy Federalism*, 72 Md. L. Rev. 773 (2013), http://digitalcommons.law.umaryland.edu/mlr/vol72/iss3/3/; Hari M. Osofsky & Hannah Jacobs Wiseman, *Hybrid Energy Governance*, U. Ill. L. Rev. (Forthcoming 2014), *available at* http://ssrn.com/abstract=2147860.
75. Wiseman, *supra* note 61, at 66.
76. *Id.* at 58, 61–66.
77. *Id.* at 63.

PART
2

Legal Issues

3

Leasing Mineral Rights
A Framework for Understanding the Dominant Estate

Chad J. Lee and Jill D. Cantway

INTRODUCTION

Natural gas production has exploded throughout the country as the industry discovers new methods of extraction. Despite the rapidly evolving technology, the oil and gas lease has changed surprisingly little in recent years and in many ways is a fairly standard contract. Oil and gas are separate hydrocarbon minerals, but are typically lumped into the same lease document, primarily because both are "fugacious" minerals, which migrate under the earth.

Oil and natural gas production has far reaching impacts, from national security to environmental integrity. While state and federal regulations more directly affect the rate of resource production, the content of individual oil and gas leases can significantly impact the effects of exploration on the real property owner, and, cumulatively, the region where exploration is taking place. In this chapter, we first discuss the nature of mineral ownership. Second, we discuss the "nuts and bolts" of oil and gas leases. Finally, we address some specific lease considerations relevant to hydraulic fracturing.

41

The oil and gas lease is both a conveyance of the mineral estate to the lessee, as well as a contractual relationship between a mineral owner (lessor) and an oil and gas company (lessee). In exchange for an initial bonus payment and/or delay rental payments to the lessor, the lessee has a temporarily vested right for a period of years (the primary term) in which to explore the mineral resource of a property and to drill a well if the lessee determines that developing the resources would be in its economic interest. The lease can be extended to a secondary term if a well is drilled within the primary term and produces oil or gas in paying quantities. This secondary term is typically indefinite in duration, so long as oil or gas is produced in paying quantities or, depending on the language of the lease, as long as drilling operations commenced within the primary term. Royalties are paid to the lessor based on production of the minerals.

The oil and gas lease is best viewed as a purely economic transaction where the oil and gas company has two main goals: (1) the right to develop the leased premises without any obligation to do so during the primary term, and (2) the right to maintain the lease for as long as production is economically profitable. The right to develop or not develop the property arises from the reality that the mineral potential of any property is, for the most part, unknown at the time the parties enter into the lease. The right to maintain the lease indefinitely upon the occurrence of certain events specified in the lease, such as oil or gas is being produced, well drilling has begun, or other exploration activities have been initiated, is justified by the significant economic risk taken by the gas company in making the investment to drill the well. Ownership of oil, gas, and other minerals in place is an interest in real property, at least until the minerals are produced, at which point it becomes an interest in personal property. Oil and gas leases reflect the realities of the gas industry, and are very different from commercial or residential leases of real estate.

MINERAL INTEREST OWNERSHIP

Legally, minerals are part of the real estate. Most lawyers are taught to think of real estate ownership as a "bundle of sticks." Each stick is a different unit of real estate with certain rights and obligations. For example, the ability to exclude third parties from one's own land is a "stick" in the bundle. Ownership of the surface, minerals, and easements are all separate sticks in the bundle. Each bundle of sticks is an "estate" in real property.

When a landowner owns all the sticks, she owns the "fee" estate, or "fee simple." More commonly, however, certain "sticks" have been conveyed to third parties in the past, like a utility easement or mineral interest. Often, the minerals have been severed from the surface, meaning the owner of the surface does not own title to the minerals. Only the owner(s) of the minerals can lease those minerals. The mineral estate can become highly complex and severely fractionated, especially in highly developed areas. Usually, the oil and gas company must hire a mineral title attorney to determine the precise interest in the mineral estate.

For example, in 1900 the federal government issued a patent, without reservation of any minerals, to Bert for a 40-acre ranch in Colorado called Blackacre. After receiving the patent, Bert owns the entire "fee estate," or 100 percent of the surface and the minerals. In 1940, Bert sells Blackacre to Andy. Understanding the value of minerals, Bert reserves half of the mineral estate to himself. After this conveyance, Andy owns 100 percent of the surface, but only a 50 percent interest in the minerals. Conveyances and reservations of minerals typically continue on down the chain of title until we get to the present day. For example, upon Bert's death, his 50 percent interest in the minerals vests in his four children, three of whom sell to third parties and one of whom conveys his interest to his four children, reserving a life estate to himself. Additionally, when Andy sells Blackacre, he reserves 50 percent of his interest in the minerals (which is actually 25 percent because he only initially owned 50 percent). Later, Andy sells only that part of his mineral interest in Blackacre above a certain horizon (or depth) under Blackacre, let's say 5,000 feet. These types of conveyances can continue, potentially resulting in very large numbers of mineral owners with each owning a different interest in the minerals under a given surface estate.

There are other potential mineral interests that can be created by specific conveyances or reservations, including various kinds of royalty interests, production payments, and net profits interest. For example, a nonparticipating royalty interest is an interest in only the percentage share of the values of the minerals sold, but without any decision-making authority regarding leasing, exploration, or development. These types of interests are all permutations of the mineral estate. Most of these interests exceed the scope of this chapter, but the reader should be aware of the variety of interests that can be created within the mineral estate.

Oil and gas companies will generally research the mineral title and obtain oil and gas leases from all mineral owners prior to drilling. If they do not obtain a lease from a mineral owner, there are force pooling statutes and other exceptions (discussed elsewhere in this book, including chapter 4) that would apply to the unleased mineral owner's share of the minerals. After the minerals are produced and sold, the lessee pays royalties to the mineral owners in proportion to their ownership of the mineral estate.

Another major "stick" in the mineral interest bundle is the implied easement to use the surface. The law implies an easement that every mineral owner (or its lessee) can use as much of the surface as is reasonably necessary to obtain the minerals under the property. This is discussed in depth below. This easement is implied by necessity; without it the mineral estate would be worthless because the surface owner would have the ultimate "veto power." In fact, in most states, courts consider the mineral estate to be even more important than the surface estate.[1] The historical justification for the superiority of the mineral estate is that the minerals cannot be moved, whereas activities on the surface can be relocated, at least temporarily, to permit the minerals to be removed.

But mineral owners (or their lessees) cannot use the surface with impunity. In most states the mineral owner is required to, at minimum, "reasonably accommodate" the surface owner. Some states have gone further and have enacted statutes codifying this doctrine and granting further rights to surface owners. For this reason, surface owners are often approached by oil and gas companies to enter into surface use agreements, which, as the name implies, dictate the oil and gas company's use of the surface of the property.

Conversely, the surface owner also typically has certain rights that extend below the surface, even if they do not own any of the minerals underlying their property. The surface owner generally has rights to potable groundwater, subsurface support, and potentially even rights to use geologic formations for the storage of natural gas.[2]

LEASING IN GENERAL

Prior to drilling, the oil and gas company will usually first obtain an oil and gas lease from each of the owners of the minerals underlying a prospective location. Depending on how fractionated the minerals are, the gas company may have to negotiate and obtain many leases. The lease gives the oil and gas company the right to explore and develop the minerals. The wording of each lease is important and determines the precise interests that are leased. As with other contracts, the parties are free to enter into whatever bargain they choose, so long as the terms are sufficiently definite to be enforceable.

LEASE FORMS AND THE MYTH OF THE "PRODUCER'S 88"

Many mineral owners are first approached by a "landman" to lease their mineral interest. A landman is either an agent of an oil and gas company or an independent contractor who will later sell the lease to an oil and gas company. Most mineral owners would be wise to consult with an attorney prior to executing any lease. Unfortunately, most do not. Most also have a mistaken assumption that there is a standard oil and gas lease form called the "Producer's 88." This myth has been perpetuated because leases commonly contain a notation in the upper margin of something like 'Producer's 88-Revised.' But there is no uniform industry standard lease, and the "Producer's 88" generally refers to a lease form with terms favorable to the gas company.[3]

BASIC PRIVATE (FEE) LEASES

Unlike commercial or residential real property leases, courts generally treat an oil and gas lease as both a conveyance of the mineral rights and a contract between the mineral owner (lessor) and the oil and gas company (lessee) for the development of the minerals. Oil and gas leases are different from real property leases in three main ways: (1) the lessee has the right not only to use the land, but also extract substances of value from it; (2) the lessee's rights are not normally limited by a specific term; and (3) the lessee's rights to use the land are not exclusive and must be shared with the surface owner.[4] Because oil and gas leases are considered to be conveyances of real property, the lease must be in writing or otherwise satisfy the Statute of Frauds. The lessee will also record either the lease itself or a "memorandum of lease" in the county records in order to provide notice of the lease to third parties.

There is some variation from state to state in the classification of the property interest conveyed by the oil and gas lease, but the interest is most commonly a conveyance of real property. In Texas, a leasehold interest is an estate in fee simple determinable to the oil and gas in place.[5] In other states, including Oklahoma and Wyoming, the lessee's interest is called a *profit a pendre*,[6] whereas Pennsylvania classifies a lessee's interest as an inchoate right, which may become vested only after production.[7] Notwithstanding this disparate legal treatment, oil and gas leases create a surprisingly uniform relationship between the lessor and the lessee, and all include a few indispensible terms.

An oil and gas lease must generally contain four clauses: the granting clause, the *habendum* clause (the term), the drilling-delay rental clause, and the royalty provision.[8] There are other miscellaneous clauses that can also be inserted into the lease and several implied covenants, some of which we will discuss below. Typical formulations of these clauses are presented below, together with a discussion of their implications.

The Granting Clause

Lessor in consideration of $_____ per net mineral acre in hand paid, of the royalties herein provided, and of the agreements of Lessee herein contained, hereby grants, leases, and lets exclusively unto Lessee for the purposes of investigating, exploring, prospecting, drilling, and mining for and producing oil, gas, and all other minerals, conducting exploration, geological and geophysical surveys by seismograph, core test, gravity and magnetic methods, injecting gas, water and other fluids, and air into subsurface strata, laying pipelines, building roads, tanks, power stations, telephone lines, and other structures thereon, and on, over, and across lands owned or claimed by Lessor adjacent and contiguous thereto, to produce, save, take care of, treat, transport and own said products, and housing its employees, the following land . . . .

or, simply:

Lessor leases to Lessee for the purposes of exploring and producing oil and gas and other liquid and gaseous hydrocarbons, compounds, and byproducts produced therewith, the following lands. . . .

The granting clause defines the specific substances and lands leased and grants the right to explore, develop, and produce oil and gas from the lands, without the obligation to do so. Because other valuable substances are produced as byproducts of oil and gas production, many courts have struggled to decide which substances are covered by oil and gas leases. To avoid disputes, oil and gas leases should be specific as to which substances are covered. In general, references to all "oil and gas and all other hydrocarbons" or "oil, gas, and all other minerals" will apply to all liquid and gaseous hydrocarbons, even if they are not considered to be oil or gas.

Further, as with all deeds conveying interests in real property, the lease must describe the leased lands sufficiently such that a reasonable person can locate the parcel. Street addresses and assessor's parcel numbers are generally insufficient, whereas metes and bound descriptions or references to specific quarter sections, townships, and ranges are preferred.

The granting clause also conveys the right to explore for and develop the minerals. We should note that in some cases, an oil and gas company will negotiate a surface use agreement with the surface owner of the lands on which they plan to drill. Such an agreement may specify the type and location of surface uses allowed. In the absence of such agreement, the oil and gas company (lessee) is accorded considerable discretion in using the surface and subsurface of the leased property. But this discretion is not unlimited. Courts have limited a lessee's activities on the leased property by at least five doctrines: (1) reasonable use, (2) the accommodation doctrine, (3) for the benefit of the minerals in place; (4) the terms of the lease; and (5) all applicable statutes, ordinances, rules, and regulations.[9]

Limitations on Oil and Gas Company Activity

An oil and gas lease conveys to the oil and gas company an implied right to reasonable use of the surface to locate, develop, and produce oil and gas from the property. The oil and gas company, in other words, has an implied easement to use the surface of the land in such ways and at such locations as may be reasonably necessary to obtain the minerals.[10] Many surface owners are surprised by the breadth of this implied easement, as it accords considerable discretion to oil and gas companies to utilize almost all aspects of the surface estate which do not directly interfere with the surface owners current uses.

Surface owners should familiarize themselves with the types of infrastructure necessary to complete a modern well. Hydraulic fracturing, in particular, adds several steps to the process, including the use of more pits, tanks, and equipment on the surface, the application of fluid and chemicals to the well after drilling, and the production of a type of waste called "flowback" water.[11] The implied easement in an oil and gas lease permits the lessee to conduct hydraulic fracturing in the absence of an express provision to the contrary. Of course, it also permits more traditional oil and gas operations. What this means for surface owners is that once the minerals are leased, the oil and gas company has a legal right to access the surface estate, conduct seismic and other exploratory tests, build roads, construct drilling sites, and erect structures associated with oil and gas production including storage tanks, compressor stations, waste pits, and pipelines.[12] It even permits the oil and gas company to use certain surface resources, such as water and building materials, in some cases.[13]

Nonetheless, any activity that exceeds the scope of the easement is a trespass, for which the surface owner can seek damages. Oil and gas companies have been held liable for a number of trespass-related claims, including negligent pollution and nuisance for failure to plug abandoned wells and remove equipment.[14] What constitutes a trespass depends on the unique facts and circumstances of the situation, which is a question of fact for a jury, and typically the burden is on the surface owner to prove any type of trespass-related action.[15] Recently, however, oil and gas companies have become acutely aware of the changing societal norms of "reasonable use" under an oil and gas lease, and typically operate accordingly.

This implied easement may be expanded, of course, by written agreement between the surface owner and oil and gas company. This could occur through a separate easement, such as a pipeline easement, a surface use agreement, or it may be included in the granting clause of the lease (if the mineral owner also owns the surface).

Under the "accommodation doctrine," mineral lessees must also accommodate surface use wherever possible. Under common law, the intent of the parties in severing the minerals was that both the mineral owner and the surface owner would have valuable estates.[16] In order to protect the value of the surface, oil and gas companies should be required to accommodate surface uses whenever reasonable. The accommodation doctrine varies state by state. For example, in Texas for the doctrine to apply (1) there must be an existing surface use; (2) the proposed mineral activity must substantially interfere with the existing surface use; and (3) the oil and gas company must have reasonable alternatives.[17] The burden is on the surface owner to prove there are alternative means to develop the mineral estate.[18] In Colorado, on the other hand, a mineral owner (or gas company) must have "due regard" for the surface estate and must select alternate methods of production which mitigate the impacts of production on the surface estate, but only if those alternatives are "economically practicable."[19]

An oil and gas company must also limit use of the surface to those uses exclusively intended to obtain minerals from under the lands leased, i.e., their activities on the surface must be "for the benefit of the minerals in place." For example, if an oil and gas company leases two adjoining tracts, it cannot install a pipeline across one tract to access minerals produced on the adjacent tract (unless it is also producing oil or gas from the first tract under a pooled unit, for example).[20]

Recent developments in horizontal drilling and hydraulic fracturing have intensified the surface operations of oil and gas drilling. Horizontal drilling permits the capture of oil and gas from a smaller footprint, though it intensifies the use of that footprint. Given the use of these techniques, the dominance of the mineral estate may become even more apparent in the future.

Lease Terms and Regulatory Restrictions

Just as in any other contract, the terms of the lease can modify the above-described common law rights and obligations between the parties. Some leases specifically limit the surface use of the parcel or contain a no surface occupancy (NSO) stipulation. An NSO stipulation is an agreement in an oil and gas lease prohibiting any sort of occupancy or disturbance on all or part of the leased lands in order to protect special values on the surface estate. Note that the lessee may develop the oil and gas estate through the use of directional or horizontal drilling from outside the area subject to the NSO stipulation. Occasionally, the parties will enter into an NSO stipulation in the lease and then enter into a surface use agreement later.

The oil and gas company's activities are also limited by statute. Local, state, and federal governments routinely impose restrictions on an oil and gas company's implied right to use the leased property. Generally, courts have held these restrictions to be valid exercises of the state's police power. In New York, for example, the courts have generally permitted municipalities to prohibit oil and gas operations within their borders under the guise of land use regulations.[21] However, some local governments may be preempted from imposing certain restrictions, especially technical restrictions.[22] In any event, preemption is a rapidly emerging field of oil and gas law, which has re-emerged in the wake of America's current "energy renaissance."

Additionally, some states have enacted surface damage acts, some of which require oil and gas companies to pay damages for their use of the surface.[23] These statutes reverse the common law that a mineral interest owner is entitled to reasonable use of the surface to obtain the minerals without the landowner's permission and without payment. Surface damages acts may become even more important now that hydraulic fracturing is mainstream. States will likely enact or update their acts in the next few years in response to the public outcry over the use of hydraulic fracturing.

The *Habendum* (Term) Clause

> This Lease shall be for a term of _____ years from this date, call the "primary term," and as long thereafter as oil or gas are produced.

or,

> This Lease shall be in effect for and during the Primary Term and as long thereafter as minerals hereunder are produced in paying quantifies from the Leased Premises or the Land Unitized herewith.

The *habendum* clause defines the term of an oil and gas lease. Typically, this clause includes a defined primary term and a contingent secondary term.[24] During the primary term, the oil and gas company may hold the lease without actually drilling. In general, the primary term is the maximum period during which the oil and gas company can hold the lease without drilling. The purpose of the primary term is to provide the oil and gas company with sufficient time to complete geologic and geophysical testing, drill a test well, or arrange for financing and other support services necessary to drill.

The length of a primary term is a function of the market. As a general rule of thumb, the primary term in non-proven or marginally producing areas is between five and ten years, and the primary term for established and proven areas is between one and five years. The primary term can be cut short by surrender of the lease by the oil and gas company or failure to pay delay rentals, if applicable.

The secondary term extends the lease beyond the primary term in the event of production in paying quantities for as long as it is economically viable to do so. Usually the secondary term is an indefinite period of time, but occasionally maximum time limits are attached to secondary terms.

Courts differ on the interpretation of "production" sufficient to extend the lease into a secondary term. In general, courts view oil and gas leases as purely economic transactions. With this in mind, the majority view requires marketing of the oil and/or gas in addition to production "in paying quantities." However, other states hold that an oil and gas lease will not terminate if oil or gas is discovered prior to the end of the primary term so long as the lessee makes diligent efforts to complete the well, produce the minerals, and market the same.[25] Production "in paying quantities" is often difficult to apply in practice. In Texas, for example, the standard is whether, under all the relevant circumstances, a reasonably prudent operator would, for the purpose of making a profit, continue to operate the well.[26] More discussion on this issue is included below regarding shut-in gas royalty clauses.

The Drilling Delay Rental Clause

If operations for drilling are not commenced on said land, or on acreage poled therewith as above provided for, on or before one year from the date hereof, the Lease shall terminate as to both parties, unless on or before such anniversary date Lessee shall pay or tender to Lessor the sum of $_____ which shall cover the privilege of deferring commencement of drilling operations for a period of twelve months. In like manner and upon the payment or tender annually, the commencement of drilling operations may be further deferred for successive period of twelve months each during the primary term hereof . . .

This clause ensures that the lessee has no obligation to drill during the primary term by negating any implied obligation to test the premises. Without this clause, many courts held that the oil and gas company had an implied duty to drill a test well on the leased premises within a reasonable time after grant of the lease.

When an oil and gas lease is extended by the drilling of a well, disputes can arise about whether drilling occurred in a timely manner (i.e., whether it occurred before the expiration of the primary term of the lease). Courts resolve these disputes by looking at the precise language of the lease, the good faith of the oil and gas company, and the oil and gas company's due diligence. To complicate matters, most leases require that the oil and gas company merely commence operations for drilling before the anniversary date to preserve its rights.[27]

A delay rental clause provides that if a well is not drilled, the lessee must make delay rental payments. Delay rental payments require strict compliance. The oil and gas company must ensure rentals are paid in the proper amount, on or before the due date, to the proper parties, and in the manner prescribed by the lease. These days, however, many leases are "Paid-Up," meaning that all delay rental payments are paid up front, as in this example:

> This is a PAID-UP LEASE. In consideration of the down payment, Lessor agrees that Lessee *shall not be obligated*, except as otherwise provided herein, *to commence or continue any operations during the primary term, or to make any rental payments during the primary term.* . . . (emphasis added).

In Paid-Up leases, all rentals are paid up front, and the lease is held for the full primary term by the initial payment to the lessor.

The Royalty Clause

> The royalties to be paid by the Lessee are: . . . (b) to pay Lessor on gas and casinghead gas produced from said land (1) when sold by Lessee at the well, 1/8 of the amount realized by Lessee, or (2) when used by Lessee off said land or in the manufacture of gasoline or other products, 1/8 of the amount realized from the sale of gasoline or other products extracted therefrom and 1/8 of the amount realized from the sale of residue gas after deducting the amount used for plant fuel and/or compression.[28]

The royalty provision is perhaps the most important clause for the mineral owner. It provides the mineral owner with a share of the production from any well drilled on the property or on lands pooled or unitized therewith. Royalties are only paid when oil or gas is actually produced in paying quantities under the lease, which means that only around 10 percent of lessors nationwide will ever see royalties.[29] Nonetheless, the potential for lucrative income makes this the most important part of the lease.

Most mineral owners think of the royalty in terms of a raw percentage. Oil and gas companies typically begin negotiations at 1/8, but royalties of up to 1/5 or more are becoming increasingly common. The flexibility of the oil and gas company depends entirely on the market and the type of "play" at issue. Higher royalties are possible in proven areas and some leases even provide for a sliding scale based on production. However, the sheer percentage of royalties is merely the first step in drafting a royalty clause. Perhaps more important is the method by which the royalty is calculated. Without this calculation, the raw percentage means little, if anything.

Gas royalty clauses generally fall in to three types: proceeds, market value, and a hybrid of these two. The "proceeds" clause makes royalties payable based on the actual proceeds received by the oil and gas company in the sale of the gas. Often, given the realities of the gas market, the oil and gas company's proceeds from the sale of gas are actually much less than the current fair market value, especially where the oil and gas company enters into a long term contract to sell to a certain supplier. The proceeds clause is preferred by the oil and gas company and is perhaps the most fair to both parties.[30]

The "market value" royalty clause makes a gas royalty payable on the market value of gas at the time it is produced from the well. Defining market value has proven difficult and is often a flashpoint between lessor and lessee.[31] Lessors argue that market value means the market value of the gas at the time it is produced and sold. Oil and gas companies, on the other side, often enter into long-term contracts to sell gas at a favorable price, and therefore as long as a lessee can demonstrate it acted prudently in entering into the long-term contract, the price received under the contract should be deemed at the market value.[32] For this reason, oil and gas companies typically disfavor market value royalty clauses, whereas mineral owners generally prefer them. The third category is simply an alternative clause, which provides a proceeds basis for some types of sales and a market value basis for others.

Another necessary consideration is whether to allow the oil and gas company to deduct certain types of expenses after the gas is produced from the proceeds before calculating the royalty. Gas produced from the well is often not marketable in its current state. The oil and gas company must expend money to treat, compress, process, transport, and dehydrate the gas. Deducting these costs from the royalties can result in much lower proceeds for a mineral owner. Under most royalty clauses, a lessee is obligated to pay all costs of production, but the lessor shares proportionately in costs after production, because these ordinarily increase the value of production. But there is dispute over when "production" has occurred. The conventional analysis holds that production occurs for royalty-calculation purposes when oil or gas is captured and held at the wellhead.[33] An increasingly popular view, on the other hand, is the "first marketable product rule," which holds that "production" is not complete for royalty-calculation purposes until a lessee has both captured and held the product and made it marketable.[34]

From the mineral owner's point of view, the ideal royalty clause would provide for a royalty based on the fair market value of the gas, calculated at the point of marketing without deductions for the costs of producing, gathering, storing, separating, treating, dehydrating, compressing, processing, transporting, or otherwise making the gas, oil, and other products produced ready for sale or use.[35] As a fallback, mineral owners could request a proceeds clause based on a gas sales contract entered into in good faith and at arm's length. In any event, the parties should find a compromise that will provide certainty, incentivize production, and avoid litigation in the long run.

Gas royalty clauses have perhaps caused more litigation than all of the other clauses combined, probably because there is so much at stake. Nonetheless, most royalty provisions remain fairly ambiguous. The technical issues surrounding royalty clauses are beyond the scope of this chapter. The reader should be mindful of the general issues surrounding the construction of a royalty clause and may consider requiring the oil and gas company to provide monthly accounting of royalties to the mineral owner.

OTHER IMPORTANT LEASE TERMS

Warranty Clauses

The oil and gas company may request a warranty of title by the mineral owner to the minerals. However, prior to warranting their interest in the minerals, a mineral owner should ensure that he does in fact own the entire mineral interest stated in the lease. If there is any uncertainty, the warranty clause should be modified or deleted. Mineral owners who are uncertain of their mineral interest are wise to include a disclaimer of warranty. For example:

> This Lease is made without any covenant of title or warranty of any kind whatsoever and without recourse against Lessor.

Typical leases also include a "lesser interest" clause, which diminishes the interest of a mineral owner down to his or her actual interest in the mineral estate. This permits the oil and gas company to pay royalties and other payments in proportion to the mineral owner's actual interest in the property. Mineral owners should ensure that a lesser interest clause applies only to the royalty and not the bonus or other rental payments.

Shut-In Clauses

> If for a period of 90 consecutive days such well or wells are shut-in or production therefrom is not being sold by Lessee, then Lessee shall pay shut-in royalty of twenty five dollars ($25.00) per acre then covered by this lease, such payment to be made to Lessor or to Lessor's credit in the depository designated below, on or before the end of said 90-day period and thereafter on or before each anniversary of the end of said 90-day period while the well or wells are shut-in or production therefrom is not being sold by Lessee; provided that if this lease is otherwise being maintained by operations, or if production is being sold by Lessee from another well or wells on the leased premises or lands pooled therewith, no shut-in royalty shall be due until the end of the 90-day period next following cessation of such operations or production.

A shut-in clause permits an oil and gas company to hold a lease during its secondary term when the well is drilled but is not producing in paying quantities. In other words, it is "shut in." If the market value of gas has significantly decreased to the point that it is no longer profitable to produce, oil and gas companies will often "shut-in" (or turn off) wells. A shut-in well could also occur where an oil and gas company is on a "wildcat" play and there is no pipeline or other infrastructure to transport the gas to market.

After undertaking substantial up-front investment to drill the well, the lease would technically lapse without production in paying quantities. To remedy this, a shut-in clause permits oil and gas companies to hold a lease during its secondary term after a well has been drilled upon payment of a certain sum to the mineral owner instead of actual production. Shut-in clauses should provide certainty and should be drafted in light of the lessor and lessee's goals.

Shut-in payments do not release the lessee from other implied obligations, such as the obligation to reasonably develop the property. The clause may contain an obligation that the oil and gas company act diligently to produce and market the gas from a shut-in well.

Pooling and Unitization

Oil and gas companies often need or desire the flexibility to combine several leased tracts into a producing unit. A producing unit is a defined geographic area, usually set by the state oil and gas commission, from which all mineral owners are paid in proportion to their ownership within the unit. Oil and gas companies accomplish this by pooling, which is the bringing together of small tracts for the drilling of a single well for production from the pooled unit. Unitization refers to combining leases and wells over a producing formation for field wide operations.

Pooling clauses are important to the oil and gas company. Without one, the oil and gas company cannot extend the lease into its secondary term without drilling a well on the actual leased property, even if spacing rules would not permit a well to be placed there or geological evidence suggests drilling would be unsuccessful (unless they receive written consent to pooling from the lessor). If a well were drilled on a lease without a pooling clause within a producing unit (or without the lessor's consent to pooling), the oil and gas company would have to account to the lessor for the entire full lease royalty on production from the well, even though the lessor may only be entitled to a portion of it.

A pooling clause modifies the *habendum* clause by stating that production or operations anywhere in the pooled unit will be considered to be production or operations on the lease premises for purposes of the secondary term. In essence, it establishes constructive production. A pooling clause obligates a mineral owner to accept a royalty proportionate to the amount of the leased land included in the pooled unit, protecting the oil and gas company from having to make double royalty payments. From a mineral owner's perspective, pooling clauses are not *per se* objectionable, but should be carefully worded. Oil and gas companies must act in good faith when pooling lands. To avoid potential problems, some mineral owners insist on simply removing the pooling clause (in which case the lessor would have to separately consent to pooling) or adding a Pugh clause.

As noted above, even if the pooling clause is removed from a lease, an oil and gas company can request that a mineral owner consent to voluntarily pooling if it is in both parties' interests. Alternatively, most states have compulsory pooling statutes that permit the oil and gas company to request that all lands within a spacing unit to be compulsorily pooled. These "Force Pooled" statutes are most often used to pool any unleased mineral interests within the pooled unit.

Pugh Clauses

A "Pugh" clause is not standard, but it can be negotiated into the lease. It limits the acreage that is held by production in the secondary term to that acreage which lies within a pooled unit. At the end of the primary term, portions which are not part of a producing well's (or a shut-in well's) spacing unit are released from the lease. Pugh clauses can be horizontal and/or vertical. A vertical Pugh clause divides the leasehold strictly on the basis of the surface acreage included in a well spacing unit. A horizontal Pugh clause limits the area held by production to the producing strata and shallower (or deeper) strata in the unit. These clauses can be difficult to negotiate. A suitable alternative could be for mineral owners to only lease their interest in and to any minerals in smaller parcels (for example, the mineral owner would execute one lease for each section, or even quarter-section, in which they own minerals), even if they own a larger parcel (mineral owners doing this should be sure that the "Mother Hubbard" clause, which automatically includes any adjacent property the lessor may own, is deleted).[36]

Force Majeure Clauses

A force majeure clause permits the oil and gas company to preserve the lease when circumstances beyond its control prevent it from operating. Commonly covered events include acts of God or war. Mineral owners should pay attention to these clauses and carefully word and define the events covered. The oil and gas company should bear the burden of market conditions or adverse government regulations. Further, these clauses should have limited time and application, such as not more than one year, and the oil and gas company should have an obligation to make a good faith effort to overcome the condition.

Implied Covenants of Oil and Gas Leases

Despite the wording of an oil and gas lease, some courts have held that oil and gas companies are bound by implied terms in addition to those written into the lease, although most states will not find an implied covenant where the lease includes an express covenant in a given area. These implied covenants are unwritten conditions by which the oil and gas company is bound. Typically these implied covenants are designed to protect lessors. At the heart of these implied covenants is that the oil and gas lease is an economic transaction and both parties should be appropriately incentivized to develop the lease in a reasonable manner. Below is a brief discussion of some of the more common implied covenants.

Lessees are required to conduct themselves as a reasonable and prudent operator under the circumstances. This requirement underlies all other implied covenants. Originally, this covenant was intended to make it clear that while the oil and gas company's obligation is less than that of a fiduciary, it is more than an obligation to act in good faith. It requires different duties in different circumstances, but it generally requires the oil and gas company to act (1) in good faith, (2) competently, and (3) with due regard for the lessor's interest.

Other covenants are also commonly implied. The implied covenant to reasonably develop imposes an obligation on the oil and gas company to reasonably develop the mineral estate in the same manner as an economically motivated prudent operator.[37] The implied covenant for further exploration imposes a general obligation on the oil and gas company to explore undeveloped parts of the leased estate or strata under the land.[38] The implied covenant to protect against drainage imposes an affirmative duty upon the oil and gas company to protect the leased lands from drainage of the minerals by adjacent parcels.[39] Finally, the implied covenant to market requires that the oil and gas company diligently market oil and gas within a reasonable time of production and at a reasonable price.[40] All of these covenants are judicially created implied obligations.

SPECIAL LEASE CONSIDERATIONS FOR HYDRAULIC FRACTURING

While some states and municipalities have begun to consider certain limitations on the use of hydraulic fracturing techniques as discussed in other chapters of this book, typically the right conveyed in the oil and gas lease encompasses the use of hydraulic fracturing techniques unless specifically prohibited by the lease. As such, mineral owners may consider negotiating special terms when hydraulic fracturing is anticipated. Hydraulic fracturing, together with horizontal drilling techniques, typically results in higher intensity use of the surface than traditional oil and gas operations. It may also pose a greater risk of surface and subsurface contamination from fracturing chemicals and flowback wastes.[41] Hydraulic fracturing operations certainly increase the potential for greater surface damage to infrastructure, such as roads, because of the larger amount of equipment and fluids that must be brought to, stored on, and removed from the site. The increased traffic associated with hydraulic fracturing may also present safety concerns and may negatively impact public and private roads.[42] Lessees may consider inserting baseline and remedial provisions to protect private roads and other infrastructure after drilling and recovery operations have completed.

In order to protect themselves, lessors and lessees alike may consider adding certain stipulations into the lease terms, such as baseline water testing and monitoring. This allows both parties to monitor the health of the ground and surface water during the lease term. Other protective terms could include remediation or bond requirements that exceed those required by the state regulatory agencies, or the requirement to disclose the types of chemicals used onsite, including in the fracturing fluid. Note, however, that some states have already begun to require the disclosure of the chemical solutions used in hydraulic fracturing operations,[43] and many industry parties are participating in voluntary disclosure programs.

A Note on Negotiation Technique

Negotiations for oil and gas leases should be collaborative endeavors, rather than adversarial. Both parties should seek to determine the other party's needs, interests, and concerns and address each in a clearly worded lease document. The oil and gas company, obviously, seeks the right but not the obligation to develop for the greatest amount of time. The mineral owner, on the other hand, seeks economic profit, but also (especially if the mineral owner is also the surface owner) domestic tranquility and minimal harm to the surface estate. A mineral owner's opportunity to negotiate many of the terms described above depends to a large extent on the type of subsurface mineral rights involved and the current oil and gas market.

Surface Use Conditions in Oil and Gas Leases

A mineral owner who also owns title to the surface estate has an opportunity to protect his or her interests in the surface estate at the time of the execution of the lease. Several considerations are discussed below. There is no common law right for a surface owner to be compensated for the oil and gas company's reasonable and necessary use of the surface. Nonetheless, in the interest of goodwill, the oil and gas company may compensate and work with the surface owner.

There are several provisions that can protect the surface estate, which may be incorporated into the lease or in a separate surface use agreement. The goal of any surface owner should be to define and locate as many of the potential uses of the surface as possible and to protect baseline resources. Some considerations include: (1) access to, testing of, and use of water resources on the property; (2) repair and compensation for surface damage to things such as timber stands and crops and other site-specific assets; (3) distance of surface operations from structures; (4) road location and construction review by landowner and a qualified engineer or forester; (5) possible timing of surface operations to allow for livestock pasturing, hunting, or other rural land activities; and (6) bonded environmental remediation requirements with firm time limitations.[44]

Many jurisdictions have passed statutes intended to protect surface owners. Some are simply codifications of the common law accommodation doctrine,[45] while others require compensation to the surface owner for surface use and damage.[46]

CONCLUSION

Oil and gas leases create a unique and often complicated relationship between the mineral owner and the oil and gas company. Mineral owners often have sufficient leverage to negotiate certain terms of the lease, but the respective party's leverage ultimately depends on market conditions.

NOTES

1. In legal terms, the mineral estate is the "dominant" estate. *See, e.g.,* Hunter v. Rosebud County, 783 P.2d 927 (Mont. 1989).
2. *See, e.g.,* Emeny v. United States, 412 F.2d 1319 (Ct. Cl. 1969) (holding oil and gas lessee did not acquire right to store in closed geological structure or underground dome underneath leased premises helium gas and pure helium produced elsewhere.); Moser v. U.S. Steel Corp., 676 S.W.2d 99, 102 (Tex. 1984) (confirming the following materials are part of the surface estate unless specifically leased: building stone and limestone; limestone, caliche,

and surface shale; water; near surface lignite, iron and coal; *cf.* Hicks Exploration v. Okla. Water Res. Bd., 695 P.2d 498, 504 (Okla. 1984) (holding owner of surface estate owns the underlying fresh groundwater, but surface estate is subject to the mineral owner's right to use reasonable amounts of the water for production of minerals).

3. The designation 'Producer's 88' derives from lease version created to circumvent a 1916 Oklahoma decision. "Producers" indicates it was used by oil producers; "88" was merely the printer's designation. The original "Producer's 88" form did spread in popularity in the early 20th Century, but each company now has its own preferred form of lease, most of which they still call the "Producer's 88." Practitioners should use caution when referring to "Producer's 88." In *Fagg v. Texas Company*, the court refused to grant specific performance on a contract that required one of the parties to enter into an oil and gas lease on an "88 form" because this was insufficient to meet the Statute of Frauds. The court noted in dicta that the "88 form" was no more descriptive than the term "oil and gas lease" used alone. Thus, despite the widespread misconception that "Producer's 88" describes some ubiquitous industry standard form, it does nothing more than indicate the form was drafted by the oil and gas company. This notation persists today only as an indication that the lease was designed with the oil and gas company (the lessee) in mind. For more information, see Owen L. Anderson, David V. Goliath: Negotiating the 'Lessor's 88' and Representing Lessors and Surface Owners in Oil and Gas Lease Plays, Proceedings of the Rocky Mountain Mineral Law Institute, Seventh Annual Institute (1982), at II (D) (discussing *Brown v. Wilson* 160 P. 94 (Okla. 1916) (holding an oil and as lease with an 'or' form rental clause was voidable at the option of both parties and merely created a tenancy at will)).

4. JOHN S. LOWE, OIL AND GAS LAW 172 (Nutshell Series, 4th ed. 2003).

5. *See* Jupiter Oil Co. v. Snow, 819 S.W.2d 466 (Tex. 1991).

6. *See* Hinds v. Phillips Petrol. Co., 591 P.2d 697 (Okla. 1979).

7. *See, e.g.,* Hite v. Falcon Partners, 13 A.3d 942 (Pa. Super. Ct. 2011).

8. *See, e.g.,* David E. Pierce, *Rethinking the Oil and Gas Lease,* 22 TULSA L.J. 445 (1987); LOWE, *supra* note 4, at 173.

9. LOWE, *supra* note 4, at 179.

10. *See* Hunt Oil Co. v. Kerbaugh, 283 N.W. 2d 131 (N.D. 1979).

11. *See* Hannah Wiseman, *Beyond Coastal Oil v. Garza: Nuisance and Trespass in Hydraulic Fracturing Litigation,* 57 ADVOCATE (Texas) 8 (2011).

12. LOWE, *supra* note 4, at 179.

13. *See generally* Douglas Hale Gross, *What Constitutes Reasonably Necessary Use of the Surface of the Leasehold by a Mineral Owner, Lessee, or Driller Under an Oil and Gas Lease or Drilling Contract,* 53 A.L.R. 3d 16 (2013); Robinson v. Robbins Petroleum Corp., 501 S.W.2d 865, 867 (Tex. 1973) (holding the lessee was entitled to "use of the salt water which was reasonably necessary to produce oil under" the surface estate, if any, but was liable to the

plaintiff for "that portion of the salt water which has been consumed for the production of oil for owners" of adjoining mineral estates); P.G. Guthrie, *Construction of Oil and Gas Lease Provision Giving Lessee Free Use of Water From Lessor's Land*, 23 A.L.R.3d 1434 (2013).

14. See, e.g., Wiseman, *supra* note 11; Brown v. Lundell, 344 S.W.2d 863 (Tex. 1961) (pollution to groundwater); *Beyond Coastal Oil v. Garza: Nuisance and Trespass in Hydraulic Fracturing Litigation*, 57 ADVOCATE (Texas) 8, 10 (2011).

15. See Key Operating & Equip., Inc. v. Hegar, 01-10-00350-CV, 2013 WL 103633 (Tex. App. 1st 2013) (imposing the burden on the landowner to prove use of road was not related to development of subsurface estate).

16. See, e.g., Moser v. U.S. Steel Corp., 676 S.W.2d 99 (Tex. 1984).

17. Getty Oil Co. v. Jones, 470 S.W.2d 618 (Tex. 1971).

18. *Key Operating & Equip., Inc.*, 2013 WL 103633.

19. Gerrity Oil & Gas Corp. v. Magness, 946 P.2d 913, 927 (Colo. 1997); COLO. REV. STAT. § 34-60-127.

20. See, e.g., Kysar v. Amoco Prod. Co., 93 P.3d 1272, 1283 (N.M. 2004).

21. See, e.g., Anschutz Exploration Corp. v. Town of Dryden, 35 Misc. 3d 450 (N.Y. Sup. Ct. Feb. 21, 2012), *aff'd sub nom.* Norse Energy Corp. USA v. Town of Dryden, 108 A.D.3d 25 (N.Y. App. Div., 3d Judicial Dept. May 2, 2013); Cooperstown Holstein Corp. v. Town of Middlefield, 35 Misc. 3d 767 (N.Y. Sup. Ct. 2013) (holding zoning ordinance effectively banning oil and gas operations within township was not preempted by the New York State Environmental Conservation Law, which expressly superseded all local laws "relating to the regulation of oil, gas, and solution mining industries," and stating "the state maintains control over the 'how' of such procedures, while the municipalities maintain the control over the 'where' of such exploration").

22. See, e.g., Colorado Mining Ass'n v. Bd. of Cnty. Comm'rs of Summit Cnty., 199 P.3d 718, 730 (Colo. 2009) (holding Summit County's ban on the use of cyanide or other toxic/acidic ore-processing reagents in heap or vat leach applications exceeded its statutory authority and was preempted by Colorado's Mined Land Reclamation Act).

23. See, e.g., N.D. CENT. CODE § 38-11.1-04 (requiring the mineral developer to "pay the surface owner a sum of money equal to the amount of damages sustained by the surface owner and the surface owner's tenant, if any, for lost land value, lost use of and access to the surface owner's land, and lost value of improvements caused by drilling operations."); MONT. CODE § 82-10-505 ("The oil and gas developer or operator is responsible for damages to real or personal property caused by oil and gas operations and production."); OKLA. STAT. tit. 52 § 318.5 (requiring the operator to negotiate with the surface owner "for the payment of any damages which may be caused by the drilling operation" prior to entering the site with "heavy equipment.").

24. *Habendum* is Latin for "that must be had."
25. Pack v. Santa Fe Minerals, 869 P.2d 333 (Okla. 1994).
26. Clifton v. Koontz, 325 S.W. 2d 684 (Tex. 1959).
27. *See, e.g.*, LOWE, *supra* note 4, at 202.
28. This is an example of a clause commonly found in many "producer's 88" leases.
29. *See, e.g.*, CORNELL UNIVERSITY COOPERATIVE EXTENSION, GAS EXPLORATION AND LEASING ON PRIVATE LAND: TIPS AND GUIDANCE FOR NEW YORK LANDOWNERS (July 2008).
30. *Id.*
31. *See, e.g.*, Scott Lansdown, *The Implied Marketing Covenant in Oil and Gas Leases: The Producer's Perspective*, 31 ST. MARY'S L.J. 297, 311–12 (2000).
32. *See, e.g.*, Tex. Oil and Gas Corp. v. Vela, 429 S.W. 2d 866 (Tex. 1968) (holding "market value" determined by comparable sales or, if comparable sales are unavailable, by working back from downstream sales to the wellhead value; Yzaguirre v. KCS Res., Inc., 53 S.W.3d 368 (Tex. 2001) (evidence of price in long-term gas purchase contract inadmissible to establish market value).
33. *See, e.g.*, Piney Woods Country Life Sch. v. Shell Oil Co., 726 F.2d 225 (5th Cir. 1984).
34. *See, e.g.*, Garman v. Conoco, Inc., 886 P.2d 652 (Colo. 1994).
35. Anderson, *supra* note 3, at II(D)(8)(b).
36. *See also* Rachel L. Allen & Scotland M. Duncan, *The Standard Oil and Gas Lease—and Why It Is Not*, 13 DUQ. BUS. L. J. 155 (2011).
37. *See, e.g.*, Lenape Resources Corp. v. Tennessee Gas Pipeline Co., 925 S.W.2d 565, 572 (Tex. 1996).
38. *See, e.g.*, Whitham Farms, LLC v. City of Longmont, 97 P.3d 135, 137 (Colo. App. 2003) (confirming that the lessor has the burden to prove breach of implied covenants.).
39. *See, e.g.*, HECI Exploration Co. v. Neel, 982 S.W.2d 881, 887 (Tex. 1998).
40. *See* Lansdown, *supra* note 31.
41. For additional information, see Angela C. Cupas, *The Not-So-Safe Drinking Water Act: Why We Must Regulate Hydraulic Fracturing at the Federal Level*, 33 WM. & MARY ENVTL. L. & POLICY REV. 605, 606 (2009); Hannah Wiseman, *Untested Waters: The Rise of Hydraulic Fracturing in Oil and Gas Production and the Need to Revisit Regulation*, 20 FORDHAM ENVTL. L. REV. 115, 121 (2009).
42. W. VA. DEP'T OF ENVTL. PROT., INDUSTRY GUIDANCE: GAS WELL DRILLING/ COMPLETION: LARGE WATER VOLUME FRACTURE TREATMENTS (Jan. 8, 2010) ("Hauling large volumes of water [for hydraulic fracturing] will result in significantly increased truck traffic that may create safety concerns, road damage, dust problems and other environmental issues."), *available at* http://www.dep.wv.gov/oil-and-gas/GI/Documents/Marcellus%20Guidance%20 1-8-10%20Final.pdf.

43. *See, e.g.*, 2 Colo. Code Regs. 404-1 (requiring the disclosure of hydraulic fracturing fluid chemicals through the "FracFocus" website, at fracfocus .org).

44. *See* Elisabeth N. Radow, *Homeowners and Gas Drilling Leases: Boon or Bust?*, N.Y. St. B.J., Nov.–Dec. 2011, at 10 (for a good discussion of other risks inherent in hydraulic fracturing operations).

45. Colorado's, for example, slightly expands the common law doctrine by requiring that the operator select "alternative locations for wells, roads, pipelines, or production facilities, or [employ] alternative means of operation, that prevent, reduce, or mitigate the impacts of the oil and gas operations on the surface, where such alternatives are technologically sound, economically practicable, and reasonably available to the operator." Colo. Rev. Stat. § 34-60-127.

46. North Dakota and Montana, for example, require the developer to compensate the surface owner for surface use and damage. N.D. Cent. Code § 38-11.1 *et seq.*; Mont. Code Ann. § 82-10-501.

4

Oil and Gas Exploration without Leases
Rule of Capture and Compulsory Integration (Forced Pooling) in New York State

Christopher Denton

INTRODUCTION

This chapter addresses the most common legal consequences to a mineral rights owner when the owner does not wish to lease his or her mineral rights or cannot come to an agreement with an oil and gas company about the terms and provisions of a lease. We will use New York State as a case study for the Northeast. The purpose of the chapter is to introduce the inexperienced reader, whether a lawyer, planner, municipal official, or environmental scientist, to one state's recent attempt to overcome the historical, adverse consequences wrought by the Rule of Capture untempered by legislative intervention. It is not intended for the experienced oil and gas lawyer.

The chapter begins by offering a simplified history of oil and gas ownership law, followed by a brief discussion of how the course of that law led to the enactment of Compulsory Integration under title 9 of

Article 23 of the New York Environmental Conservation Law (ECL). The last portion of the chapter offers a brief explanation of how Compulsory Integration functions in New York.

Most people are surprised to learn that if a mineral rights owner refuses to lease or develop his or her land for oil and gas, an oil and gas company may lease from the owner's neighbors. By doing so, the company may take possession of the oil and gas without the owner's permission. Additionally, the gas company may be able to keep up to 87.5 percent of the owner's oil and gas, or may instead be able keep so much oil and gas as guarantees that the company recovers all of its drilling and development costs plus a profit of 200 percent, albeit prorated to the landowner's acreage.[1]

Whether this is fair to all parties and whether this is constitutional are not the concern of this chapter. We leave those discussions to other writers in other forums. Our purpose here is to write about what exists now. The process by which an oil and gas company can legally take a landowner's oil and gas without permission began with the judicial "rule of capture" and has been augmented over time with the addition of statutory provisions known as "compulsory integration" (sometimes known as "forced pooling").

ORIGINS OF THE RULE OF CAPTURE

To understand the Rule of Capture and Compulsory Integration, we need to briefly review the evolution of the law governing the ownership of oil and gas in the United States. In most states, the Rule of Capture governs oil and gas ownership and has generally been defined by judicial decisions and not by statutes. Most non-lawyers are surprised that a whole body of law defining the ownership of oil and gas could be created by judicial decisions (called common law) without any input from a legislature. It is important to note, however, that if a legislature passes statutes modifying judicial decisions and then later repeals those statutes, the original judicial decisions become controlling law again.

The judicial Rule of Capture arose from the fact that oil and gas flow under ground and geology as we know it today was not well understood at the time that judges were first asked by disputing landowners to decide who owned the gas and oil beneath their respective parcels. These problems of ownership first became evident when landowners discovered that if each of them drilled wells on adjacent land, the production from the first well would immediately decline at the moment production commenced on the neighbor's well. The wells were said to be "communicating," i.e., gas and oil were migrating underground.

For non-lawyers, the question of ownership of minerals would seem apparent. In states where the federal or state government does not own the mineral rights and in the absence of the severance of mineral rights from the fee estate, whoever owns the fee estate (land) owns the minerals directly under the surface. This seemingly self-evident assertion holds true for gypsum, limestone, or bluestone, for instance. It does not hold true for oil and gas, which tend to flow underground. The question of oil and gas ownership, therefore, reduces itself to a single basic question: who owns a natural resource that does not stay in one place, or in other words, tends to flow to the nearest well bore?

Using hunting and game law as an analogy, the courts settled on a Rule of Capture. Courts ruled that oil and gas were fugitive and therefore were not owned until captured, much like a wild deer running across a farmer's land. If the farmer shot it on his or her land, the deer belonged to the farmer. But if the deer left the farmer's land unharmed, the farmer had no right to shoot it on the land of another without the other landowner's permission. Therefore, a landowner who drilled the well on his or her own land had the right to keep anything that came out of the well. By capturing it, he or she gained ownership of it. As such, some courts have decided that a landowner only owns the gas and oil when he or she takes possession of it at the surface. Other states have alternatively held that one may actually own the oil and gas in the ground, subject to defeasance (loss of ownership) by someone lawfully draining it on his or her own land.

In New York, the Rule of Capture specifically states that each landowner who owns land with the mineral rights intact has the right to own so much of the oil and gas as he or she actually takes from the ground. Accompanying this principle is the principle that the landowner has the right to access oil and gas by drilling on his or her own property. Until the oil and gas is removed from the ground and reduced to actual physical possession above ground, the permanency of the ownership of the oil and gas will not have been established. In other words, if your neighbor drills a well on his or her property and in taking the oil and gas from that property drains the oil and gas from your property, the neighbor becomes the owner of all the oil and gas that comes out of his or her well, regardless of its source. The neighbor has no responsibility to pay you for it. The neighbor is not taking your oil and gas. The neighbor is simply exercising his or her rights to drain the pool of oil and gas that lies beneath the surface.

Consequences of the Application
of the Rule of Capture

The consequences of the Rule of Capture include the incentive to drill an excessive number of wells along the borders of the landowner's property in order to prevent drainage by the neighbor and a rush to produce as much oil or gas as possible in the shortest time. This was common in the past because, unlike the present, landowners once had the right to drill innumerable wells on their property, regardless of the size of the property. Under an unmodified Rule of Capture, landowners were compelled by economics to drill as many wells as possible on their land and to drill them as close to their boundary lines as possible to prevent the neighbor from legally capturing all the gas and oil in the common pool. Drainage by a neighbor was therefore a point of serious economic concern.[2] These drilling incentives caused by the Rule of Capture also resulted in severe overproduction, which resulted in a glut of oil and gas on the market. This in turn caused massive swings in prices, which produced boom and bust years.[3]

The right to protect the oil and gas beneath the surface of landowners' property was substantially influenced by their economic means. If they had the money to drill, they could protect their oil and gas by drilling wells to drain as much as the wells would allow. If they had no money, then the neighbor's wells would instead drain the gas and oil pool beneath the property. Regardless of their financial capacity, however, landowners always had the right to drill on their own property. Ironically, too many wells on too little space resulted in a second kind of economic loss—the loss of well bore pressure that caused much oil to be trapped in the ground, unrecoverable. This loss was considered "wasteful" and became one of the prime rationales for subsequent laws enacting unitization and well spacing rules.

Although the Rule of Capture essentially leaves landowners with the right to drill and remove oil and gas, it also required that the well and the well bore be located exclusively on landowners' property. Landowners could not legally drill under a neighbor's property without the neighbor's permission. Such drilling would constitute a trespass. In the highly technical age in which we live and with the rise of geology, geophysics, geochemistry, and highly efficient drilling techniques, the issue of trespass was sure to arise. In Texas, the supreme court was asked to decide whether the fracturing of a well that causes the fractures to extend on to the neighbor's property is a trespass.[4] The court decided that, for Texas, the Rule of Capture is so strong that when the hydraulic fractures extend into another owner's property, the owner may not be able to legally recover damages for the gas drainage caused by such fractures. The issue concerned lines of fracture, not the well bore. A well bore entering a neighbor's land without his or her consent would still constitute a trespass. As recently as April 2013, a West Virginia federal district court disagreed, stating "that hydraulic fracturing under the land of a neighboring property without that party's consent is not protected by the 'rule of capture,' but rather constitutes an actionable trespass."[5]

SOLUTIONS TO THE ADVERSE ECONOMIC CONSEQUENCES OF THE RULE OF CAPTURE

The oil and gas industry for its first fifty years of life either boomed with great profit or busted horribly with many operators bankrupted. After another round of losses in the Depression and to alleviate the wild market fluctuations in the price of oil and gas and to stabilize production, several producing states agreed to form the Interstate Oil and Gas Compact Commission, (initially founded as the Interstate Oil Compact Commission). Although this body has no enforcement power, it has been said that it is "the most powerful powerless organization in the world."[6]

The member states, in an attempt to rein in these destructive swings in the market and to prevent the waste of oil and gas caused by excessive drilling, instituted a number of reforms. These included setting distances between wells (spacing to prevent communication and drainage), establishing units (in order to determine correlative rights), limiting the number of wells in the unit (to prevent waste of capital and product), forcing "unleased" mineral owners into a single unit for drilling purposes (to prevent landowners from holding out), and above all, requiring that no well be drilled without first obtaining a permit. These measures helped to stabilize the economics of oil and gas.

Thus Compulsory Integration must be viewed from the larger perspective of market stabilization, statewide spacing, unitization, and correlative rights guarantees. Our case study state, New York, also eventually signed the Interstate Oil and Gas Compact.[7] Embracing the policies promoted therein, New York State in section 301 of the ECL set forth the following statement of the purposes of its Oil and Gas Policy: "To regulate the development, production, and utilization of natural resources of oil and gas in this state in such a manner as will prevent waste; to authorize and to provide for the operation and development of oil and gas properties in such a manner that a greater ultimate recovery of oil and gas may be had; and that the correlative rights of all owners and the rights of all persons including landowners and the general public may be fully protected."[8] Among these policies, the ones that lead most inevitably to compulsory integration are the policies toward "a greater ultimate recovery of oil and gas" and the full protection of correlative rights.

The correlative rights guaranteed in the ECL are essential to the notion of Compulsory Integration and can be stated two ways: (1) "an owner who exercises the right to capture oil and gas is subject to the concomitant duty to exercise the right without negligence or waste"; and from a more positive perspective, (2) "the correlative-rights doctrine provides that each owner of minerals in a common source of supply has the right to a fair chance to produce oil and gas from the reservoir substantially in the proportion that the quantity of recoverable oil and gas under his or her land bears to the quantity in the reservoir."[9] Once correlative rights had been recognized by judges and in policy statements, it followed that the legislature would enact a compulsory integration statute.

INTRODUCTION TO COMPULSORY INTEGRATION IN NEW YORK STATE

The statute regulating oil and gas development in New York State is Article 23 of the ECL, entitled the Oil, Gas, and Solution Mining Law, and it is administered by the New York State Department of Environmental Conservation (DEC). Permitting and statewide well spacing proceed under Title 5, voluntary integration and unitization under Title 7, and compulsory integration and correlative rights under Title 9. Well spacing in New York is determined by the targeted formation and the depth drilled. Although New York has chosen a multi-faceted approach, this chapter will concentrate only on Title 9 and Compulsory Integration.

As currently enacted, Article 23 section 0901 of the ECL attempts to establish a system that will allow a driller/operator to drain an entire unit without the permission of every landowner in it, while attempting to protect an unleased landowner's correlative rights by offering three different forms of compensation for the loss of the rights to drill, to take and keep oil and gas, to prevent drainage, to decide when a well will be drilled on the owner's property, and to determine the competence of a well driller, i.e., to decide by whom and how a well will be drilled.

The statute attempts to accomplish these goals of orderly development, non-wasteful drilling, and the prorata distribution of oil and gas production by first requiring that a single permit be issued and that a spacing unit be formed, all prior to drilling. Enormous amounts of capital are preserved by these requirements. Under current law, no wells need to be drilled along a boundary line. One well, properly located, can drain the entire unit. To qualify for a permit, the driller must control by ownership or lease at least 60 percent of the acreage included in the unit. The permit will be limited to the one unit, to the one depth, and to the one target formation named in the application. Any landowner/mineral rights owner who is in the unit and who is not "controlled" by the driller/operator must then be Compulsorily Integrated by the driller/operator under the proceeding set forth in Title 9 of the ECL.

The unit is formed and the mineral rights owners are identified in the application for the permit. The driller is permitted to commence drilling as soon as the permit has been issued and the unit map approved but cannot drill under any unleased or "uncontrolled" property until a Final Order of Integration has been issued by DEC. If the well is successful, the driller/operator can commence production immediately, not having to pay the unleased landowners until the Final Order of Integration is issued, which can be years away.

Compensating a Landowner in Compulsory Integration

How is a landowner compensated under involuntary integration? Without identifying for which losses the landowner will be compensated nor allocating the compensation for those losses, Title 9 of the Article 23 of the ECL sets forth three exclusive classes that may provide compensation to the landowner, but the owner must choose among them within 21 days of receiving notice of the Compulsory Integration Hearing. They are (1) the Integrated Royalty Owner, (2) the Integrated Non-Participating Owner, and (3) the Integrated Participating Owner. Of the three, the Integrated Royalty Owner is the default status. If the landowner does nothing or ignores the proceeding, the statute designates him or her as an Integrated Royalty Owner.

A landowner who has the financial wherewithal and can access it within thirty days of receiving the notice of the Compulsory Integration Hearing can "participate" in the well as an Integrated Participating Owner (IPO). This means that he or she will contribute a prorata share of the capital costs of that well (as shown in the document called an Authorization For Expenditure, AFE). The owner will assume proportionate liability in contract and tort and will be obligated to contribute more funds when additional capital is needed for the well. In other words, the owner can engage in a high-stakes poker game for which he or she has had no reasonable time to raise the necessary funds (which has unlimited raises), for which he or she has enormous liability beyond the capital costs, and in which he or she has no voice in any decisions whatsoever. The upside is that from the first day of production the owner is entitled to a proportionate share of the profits. The down side is self-evident—the loss of the owner's entire investment.

A landowner who does not have access to such funds can elect to become an Integrated Non-Participating Owner (INPO). With this election he or she does not need to advance any funds whatsoever. However, the production profits that are attributable to the owner's portion of the unit are subject to a "risk penalty." The statute does not define the risk penalty nor explain its rationale. It does, however, clearly state the amount of the penalty as 300 percent of the costs of the well, prorated to the landowner's acreage in the unit. Furthermore, the INPO is not entitled to a prorata portion of the production profit until the 300 percent has been entirely recovered by the driller/operator from the well's production. In effect, this means that the well operator is entitled to a guaranteed recovery of all of the landowner's prorated well costs plus a 200 percent prorated profit.

Yet this doesn't tell the whole story. Another way to view the driller's benefit is to calculate the driller's profit in those circumstances where the driller holds leases for the bare minimum—60 percent of the acreage of the unit. If all the "uncontrolled landowners" elected Integrated Non-Participating Owner status, the driller would recover 120 percent (i.e., 40 percent × 300 percent) of the full cost of the well, regardless of any proration of the costs to those landowners. In other words, the uncontrolled landowners would be paying 120 percent the entire costs of the well, not just their prorata portion. If the well produces marketable oil or gas of sufficient value, the driller/operator could literally drill and complete the well without any cost to it. This raises the question of whether there is any incentive remaining for the driller/operator to continue to acquire leases once it has achieved the 60 percent ratio.

It is likewise possible that the INPO will never receive a cent for the loss of his or her right to drill or to prevent drainage, the loss of his or her rights to the oil and gas, the loss of his or her right to decide when or how to drill, and the loss of time needed to obtain investors to drill. In other words, because of the statute, the driller/ operator could end up with all the landowner's gas or oil for free, and without having to pay for any of the well costs.

There is a final irony. If the well bore travels under the uncontrolled landowner's land pursuant to the permission granted in the Final Integration Order, then the landowner will not be paid for that permanent invasion of his or her subsurface rights. Yet if the same oil and gas company tried to construct a gas-gathering pipeline beneath the surface of the same landowner's property, it would be a trespass unless the company had the power of eminent domain and paid the fair market value for the pipeline easement.

The third statutory election is the Integrated Royalty Owner (IRO). If the landowner ignores the proceeding, he or she is deemed an IRO and gets the lowest royalty of all the leases in the unit, but not less than 12.5 percent. DEC has ruled in administrative hearings that the royalty is calculated without deducting any costs. The statute also specifically insulates the IRO from any liability related to the well and denies the driller any use of the surface of the IRO's property.

We take special note that at the end of Title 9, the statute contains a provision that saddles the buyer of a compulsorily integrated real property with the election of the previous owner, including the liabilities thereunder. The provision states, "Any person taking title by operation of law to any oil and gas interests integrated into a spacing unit pursuant to an order of integration, shall take such interests subject to the terms and conditions of the final order of integration issued by the department duly recorded in accordance with the provisions of this section and shall be subject to all liabilities and benefits associated therewith, unless such person, within sixty days of the taking of such interest, elects to be an integrated royalty owner and notifies the well operator of such decision."[10]

When the Compulsory Integration Proceeding actually commences, the driller/operator must give 30 days' actual notice to any unleased landowner in the unit. The hearings are held exclusively in Albany, NY, and the unleased landowner has only 21 days to file his or her election with DEC or be deemed an IRO. It has been the practice of oil and gas investors who have acquired leases, and thereafter find themselves compulsorily integrated, to request and litigate detailed modifications and amendments to the Integration Order on the grounds that the statute requires that the integration order be "upon such terms and conditions that are just and reasonable."[11]

There is a quirk in Title 9 that states that if you are a lessee when the integration hearing is held and if you elect the Integrated Non-Participating Owner status, then you, as lessee, are entitled to a special graduated royalty interest in the well until the 300 percent risk penalty has been paid in full from the landowner's portion of the production proceeds. This loophole was written for the industry, which sometimes holds leases but not the permit. The loophole would give those companies some extra money. Normally the INPO receives no proceeds until the risk penalty has been paid in full. But if the landowner forms a Limited Liability Company (LLC) wholly owned by the landowner, he can then lease to his or her own LLC. The LLC thereby qualifies as a lessee and receives the graduated royalty during the risk penalty phase. DEC administrative law judges have upheld this practice by INPOs.

There is a fifth option that has grown out of a unique practice of some landowner attorneys, which is unofficially called the Compulsory Integration Lease. Once the unleased landowner is notified of the Compulsory Integration hearing, he or she is often approached by investor companies who want "into the game" by leasing from the owner. If the investors have oil and gas leases in a unit but not enough leases to qualify to be the permit holder, then they will be integrated by the permit holder and can themselves elect to be a "participating owner," i.e., a partner. Like any other IPO, they must front all the money immediately (at the hearing). The driller cannot refuse to take them as an IPO, and the investors will receive their net profits from the first day of production (see figure on opposite page).

In the Compulsory Integration Lease model, the landowner only leases the target formation to which the permit has been granted, leases no surface rights, and usually receives no bonus. The lease lasts only the duration of the permit and covers only the acreage included in the unit. It is specific to the permit, the unit, and the target formation. It is an unusual compromise by a landowner and a company that has been competing with the permit holder. The typical royalty of this kind of lease is usually higher than the royalty of a landowner who signed a lease with the permit holder. This constitutes an easy short-cut for an investor to get into a well as a partner without the necessity of signing a Joint Operating Agreement with the permit holder. Moreover, an Integrated Participating Owner is entitled to well log data (the essential raw geologic data recorded during the drilling process), as well as production figures, etc. That data has value. Under New York law the public can be stopped from obtaining that information for up to two years, but not so for the IPO. He or she is entitled to it upon paying the upfront money.

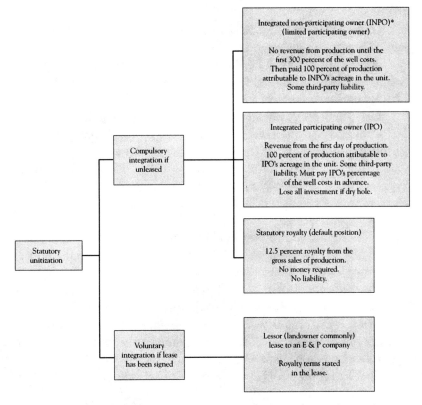

Outline of Statutory Unitization

* Exception when the NPO is a lessee, then the NPO receives a graduated royalty:

  a. On production equaling 100% of the cost of the well—6.25%

  b. On production equaling the second 100% of the cost of the well—9.38%

  c. On production equaling the third 100% of the cost of the well—12.5%

Non-Statutory Alternative: Lease to an investor only so much of the target formation as is included in the compulsory integration notice, for the life of the permit and the life of the unit, reserving all other formations and rights and granting no surface rights. In other words lease the same amount of mineral rights as are covered by the compulsory integration proceeding. This allows one to participate and still be able to lease the remainder of the rights to others.

THE MATHEMATICS OF COMPULSORY INTEGRATION

Here is how the math would work in New York for a typical Compulsory Integration Proceeding. Our figures and location are taken from an actual Authorization For Expenditure (AFE) and an actual Spacing Unit Map (Unit Map) in a completed Compulsory Integration Proceeding, but we shall use a fictitious landowner and a fictitious exploration and production company.

Act I:

Ms. Carey Drake and her husband, Grant Drake, own 100 acres of land. They have not leased their land to anyone.

The permit holder is E&P Resources, Inc. (E&P) of Tulsa, Oklahoma, which has obtained leases from everyone around the Drakes. The lowest royalty rate in the leases is 12.5 percent.

E&P filed an application showing the Spacing Unit Map of 160 acres and that the Drakes were not "controlled." DEC issued the permit and ordered E&P (now called the operator) to commence a Compulsory Integration hearing. The Notice of Hearing was served in person upon both Drakes along with an AFE and an Election Form, the template for which is located on the website of DEC. E&P has already started to drill.

14.38 acres of the Drake's land have been included in the Weston #1 well, API # 31-107-73406-00-00. (Wells are often named after the landowner on whose land they are located.)

The API number can be read as follows: the first two digits identify the state, the second two digits identify the county, the next five-digit group is the unique well number, the next two digits identify the number of sidetracks, and the last two digits indicate the number of operations had on a single well bore.

The Drakes own 8.9875 percent of the acreage in the well.

14.38 acres / 160 acres = 8.9875% of the acreage

In the first year the well produces gross sales of $1,000,000.00 from the sale of natural gas from the Weston #1 well.

The AFE is $344,474.99. This constitutes the projected cost of all the drilling and completion. The prorated costs to the landowner is $344,475.00 × 8.9875% = $30,959.69, which is the amount that the landowner as IPO would have to pay at or before the Compulsory Integration Hearing.

Act II:

A. The Drakes have 21 calendar days from receipt of the Notice of Hearing to file an election on the Election Form supplied by E&P. If the Drakes do nothing, they will become an Integrated Royalty Owner at 12.5 percent without any deductions for any costs of transportation or preparation for market. They will have no liability for any matters arising out of the permit and the election.

Their return at the end of the first year will be 12.5% royalty × (8.9875% of the acreage × $1,000,000.00 gross sales for the unit) = $11,234.375.

If the well is a "duster," there is no loss as the Drakes paid in no money.

B. The Drakes can pay to E&P the sum of $30,959.69 (their prorata share of drilling and completion costs) before the end of the hearing by certified funds to become an Integrated Participating Owner. By doing so the Drakes must now pay more money to E&P each and every time the costs of the Weston #1 well exceeds the AFE and all funds collected thereafter. If the Drakes do not pay, then they will lose all the money they have paid, and they will be involuntarily converted to an IRO with no way of recovering their investment. They will have "folded" in this high stakes poker game. If on the other hand they always make the payments demanded and on time and the well produces gas in paying quantities, the Drakes will receive 100 percent of the sales price of the gas attributable to their percentage of the acreage in the unit, less the costs of transportation, preparation, and operation of the well. The return on investment could be high. The losses could be crippling.

Calculating returns based on first year's sales of $1,000,000.00, the profit would be as follows:

$$(\$1,000,000.00 \text{ gross sales} - 10\% \text{ overhead at } \$100,000.00) \times$$
$$8.9875\% \text{ of ac.} = \$80,887.50$$

Losses could be the full $30,959.69 plus any "calls" for more capital on a "dry hole."

C. The Drakes can elect the Integrated Non-Participating Owner and pay in nothing. They will not receive a penny until the well sales have achieved at least 3 × $344,475.00 or $1,033,425.00. In this circumstance, an INPO would receive nothing the first year, while the company received all of the INPO's gas for free.

If the Drakes had formed an LLC and had then leased to their own LLC before the election period expired, they would have achieved a graduated royalty return as follows:

On the first $344,475.00 of gross sales: ($344,475 × 6.25%) × 8.9875% = $1,934.98

On the second $344,475.00 of gross sales: ($344,475 × 9.38%) × 8.9875% = $2,904.02

On the third $344,475.00 of gross sales: ($311,050.00 × 12.5%) × 8.9875% = $3,494.45

Totaling: $8,333.45 in graduated royalties

Once the 300 percent penalty has been paid then the INPO effectively becomes an IPO.

D. Once the final compulsory integration order is issued, the landowner or his or her successor remains in the unit and bound by the order until the permit is surrendered or revoked.

CONCLUSION

The benefits and liabilities of compulsory integration vary in risk and reward. But in the end, Compulsory Integration, Forced Pooling, Drainage Protection, Spacing Rules, Correlative Rights, and Unitization come into existence because of the economic pressures on mineral rights owners from the application of the Rule of Capture. As long as the Rule of Capture is the controlling principle of oil and gas ownership, there will be a need for some modifying influences to ameliorate the irrational and wasteful habits generated by the economics of its raw application.

As a consequence, repealing, amending, or modifying any or all of these concepts will have a direct impact on the rights of mineral owners and on the economics of oil and gas development. The advisability or merits of repealing or altering these legal concepts is reserved for another forum.

Notes

1. N.Y. Envtl. Conserv. Law § 23-0901.
2. Terence Daintith, Finders Keepers?: How the Law of Capture Shaped the World Oil Industry (2010). The historical background set forth in this chapter is derived from N.Y. Envtl. Conserv. Law § 23-0901 and from Daniel Yergin, The Prize: The Epic Quest for Oil, Money and Power (2008).
3. Daintith, *supra* note 2.
4. Coastal Oil and Gas Corp. v. Garza Energy Trust, 268 S.W.3d 1 (Tex. 2008).
5. Stone v. Chesapeake Appalachia, LLC, No. 5:12-cv-102, at 16 (N.D. W. Va. Apr. 10, 2013) (order denying defendant's motion for summary judgment).
6. Daintith, *supra* note 2, at 376.
7. N.Y. Envtl. Conserv. Law art. 23, tit. 21, § 2101.
8. N.Y. Envtl. Conserv. Law art. 23, tit. 3, § 0301.
9. John S. Lowe, Oil and Gas Law 15–16 (5th ed. 2003).
10. N.Y. Envtl. Conserv. Law art. 23, tit. 9, § 0901(13).
11. *Id.* § 0901(3).

5

Getting Gas to the People
The Federal Energy Regulatory Commission's Permitting Process for Pipeline Infrastructure

Suedeen Kelly and Vera Callahan Neinast

Natural gas is a gaseous hydrocarbon mixture consisting primarily of methane. Unlike oil, which comes out of the ground in a liquid form that can be easily transported by truck, rail or pipeline, natural gas (in its gaseous form)[1] can only be transported by pipeline. Therefore, getting natural gas from the wellhead to the ultimate consumer requires a great deal of infrastructure. The recent surge in natural gas production from shale gas formations has resulted in a boom in pipeline construction. That is because many shale gas formations are located in areas that do not have an established pipeline infrastructure, such as North Dakota, or in areas where the existing pipeline infrastructure does not have sufficient capacity to accommodate the increased production. Where pipeline infrastructure is insufficient or nonexistent, oil well producers may simply burn, or "flare," gas that is produced with oil. Flaring gas wastes an otherwise valuable resource. This chapter explores the types of infrastructure necessary to transport natural gas to its ultimate destination and describes the regulatory framework applicable to each phase of movement—production, gathering, transmission, distribution, and storage. Additionally, the chapter will discuss how concerned members of the public can obtain information about and become involved in the pipeline construction approval process.

OVERVIEW

The natural gas industry is highly regulated, with different aspects regulated by the states and the federal government. The states regulate the production of gas. A producer must obtain a permit from the applicable state agency to drill and operate wells. Once the natural gas comes to the surface, it is moved through a series of pipelines, which are subject to different regulatory regimes. Gas is first transported from the well via small production pipelines. The production pipelines take the gas to larger gathering pipelines. Gathering pipelines gather gas from a number of wells and generally transport the gas to a processing plant where it is processed to pipeline quality and then delivered to a high-pressure transmission pipeline. Processing plants remove liquefiable hydrocarbons (ethane, butane, propane, pentanes, and other heavier hydrocarbons) from the natural gas, and impurities such as water, carbon dioxide, hydrogen sulfide, or nitrogen. The purpose of processing is to make the gas suitable for industrial and residential use and to separate out heavier hydrocarbons that can be sold as separate products. If processing is not required (for example, if the gas is "dry" gas containing few hydrocarbons or impurities), the gathering pipeline may deliver the gas directly to a transmission line or to a local distribution company. The transmission pipeline moves the gas directly to customers (typically industrial customers) or to local distribution companies, which then deliver gas to residential, commercial, and industrial customers for ultimate consumption.

It may be helpful to visualize the pipeline system by comparing it to a road system—which, in a sense, it is. The gas leaves its house (the well) and travels along a driveway (production line) to the street (gathering line). The street feeds into a larger street or highway (transmission line), which takes the gas across the state or across the country to another town. At that point, the gas leaves the highway (transmission line) and enters a smaller road system (local distribution company), which then delivers the gas to its destination: residential, commercial, or industrial consumers. Similar to a road network, there are quantitatively more smaller production, gathering, and distribution pipelines than there are larger transmission lines.

Regulatory oversight over pipelines is based on the function performed by the particular pipeline. Production lines, gathering lines, transmission lines, and distribution lines are all subject to different regulatory requirements.

THE NATURAL GAS ACT OF 1938

Natural gas has been moved by pipeline in the United States since the mid-1800s. In the early days, pipelines were relatively short, delivering natural gas in the vicinity of its production. These pipelines were regulated by local governments, which realized that without regulation, pipelines as "natural monopolies" could exert market power to charge high rates. By the early 1900s, advances in technology enabled the construction of pipelines that could carry natural gas long distances. After a series of U.S. Supreme Court decisions determined that local government regulation of interstate pipelines would violate the commerce clause of the U.S. Constitution, Congress passed the Natural Gas Act, or NGA, in 1938 to provide for federal regulation of interstate pipelines.

Section 1(b) of the NGA sets forth the scope of federal regulation, which applies to (1) the transportation of natural gas in interstate commerce, (2) the sale in interstate commerce of natural gas for resale, (3) natural gas companies engaged in such interstate transportation or sales, and (4) the importation or exportation of natural gas in foreign commerce and to persons engaged in such importation or exportation. Section 1(b) specifically exempts from federal regulation "any other transportation or sale of natural gas or . . . the local distribution of natural gas or . . . the facilities used for such distribution or . . . the production or gathering of natural gas."[2]

As a result of the NGA, the federal government regulates interstate transportation of natural gas, while the regulation of production, gathering, intrastate transportation, and local distribution of gas is left to the states. The primary federal agency charged with administration of the NGA is the Federal Energy Regulatory Commission, or FERC, which is an independent agency under the Department of Energy umbrella.[3] While it may appear that the jurisdictional boundaries between federal and state regulation are clear cut, in fact they are not, because the NGA does not define the terms "production," "gathering," "transportation," or "local distribution."

WHAT TYPES OF PIPELINES ARE THERE, AND HOW ARE THEY REGULATED?

Production Pipelines

Although the NGA does not define the term "production," the industry has developed general guidelines for determining what constitutes a production pipeline. These guidelines are set forth in the American Petroleum Institute's Recommended Practice 80,[4] or API RP 80. According to API RP 80, production pipelines are generally considered to be those pipelines that relate to the extraction and recovery of natural gas, and may include individual well flowlines, equipment piping, transfer lines between production operation equipment elements and sites, and tie-in lines to connect to other pipelines, such as gathering, transmission, or distribution pipelines.[5] Production pipelines are not regulated by FERC and are not subject to federal pipeline safety requirements.[6] Production pipelines are subject to state regulation, but most states impose minimal, if any, regulatory requirements on production pipelines.

Gathering Pipelines

If natural gas crosses a state boundary in its journey from wellhead to consumer (even if this journey takes place on multiple pipelines, some of which may not cross state lines), then federal jurisdiction generally attaches to all of the facilities used for the transportation of such gas and to all of the companies engaged in such transportation. However, natural gas may be gathered across state lines without federal jurisdiction attaching to the gathering facilities, because the FERC has no jurisdiction over the gathering of natural gas under the NGA.[7] FERC jurisdiction attaches once gathering stops and transportation begins.[8] Thus, it is important to understand how the distinction is made between gathering and transportation (transmission) pipelines.

Because the terms gathering and transportation are not defined in the NGA, the FERC has developed several legal tests over the years to determine which facilities should be deemed to be non-jurisdictional gathering facilities and which facilities should be considered to be jurisdictional transmission facilities. The FERC currently relies on the modified "primary function test" to delineate between gathering and transportation.[9] This test considers six physical and geographic factors, including: (1) the length and diameter of the pipelines, (2) the extension of the facility beyond the central point in the field, (3) the facility's geographic configuration, (4) the location of compressors and processing plants, (5) the location of the wells along all or part of the facility, and (6) the operating pressure of the pipelines. In addition, the FERC also considers the purpose, location, and operation of the facilities; the general business activity of the owner of the facilities; and whether the jurisdictional determination is consistent with the NGA and the Natural Gas Policy Act. The FERC does not consider any one factor to be determinative and recognizes that all factors do not necessarily apply to all situations. In short, the FERC's modified primary function test is a subjective test. Until the FERC scrutinizes specific facilities under this test, the actual jurisdictional status of a particular pipeline cannot be definitively determined. As a rule of thumb, it is generally accepted that pipelines upstream of a processing plant are considered to be engaged in the gathering of gas.[10] If there is no processing plant in the field, then it is less predictable where the FERC would place the point of demarcation between the gathering and the transportation functions on a particular pipeline system.

States generally apply light-handed regulation to gas gathering pipelines, unless such pipelines are regulated as gas utilities, in which case service obligations and rate oversight may apply. Construction authorization is generally not required.

Transmission Pipelines

Once gathering has ended, then transportation or local distribution begins. Transmission pipelines generally are high-pressure, large-diameter pipelines that transport natural gas long distances. These pipelines are typically 24 to 42 inches in diameter and may operate at pressures in excess of 1000 pounds per square inch. The large size and high pressure is necessary to move large quantities of natural gas efficiently. Compressor stations placed along the pipeline keep the gas pressurized and moving. The U.S. Energy Information Administration, or EIA, estimates that the United States has more than 300,000 miles of interstate and intrastate transmission pipelines. If a transmission pipeline crosses a state line, then it is considered to be an interstate pipeline subject to FERC jurisdiction. However, even transmission pipelines that are wholly located in one state may become subject to FERC jurisdiction if they transport gas as part of a chain of movements in interstate commerce from the wellhead to the burner tip. Thus, if gas is produced and gathered in Texas and is delivered to an intrastate pipeline, which then delivers the gas to an interstate pipeline that delivers the gas to a customer in Louisiana, the Texas intrastate pipeline would be considered to be engaged in the interstate transportation of gas and subject to FERC jurisdiction.[11]

Local Distribution Pipelines

Local distribution pipelines tend to be lower in pressure and smaller in diameter than transmission lines. A local distribution company is the local gas company or municipality that provides gas utility service to end users. A local distribution company typically receives gas from a transmission line and steps down the operating pressure to 200 pounds per square inch or less. By the time natural gas is delivered to a residence, the pressure has been reduced through regulators to less than one-quarter pound per square inch. These pipelines are not regulated by FERC, but are subject to varying degrees of state regulation. PHMSA estimates there are more than two million miles of gas distribution pipelines in the U.S.

Storage Facilities

Natural gas can be stored in underground caverns for later use. Most storage facilities are depleted natural gas or oil fields, but aquifers and salt caverns are also used to store natural gas. Many local distribution companies and other large gas users contract for gas storage to supplement their gas supplies during periods of high demand, such as very cold winter days or very hot summer days.

Natural gas can also be stored as liquefied natural gas (LNG), by cooling it to approximately −260 degrees Fahrenheit. LNG is kept in specially built storage tanks. When it is needed for periods of peak demand, then the LNG is regasified and transported by pipeline where needed. A benefit of LNG storage is that it can be placed close to market areas, and is therefore valuable to ensure reliability of service during periods of peak demand.

FERC considers storage to be a form of transportation. Thus, if a storage facility is used to store gas that has been or will be transported in interstate commerce, then the storage cavern and associated piping is likely to be subject to FERC regulation as an interstate pipeline facility.[12] According to the EIA, there are currently approximately 400 active storage facilities in the continental United States, with about 200 of these subject to FERC regulation. Pennsylvania, West Virginia, and New York have the most FERC-jurisdictional storage facilities, with 40, 26, and 25, respectively. Intrastate storage facilities are subject to varying levels of state regulation.

WHAT TYPE OF REGULATORY APPROVAL PROCESS IS REQUIRED TO CONSTRUCT A PIPELINE?

The type of regulatory approval process that is required to construct a pipeline depends on the type of pipeline that is being constructed. Production, gathering, intrastate transmission, and local distribution company pipelines are subject to state regulatory requirements. Thus, most of the pipelines that will be constructed to support the shale gas boom will be subject to state regulatory oversight, which varies greatly from state to state. Some state commissions may require pipelines to obtain construction permits, while other state commissions simply require notification of construction, or have no requirements. Some states may regulate the construction of transmission pipelines, but not gathering pipelines. It is not possible to make any generalizations regarding state regulation. The best way to determine what a particular state's requirements are is to visit the state regulatory agency's website. Most state agency websites have links to the governing state statutes and their administrative rules, which would provide more detailed information.

Unlike the states, the federal government has a well-established approval process for construction of interstate natural gas pipelines. Under the NGA, a pipeline must obtain prior approval from the FERC, called a "certificate of public convenience and necessity," before construction may commence.[13] Helpfully, the FERC issued a Statement of Policy in 1999[14] concerning certification of new interstate pipeline facilities that sets forth the principles applicable to the FERC's review of interstate pipeline certificate applications, including the overarching principle that the public benefits must outweigh the adverse effects of the proposed construction. The Statement of Policy and the FERC's regulations provide the framework for FERC review of pipeline construction projects.

The FERC Process

The determination of need for new interstate pipeline facilities starts with the pipeline and its existing or potential customers. Gas producers or potential gas users may approach a pipeline to inquire whether the pipeline has sufficient existing capacity to transport additional gas supplies. Because of the lead time necessary to obtain construction permits, these communications typically occur before wells are drilled. Obviously, it does not make sense to drill a well and then not be able to move the gas to market. A pipeline company that receives expressions of interest will conduct an "open season" to determine whether there is a market need for additional pipeline infrastructure. The company publishes details about its proposed construction, and all interested customers have the opportunity to sign up for service. In addition to being required by FERC, the open season is useful for the pipeline's planning purposes, as it enables the pipeline to adjust the scope of its project to meet the expected demand for pipeline capacity. For example, if there is greater demand than the pipeline had anticipated, the company may decide to construct a larger-diameter pipeline. Conversely, if there is less demand than anticipated, the pipeline may be able to meet the expected level of new demand by adding compression or looping the existing line, instead of laying a new line.

Following the open season, the pipeline company selects its proposed pipeline route and meets with landowners along the route. The FERC encourages pipeline companies to secure easements and rights-of-way by negotiation with landowners. The pipeline company may also hold public meetings along the proposed pipeline route to educate the public about the proposed project at this stage.

Pipeline companies have the option to utilize the FERC's "prefiling" procedures for construction of new pipeline facilities (such procedures are mandatory for construction of liquefied natural gas terminal and related pipeline facilities). Under these procedures, the pipeline requests the FERC to open a prefiling docket. The prefiling process provides for a 180-day period for the pipeline, the public, and the FERC to hold scoping meetings and review information from the pipeline about the proposed pipeline project. As part of the prefiling process, the pipeline company files draft environmental resource reports, which are available for public review. The prefiling process is intended to be a vehicle for addressing and resolving public concerns about a proposed pipeline construction project before the formal FERC certificate application is filed. Less controversy and public outcry generally results in a quicker approval process once the formal application is filed.

If the prefiling process is not used, then after the open season the pipeline company sets about assembling the information necessary to file a certificate application with the FERC. This includes information about the pipeline company, maps, flow diagrams, market data, information on costs and financing, and an environmental report, which is normally prepared by environmental consultants. The environmental report consists of 12 resource reports sufficient to meet the requirements of the National Environmental Policy Act (NEPA). The FERC will conduct an environmental study of the applicant's proposed project and either prepare an Environmental Assessment (EA) for more minor projects, or an Environmental Impact Statement (EIS). Underground storage facility projects and major pipeline construction projects using rights-of-way in which there is no existing natural gas pipeline require the FERC to prepare an EIS.

After the necessary information is assembled, the pipeline company files its application with the FERC. The FERC issues a notice of the application in the Federal Register shortly after the application is filed, usually within a week or two. The Federal Register notice provides information concerning the proposed construction project, identifies a contact person for the applicant, sets forth a projected timetable for the FERC's environmental review, and provides information about how to file comments about the application or become a party to the proceeding.

After the notice is issued, the pipeline is required to publish newspaper notice of the application, notify all affected landowners, towns, communities, and local, state, and federal government agencies involved in the project, and provide such entities copies of the most recent version of the FERC's pamphlet that explains the FERC's certificate process.[15]

Next, the FERC conducts public scoping meetings to determine the extent of environmental issues related to the proposed project. The FERC reviews the application, and may request additional information from the applicant. The FERC may issue an order on the project's nonenvironmental factors, such as rate design, before it completes its environmental review.

The FERC then determines whether it needs to complete an EA or an EIS. When completed, a draft of the EA or EIS is sent to other federal agencies for their review and input. The FERC is the lead permitting agency for pipeline construction projects, but other federal agencies, such as the U.S. Environmental Protection Agency, the U.S. Fish and Wildlife Service, or the Army Corps of Engineers, may also have permitting authority over aspects of the project. Following their review, the FERC will issue a draft EIS or EA for public review and comment. If the FERC issues a draft EIS, the FERC will also hold meetings in the project area to take public comments on the draft. After the close of the public comment period, the FERC will respond to comments received and prepare a final EIS or EA. Following the issuance of the final EA or EIS, the FERC will issue an order either approving or denying the certificate application. Typically, the FERC order approving an application will require the applicant to comply with a number of conditions, including completion of the construction within a set period of time, compliance with all FERC regulations, and compliance with environmental conditions listed in an appendix to the order. The environmental conditions will include a condition that the applicant submit proof to the FERC that it has secured all other required federal permits before construction may commence.

How Can the Public Effectively Convey Concerns about Proposed Pipeline Projects?

The relatively recent discovery of shale gas and the rush to develop and produce this resource means that a large network of new pipeline infrastructure will be needed to gather and transport the gas to market. Some shale gas is located in traditional gas producing areas, but some is not. Where new pipelines are being proposed in areas where pipelines have never been built before, or at least not recently, the public may be understandably concerned about the potential impacts of having a natural gas pipeline and appurtenant facilities nearby.

The ability of the public to obtain information about proposed pipeline construction projects or to participate in the approval process depends on the type of pipeline that is being constructed. As previously noted, production, gathering, and intrastate transmission pipelines are subject to state jurisdiction. There may or may not be a formal construction review process for such pipelines. Because production and gathering pipelines tend to be low pressure pipelines, they generally cause less public concern than high-pressure transmission lines. In states where there is no formal review process by the state regulatory commission, there may be no public notice of the construction at all. There may be no opportunity for the public to obtain any information about the project or become involved with issues such as siting. In such cases, only affected landowners would be aware of the proposed construction.

Even when no formal permission from a state regulatory agency is required, a pipeline company may not lay a pipeline without permission to do so from the affected landowners along the entire pipeline route. Usually, a company representative will contact the landowner, describe what the company wants, and make an offer for the use of a strip of land 50 to 100 feet wide, depending on the type of pipe. This right-of-way or easement is a formal property document filed at the courthouse with other real property documents that authorizes the pipeline to use a specified parcel of land for a specified purpose for a specified term of years. The landowner can negotiate with the company over the terms of the right-of-way or easement, including the location, price, and duration. However, if the landowner refuses to negotiate, that does not mean that the pipeline will not be constructed over the landowner's land. In most if not all states, pipelines have the right of eminent domain to acquire property to lay their pipelines. This is accomplished through a state court proceeding, where the burden of proof to establish the value of the right-of-way or easement is likely to be on the landowner.

High-pressure interstate natural gas pipeline facilities tend to cause the most public concern. As previously noted, the FERC has an established process for certificating such pipelines, and the FERC requires that there be public notice of the pipeline's proposal. The pipeline company is required to publish notice of its proposed construction in local newspapers all along the pipeline route. The company is also required to notify all affected landowners, including landowners whose property abuts the proposed right-of-way, is within one-half mile of proposed compressors, or contains a residence within 50 feet of a proposed construction work area. The pipeline company will also be conducting scoping meetings to discuss the pipeline project, and there must be public notice about the scoping meetings. This means that a member of the public is likely to have actual notice that a new interstate pipeline is being proposed.

What Are the Opportunities for Public Involvement in a FERC Certificate Proceeding?

There are several ways that members of the public can participate in the certificate process at FERC. It is important to get involved early. If a pipeline company is conducting a scoping meeting in a community, then concerned citizens should attend. This is the first opportunity to obtain information about the project and its potential impacts. Further, the level of citizen participation in the scoping meeting will help the pipeline decide whether it should ask the FERC to open a prefiling docket. Members of the public can also request the pipeline to initiate the prefiling process, although it is up to the pipeline whether it decides to do so. During the prefiling process, the pipeline will be conducting scoping meetings and making its draft environmental reports available to the public. This provides more opportunity for the public to become informed about the project, ask questions, and explore whether modifications to the project might be appropriate. It is always easier to make changes earlier in the process than later.

The next opportunity for public involvement occurs once the formal application is filed. The FERC's Federal Register notice will provide the deadline for filing a motion to intervene, which makes the filer a party to the certificate proceeding. If a person or entity wants to have the ability to file a request for rehearing of the FERC order on the certificate application or to challenge the FERC's order in court, then that person or entity needs to file a motion to intervene and become a party to the proceeding. A motion to intervene may also include comments or a protest. If the person or entity only wants to file comments on the pipeline's proposal, and does not wish to formally become a party, that is also permissible. The FERC's certificate order will consider and address all comments filed, whether or not the filer is a party to the proceeding.

After the FERC publishes notice of the application, the FERC will conduct scoping meetings to determine the environmental issues associated with the proposal. Representatives of the pipeline will also be in attendance. This provides opportunities for interested members of the public to ask questions and place their concerns in front of the FERC staff for consideration at an early phase of the proceeding.

The next public input opportunity occurs after the FERC issues the draft EIS or EA. The FERC provides a public comment period of at least 30 days.

After the FERC issues its order approving or denying the project, parties to the proceeding may file for rehearing of the FERC order and pursue court appeals. Commenters do not have these rights.

What Criteria Does the FERC Use to Evaluate a Project?

In order for a member of the public to determine how best to become involved in a pipeline certificate application, it is helpful to understand how the FERC evaluates certificate applications. The 1999 Policy Statement is the latest expression of the FERC's policy.

Under the Policy Statement, the threshold requirement for an applicant to establish is that the new pipeline can be constructed without subsidization by existing customers. The "no subsidy" prong is generally satisfied by pricing the services to be rendered through the new facilities on an incremental basis, i.e., the cost of transportation through the new pipeline is based on the construction cost of the new pipeline. Assuming this requirement is satisfied, then the FERC considers whether the applicant has made efforts to eliminate or minimize adverse effects on the applicant's existing customers, existing pipelines in the market and their captive customers, and landowners and communities affected by the construction. If there are residual adverse effects on these interest groups after efforts have been made to minimize them, the FERC will evaluate the project by balancing the evidence of public benefits to be achieved against the residual adverse effects. This is essentially an economic test. Only when the benefits outweigh the adverse effects on economic interests does the FERC proceed to environmental analysis of the project.

The FERC's environmental analysis of the application starts with the company's environmental report submitted as part of the certificate application. But the FERC conducts its own environmental review to prepare the EA or EIS with the assistance of a third-party environmental consultant contractor, which the FERC selects and the applicant pays for. The FERC's environmental review is thorough and addresses all comments received by government agencies and members of the public. If the EA or EIS results in a finding of no significant impact, then it is fairly certain that the FERC will approve the project. The environmental review may also reveal that an alternate route is environmentally preferable for the project to avoid sensitive areas or mitigate environmental impacts, in which case the FERC order on the application is likely to condition approval of the application on use of the alternate route or certain mitigation measures.

Issuance of a certificate of public convenience and necessity by FERC does not mean the applicant may commence construction immediately. The FERC order may be issued before the applicant has received other required federal agency approvals. The environmental conditions attached to the FERC order will require that all such approvals be obtained prior to the commencement of construction. The applicant will have to obtain written authorization from the FERC's Director of the Office of Energy Projects to commence construction.

If the applicant receives all of the requisite permits but has not been able to acquire all of the necessary rights-of-way or easements through negotiation, the applicant can exercise eminent domain to acquire the land rights. The NGA confers eminent domain authority on holders of a FERC construction certificate.

Case Study

A recent FERC order is illustrative of the FERC's approach to certificating a pipeline project in the face of significant public opposition.[16] In that proceeding, the pipeline company proposed to put a compressor station close to a small Maryland town, next to a wastewater treatment plant and gas station, and adjacent to an interstate highway. A compressor station is an above-ground facility, and is used to facilitate movement of gas through the pipeline. As previously noted, compressor stations are spaced along the route of the pipeline. The townsfolk vigorously protested the location of the compressor station in their town. More than 650 individuals filed comments opposing the proposed location, contending it was incompatible with their rural community and would result in irreversible damage to their quality of life. Concerns were also expressed with respect to construction traffic, road damage/repairs, and dust, as well as operational aspects of the compressor station, such as noise.

The FERC order explained that FERC looked at eight alternative compressor sites in addition to the pipeline's proposed site. Three were eliminated due to engineering requirements. Three others were eliminated due to constructability and/or residential impact issues. The FERC also considered a pipeline looping alternative and an electric compression alternative. The two remaining alternative sites were thoroughly analyzed in the EA, and the FERC determined that the proposed site offered environmental advantages the two alternatives did not. Accordingly, the FERC order approved the applicant's proposed compressor station site.

Instructive findings by the FERC include:

1. *Need for the project.* Because the capacity of the proposed project was fully subscribed, the FERC concluded there was a need for the pipeline, including the compressor station.

2. *Town's rejection of zoning request.* The FERC stated that while it encourages cooperation between pipeline companies and local authorities, this does not mean that state or local laws can be used to prohibit or unreasonably delay construction or operation of FERC-approved facilities. FERC stated, "While applicants may be required to comply with appropriate state and local regulations where no conflict exists, state and local regulation is preempted by the NGA to the extent they conflict with federal regulation, or would delay the construction and operation of facilities approved by this Commission."[17]

3. *Air permits.* Compressor stations require Clean Air Act permits. These are federal permits, but are administered by the state environmental agency if the state has a federally approved state implementation plan. The FERC declined to address air quality permit issues because they are outside the FERC's jurisdiction, but noted that the EA concluded that air impacts would be within environmentally acceptable limits. The FERC further noted that its order was conditioned on the pipeline company obtaining all applicable authorizations required under federal law. Thus, if the state of Maryland did not issue the air quality permit, it would be up to the pipeline company to determine how to proceed.

4. *Unavailing arguments.* The FERC considered and dismissed arguments raised concerning the following: impact on historical properties (none); visual impacts (sufficiently mitigated); property values (subjective and adequately mitigated through visual screening and noise mitigation measures); economic issues (speculative); air quality impacts (compliance with

federal and state air quality regulations are required by the order); noise impacts (mitigation adequate); public safety (adequate control systems, compliance with safety regulations required); landowner impact (FERC declined to expand the impact zone beyond the one-half mile radius required by FERC regulations); water quality (adequate mitigation, plus compliance with the Clean Water Act is required by the order); invasive species (adequate mitigation); and migratory birds (no adverse effect).

It can be expected that because FERC does a thorough environmental review, the FERC's order will defend the conclusions of the EA or EIS against challenges. Further, if the FERC finds that adverse impacts can be mitigated through adoption of reasonable measures such as planting trees or installation of sound control equipment, then the FERC is not going to be receptive to concerns about such adverse impacts. This means that any project concerns should be communicated to the FERC early on, before the final EA or EIS. The FERC might not agree with the concerns expressed, but the FERC will consider and respond to them. This provides the concerned citizen with the maximum opportunity to be heard.

Many of the Maryland citizens were generally opposed to the compressor station on generic quality of life grounds. In essence, these are "not in my back yard" arguments. The FERC is not receptive to these sorts of complaints. Local opposition will not deter the FERC from its mission, which is to evaluate the pipeline project in accordance with FERC's policies and regulatory requirements.

The bottom line is that a concerned citizen may not have the ability to prohibit certification of an interstate pipeline, but he or she will have the opportunity to express his or her concerns and have them addressed in the certificate proceeding. Public input may cause the FERC to require the applicant to take measures to minimize adverse impacts associated with construction and/or operation of the pipeline and associated facilities. Active participation early in the project may even influence the siting of an interstate pipeline facility if there are environmental issues that can be mitigated though relocation. For these reasons, it is worthwhile for members of the public to become involved in FERC certificate proceedings. The public interest is advanced when pipeline projects are subjected to vigorous examination.

Notes

1. Natural gas can be converted to a liquid by cooling the gas to approximately –260 degrees Fahrenheit. Liquefied natural gas, or LNG, takes up 1/600th the space of natural gas at atmospheric pressure. In this condensed form it can be stored in above-ground storage tanks until it is needed, at which time it is regasified for transportation in pipelines. LNG can also be shipped in special tankers across the oceans to LNG storage tanks and regasification terminals in other countries.

2. Section 1(c) of the NGA, 15 U.S.C. § 717c, contains an additional exemption from federal regulation for intrastate pipelines that receive their gas supplies within or at the boundary of a state and all the gas is ultimately consumed within such state, provided that the rates and services provided by such pipelines are subject to regulation by a state commission.

3. The Department of Energy's Office of Fossil Energy, or DOE/FE, is responsible for approving imports and exports of natural gas, including LNG, but FERC has jurisdiction over the siting of natural gas pipelines used to import or export natural gas, and the siting of LNG terminals.

4. Am. Petrol. Inst., AMERICAN PETROLEUM INSTITUTE RECOMMENDED PRACTICE 80: GUIDELINES FOR THE DEFINITION OF ONSHORE GAS GATHERING LINES, (1st ed., Apr. 2000) [hereinafter API RP 80].

5. API RP 80 at Section 2.4.4.

6. The U.S. Department of Transportation's Pipeline and Hazardous Materials Safety Administration, or PHMSA, has jurisdiction over pipeline safety and integrity. Production pipelines are not presently subject to PHMSA regulation.

7. Natural Gas Act of 1938 § 1(b), 15 U.S.C. § 717b.

8. In contrast, federal regulation over pipeline safety starts with gathering pipelines. PHMSA's regulations generally define the term "gathering line" as "a pipeline that transports gas from a current production facility to a transmission line or main." Under the PHMSA regulations, the pipeline operator must determine whether a pipeline is a gathering line by consulting API RP 80, then applying additional considerations and limitations imposed by the PHMSA regulations.

9. *See, e.g.*, Stingray Pipeline Co., LLC, 142 FERC ¶ 62,069 (2013).

10. Processing plants are not subject to FERC jurisdiction under the NGA.

11. Under Section 311 of the Natural Gas Policy Act, however, intrastate pipelines may participate in interstate transportation without becoming interstate pipelines subject to the full panoply of FERC jurisdiction, so long as they follow the FERC regulations and policies applicable to Section 311 service.

12. LNG terminal facilities are subject to FERC siting regulation, but not all LNG terminals are subject to rate regulation.

13. NGA § 7(c).
14. Certification of New Interstate Natural Gas Pipeline Facilities, 88 FERC ¶ 61,277 (1999).
15. This pamphlet, called, AN INTERSTATE NATURAL GAS FACILITY ON MY LAND? WHAT DO I NEED TO KNOW? can also be downloaded from the FERC website, www.ferc.gov.
16. Dominion Transmission, Inc., 141 FERC ¶ 61,240 (2012).
17. *Id.* at P 68.

6

Anticipating Problems
Road Agreements, Performance Bonds, and Enforcement

Heather M. Urwiller

Local governments must balance the needs of job creation and economic development with the responsibility to protect the health, safety and welfare of local residents and stakeholders. As detailed in chapter 11, the activities that accompany unconventional oil and gas development can have significant impacts on roads, public safety, emergency responder workload, and other public services. Municipalities are primarily responsible for providing these services and must budget for them in their staffing and tax plans. They are implementing strategies to protect themselves from unfunded liabilities in the face of rapid development of oil and gas. Municipalities have long used road agreements and proof of insurance and performance bonds to manage negative impacts of many kinds of development and are now tailoring these tools for use with oil and gas development. This chapter will use case studies to illustrate how these tools can be used to maintain some control over the impacts of oil and gas development activity.

Performance bonding, insurance requirements, and road agreements can be used to ensure that municipalities are able to address adverse conditions that could arise as a result of oil and gas development. Performance bonds are often used to ensure that developers comply with state and local regulations. Road maintenance agreements are specifically applicable to jurisdictional highways—often the greatest percentage of local appropriations and expenditures in rural municipalities.[1]

PERFORMANCE BONDS

Performance bonds are a useful instrument to protect communities against abandonment of projects and to ensure compliance with preapproved development plans. Typical examples of areas outside of oil and gas development where bonding is commonly employed include projects like subdivision development and extraction of sand and gravel.

In oil and gas drilling, performance bonds are required by local governments to guarantee that drilling and reclamation of wells is done in compliance with both state and local permit requirements. Should a drilling company fail to restore a well site, the cost of reclamation could potentially bankrupt a small community (not to mention a landowner), and bonds can help to indemnify the community (or individual) against such costs.

The bonds are generally delivered to the municipality by drilling operators as the final step in the permit process before drilling commences. Bond amounts can range from a few thousand dollars to over a million dollars. For example, the City of Pine Haven, Wyoming, requires both a minimum surety bond of $200,000 and a one million dollar bond or policy of liability insurance to cover hazardous accidents, including blowout preventer malfunctions. In addition, the applicant must carry standard public comprehensive liability coverage.[2] For additional examples of communities that require bonding or insurance provisions, see Tables 6.1 and 6.2.

Performance bonds are generally held by the municipality until the well sites are completely reclaimed. Defined criteria and performance measures often must be achieved before the bonds are released by municipalities. Performance measures may include total reclamation, partial site reclamation, satisfactory water quality tests, or other environmental measures. Operators may request, and municipalities

Table 6.1. County Government Efforts to Regulate Oil and Gas Development

COUNTY	ACTIONS TAKEN	SOURCE
Garfield County, Colorado	Draft regulation and Oil and Gas Department. Permits for overweight vehicles are required	http://www.oilandgasbmps.org /law/colorado_localgovt_law.php http://www.garfield-county.com /oil-gas/index.asp
Gunnison County, Colorado	Regulations for well facilities and include requirement to pay mitigation for impact of operations	http://www.oilandgasbmps.org /law/colorado_localgovt_law.php http://www.gunnisoncounty.org /planning_regulations_guidelines .html#Oil_Gas
La Plata County, Colorado	Regulation of well facilities and differentiate between minor and major facilities & impacts must be mitigated	http://www.oilandgasbmps.org /law/colorado_localgovt_law.php http://www.co.laplata.co.us /departments_and_elected _officials/planning/natural _resources_oil_gas
Pitkin County, Colorado	Regulation of oil and gas facilities and include provisions to protect Roads and Access	http://www.oilandgasbmps.org /law/colorado_localgovt_law.php
Saguache County, Colorado	Regulation of oil and gas well facilities and include Road Access and Transportation Route Plans	http://www.oilandgasbmps.org /law/colorado_localgovt_law.php
Yuma County, Colorado	Regulation of oil and gas well facilities and include Road/ Improvement Agreements	http://www.oilandgasbmps.org /law/colorado_localgovt_law.php
Duchesne County, Utah	Oil and Gas drilling requires a conditional use permit and road permits, encroachment permits are required and County must be named as an additional entity on State required performance guarantees	http://www.oilandgasbmps.org /law/utah_localgovt_law.php
Emery County, Utah	Oil and Gas Wells require a conditional use permit and a road encroachment permit	http://www.oilandgasbmps.org /law/utah_localgovt_law.php
Grand County, Utah	Oil and Gas Wells require extensive review of haul route, restriction maybe placed on haul routes and operator are restricted to daytime	http://www.oilandgasbmps.org /law/utah_localgovt_law.php

Source: Intermountain Oil and Gas BMT Project: Getches-Wilkinson Center for Natural Resources, Energy and the Environment/University of Colorado Law School http://www.oilandgasbmps.org/laws/index.php.

Table 6.2. City Government Efforts to Regulate Oil and Gas Development

CITIES	ACTION TAKEN	SOURCE
Gillette, Wyoming	City has insurance requirements and speaks to maintaining of roads. All loads are to be within limitation set by city and average load weights and number of projected loads are to be included as part of application	http://www.oilandgasbmps.org /law/utah_localgovt_law.php http://www.ci.gillette.wy.us /Modules/ShowDocument .asp?documentid=54
Pine Haven, Wyoming	City requires a statement a map what routes will be utilized for transportation of equipment and supplies and approximate weight of each load. All loads shall be within weight limits set by city.	http://www.oilandgasbmps.org /law/utah_localgovt_law.php http://pinehaven.wy.govoffice2 .com/index.asp?TYPEB -BASIC&SEC={68E82548-2404 -4AE9-BD74-C2E91A178F69}
Fort Worth, Texas	City regulates oil and gas wells through permitting Truck routing information must be provided including both use of commercial and non-commercial routes along with a road agreement	http://forthworthtexas .govuploadedFiles/Gas _Well/09012_gas _drilling_final .pdf
Arlington, Texas	City requires payment of a road damage fee based on the City's Road Damage Assessment. The fee is calculated using a formula.	http://www.arlingtontx.gov /planning/pdf/Gas_Wells/Final _Gas_Drilling_Amendments _Ordinance.pdf
Aurora, Colorado	Oil and Gas Facilities in the city	Ch.146, Art 2, Sec.7 (146-1207): http://library.municode.com/index .aspx?clientID=13725
Lafayette, Colorado	Oil and Gas Development specific standards for road and road access agreements required	§26.22-1: http://library .municode.com/index .aspx?clientID=10101
Louisville, Colorado	Oil and Gas Regulations	Ch. 17.68: http://library .municode.com/index .aspx?clientID=13149
Thornton, Colorado	Oil and Gas Regulation	Ch.18, Article X: http://library .municode.com/index.aspx?clien tID=15041&StateID=&Statenam e=Colorado

Source: Intermountain Oil and Gas BMT Project: Getches-Wilkinson Center for Natural Resources, Energy and the Environment/University of Colorado Law School http://www.oilandgasbmps.org/laws/index.php.

often grant, partial bond releases upon completion of stages of reclamation. This type of practice is especially important in the context
of industries, such as unconventional oil and gas development, where
accidents and negligence can result in extreme impacts to communities and stakeholders. Most state governments also require bonding by
oil and gas companies. Table 6.3 provides statutory locations of state
bonding requirements.

Many municipalities are not satisfied with state bonding requirements for oil and gas operators and with increasing frequency are
requiring bonds and liability insurance beyond what states mandate.
Table 6.1 provides examples of county governments that require local
bonds. Table 6.2 provides examples of cities that require bonds as part
of the local permit application. Some municipalities are more aggressive than others in the type of insurance and bonding they require
operators provide to secure a local well drilling permit. In Colorado,
Gunnison and Mesa Counties have explicit requirements for financial security,[3] which is usually accomplished through bonds or letters
of credit. In contrast, Campbell County, Wyoming, has no bonding
requirements in relation to oil and gas well development.[4]

INSURANCE

While most operators carry a variety of insurance—whether it is
required or not—municipalities are increasingly requiring operators
to carry additional insurance to further indemnify the community
against potential loss and increase compliance. Insurance protects
the operators, landowners, and municipalities from catastrophic loss
if something unintended occurs on the well site. For instance, chapter
12 of the Oil and Water Well section of the city of Gillette's code
requires applicants to a provide a minimum of one million dollars
in liability insurance and deposit $16,500 in lawful currency, letter
of credit or surety bond for each well. Any violation of the permits
results in the forfeiting of the deposit.[5]

ROAD MAINTENANCE AGREEMENTS

Bonding requirements can be extended to road maintenance. Many
municipalities include provisions in drilling applications that allow
the use of bonds, letters of credit or insurance claims to pay for damage

Table 6.3. Oil and Gas Regulations in Various States

STATE	STATE REGULATORY AUTHORITY	MAJOR REGULATIONS	SOURCE
Pennsylvania	Pennsylvania Department of Environmental Protection	Title 58, 78, 79, 91, 95 & 102 PA Consolidated Statutes	http://www.portal.state.pa.us /portal/server.pt/community /oil_and_gas/6003 http://www.portal.state.pa.us /portal/server.pt/community /law%2C_regulations _guidelines/20306 http://www.legis.state.pa.us /WU01/LI/LI/CT/HTM/58/58.HTM
Texas	Railroad Commission of Texas	Chapter 52, 71, 81, 85 ,86, & 89 TX Natural Resources Code	http://www.statutes.legis.state .tx.us http://www.rrc.state.tx.us/index .php
Colorado	Colorado Oil & Gas Conservation Commission	Title 34 Colorado Revised Statutes	http://www.legisnexis.com /hottopics/Colorado/ http://www.oilandgasbmps.org /law/Colorado_law.php http:cogcc.state.co.us
Utah	Utah Division of Oil, Gas & Mining	Title 40 Utah Statutes	http://le.utah.gov/Utah code /chapter.jsp?code=40 http://www.oilandgasbmps.org /law/Utah_law.php http://linux1.ogm.utah.gov/web stuff/wwwroot/division/tabs/html
Louisiana	Department of Natural Resources	Titles 30 and 31 Revised Statutes	http://www.legis.la.gov /legis/laws_toc.aspx?folder= 75&level=parent http://dnr.louisiana.gov/index.cfm ?md=pagebuilder&tmp=home&pi d=301&ngid=1
Wyoming	Wyoming Oil and Gas Conservation Commission	Title 30 Chapter 5 Wyoming Code	http://legisweb.state.wy.us /statute/statute.aspx http://www.oilandgasbmps.org /law/Wyoming_law.php http://wogcc.state.wy.us
Montana	Montana Board of Oil and Gas Conservation	Title 82, Chapter 10-11 Montana Code	http://data.opi/mt.gov/bill /mca_toc/82.htm http:// www.oilandgasbmps.org /law/Montana_law.php http://bogc.dnrc.mt.gov

Source: Intermountain Oil and Gas BMT Project: Getches-Wilkinson Center for Natural Resources, Energy and the Environment/University of Colorado Law School, http://www.oilandgasbmps.org/laws/index.php.

to local infrastructure. Municipalities commonly use road agreements for trucking and distribution facilities, commercial wind farms, and large commercial and industrial campuses. Municipalities have extended these common provisions from more conventional types of local development to unconventional oil and shale gas development.

Roads are built to specific standards, and heavy loads that exceed design standards can cause the failure of the road surface as well as bridge collapse. Many local roadways and bridges are not designed to handle large volumes of overweight loads, posing logistical and compliance problems for operators. Road failure can lead to costly road reconstruction or redesign. Even modest increases in this type of traffic can severely impact local communities. If developers and operators of well sites are not monitored for their impacts on roadways, the municipality can be forced to bear costs associated with road damage—costs that, were they anticipated, can be avoided or minimized.

To avoid or minimize these problems, operators are generally required to get permits at both the state and local level for overweight vehicles. Where prevention does not suffice to avoid damage, carefully executed road agreements can help to ensure repair or replacement of road surfaces or bridges in the event they are damaged due to a developer's actions.

Road impacts include not only damage to road surfaces but include broad impacts on road right of ways like concentrated traffic requiring road improvements. Concentrating traffic can require the following types of improvements: road widening, vertical realignment of highways to improve grades for heavy vehicles, horizontal realignment of highways to accommodate curve radii for large vehicles, drainage improvements associated with road widening and/or vertical/horizontal realignments, or legal and property rights transactions associated with temporary or permanent property acquisitions or easements.[6] Road agreements are common in any type of extractive use. The local municipality will review the developer's application and determine the loading and types of equipment that will be hauled on local roadways. The agreements generally delineate preferred or required truck haul routes and define the maximum number and weight of truckloads in the haul route schedule.

Because these costs can be significant, many local communities are working with the industry on issues related to road conditions by, for example, requiring that industry use designated truck haul routes and estimate weight and number of loads. Tables 6.1 and 6.2 provide information on counties and cities currently requiring road impacts to be addressed as part of the drilling permit process.

Deliberate use of haul routes and other best management practices can protect operators and their subcontractors from being forced to provide new road surfaces. Drilling and fracturing processes are temporary and intermittent. Therefore, when best management practices are used, operators need not provide costly repairs to infrastructure. Yuma County and Pitkin County, Colorado, both require road agreements as part of the permit application process (see Table 6.1). The agreements generally look at the prior conditions of roadways, truck hauling routes, and the number and average weight of overweight loads. Both communities also require overweight vehicle permits and local road or encroachment permits.

The cities of Lafayette, Wyoming, and Forth Worth, Texas, require road agreements as part of the permit application process (see Table 6.2). These communities look at the impact of overweight vehicle and truck haul routes on local roadways. The city of Arlington, Texas, has a different approach. It has adopted a road damage fee based on the City's Road Damage Assessment (see Table 6.2), which are used to pay for improvements to local roadways. Fees are calculated based on access of lane mile for appropriate road type, assessment per land mile, and number of lane miles included in each gas permit.[7]

Enforcement against violators of permits or posted weight limits is an additional mechanism used to deter road damage and raise dollars to fund repairs. In addition to permits, Caddo Parish, Louisiana, has successfully used fines for overweight vehicles and other penalties in an effort to stem road damage. According to the parish attorney, the parish determined early in the shale gas boom that revenue from fines would exceed permit fees for overweight vehicles transporting materials to and from well sites. Over time the parish has seen a reduction in the number of fines as truck haulers and operators increase compliance with local laws and seek permits prior to moving materials to and from well sites. By requiring permits, the parish can provide guidance to operators and truck haulers on which roads and routes to use for overweight vehicles. This minimizes the damage that operators must repair.[8]

Some states, like Pennsylvania, have taken unique approaches to provide resources for infrastructure maintenance and repair. Title 58 of the Pennsylvania Consolidated Code allows counties to levy well fees specific to unconventional gas wells. If counties opt out of levying these additional fees, local municipalities are authorized to levy the fee.[9] This unconventional well fee is in addition to any local application fees or state taxes. The fees collected are used to support a variety of state goals, such as providing additional funds to the state's road and bridge program and improving environmental quality and stewardship among local communities that have active unconventional oil and gas resources extraction.

As unconventional oil and gas development expands, local communities will have to work with operators to develop provisions to protect infrastructure and foster environmental stewardship. Damage from nonperformance and/or accidents can be anticipated and mitigated through the use of bonding and insurance requirements. Road agreements and regulation can put the onus on the industry to repair infrastructure damage caused by shale oil and gas exploration and development. While this development brings some new challenges, many of the types of impacts are similar to those experienced with any large-scale extractive industry; the tools available to municipalities for dealing with these issues—bonding, insurance requirements, and contractual agreements governing infrastructure use—are variations on tools that municipalities have been using for a long time.

NOTES

1. Author's personal communication with Adam Yagelski (May 2013).
2. For Pine Haven, Wyoming, local insurance provisions see: http://www.oilandgasbmps.org/law/utah_localgovt_law.php and http://pinehaven.wy.govoffice2.com/index.asp?TYPEB-BASIC&SEC={68E82548-2404-4AE9-BD74-C2E91A178F69}.
3. For Gunnison County and Mesa County, Colorado, ordinance provisions see: http://www.oilandgasbmps.org/law/colorado_localgovt_law.php.
4. Conversation with Building and Planning Department Staff, Campbell Cnty., Wyo. (May 9, 2013) (verified that the County does not have bonding requirements for oil and gas development).
5. Gillette, Wyoming: Chapter 12 Oil and Water Wells provision B and D cover the liability insurance and additional surety requirements: see http://www.oilandgasbmps.org/law/wyoming_localgovt_law.php. Cities are discussed at the bottom of the page.
6. C. J. Randall, *Hammer Down: A Guide to Protecting Local Roads Impacted by Shale Gas Drilling* (Working Paper Series: A Comprehensive Economic Impact Analysis of Natural Gas Extraction in the Marcellus Shale, 2010),

available at http://www.greenchoices.cornell.edu/downloads/development /shale/marcellus/Protecting_Local_Roads.pdf (citing, in a broad way, considerations pertaining to preparing and implementing a "comprehensive traffic impact study"). *See also* Powerpoint: Delta Engineers, Architects, & Land Surveyors P.C., *Delta Road Protection Program* (June 24, 2011), *available at* http://www.co.chenango.ny.us/planning/education/documents /AOTC/Marcellus%20Roads%20-%20Messmer%20Delta%20Eng.pdf (Chenango County from the Engineering Company—see the map of participating towns at the end); Oneonta, N.Y., Local Road Use and Preservation Law, Local Law No. 3 (2012), *available at* http://townofoneonta.org /site%20elements/LocalLawNo3_2012.pdf (implementing legislation).

7. Arlington, Tex., Ordinance No. 11-068, § 5.01(I) (Dec. 6, 2011). *See* Arlington, Tex., Ordinance No. 07-074 (Oct. 23, 2007), *available at* http://www.arlingtontx.gov/planning/pdf/Gas_Wells/Final_Gas_Drilling _Amendments_Ordinance.pdf.

8. Telephone Conversation with Charles Grugg, Attorney, Caddo Parish, La. (Apr. 1, 2013). As part of the permit process operators, and contractors must seek approval for the routes used by trucks for construction and well drilling. The Parish takes video evidence to road conditions prior to well development. Operators are held accountable for any damage to roads and bridges and required to repair damage. The Parish, through enforcement of the laws, uses fining and prior permitting as a means to control damage to public infrastructure. "They have found this to be effective." The Parish employs a full time employee who has a portable scale that he tows around, using random truck weighing to enforce the overweight truck regulations. The enforcement is mean to collect fines from cross-state independent haulers. The employee patrols the back roads looking for violators. The Parish determined early in the shale gas boom that revenue from fines would exceed permit fees for vehicles transporting materials to and from well sites. Over time, the Parish has seen the number of fines decrease as haulers and operators become more compliant and seek permits prior to moving materials to and from well sites. The permitting process allows the Parish to provide guidance to operators and haulers on which roads and routes to use for overweight trucks, minimizing damage that operators must repair.

9. Unconventional Gas Well Fee, 58 PA. CONST. STAT. §§ 2301–2318, *available at* http://www.legis.state.pa.us/WU01/LI/LI/CT/HTM/58/58.HTM.

7

Clearing the Air
Reducing Emissions from Unconventional Oil and Gas Development

Beth E. Kinne

The debate on air pollution impacts from unconventional gas development via hydraulic fracturing has focused on two related yet quite distinct areas. The first involves broader climate impacts that may be geographically and temporally removed from the locus of drilling activity. The second, which involves the health impacts of more or less immediate localized exposure to pollutants such as volatile organic compounds, ground level ozone, and smog, is the primary focus of this chapter.

In response to these concerns, some state governments, such as Colorado, Wyoming, Texas, and Pennsylvania, and more recently the U.S. EPA, have promulgated regulations aimed at reducing emissions of air pollutants from oil and gas wells (see state-by-state discussion below). Industry has also developed new technologies to reduce emissions. Many of these changes have enabled the capture of significant amounts of valuable hydrocarbons, resulting in economic gains and reasonably short payback periods. The willingness of industry and regulators to embrace advances in technology and work practices will shape the overall impact of oil and gas development on air quality, public health, greenhouse gas emissions, and the public's perception of the industry and regulators.

This chapter begins with an overview of the types of air pollution created by oil and gas drilling. It then addresses the human health and air quality concerns created by oil and gas development, particularly from unconventional drilling. This is followed by a discussion of some key technologies available to reduce emissions. The final section explains some voluntary initiatives and regulations that are promoting the use of these key technologies and provides some examples of air quality monitoring programs that are being used to better understand emissions from oil and gas development.

AIR POLLUTION FROM OIL AND GAS DRILLING

Known air pollutants associated with hydraulic fracturing activities include particulate matter, methane, and a variety of other volatile organic compounds (VOCs), including benzene, toluene, ethylbenzene, and xylene, which are sometimes collectively referred to as BETEX or non-methane hydrocarbons (NMHCs).[1] When combined with sunlight, water, and nitrogen oxides (the primary source of which is combustion of diesel fuel by large trucks and generators at the well pad site), VOCs create ground-level ozone, which has well-documented consequences for human and plant health. The oil and gas industry is the largest industrial emitter of VOCs, emitting an estimated 2.2 million tons in 2008.[2]

Natural gas development is frequently not the only exposure pathway to these chemicals for most people. For example, people are regularly exposed to small amounts of benzene from motor vehicle exhaust, tobacco smoke, and many solvents, paints, and detergents.[3] However, long-term, chronic, high-level exposure in areas experiencing intensive development can significantly impact human health and the quality of life of gas industry workers and of individuals living near these operations.[4]

Data on fugitive methane emissions from oil and gas production is somewhat limited, although recent studies are contributing significantly to the creation of a more comprehensive understanding of this issue.[5] However, fugitive emissions have been documented during the drilling process, during completion (the period of time after the well is drilled, but before it is attached to a production line), and from compression, transmission, storage, and consumer distribution processes.[6] During drilling of the well, emissions from the target layer and/or other shallower layers may escape.[7] In addition, if flowback is returned to open pits, volatile compounds can evaporate from those pits into the air.

Steps used to maintain the productivity of the well can also result in fugitive emissions. Over the life of the well, smaller amounts of water continue to be produced along with the gas. After a well has been in production for some time, the rate of gas flow declines as the pressure in the system is reduced. Water can build up in the wellbore and reduce the productivity of the well. In these cases, taking the well offline to vent it to atmospheric pressure can allow the pressure of the gas to lift the accumulated water out of the well in what is called well deliquification or "blowdown." The EPA estimates that 9.6 Bcf of methane per year is lost during well blowdowns.[8] During this process, the gas must be either vented (released) to the atmosphere or flared (burned on site), thus producing either methane (with venting) or carbon dioxide (with flaring). Methane and other hydrocarbons can be captured using specialized equipment. Alternative technologies to blowdown are available (as detailed below) and can significantly reduce air emissions.

Releases can also occur at many other points along the process as well, either from leakage (fugitive emissions) or by design (venting). For example, faulty construction and wear and tear can result in fugitive emissions from pipeline connections, valves, compressor stations, and storage facilities. Routine maintenance and repair activities often require depressurization of a component of the system, which can be quickly and easily accomplished by venting.

The EPA's 2011 Greenhouse Gas Inventory Report, released in spring 2013, reported that overall emissions from natural gas systems (including production, transmission, storage, and distribution) decreased by 10.2 percent between 1990 and 2011.[9] Recent research tracking actual emissions of air pollutants by the oil and gas industry and industry-reported emission reductions under the EPA Natural Gas STAR program (discussed below) suggest that losses of methane, benzene, and other compounds may be significantly underestimated in both industry and government studies.[10] Currently, over 20,000 oil and gas wells are hydraulically fractured or re-fractured each year.[11] While some states, such as Colorado,[12] are utilizing increased setbacks to reduce risks presented by gas drilling, setbacks alone will likely be insufficient to mitigate chronic exposure of the public from cumulative sources over long periods of time and will certainly not reduce workers' exposure to these pollutants.[13]

HEALTH IMPACTS OF EMISSIONS FROM OIL AND GAS DRILLING

In a recent policy statement, the American Public Health Association asserted, "The onset of HVHF in many parts of the country represents a new industrial, environmental, and land use development pattern with significant potential for impacts on public health."[14] As development of unconventional shale plays for oil and gas expands, the number of wells hydraulically fractured annually will likely rise. Increases in oil and gas development near urban and suburban populations will result in increased exposure rates unless emissions are reduced by the application of appropriate technology and work practices. While drilling activity could affect health in multiple ways, air pollution concerns mainly include ground-level ozone, particulate matter, and air toxics.

Ground-level ozone is a very strong oxidant. It is damaging to lung tissue and can have particularly significant impacts on children, the elderly, and people who spend a lot of time outdoors. The EPA states that ground-level ozone "is linked to a wide range of health effects, including aggravated asthma, increased emergency room visits and hospital admissions, and premature death."[15] When ground-level ozone combines with small particulates (<2.5 microns in diameter), it produces smog. In addition to aesthetic concerns, high smog levels are known to correlate with increases in respiratory distress in vulnerable populations such as children, the elderly, and people with diabetes and heart disease.[16] In a 2012 report, the American Lung Association estimated that over 43 million people under the age of 18 and over 20 million people over the age of 65 in the United States are at higher risk for health complications due to exposure to unhealthy levels of ozone or particulate.[17] Aside from human health impacts, ground-level ozone causes more damage to plants than all other air pollutants combined and can have significant impacts on crop productivity for some important food and feedstock crops, such as soy and peanuts.[18]

Exposure to VOCs released by wells is of particular concern for those living nearby and downwind of gas development activities, including open flowback pits. A Colorado School of Public Health study of Garfield County, Colorado, concluded that residents living within a half-mile from a well site where completion activities were occurring had exposure levels to toxic and carcinogenic chemicals that warranted further research into cumulative effects and effects over time.[19] Intensive development of natural gas resources without minimizing releases of VOCs could increase the number of people at risk for health complications from poor air quality and/or put already at-risk citizens at further risk.

In addition to the localized impacts in the immediate vicinity of drilling sites, the upstream and downstream processes involved with oil and gas development also contribute to air pollution. In response to the great increase in demand for silica sands for proppants, for example, sand mining has rapidly increased in certain areas of Wisconsin and Minnesota,[20] resulting in air pollution in those regions and potential increases in asthma and other respiratory ailments in nearby residents. While not classified as a hazardous air pollutant (HAP) by the EPA, respirable crystalline silica is classified as a human carcinogen by the International Agency for Research on Cancer. It can cause silicosis and is also associated with emphysema, bronchitis, and kidney and immune system diseases.[21] The persons most at risk are those working with silica, but high ambient levels could also pose nonoccupational risks.

Key Emission Reduction Technologies

According to a 2012 report by the Natural Resource Defense Council (NRDC), application of just two technologies—green completions and plunger lift systems—could eliminate almost 40 percent of methane emissions from oil and gas drilling activities.[22] If all existing emission-reduction technologies were employed and applied to existing as well as future infrastructure, emissions levels reported by the EPA in 2011[23] could be reduced by more than 80 percent.[24] If the trend toward increased regulation of emissions continues, drillers will increase application of recapturing technologies, thereby eliminating much of the need for flaring, which will bring the same benefit of better community relations as venting while providing additional revenue for the industry.

Green Completions

During the well completion phase, the operator may choose one of three options for the escaping gases: venting, flaring (both described above), or capture via a green completion. With green completions, also known as reduced emission completions (RECs), sand, gases, water, and other chemicals are contained and separated, and then methane and other hydrocarbons are directed to a sales line. When done properly, green completions can eliminate most of the need for flaring or venting.[25] The figure below illustrates the steps in a green completion process. A sand trap removes the proppant from the liquids, then the water is separated out and sent to recycle or disposal. The various hydrocarbons are separated and moved to sales lines or flared. Wastewater and condensate are recycled if their chemistry and quantities make recycling possible or disposed of, usually in deep injection wells. In contrast to conventional vertical wells where methane emissions during completion are small, unconventional wells are high-pressure systems and may release significant amounts of methane, making green completions economically feasible in ways they might not (yet) be on lower-pressure systems that are less prone to large-volume emissions.[26] Green completions can also reduce exposure to hydrocarbons and fracturing chemicals by oil and gas company workers and nearby residents.[27]

Once separated, the various products available in considerable quantity from many gas and oil wells (such as propane, butane, benzene, and other hydrocarbons) can be sold, but the cost of collection and distribution is a key factor affecting whether a company will invest in the technology required to recapture hydrocarbons other than the primary target oil or methane. In wells that primarily produce methane, the economic benefit of green completions may be clear since gas production lines will already be in place. In areas like the Bakken Shale in North Dakota where oil is the target product and methane is a byproduct, the economics may be less compelling. Thirty percent of the methane produced is flared because there is no infrastructure to collect and transport it to natural gas refineries.[28] While proper flaring eliminates methane as a climate and health hazard, it produces CO_2 and other pollutants such as carbon monoxide.

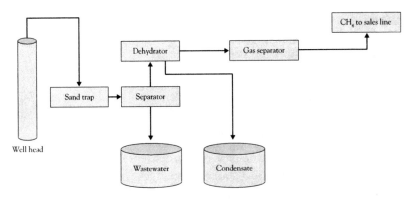

Green completion process
Source: Adapted from Susan Harvey, Vignesh Gowrishankar and Thomas Singer, Natural Res. Def. Council, Leaking Profits: The U.S. Oil and Gas Industry Can Reduce Pollution, Conserve Resources, and Make Money by Preventing Methane Waste 19 fig. 11 (March 2012).

Plunger Lift Systems

Plunger lift systems are another technology that can significantly reduce methane and other VOC losses to the atmosphere. As explained above, after a well has been in use for some time, the accumulated liquids inhibit gas movement out of the well. One way to remove the fluids is to deliquify the well by venting it to atmospheric pressure—blowing down the well. This process uses the gas in the well to force liquids out of the well. Once those liquids are removed, the well produces more easily. This type of well deliquification can result in venting of significant amounts of methane as well as other VOCs to the atmosphere. However, with a plunger lift system, a metal plunger is placed in the well annulus and the pressure built up by gas in the wellbore is used to lift the plunger out of the well, along with a column of fluid. This system uses the well's own pressure for simultaneously removing accumulated fluids and recapturing methane, non-methane hydrocarbons, VOCs, and HAPs that otherwise would be vented.[29]

Other Opportunities for Emissions Reductions

Valves and devices that control pressure by intentionally releasing methane can be replaced with technologies that control pressure by other means or that reroute released methane back into the system. System-wide leak detection and repair programs are also key to reducing losses. Regulations at the state and federal level are target-ing not only wellhead emissions, but also emissions from transmission lines and compression and storage facilities.

THE REGULATORY FRAMEWORK

Oil and gas development is primarily regulated at the state level, but air pollution is primarily regulated at the federal level. States manage implementation of federal standards through State Implementation Plans (SIPs) in accord with the Clean Air Act, (CAA) 42 USC 85. At the federal level, the key regulations are found in the New Source Review Performance Standards (NSPS) and the National Emissions Standards for Hazardous Air Pollutants (NESHAP).[30]

There are some limitations on the efficacy of the CAA with respect to oil and gas emissions. Oil and gas wells are typically con-sidered minor sources of emissions and therefore not regulated under many parts of the CAA. A recent Supreme Court case, *Summit Petro-leum Corp. v. United States EPA*, vacated the EPA's decision to treat related emission sources as a single stationary source under the CAA's Title V permitting program.[31] SIPs and rules by state oil and gas con-servation commissions (or similar state regulatory bodies) may include emissions reduction requirements, which sometimes only apply to cer-tain geographical areas or types of wells drilled in the state.

Methane emissions reduction is a logical target for "greening" natural gas. First, methane leaked from oil and natural gas systems represents about 40 percent of the total methane emissions from all sources in the United States.[32] Second, methane is economically valuable. Oil and gas companies have an incentive, at least at cer-tain price points, that could be moved through targeted regulatory frameworks to employ technology to maximize its capture. Third, high concentrations of ambient methane increase risk of explosions. Explosions at the well site are, of course, highly undesirable for obvi-ous reasons. Methane emission reduction is achieved through regula-tions that target VOCs generally and HAPs, as opposed to regulations specifically focused on methane.

The 2012 Federal Air Regulations for the Oil and Gas Industry

On April 17, 2012, the EPA issued the final amendments to Air Reg-ulations for the Oil and Gas Industry, pursuant to a consent decree issued in February 2010 by the District Court of the District of Columbia.[33] The regulations are the first to cover unconventional gas development specifically and include revisions to NSPS and the NESHAP standards for the oil and gas industry.[34] The new regulations cover production, processing, transmission, and storage of natural gas. They do not cover crude oil refineries or distribution mains that transport gas to the commercial or residential customers.[35]

The EPA predicts implementation of the NSPS standards will result in a $15 profit for the industry (from captured salable hydrocarbons) along with reductions in VOCs (190,000 tons), HAPs (11,000 tons), and methane (1M tons). The NESHAP standards will cost the industry $3.5 million and result in reductions in VOCs (1,200 tons), HAPs (670 tons), and methane (420 tons).[36] While the rules do not directly target methane, EPA claims they will result in a 95 percent reduction in methane emissions for the predicted 11,000 wells drilled per year after 2015 (the first year the rules are in full effect) and will reduce air emissions of toxins such as benzene, ethylbenzene, and n-hexane,[37] substances with known carcinogenic and health impacts.[38] The EPA also anticipates these rules will significantly reduce small (<2.5 micron) particulate matter, ground-level ozone, and greenhouse gas impacts,[39] thereby reducing negative impacts of oil and gas drilling on human health, vegetation, and climate change.

Implementation of the new rules is predicted to have some negative impacts, or "disbenefits," in the form of creating an additional 1.1 million tons of CO_2, 550 tons of nitrogen oxides (NOx), 19 tons of particulate matter (PM), 3,000 tons of CO, and 1,100 tons of total hydrocarbons (THC).[40] However, overall, the EPA calculates net CO_2-equivalent emission reductions of 18 million metric tons (19.8 million tons) for the final NSPS and 8,000 metric tons for the final NESHAP.[41]

As noted earlier, green completions may not be feasible where wells are not near sales lines or are not of sufficiently high pressure to result in significant production of methane during the cleanout process. Similar to those in existing state regulations, the federal Reduced Emissions Completions requirements (RECs) do not apply to all oil and gas wells. Wildcat wells (also known as exploratory wells), delineation wells (those used to identify the border of a natural gas reservoir or productive shale play), and most coal-bed methane wells are exempt from the green completion requirements.[42] However, the standards in the rules that require emission reductions in downstream steps in processing and transmission, such as pneumatic controllers and storage vessels (discussed more below) apply equally to oil and gas wells.

Once collected, gas must be compressed and transmitted through pipelines. The new rules governing gas collection, transmission, and storage are aimed at reducing emissions from high-bleed valves (defined as those that release >6 cubic feet/minute), glycol dehydrators (which remove water vapor from gas), and storage components with annual emissions of 600 tons or more of VOCs per year.[43] In particular, the 2012 regulations apply to centrifugal compressors with "wet" seals in which oil is used as a sealant, requiring 95 percent reduction in VOC emissions from wet seal compressors.[44] Reciprocating compressors are subject to requirements for regular replacement of parts that wear out. Testing, record-keeping, and reporting requirements were added to document compliance.[45]

Glycol dehydrators are used to separate water vapor from methane and other hydrocarbons. The 2012 rule maintains the existing air toxics regulation for large glycol dehydrators (those producing more than 1 ton of benzene per year) and adds limits on VOC emissions from small glycol dehydrators (<85,000 standard cubic meters per day of gas throughput or annual benzene emissions of <1 ton) based on volume of gas throughput.[46]

The new rules allow operators until April 2013 to reduce emissions by 95 percent on storage vessels with greater than six tons per year of VOC emissions. The majority of these VOC reductions will be accomplished through the use of combustion devices (e.g., flares) that, although not an ideal method since they still produce CO_2 and other pollutants, were deemed by the EPA to be a reasonable short-term fix until better regulations could be developed.[47] The Texas Commission on Environmental Quality expressed some concerns regarding the rules, including: (1) requiring flaring in lieu of green completions near populated areas might increase risk of fires, (2) the cost of regulation for states would increase, and (3) it was unclear which wells actually fell into the exempt categories of "delineation" and "exploratory."[48]

Self-Regulation through Voluntary Programs

The U.S. EPA has been working with the oil and gas industry since 1993 to encourage voluntary testing and adoption of technologies designed to reduce releases of methane and other hydrocarbons and

VOCs from the gas exploration and production processes. The EPA Natural Gas STAR program (formerly the Methane to Markets program) and the Global Methane Initiative (GMI) are two efforts to encourage voluntary implementation of methane capture technologies and work practices. The Natural Gas STAR program was initiated in 1993 as collaboration between the EPA and industry to reduce methane emissions. The Global Methane Initiative began in 2004 as an international, public-private collaboration with 14 member countries. As of 2012, it has expanded to include 21 countries and the European Commission as well as over 850 organizations from both the public and private sectors.[49] According to the EPA, the success of the domestic Natural Gas STAR program and a commitment to the GMI prompted the EPA to create Natural Gas STAR International in 2006, a program through which the EPA works with oil and gas companies to reduce emissions globally.[50] These programs may play an important role in creating international standards for technology and work practices that will help minimize methane losses and other emissions from oil and gas development.

The STAR program provides a framework through which companies can create emission-reduction plans, share technologies, access technical assistance, network with other companies, and record emission reductions.[51] All reporting is voluntary, and participant companies can engage at various levels with the program—from running pilot programs on one or more wells, to broad-scale implementation across operations. In 2010 alone, STAR program participants reported reduction of 94 billion cubic feet (Bcf) of methane emissions. According to the EPA's calculations, this greenhouse gas emissions reduction equates to removing over seven million passenger vehicles from the road for one year. The profits gained equal about $376 million in additional natural gas sales for the industry.[52] This amount was greater than the EPA had previously predicted was being lost.[53] Upward adjustments of estimates of methane losses from gas drilling activity are also supported by empirical studies of air emissions downwind of active drilling sites in Colorado and Utah.[54] However, it is important to note that these analyses include emissions from a variety of sources in the gas recovery and transmission process, not just well completion. While the reported numbers for methane capture and the empirical data for regional air emissions may not be directly comparable, both may be useful to the EPA in increasing the accuracy of its estimation of how much methane loss is actually occurring during natural gas operations.

Air Emissions Regulation and Monitoring Approaches Taken by States

Alongside recent steps to actively reduce well field emissions such as those detailed above, several states have promulgated stricter emissions regulations and undertaken air monitoring projects in shale gas development areas. Drilling regulations in Wyoming and Colorado have required green completions in certain areas since 2004[55] and 2008,[56] respectively, and some cities in Texas, such as Fort Worth and Southlake, also require them.[57] States like Pennsylvania are increasing monitoring, partially in response to the EPA's new Air Emission Rules and reporting requirements under the CAA. These regulations address concerns for health as well as non-attainment areas for federal limits for ozone, nitrogen oxides, and other pollutants. Monitoring programs help to identify air quality issues before they create health impacts and to allay unfounded fears. The paragraphs below give an overview of the regulatory and monitoring programs implemented in four states with significant gas development projects.

Colorado

The Colorado Oil and Gas Conservation Commission (COGCC) rules, like the recent federal rules, reflect the reality that green completions are not practical in every instance. The COGCC rules require green completions when conditions are likely to produce "naturally flowing hydrocarbons in flammable or greater concentration; in other words, where there is risk of fire or explosion if the hydrocarbons are vented directly to the atmosphere."[58] Green completion practices are not required for wildcat wells, wells not near sales lines, or where they are not "technologically or economically feasible."[59] These terms leave operators considerable flexibility in deciding whether to implement green completion technologies.

It is currently difficult to determine the impact of green completions on regional air quality due to lack of centralized records indicating where green completions have been utilized. Although Colorado state law has required the use of green completions since 2009, only in June 2012 did the COGCC change its record-keeping requirements for operators to include recording of whether green completions were used for a given well.[60] Records are kept on a well-by-well basis, rather than in a comprehensive, searchable database, so it is no small task to determine what percentage of wells have been completed using green completions since the change in the recording requirement. For the period prior to June 2012 and the change in the state's reporting form, it is even more difficult to determine what percentage of wells used green completion technologies.

As a public resource, the Colorado Department of Public Health and Environment maintains an air pollutants emissions inventory by county for the following six key pollutants: CO, SO_2, NO_2, Particulate matter less than10 microns, VOCs, and benzene. For each pollutant in each county, interactive maps allow a user to see what types of sources are responsible for the pollutant and in what proportion. For example, in Garfield County, the lion's share of benzene (178 tons per year (TPY) out of the total 267 TPY) is produced by oil and gas point sources. In contrast, in Montrose County, a western slope county without significant oil and gas drilling activity, the majority of benzene (38 out of 79 TPY) is due to forest and agricultural fires.[61] These monitoring frameworks allow the public to access air quality information and potentially provide data that can be compared to oil and gas activity data to draw some conclusions about impacts of the industry on air quality.

Texas

Green completions are required in South Lake, Fort Worth, and Forth Worth International Airport areas in Texas, where gas drilling is taking place close to large population centers. They are not yet required in the remainder of the Barnett Shale or in the state in general.[62]

The Barnett Shale development area in Texas boasts one of the most developed air emissions monitoring projects is in the country. The Texas Commission on Environmental Quality (TCEQ) initiated the Automated Gas Chromatographs (AutoGCs) Barnett Shale Monitoring Network to document air quality changes in the Barnett Shale area. The AutoGCs collect air quality measurements at 12 different sites around the clock for some 70 compounds related to natural gas development. The user interface allows anyone to create reports of the data for the various test sites.[63] In addition to the AutoGCs, the TCEQ conducted extensive canister testing (manual collection of air samples for constituent analysis) to determine the existence of air pollutants in excess of short-term and long-term health-based comparison values. Testers found levels of benzene higher than short-term exposure limits at some sites.[64] In August 2012, the Alamo Area Council of Governments and the TCEQ published a plan to create an unconventional oil and gas well emissions inventory for the Eagle Ford play, which produces wet gas (mixtures of methane and other hydrocarbons) and oil, in order to better understand the emission footprint of that development and to attempt to prevent San Antonio from violating ozone standards.[65]

Wyoming

Green completions are required in some areas of Wyoming, such as the Jonah Field, where high-density well development is taking place and sales lines are readily available.[66] Drillers and operators are required to apply for a permit from the Oil and Gas Conservation Commission (WOGCC) if they wish to flare hydrocarbons. However, they do not have to report use of green completion technologies.[67] Therefore, data on how many wells included green completions is not readily available.

From a monitoring perspective, the Air Quality Division of the Wyoming DEQ publishes real-time data on visibility, particulate, and ozone levels for each of three mobile and sixteen stationary monitors throughout the state.[68] On December 17, 2012, the Wyoming DEQ began use of an air quality mobile monitoring station in Converse County in eastern Wyoming, an area of active gas drilling. Among other things, the device will measure ozone, nitrogen oxides, particulate matter, methane, and nonmethane hydrocarbons in a rural area where residences are near gas drilling.[69] Analysis of data from air emissions monitors in drilling areas promises to be useful in the creation of appropriate regulations.

Pennsylvania

In 2011, Pennsylvania initiated an air emissions inventory database to collect data on air emissions from the oil and gas industry—the Shale Gas Emissions Data Management System. Oil and gas drillers and operators are requested to provide annual total emissions reports for carbon monoxide, nitrogen oxides, particulate matter less than 10 microns (PM10), particulate matter less than 2.5 microns, (PM2.5), sulfur oxides, VOCs, and HAPs. The first reporting deadline was March 2012 for year 2011. Reports are uploaded into the Oil and Gas Electronic system (OGRE) by drillers and operators.[70]

In July 2012, the DEP initiated a one-year ambient air monitoring program for areas of Marcellus Shale drilling activity in southwestern Pennsylvania.[71] The protocol uses mobile monitors to sample 48 VOCs from facilities identified in a pilot monitoring program as having some fugitive emissions. The purpose of the study is to help determine if cumulative impacts of emissions from oil and gas operations may present threats to human health and welfare.[72]

CONCLUSION

Gas has been cited by industry representatives, politicians, and academics as greener than coal and a necessary "bridge fuel" to assist in the transition from coal and oil to technologies such as solar, wind, hydroelectric, and others having fewer climate and health impacts. As with other fossil fuels, recovery of natural gas results in some pollution. Air emissions from the oil and gas industry have not received the amount of attention that water contamination has garnered. However, the impacts of these emissions on human health and climate change could be quite costly to individuals and state and federal governments. There is much room for additional study and understanding of quantity and quality of air emissions from unconventional oil and gas development, and many states are initiating monitoring programs to this end. Technologies for reduction of emissions are currently available for the exploration, production, transmission, and storage stages. With increased use, they can provide significant improvement in the capture of methane, other VOCs, and HAPs. Existing data supports the conclusion that further reductions in air emissions are a worthy target for regulators, an economical choice for industry, and could result in gains for human health and environmental protection and better industry-community relations.

NOTES

1. Theo. Colborn, et al., *An Exploratory Study of Air Quality Near Natural Gas Operations*, HUM. & ECOLOGICAL RISK ASSESSMENT (2012), *available at* http://www.endocrinedisruption.com/chemicals.air.php.

2. *Oil and Natural Gas Air Pollution Standards*, EPA, http://www.epa.gov /airquality/oilandgas/basic.html (last visited Sept. 22, 2013).

3. *Benzene*, AM. CANCER SOC'Y (last revised Nov. 5, 2010), http://www.cancer .org/cancer/cancercauses/othercarcinogens/intheworkplace/benzene.

4. Theo Colborn et al., *Natural Gas Operations from a Public Health Perspective*, 17 HUM. & ECOLOGICAL RISK ASSESSMENT 1039 (2011).

5. Gabrielle Petron et al., *Hydrocarbon Emissions Characterization in the Colorado Front Range: A Pilot Study*, 117 J. GEOPHYSICAL RES. D04304 (2012). *See also,* Michael A. Levi, *Comment on "Hydrocarbon emissions: characterization in the Colorado Front Range: A Pilot Study,"* 117 J. GEOPHYSICAL RES. D21203(2012).

6. SUSAN HARVEY, VIGNESH GOWRISHANKAR & THOMAS SINGER, NATURAL RES. DEF. COUNCIL, LEAKING PROFITS: THE U.S. OIL AND GAS INDUSTRY CAN REDUCE POLLUTION, CONSERVE RESOURCES, AND MAKE MONEY BY PREVENTING METHANE WASTE (March 2012) [hereinafter NRDC]; Nathan Phillips, et al., *Mapping Urban Pipeline Leaks: Methane Leaks Across Boston*, 173 ENVTL. POLLUTION, Feb. 2013, at 1.

7. Webinar: Mark K. Boling, *Balancing Environmental, Social and Economic Impacts of Shale Gas Development Activities* (Yale Center for Environmental Law and Policy Webinar Series, Jan. 23, 2013), *available at* http://envirocenter.yale.edu/calendar/63/126-Balancing-Environmental-Social-and-Economic-Impacts-of-Shale-Gas-Development-Activities.

8. EPA, OPTIONS FOR REMOVING ACCUMULATED FLUIDS AND IMPROVING FLOW IN GAS WELLS, LESSONS LEARNED FROM NATURAL GAS STAR PARTNERS (2011), *available at* http://www.epa.gov/gasstar/documents/ll_options.pdf.

9. All data reported here and in the 2011 Greenhouse Gas Inventory Report are in carbon dioxide equivalents.

10. Gabrielle Petron et al., *Hydrocarbon Emissions Characterization in the Colorado Front Range: A Pilot Study*, 117 J. GEOPHYSICAL RES. D04304 (2012). *See also* EPA, REDUCED EMISSIONS COMPLETIONS FOR HYRDAULICALLY FRACTURED NATURAL GAS WELLS (2011), *available at* http://www.epa.gov/gasstar/documents/reduced_emissions_completions.pdf.

11. David Doniger, *Leading Companies Already Meet EPA's "Fracking" Air Pollution Standards*, SWITCHBOARD: NATURAL RES. DEF. COUNCIL STAFF BLOG (Apr. 18, 2012), http://switchboard.nrdc.org/blogs/ddoniger/leading_companies_already_meet.html.

12. *Setback Rulemaking 2012: Establishing New and Amended Rules for Statewide Setbacks*, COLO. OIL AND GAS CONSERVATION COMM'N, http://cogcc.state.co.us/RR_HF2012/setbacks/setbacks.htm (last visited Sept. 22, 2013).

13. ROXANA WITTER ET AL., HEALTH IMPACT STATEMENT FOR BATTLEMENT MESA, GARFIELD COUNTY COLORADO, (Sept. 2010), *available at* http://www.garfield-county.com/public-health/documents/1%20%20%20Complete%20HIA%20without%20Appendix%20D.pdf.

14. AM. PUB. HEALTH ASS'N, POLICY NO. 20125, THE ENVIRONMENTAL AND OCCUPATIONAL HEALTH IMPACTS OF HIGH-VOLUME HYDRAULIC FRACTURING OF UNCONVENTIONAL GAS RESERVES (Oct. 30, 2012), *available at* http://www.apha.org/advocacy/policy/policysearch/default.htm?id=1439 (last visited Dec. 10, 2012).

15. *Oil and Natural Gas Air Pollution Standards*, EPA, http://www.epa.gov /airquality/oilandgas/basic.html (last visited Sept. 22, 2013).
16. Theo Colborn et al., *Natural Gas Operations from a Public Health Perspective*, 17 Hum. & Ecological Risk Assessment 1039 (2011). *See also* Am. Lung Ass'n, State of the Air 2012 (2012) (covering 2008–2010 data), *available at* http://www.stateoftheair.org/2012/key-findings/2008-2010/people-at-risk .html.
17. Numbers calculated from data found in the American Lung Association, State of the Air 2012 Report, People at Risk (covering 2008–2010 data).
18. Ground-level ozone pollution has significant crop yield impacts on cotton, soy and peanuts. *Effects of Air Pollution on Plants*, USDA Agric. Research Serv. (last modified Mar. 17, 2012), http://www.ars.usda.gov/Main/docs .htm?docid=12462.
19. Lisa McKenzie et al., *Human Health Risk Assessment of Air Emissions from Development of Unconventional Gas Drilling*, 424 Sci. Total Env't. 79 (2012).
20. Sand mining in Wisconsin is estimated to exceed 12 million tons/year. Wis. Dep't of Natural Res., Silica Sand Mining in Wisconsin (Jan. 2012), *available at* http://dnr.wi.gov/topic/mines/documents/silicasandminingfinal .pdf.
21. *Safety and Health Topics: Silica, Crystalline*, Occupational Safety and Health Admin., http://www.osha.gov/dsg/topics/silicacrystalline/health _effects_silica.html (last visited Sept. 22, 2013).
22. NRDC, *supra* note 6.
23. *See* EPA, Inventory of U.S. Greenhouse Gas Emissions and Sinks: 1990–2009 (2011), *available at* http://www.epa.gov/climatechange/Downloads /ghgemissions/US-GHG-Inventory-2011-Complete_Report.pdf.
24. NRDC, *supra* note 6.
25. EPA, Lessons Learned from Natural Gas STAR Partners, Reduced Emission Completions for Hydraulically Fractures Natural Gas Wells (2011), *available at* http://www.epa.gov/gasstar/documents/reduced _emissions_completions.pdf.
26. Francis O'Sullivan & Sergey Paltzev, *Shale Gas Production: Potential Versus Actual Greenhouse Gas Emissions*, 7 Envtl. Res. Letters 044030 (2012), *available at* http://m.iopscience.iop.org/1748-9326/7/4/044030/pdf/1748-9326_7_4_044030.pdf (citing EPA, Greenhouse Gas Emissions Reporting from the Petroleum and Natural Gas Industry: Background Technical Supporting Document (2010)).
27. NRDC, *supra* note 6.
28. Robert Krulwich, *A Mysterious Patch of Light Shows up in the North Dakota Dark*, Nat'l. Pub. Radio Blogs (Jan. 16, 2013, 1:58 PM), http://www.npr.org /blogs/krulwich/2013/01/16/169511949/a-mysterious-patch-of-light-shows

-up-in-the-north-dakota-dark; *see also* Brian Hansen, *North Dakota's Oil/Gas Boom to get Even Bigger, Official Says,* PLATTS, (Aug. 5, 2012, 2:03 PM), http://www.colorado.gov/cs/Satellite/CDPHE-AP/CBON/1251596446069.

29. NRDC, *supra* note 6.

30. The EPA estimated that the O&G industry reduced emissions by 168 Bcf in 2009, attributing 39Bcf of that to compliance with NESHAPs and 129 Bcf to voluntary emissions reductions under the EPA Natural Gas STAR program. *See EPA, supra* note 23.

31. Summit Petroleum Corp. v. U.S. EPA, 690 F.3d 733 (6th Cir. 2012).

32. Robert Howarth, et al., Methane Emissions from Natural Gas Systems (Background Paper Prepared for the National Climate Assessment, Ref. No. 2011-0003, 2012), *available at* http://www.eeb.cornell.edu/howarth/Howarth%20et%20al.%20—%20National%20Climate%20Assessment.pdf. The next largest contributors of methane to the atmosphere are agriculture (about 25%) and landfills (about 15%). *Id.*

33. Oil and Natural Gas Sector: New Source Performance Standards and National Emission Standards for Hazardous Air Pollutants Reviews, 40 CFR part 63, subparts Hh and Hhh, *available at* www.epa.gov/airquality/oilandgas/pdfs/20120417finalrule.pdf.

34. Under section 111 of the Clean Air Act (42 U.S.C. § 7411), the EPA is required to set new source performance standards (NSPS) for categories of industry that cause or significantly contribute to air pollution that may endanger public health or welfare, and there is a general requirement to review these standards every eight years. Under section 112 of the CAA (42 U.S.C. § 7412), the EPA must do the same for air toxics. The EPA last reviewed and issued NSPS standards (for VOCs) and for and air toxics in 1985 and 1999, respectively. In 2009, WildEarth Guardians and San Juan Citizens Alliance sued the EPA for its failure to timely review both the NSPS and air toxics standards for the oil and gas industry.

35. 77 FR 159 (Aug. 16, 2012). *See also* EPA, Presentation: Reducing Air Pollution from the Oil and Gas Industry (Apr. 17, 2012), *available at* http://www.epa.gov/airquality/oilandgas/pdfs/20120417presentation.pdf.

36. 40 CFR part 63, *supra* note 33.

37. EPA, OVERVIEW OF FINAL VERSIONS OF THE AIR REGULATIONS FOR THE OIL AND GAS INDUSTRY (2012), available at http://www.epa.gov/airquality/oilandgas/pdfs/20120417fs.pdf.

38. *Id.*

39. EPA, REGULATORY IMPACT ANALYSIS: FINAL NEW SOURCE PERFORMANCE STANDARDS AND AMENDMENTS TO THE NATIONAL EMISSIONS STANDARDS FOR HAZARDOUS AIR POLLUTANTS FOR THE OIL AND GAS INDUSTRY (2012), *available at* http://www.epa.gov/ttn/ecas/regdata/RIAs/oil_natural_gas_final_neshap_nsps_ria.pdf.

40. *Id.*

41. *Id.*

42. EPA, Summary of the Key Changes to the New Source Performance Standards (2012), *available at* http://www.epa.gov/airquality/oilandgas /pdfs/20120417changes.pdf.

43. *Id.*

44. The regulations exempt dry-seal compressors, which do not have the same VOC emission problems as wet-seal compressors.

45. EPA, Summary of Requirements for Processes and Equipment at Natural Gas Gathering and Boosting Stations (2012), *available at* http:// www.epa.gov/airquality/oilandgas/pdfs/20120417summaryboost.pdf.

46. *Id.*

47. *Id.*

48. Tex. Comm'n on Envtl. Quality, Comments in response to proposed EPA rule, Docket ID No. EPA-HQ-OAR-2010-0505.

49. Global Methane Initiative, http://www.globalmethane.org/index.aspx (last visited Sept. 22, 2013); *EPA Natural Gas STAR International*, EPA, http://www.epa.gov/gasstar/international/index.html, (last visited Sept. 22, 2013).

50. *EPA Natural Gas STAR International*, EPA, *available at* http://www.epa.gov /gasstar/international/index.html.

51. *EPA Natural Gas STAR Factsheet*, EPA, *available at* http://www.epa.gov /gasstar/documents/ngstar_mktg-factsheet.pdf.

52. *Id.*

53. NDRC, *supra* note 6.

54. Gabrielle Petron et al., *Hydrocarbon Emissions Characterization in the Colorado Front Range: A Pilot Study*, 117 J. Geophysical Res. D04304 (2012); *See also* Jeff Tollefson, *Air Sampling Reveals High Emissions from Gas Field*, 482 Nature 139 (2012); *and* Jeff Tollefson, *Methane Leaks Erode Green Credentials of Natural Gas*, 493 Nature 12 (2013).

55. Fred Krupp, *Review of Recent Environmental Protection Agency's Air Standards for Hydraulically Fractured Wells*, Testimony before the United States Senate Subcommittee on Clean Energy and Nuclear Safety (July 19, 2012), *available at* http://www.epw.senate.gov/public/index.cfm?FuseAction=Files .View&FileStore_id=bc4a4812-ca46-4d22-b593-e3929c2c64a6 (last visited Sept. 22, 2013).

56. Colorado Oil and Gas Conservation Commission Rules, Section 800.3.

57. EPA, Overview of Final Versions of the Air Regulations for the Oil and Gas Industry, *available at* http://www.epa.gov/airquality/oilandgas /pdfs/20120417fs.pdf.

58. Colorado Oil and Gas Conservation Commission Rules, Section 800-3, *available at* http://cogcc.state.co.us/.

59. *Id.*

60. Author's communication with staff in COGCC well permitting department (Nov. 2012).

61. Colo. Dep't of Pub. Health and Env't, Air Pollution Control Division, 2008 Air Pollution Emissions Inventory, *available at* http://www.colorado.gov/airquality/inv_maps_2008.aspx.

62. *Overview of Final Amendments to the Clean Air Act and the Oil and Gas Industry*, U.S. EPA, http://www.epa.gov/airquality/oilandgas/pdfs/20120417fs.pdf (last visited Sept. 22, 2013); and *Green Completions Now the Standard in the Barnett Shale*, Devon Energy, http://www.dvn.com/CorpResp/initiatives/Pages/GreenCompletions.aspx (last visited Sept. 22, 2013).

63. *Auto GC Data by Day by Site*, Tex. Comm'n on Envtl. Quality, http://www.tceq.state.tx.us/cgi-bin/compliance/monops/agc_daily_summary.pl?user_site=48_121_1013 (last visited Sept. 22, 2013).

64. For one example, see Texas Commission on Environmental Quality, Interoffice memorandum, Health Effects Review of Barnett Shale Formation Area Monitoring Projects, Jan. 27, 2010, *available at* http://www.tceq.state.tx.us/assets/public/implementation/tox/barnettshale/healtheval/co/multi/mm1.pdf.

65. Alamo Area Council of Gov'ts, Oil and Gas Emission Inventory Improvement Plan, Eagle Ford (2012), *available at* http://www.aacog.com/DocumentCenter/View/8286.

66. Author's Communication with Bob King, Interim Director, Wyo. Oil and Gas Cons. Comm'n, (Nov.–Dec. 2012).

67. *Id.*

68. *See* Wyo. Dep't of Envtl. Quality, *Wyoming Visibility Monitoring Network*, WYVISNET, http://www.wyvisnet.com (last visited Sept. 22, 2013).

69. *See* News Release, Wyo. Dep't of Envtl. Quality, ADQ Installs Mobile Monitoring Device in Converse County (Dec. 17, 2012), *available at* http://deq.state.wy.us/out/downloads/PressReleaseAQMonitorDEC2012.pdf.

70. Pa. DEP Bureau of Air Quality, Initial Notification Concerning Source Reports and Annual Air Emissions Inventories, Dec 6, 2011, *available at* http://files.dep.state.pa.us/AboutDEP/AboutDEPPortalFiles/RemarksAndTestimonies/AirEmissionsInventory/VanOrdenMarcellusShaleLtr.pdf.

71. Pa. Dep't Envtl. Prot., Bureau of Air Quality, Long-term Ambient Air Monitoring Project Near Permanent Marcellus Shale Gas Facilities Protocol (2012), *available at* http://files.dep.state.pa.us/Air/AirQuality/AQPortalFiles/Long-Term_Marcellus_Ambient_Air_Monitoring_Project-Protocol_for_Web_2012-07-23.pdf.

72. *Id.*

8

Western Water Law
Differing Approaches to Planning for Unconventional Oil and Gas Development in Colorado, Texas, Oklahoma, and Wyoming

Kevin Patrick and Laurie Stern

INTRODUCTION

States are confronting a relatively new water use with hydraulic fracturing that requires large volumes of water and, in some instances, strains local resources. The western United States faces a particular challenge because of its limited water resources. This chapter is intended to impart an understanding of how much water hydraulic fracturing requires, available water resources in western states, and how states manage their water resources in conjunction with hydraulic fracturing operations. This chapter also discusses how oil and gas companies conducting hydraulic fracturing operations (hydraulic fracturing operators) obtain the water they require by working within these state systems. Because each state differs in terms of its allocation and administration of water resources, it is helpful to review a sampling of state regulatory schemes with regard to the hydraulic fracturing industry. This chapter will provide an overview of Colorado, Oklahoma, Texas, and Wyoming as case studies.

HYDRAULIC FRACTURING'S WATER NEEDS AND CONSUMPTION

Water is essential to the hydraulic fracturing process. Hydraulic fracturing fluids, the mixture of water and chemicals that operators pump into wells at high pressure to create fractures in the rock, are 99 percent water. A well may be hydraulically fractured up to 100 times throughout its production years, and each round of hydraulic fracturing requires a large amount of fluid. The specific volume of water needed varies from well to well and depends on factors such as the depth of the well, the target mineral, the geology of the formation, and how many times the well has been previously fractured. For example, hydraulically fracturing a well in portions of Wyoming can require one to two million gallons of water per well (three to six acre feet), while hydraulic fracturing in the Woodford Shale in Oklahoma may take up to six million gallons per well (18.4 acre feet).[1] Operators may require additional water for activities related to hydraulic fracturing such as dust suppression on drilling sites and the heavily traveled roads leading to them. These uses are in addition to the initial amount of water that is used to make drilling mud in order to drill the well.[2] Although it is possible for hydraulic fracturing operations to reuse fracturing fluids after a sufficient fluid-treatment process, most often the operators inject leftover fracturing fluids into hydrologically isolated wells or store hydraulic fracturing fluids for disposal by evaporation. Injected fluids remain trapped underground in formation and water allowed to evaporate is water lost to the watershed.

Although hydraulic fracturing requires a large amount of raw water, these operations account for only a small percentage of the United States' overall water use. The United States Geological Survey (USGS) issues reports on the nation's water use every five years. The USGS's most recent report from 2005 reveals that all forms of mining accounted for only 1 percent of the country's total water use.[3] By contrast, irrigation of farmland accounted for 31 percent of water, and thermoelectric power generation accounted for 49 percent. "Mining" is a broad category that includes the extraction of solid minerals such as coal, iron, sand, and gravel, as well as liquid/gas minerals, such as oil and gas. Thus, hydraulic fracturing for natural gas accounts for only a fraction of the mining that used 1 percent of our nation's water in 2005.

In 2011, the U.S. EPA released the Draft Plan to Study the Impacts of Hydraulic Fracturing on Drinking Water Resources.[4] In its report, the EPA estimated that hydraulic fracturing operations may use approximately 70 to 140 billion gallons of water annually. This figure did not distinguish water diverted and used (recyclable water) from water consumed (lost water),[5] but it does give one an idea of the increasing demand placed on our nation's water supply by domestic energy development. The final draft of the EPA's ongoing study is expected to undergo public comment and peer review in 2014 and will contain specific findings on the impact that hydraulic fracturing is having on water availability.

States often provide more precise data on how much of their waters go toward hydraulic fracturing. Colorado authorities report that in 2010, hydraulic fracturing used approximately 13,900 AF of water, or slightly less than 0.1 percent of the overall statewide water use. Colorado expects that by 2015, hydraulic fracturing operations will increase by 35 percent and will use 18,700 AF annually, Even then, though, hydraulic fracturing will only account for slightly more than 0.1 percent of Colorado's water use.[6] Numbers are similar in Texas, where the state reports that in 2010, hydraulic fracturing used 35,800 AF of water in the state, with the majority of that water going to use in the Barnett formation. The state total for water use that year was 18,010,599 AF, meaning that hydraulic fracturing accounted for just over 0.1 percent of total water use in the state.[7] In Oklahoma, a typical well in the Woodford Shale formation can use up to six million gallons of water (18.4 acre feet)—or the amount of water needed to fill nine Olympic-size swimming pools.[8] Oil and gas production within Oklahoma as a whole accounts for 2 percent of the state's annual water use. Thus, the overall use may not be substantial, but the impacts on a localized scale can impact other water users and water availability. Since shale plays are concentrated in portions of states, energy industry water use in select watersheds is greater than the statewide average, which can contribute to local strains on water resources.

HYDRAULIC FRACTURING AND WATER CHALLENGES IN THE WEST

Operators wishing to obtain water for hydraulic fracturing in the West face a specific set of challenges. The first challenge comes from the western system of water allocation, known as the "prior appropriation system." Because western water resources are relatively scarce (compared to the eastern United States), the prior appropriation system awards water rights to whoever first diverts water from a waterbody and puts it to beneficial use. The definition of beneficial use traditionally included uses such as domestic, agricultural, industrial, and mining. Hydraulic mining in another form (sluices and hydraulic drills) was the original means by which the settlers separated gold and silver from ambient minerals. The prior appropriation system is often summarized by the phrase "first in time, first in right," stemming from the West's mining heritage. At this point in our history, much of the West's water is spoken for, which makes it difficult for new water users—such as hydraulic fracturing operators—to come into a state and obtain the water they need by applying for new water rights.

Instead, hydraulic fracturing operators typically need to buy or lease water from existing water rights holders and change the use or location of use to meet the new goals. Commonly, companies buy or lease water from municipalities, but it is also possible to obtain water from agricultural water rights holders or private citizens.[9] The process of obtaining water is becoming more complex for some operators as some municipalities are contemplating moratoriums on water sales for hydraulic fracturing or having to reduce water sales to meet shortages for municipal deliveries. For example, in July 2012, the Boulder County Planning Committee began contemplating an update to the Boulder County Comprehensive Plan that would include a policy prohibiting the county from leasing or selling any of its water rights to companies that would use that water in drilling oil and gas wells. Other municipalities that traditionally sold water for hydraulic fracturing as a source of revenue were forced to curtail sales to meet municipal demands during the 2012 drought. Although some question the authority of municipalities to enact such prohibitions, these legal and practical obstacles make it more difficult for oil and gas companies to obtain the water they need for their hydraulic fracturing operations.[10]

Compounding the difficulty of obtaining water is the reality that hydraulic fracturing's water demands are steadily increasing at a time when water availability in the West is increasingly a concern. The shift in population from the Northeast United States to the West has compounded water availability problems.[11] Currently, the West is experiencing long-term water shortages as a result of competing demands and drought. Arizona, for example, is in its fifteenth year of drought. Texas is in the midst of a multi-year struggle to meet its population's needs. Climate scientists predict that droughts will worsen in severity and duration as the effects of climate change take hold. As drought and increased population contribute to water stress, hydraulic fracturing technology is advancing and allowing oil and gas operations to reach new and more remote shale plays, which increases hydraulic fracturing water demand. At this time it is more important than ever for states to have a firm grip on how they regulate hydraulic fracturing's water use within their boundaries. Increasingly, states will need to address how changing climate patterns may affect future water supplies as the energy industry's demand for water increases.

HOW IS HYDRAULIC FRACTURING REGULATED? A LOOK AT SELECT WESTERN STATES

The water issues hydraulic fracturing creates revolve around both water quantity and water quality. While water quantity issues are almost exclusively within states' domain, water quality is largely regulated by federal standards and implemented by the states. Understanding the interplay of quantity and quality by state is critical to an understanding of how hydraulic fracturing affects water. We look to how select states address these issues.

Colorado

Colorado is the nation's fourth highest producer of natural gas. Colorado's first oil and gas well was drilled in 1826, and hydraulic fracturing has occurred in the state since 1947. In January 2012, Colorado had around 45,000 active wells, with nearly all of them having been hydraulically fractured. Over a million Colorado wells have been hydraulically fractured since 1947. These numbers will likely increase throughout the next decade as hydraulic fracturing allows new areas to be productive.

The newest and largest shale play in Colorado is the Niobrara formation. The Niobrara formation is a shale rock formation located in northeast Colorado and extending into northwest Kansas, southwest Nebraska, and southeast Wyoming. The target minerals are found at depths of 3,000 to 14,000 feet.[12] In 2011, Anadarko Petroleum announced that it assessed the Wattenberg field in the Niobrara formation to hold up to 1.5 billion barrels of oil equivalent (BOE).

The Wattenburg field sits just north of Denver in relatively populated counties. This area is in the South Platte River watershed, which is the most populated and over-appropriated river basin in the state. In addition, hydraulic fracturing is also prevalent in the Piceance Basin on the Western Slope of Colorado, and coalbed methane (CBM) mining[13] occurs in the Paradise Basin in the southwest corner of Colorado.

Colorado is unusually situated in terms of its water resources. Colorado experiences a semiarid climate and is a "headwaters state." The Rocky Mountains snowpack forms several major western rivers, including the Colorado, Arkansas, Platte, and Rio Grande Rivers. While these rivers originate in Colorado, Colorado does not have exclusive rights to their flows. Rather a series of interstate compacts allocate each of these rivers' flows between Colorado and each of the different states that the rivers pass through.[14] Further, no rivers flow into Colorado. Thus, interstate compacts and a lack of inbound water limit Colorado's available water resources. Colorado geography further complicates and influences water usage: approximately 80 percent of the state's precipitation falls on the area west of the Continental Divide, and 80 percent of the population resides east of the Continental Divide.

Colorado manages its water resources in a unique way. While most western states have vested state agencies with control over the prior appropriation system, Colorado is the only remaining prior appropriation state that grants and determines water rights in a purely judicial manner.[15] Each of the state's major basins has a "water court," which has exclusive jurisdiction over "water matters" and is headed by water referees and water judges with particular expertise in water law. These water courts decree new water rights, modify how existing water rights holders use their rights, and adjudicate disputes between water users.

However, it is not just water courts that regulate the water resources used for hydraulic fracturing. Once water courts issue water rights decrees, the administration of those decrees shifts to the Colorado State Engineer's Office (SEO). The SEO regulates hydraulic fracturing operations in two ways.[16] First, once hydraulic fracturing operators buy or lease water rights, they become water rights holders and thus must comply with the SEO-administered state priority system. To ensure that other water rights holders are not injured, the SEO administers water rights in priority. Thus, with few exceptions, water rights decreed in one year are "junior" to water rights decreed in prior years. The priority system allows the senior right to divert and be used, without waste, fully before the next most senior water right may receive water, curtailing fully junior rights in times of sharing.[17] Because new uses are junior to senior uses, they are compelled to acquire more senior water rights and adapt, or change, the rights to meet the new demand, which is allowed provided injury or impairment does not occur to other rights. Water supply arrangements that ensure noninjury are therefore often necessary. The SEO may require water rights holders to develop augmentation plans, substitute water supply plans, and/or exchange plans, where water is removed from one place in the system and replaced at another to allow out of priority diversion. Second, the SEO has authority over groundwater, and this authority extends to water produced from mining operations. In this way, the SEO regulates water quantity rather than water quality. The SEO permits all "wells"—defined as structures that expose groundwater to the atmosphere or obtain groundwater for beneficial use[18]—and ensures that groundwater extraction occurs in a way that does not injure other water rights holders. Over the last few decades, the definition of what constitutes a "beneficial use" has evolved to include uses that create economic benefits, such as water used to produce oil and gas. Thus, wells drilled either to provide water for hydraulic fracturing or which produce water from hydraulic fracturing must obtain an SEO permit.

The SEO's power over groundwater resources used for hydraulic fracturing expanded in the 2009 Colorado Supreme Court case *Vance v. Wolfe*.[19] In this case, operators were dewatering CBM mines in the San Juan Basin.[20] This mining depleted surrounding groundwater resources and injured the water rights of farmers and ranchers. The injured parties asked a Colorado court to declare that pumping produced water from a well in order to obtain minerals is a beneficial use of groundwater and thus subject to the SEO's permitting power. The Colorado Supreme Court reasoned that the CBM process "uses" water by removing it from the ground in order to accomplish a "benefit"—extracting gas. Because it found produced water to be a beneficial use of groundwater, the court held that the State Engineer must permit wells that extract produced water. In effect, the *Vance* decision ordered the SEO to permit in excess of 35,000 oil and gas wells throughout the state.

To simplify the task of permitting all Colorado oil and gas wells, the SEO's post-*Vance* regulations focus on the distinction between tributary and nontributary groundwater.[21] All Colorado groundwater is presumed tributary; however, users that can overcome this presumption may extract nontributary groundwater without a SEO permit and may use the water outside the prior appropriation system. The post-*Vance* regulations allow the SEO to designate entire geological formations as nontributary for permitting purposes. Under the new permitting regulations, oil and gas wells that produce water from nontributary groundwater formations may operate without an SEO permit and are not subject to Colorado's prior appropriation system. Thus, when a hydraulic fracturing operator wishes to drill wells, whether it will need an SEO permit will depend on the well's location. If the well will pump tributary groundwater, the hydraulic fracturing operator will need an SEO permit; however, if the well is located within a "nontributary" area, the hydraulic fracturing operator will not need a permit. By statute, nontributary water in Colorado is generally the property of the overlying landowner who has the right to quantify and extract such at the rate of not more than 1 percent per year.[22]

A second Colorado agency, the Colorado Oil & Gas Conservation Commission (COGCC), also regulates water resources used in hydraulic fracturing, albeit from a water quality standpoint. This agency seeks to prevent injury to Colorado's freshwater resources throughout the mining process.[23] At the outset, mining companies must apply to the COGCC for a permit to drill a mine. In evaluating the permit application, the COGCC determines the mine's proximity to surface water and underground aquifers, and the COGCC may grant the permit with site-specific conditions, such as minimum casing depths[24] or freshwater sampling/testing requirements. The COGCC also has geographically specific standards that cater to the individual characteristics of different basins. For example, in the San Juan basin, where CBM mining is widespread, CBM mining operators must conduct baseline and continued water sampling and testing from surrounding water bodies to ensure their integrity. During production, operators must keep track of which chemicals they pump into which wells and disclose this information to the COGCC and to the public via the FracFocus website.[25] The COGCC also requires operators to monitor internal well pressure to prevent blowouts, responds to any environmental incidents concerning oil and gas wells, and sets standards for the pits and tanks used for the temporary storage of hydraulic fracturing fluids and produced water during the hydraulic fracturing process. Once the mining process is complete, the COGCC also governs what companies do with waste. COGCC allows operators to dispose of hydraulic fracturing fluids and produced water by underground injection into Class II wells, evaporation in lined pits, disposal at commercial facilities, application to land for dust suppression, or recycling.

Texas

Texas contains more oil and gas reserves than any other state in the country and is the United States' top-producing state.[26] Texas' history cannot be separated from energy production. The first well to strike oil was in Nacogdoches County, Texas, in 1866. The first known gas production occurred near Graham in 1872. Although Texas has been producing oil since the late 1800s, it is estimated that the state has remaining oil reserves of 4.9 billion barrels and remaining gas reserves of 40.8 trillion cubic feet.

Although Texas made its name in traditional oil production, today Texas contains some of the most productive shale plays in the country. The Barnett Shale, located in the Fort Worth Basin in northern Texas, is the major hotbed of hydraulic fracturing activity in Texas. It was one of the first major shale plays recognized by industry. Although industry knew of the Barnett's reserves as early as 1981, it was not until 1995 that technology made it possible to profitably produce its minerals. Today, the Barnett produces an estimated 2 percent of all the natural gas used daily in the United States,[27] and industry estimates that the Barnett shale still has trillions of cubic feet of reserves. Another major shale play in Texas is the Eagle Ford in Southern Texas. This crescent-shaped formation is 400 miles long and 50 miles wide, and touches the Mexican border and eastern Texas. The Eagle Ford formation is highly productive and industry estimates it will continue to be productive for years to come.

Hydraulic fracturing operators seeking water for their operations in Texas must operate within the state's water allocation system. Texas manages its water resources in a unique way, regulating groundwater and surface water in significantly different ways.

Groundwater supplies much of the water needed for hydraulic fracturing operations. Under Texas law, the state does not own groundwater; rather, groundwater belongs to the overlying property owner who owns the resource "in place." Water is produced under the "rule of capture," which allows a property owner to freely pump groundwater from underneath his or her land, even if such pumping impacts groundwater resources underneath neighboring properties.[28] The rule of capture has several limitations, including: (1) pumping may not intentionally and maliciously injure a neighbor, (2) pumping may not waste water, and (3) if pumping groundwater causes a neighboring property to subside, the person pumping the water may be liable to the neighbor for damages.[29]

To obtain groundwater, oil and gas companies may drill groundwater wells on property they own. Operators may also purchase water from private property owners with groundwater wells. The state of Texas does not limit the amount of groundwater that operators may extract for (or that private property owners may sell to) hydraulic fracturing. However, under recent hydraulic fracturing fluid disclosure regulations, the operators must disclose how much water they use. Increasingly, groundwater management districts play a role in the limits of water use for the industry.

To a lesser extent, hydraulic fracturing operators in Texas also use surface water to meet their needs. Texas' surface water resources vary throughout the state. Texas' southeastern border is the Gulf of Mexico, and this area receives a relatively high amount of annual rainfall. In contrast, the central-western half of the state experiences an arid climate. Unlike groundwater, surface water within Texas is the property of the state, subject to the right of appropriation. Historically, Texas followed the riparian[30] system of water law, but today, while still recognizing riparian rights for some lands and for limited purposes, Texas issues appropriative water rights for surface water.

Operators that withdraw surface water for hydraulic fracturing must first obtain a water right permit from the Texas Commission on Environmental Quality (TCEQ). The TCEQ issues water rights and oversees the permitting system. The TCEQ also regulates water quality within the state. However, when it comes to the oil and gas industry, the TCEQ shares water quality control with the Texas Railroad Commission (RRC).[31] The RRC is responsible for the discharge of wastes and the abatement and prevention of water pollution resulting from oil and gas exploration and production, including hydraulic fracturing.[32] The RRC holds regulatory authority over these activities but enforces TCEQ-issued water quality standards.

In all other areas of hydraulic fracturing regulation relevant to this chapter, the RRC holds sole regulatory authority over hydraulic fracturing. The RRC was established in 1891 to oversee the state's railroad operations. In 1917, the Texas legislature gave the RRC authority over the state's oil and gas operations. The state did so because it recognized that oil pipeline operators had the same control over oil fields that the railroad companies once had over Texas' farmers and ranchers who needed to transport their goods to market. Today, the RRC has broad regulatory power over hydraulic fracturing operations. The RRC provides structural requirements for wells from start to finish, including casing and cementing regulations to protect freshwater resources.[33] The RRC's authority also extends to the disposal of hydraulic fracturing byproducts into wells.[34] Operators must disclose information about their operations to the RRC and also to FracFocus.org. Such disclosures include the quantity of water and the chemicals operators used.[35]

Municipalities in Texas also enact ordinances that regulate hydraulic fracturing's impact on their territories. For example, the city of Fort Worth, Texas, which sits in the hotbed of Barnett shale activity, has enacted ordinances that seek to prevent operators from drilling wells within 600 feet of a residence, school, or other public buildings.[36] Operators may only drill within set-back limits if the city council approves or all affected property owners consent. The city regulations also require operations within the city to use a "closed-loop" system for disposing of hydraulic fracturing byproducts.[37]

Oklahoma

Oklahoma has been producing oil and gas since the early 1900s. There are 137,800 active wells in the state. Over the last 60 years, more than 100,000 wells have been hydraulically fractured in the state. Hydraulic fracturing within the Woodford Shale formation has become an important source of natural gas in recent years. Pressures on water in Oklahoma may be less than in other states, as Oklahoma is a relatively water-rich state when compared to its western neighbors. Annually, after Oklahoma has met all its instate needs with its water resources, it still discharges some 36 million AF from its borders.[38]

Hydraulic fracturing operators in Oklahoma may obtain permits for water from the Oklahoma Water Resources Board (OWRB).[39] The ORWB regulates water use and water quantity/availability in Oklahoma. Its primary responsibilities include administering the prior appropriation system under Oklahoma law and issuing permits to those who make beneficial use of the state's water resources, both surface and groundwater. Because of the relative abundance of water in Oklahoma, the OWRB does not actively administer water permits. Rather, permitting assumes water being available to all without active permit administration. Because water used for oil and gas production is a recognized beneficial use in Oklahoma,[40] hydraulic fracturing operators may receive permits from the OWRB for their water needs. Hydraulic fracturing operators may also contract with existing water rights holders to obtain water.

Operators may also obtain their own groundwater permits. The law of groundwater in Oklahoma is unique. Water outside the cut-bank of a stream is presumed to have little or no hydraulic connection to a surface stream. Similar to the law of capture in Texas, a landowner has the right to withdraw groundwater "in place" beneath his land in an amount which would exhaust the resource over a legislatively mandated period, which is arbitrarily set at 2 AF/acre in most areas of the state. The OWRB issues four types of groundwater permits: regular, temporary, special, and provisional temporary.[41] Most often, hydraulic fracturing operators seek a "provisional temporary" permit. Operators can quickly obtain these permits, as they do not require public notice and hearing. These permits also fit hydraulic fracturing's short-term needs, as they allow groundwater extraction for up to 90 days.[42]

Once permitted, the Oklahoma Corporation Commission (OCC) is responsible for regulating hydraulic fracturing in a way that safeguards Oklahoma's natural resources (including water from a water quality perspective).[43] To protect groundwater, the OCC imposes minimum cementing and casing requirements, as well as pressure-testing rules. The OCC also regulates the pits that operators may use for temporary storage of hydraulic fracturing fluids, flowback, and produced water. The OCC regulations cover pit linings, runoff prevention, and flood protection, closure requirements, and post-closure monitoring. When hydraulic fracturing operations are complete, the OCC provides for many disposal methods for produced water, including evaporation in pits, soil farming, recycling, underground injection into certain types of wells, and commercial disposal. The OCC allows land application of produced water as a disposal method, but the agency regulates this method heavily, setting conditions and set-back requirements. The OCC is also the agency responsible for responding to contamination reports.

On the whole, Oklahoma recognizes that it needs to create a long-term plan for oil and gas water use within its state. OWRB plans for the state's long-term water needs via the periodically updated Oklahoma Comprehensive Water Plan.[44] This document addresses water needs and resources across the state. The Comprehensive Water Plan recognizes that the demand for water from oil and gas operations will be increasing in the decades ahead by as much as 200 percent. Nevertheless, given the tremendous quantities of unappropriated water in Oklahoma, this demand will not "cut-into" water for other beneficial uses.

In response to growing demands and a limited supply of water, the Oklahoma legislature instructed the OWRB to establish a technical workgroup to analyze the potential for expanded use of "marginal quality water" (MQW).[45] The goal of this workgroup is to look to non-traditional sources of water to meet new demands. The OWRB identified flowback and produced water from oil and gas operations as a potential source of MQW. The Comprehensive Water Plan recognized that using this water will include challenges, such as the fact that "utilization of this resource is likely to be limited by temporal, location, and water quality issues" and that "treatment requirements, storage needs, and the location of significant water users' demand relative to oil and gas production activities may negatively impact the cost-effectiveness of using the water resource."[46] However, the OWRB was hopeful that reusing flowback and produced water to support the water needs of nearby oil and gas drilling operations could be a viable opportunity for meeting growing water needs.[47]

Wyoming

Behind Texas, the state of Wyoming is number two in the nation for natural gas reserves. Wyoming contains some of the most productive fields in the country. The Pinedale field in Sublette County has 1,851 active wells and produces 1.5 billion cubic feet of natural gas per day, which is approximately 2.5 percent of the total U.S. onshore production.[48] Wyoming also conducts CBM mining. In 2003 alone, the total value of Wyoming's CBM production was $1.5 billion. Wyoming regulates hydraulic fracturing through three agencies: the Wyoming State Engineer's Office (WSEO[49]), the Wyoming Oil and Gas Conservation Commission (WOGCC), and the Department of Environmental Quality (DEQ).

The WSEO oversees and administers Wyoming's water resources, primarily from a water quantity standpoint. Water users obtain water rights to both surface and groundwater through the WSEO. As such, the WSEO comprehensively regulates the water supply necessary to the hydraulic fracturing industry in Wyoming. According to the

WSEO, hydraulic fracturing operations in Wyoming require about 9 to 15 acre feet of water per operation per well. Most often, this water supply comes from groundwater wells.[50]

The WSEO grants three types of groundwater well permits. Each is available to oil and gas operators, but what type of permit an operator will seek will depend on its needs. There are two types of long-term permits. First, operators can apply for a new permit. In most areas of Wyoming, water is available for appropriation, and new users can obtain a water right within six months. In areas of southeast Wyoming where water is scarcer, getting a new permit can take up to a year. Second, operators can buy water from an existing water rights holder and apply for a "Permanent Change of Use for Existing Water Right" permit. These permits are time-intensive as well, and it can take over a year for an operator to receive WSEO approval. A long wait for permit authorization is less than ideal for most oil and gas operators; they typically need water on an immediate, short-term, and temporary basis. Thus most often operators apply for the third type of permit available, called a "Temporary Change of an Existing Water Right" permit.[51] Under these permits, operators can buy or lease water rights from existing water rights holders, such as farmers or ranchers, and apply to the WSEO for a temporary change-of-use permit. The WSEO typically grants these permits in less than a month. These permits allow temporary water rights holders to use their allotted water for up to two years. During this time, the oil and gas operators' water rights will be administered in accordance with the priority system, meaning that a senior water rights holder can prevent the hydraulic fracturing operator from continuing to use water if it is impairing the senior use.

Once oil and gas companies have the water they need to complete their hydraulic fracturing operations, the operators fall under the purview of the WOGCC. The WOGCC seeks to ensure that operators protect the state's water resources from a water quality perspective. To apply for a permit to drill, operators must provide the WOGCC with three categories of information: site information, a well integrity plan, and chemical disclosure. Regarding site information, an operator must list all wells within a quarter mile of the proposed hydraulic fracturing site, identify any aquifers in the area, and discuss how it will safeguard groundwater resources. Operators must also provide a well integrity plan that creates a casing and cementing design customized to their mine's particular geologic formation and potential groundwater impact. Finally, the WOGCC requires operators to disclose what chemicals are in their hydraulic fracturing fluids. After hydraulic fracturing operations are complete, byproducts are typically injected underground. Hydraulic fracturing fluids and produced water can also be recycled.

Wyoming has been getting some recent national attention regarding hydraulic fracturing due to an EPA groundwater contamination study that took place near Pavillion, Wyoming.[52] The EPA's draft report, released in 2011, seemed to indicate that hydraulic fracturing did indeed cause groundwater pollution. This report marks the first time that the federal government has recognized groundwater pollution as a hazard of hydraulic fracturing. Some experts challenged the EPA's study arguing that the study was skewed because the EPA studied a hydraulic fracturing site that is not geologically representative of most hydraulic fracturing operations throughout the country. The Pavillion site is unusual in that the aquifer and gas-producing formations occur within the same geologic unit, whereas most freshwater aquifers do not extend below 1,500 feet below ground while hydraulic fracturing occurs between 5,000 and 8,000 feet. Regardless of its flaws, the EPA study reflects the first time that the federal government has taken an in-depth look at hydraulic fracturing. Some see the Wyoming study as the first step toward federal regulation of hydraulic fracturing. However, in September 2013, EPA announced that it was discontinuing its plan to finalize the study or seek peer review and was deferring groundwater investigations to the State of Wyoming.

MOVING FORWARD

Although a relatively new method of extracting natural gas, hydraulic fracturing is, has been, and will be commonly employed as a means of extracting hydrocarbons. Hydraulic fracturing technology is improving all the time. With each new chapter in the technology, new and more difficult formations will become profitably productive, and the amount of water used for hydraulic fracturing will increase. Although the industry is researching new hydraulic fracturing methods that do not use water—such as gel-based and sonic wave fracturing—these technologies will require years, if not decades, of refinement before operators can economically put them into place.

Instead of relying on the new technologies that might come in the future, western states must confront the new challenges regarding how to allocate and adapt their existing and scarce water resources in the face of hydraulic fracturing's demands. States routinely assess their existing water resources and competing demands through state water comprehensive plans. Nearly all the state water resource planning documents consulted for this chapter recognize that although the water used for hydraulic fracturing accounts for only a small percentage of the water used statewide, this percentage is increasing. However, few of these documents provided a plan for how to satisfy these increasing demands. In places like Colorado, a few municipalities are not willing to wait on the state to address competing water resource needs, and these municipalities are attempting to curtail water use via their own limited authority. States must move to leave these state-versus-local battles behind and strive to keep up with the rapidly expanding landscape of hydraulic fracturing's water demands. However, the West, driven by both the nature of the prior appropriation doctrine and its independent streak, places the ability to acquire and transfer of water within the open market, making market-based solutions the means for allocating scarce water resources. With this in mind, there is little doubt that the value of water for hydraulic fracturing will ensure the availability of water for the energy industry.

As the value of water has been increasingly appreciated by users in the West, reuse and recycling have become more prevalent. Although existing state regulations allow for limited recycling of hydraulic fracturing water, from a practical standpoint, most leftover hydraulic fracturing fluids and produced water is injected into underground wells, which are then sealed. This water is effectively removed from the hydrologic cycle. Although onsite water purification systems do exist, this technology is only beginning to evolve. States are increasingly devoting their efforts toward studying and adopting rules for the recycling or reuse of hydraulic fracturing water.

The oil and gas industry must also prepare to deal with the water-based challenges ahead. Industry may need to comply with an increasingly complex web of federal-state-local jurisdiction laws. Population growth and climate change will decrease water availability, which will put additional pressure on the energy industry and other water users alike. The industry should continue to devote efforts to develop technologies that either decrease the amount of water required to hydraulically fracture or increase the reuse and recycling potentials of hydraulic fracturing operations.

Underlying the challenges faced by both states and industry is the possibility of federal water quality regulation of hydraulic fracturing. As of now, the federal government has little or no control over hydraulic fracturing operations. However, the EPA's Pavillion, Wyoming study indicates that the EPA is taking an interest in how hydraulic fracturing affects our nation's water resources.[53] There are two sides to federal hydraulic fracturing regulation. On one hand, federal regulation would simplify standards by creating a uniform body of law that hydraulic fracturing operators would need to comply with no matter where their productions took place. On the other hand, many argue that the "one-size-fits-all" approach has no place in water or energy management due to the differing legal frameworks that the states employ and the unique geologic attributes of each shale play. Although this chapter explored four western states, it reveals the different ways which the states manage their water resources. The abundance and management of water resources varies even more greatly when comparing hydraulic fracturing operations and water implications discussed in this chapter to those of the eastern United States.

Conclusion

On a statewide and national level, the use of water for hydraulic fracturing is very small—less than 0.5 percent of all water use. However, the use of water can be concentrated in the shale play areas such that the percentage of water used for hydraulic fracturing on a local level may be many times higher. The arid West has seen an explosion in population in the last two decades competing with new water demands for water such as hydraulic fracturing. The western United States employs the prior appropriation doctrine for the allocation and administration of water, which is founded on the principles of first in time, first in right, and the maximum beneficial use of water. Since many streamcourses are over-appropriated, water for new uses such as hydraulic fracturing must be secured by lease or purchase from other water holders. Often these rights are decreed for uses other than mining purposes and must be adapted or changed to the new beneficial use of mining. The process of adapting and changing water rights is a state issue with each state having their own laws and regulations. Most states employ administrative agencies to allocate and administer water, while Colorado stands alone in allocating water through the judicial process, leaving administration of the water rights once decreed to administrative means.

Water quantity considerations are distinct from water quality ones. State law now, and in the future, will govern the acquisition and administration of water resources. Market-based solutions are components of the prior appropriation system, which allocates water based on beneficial use rather than political or geographical preference. Like all new uses of water, the energy industry is on an equal footing to participate in such allocations and transfers ensuring that adequate water resources will be available for the industry. Water quality aspects of the use of water for hydraulic fracturing on the other hand must comply and take into account a mesh of federal, state, and local jurisdiction concerns, interests, and regulation, which will undoubtedly increase over time.

NOTES

1. An AF is the measure of water it would take to flood one acre of land with one foot of water. An acre foot (AF) is equal to 325,851 gallons.
2. Water-based drilling mud is a fluid mixture of water and clay that is utilized to carry rock cuttings from the bottom of the wellbore to the surface, while at the same time cooling and lubricating the drillbit as it rotates. The amount of water required for drilling operations, while not insignificant, is much less than the amount required for hydraulic fracturing and completion processes. For example, Chesapeake Energy estimates that drilling a typical deep shale oil and gas well requires between 65,000 and 600,000 gallons of water. CHESAPEAKE ENERGY, WATER USE IN DEEP SHALE GAS EXPLORATION FACT SHEET (May 2012), *available at* http://www.chk.com/media/educational-library/fact-sheets/Pages/default.aspx.
3. The USGS 2010 report is late. Due to administrative delays, the agency estimates that the 2010 report will not be available until 2014. Because hydraulic fracturing has been on the rise since 2005, it is possible that the 2010 report may reflect an increase in the percentage of the nation's waters used for mining. For more information, see http://water.usgs.gov/watuse/. However, State reports demonstrate that water use for hydraulic fracturing is not excessive. For example, the Colorado State Engineer confirmed that less than 1% of state-wide water use is attributable to water for oil and gas exploration and production uses in 2012. Kevin Rein, Presentation at Niobrara Infrastructure Development Summit (Mar. 2013).
4. EPA, DRAFT PLAN TO STUDY THE IMPACTS OF HYDRAULIC FRACTURING ON DRINKING WATER RESOURCES (Feb. 2011), *available at* http://water.epa.gov/type/groundwater/uic/class2/hydraulicfracturing/upload/HFStudyPlanDraft_SAB_020711-08.pdf.

5. Generally, figures measured in terms of "water used" may include some portion of water that is ultimately returned to the hydrologic cycle by way of surface water return flow into a stream, or by infiltration and percolation to shallow ground water aquifers. Consequently, this water may be utilized by other downstream appropriators or users. On the other hand, figures measuring "water consumed" more accurately refer to water that is not returned to the hydrologic cycle and thus lost for future use. Flowback water may be consumed, for example, by evaporation in open pits, or by disposing of it through injection into deep wells that are tens of thousands of feet beneath the water table. When left to natural processes, water injected to these depths may take geologic time periods before it returns to the water cycle. *See, e.g.*, ANDY D. WARD & STANLEY W. TRIBLE, ENVIRONMENTAL HYDROLOGY 4–6 (CRC Press, LLC 2d ed. 2004).

6. The Colorado Oil & Gas Conservation Commission's full report on water quantity needed for hydraulic fracturing in Colorado is available at http://cogcc.state.co.us/Library/Oil_and_Gas_Water_Sources_Fact_Sheet.pdf.

7. The Railroad Commission's full report to the Texas State Senate on water quantity needed for hydraulic fracturing in Texas is available at http://www.senate.state.tx.us/75r/Senate/commit/c510/handouts12/0110-RRC.pdf.

8. Statement of Richard Luedecke, Presenter at the 2010 Oklahoma Governor's Water Conference (Oct. 27, 2010). PowerPoint presentation *available at* http://www.owrb.ok.gov/news/news2/pdf_news2/conference/2011_GWC__Presentations/Luedecke.pdf.

9. A recent trend in Colorado is for hydraulic fracturing operators to buy water from farmers who are hurting for cash during times of drought. Without water to keep the land fertile, these farmlands fallow. The concerned agricultural lobby is seeking new solutions wherein these competing water uses can coexist. The Arkansas Valley "Super Ditch" is one such solution. *See generally, Super Ditch*, THE WATER INFO. PROGRAM, http://www.waterinfo.org/super-ditch.

10. Boulder County's proposed policy is the latest development in a recent trend wherein local governments have attempted to regulate hydraulic fracturing. Some local governments wish to completely ban hydraulic fracturing within their territories. However, because Colorado state law regulates oil and gas operations, including hydraulic fracturing, the state laws on hydraulic fracturing preempt local laws, and thus local bans on hydraulic fracturing would be illegal and ineffective. Using another approach, local governments have enacted temporary moratoriums on issuing new permits for oil and gas operations within their territories. In 2012, the Boulder County Commissioners, Loveland City Council, and Erie Board of Trustees each enacted 6- to 9-month moratoriums. The local entities say that the moratoriums allow the counties and cities to assess local land-use regulations to determine whether these regulations need to be updated in light of the recent surge in

hydraulic fracturing. Although the state has not struck down these moratoriums on preemption grounds, there the state legislature is contemplating
bills that would similar outlaw future local-level moratoriums.

11. For example: Since 1990, Colorado has grown in population by 40 percent,
Texas has grown by 50 percent, and other western states have gained significant populations.

12. *Niobrara Shale Formation,* Oil Shale Gas, http://oilshalegas.com
/niobrarashale.html.

13. CBM mining is unique in that the methane usually lies at a much shallower depths than other natural gas deposits. The shallow depth of the
wells means that the production activities, including hydraulic fracturing,
if hydraulic fracturing is necessary in formation, take place closer to the
surface water and shallow freshwater aquifers. Sometimes, mining CBM
involves pumping produced water without hydraulic fracturing. Because of
its unique characteristics, CBM mining is often placed in a category all its
own when it comes to state regulation.

14. Perhaps the most famous of these Compacts is the Colorado River Compact, which allocates water between Colorado, Wyoming, Utah, Nevada,
Arizona, New Mexico, and California and has been a source of conflict
between the signatory states since its signing in 1922.

15. *See* the Water Right Determination and Administration Act of 1969,
Colo. Rev. Stat. § 37-97-101 *et seq.*

16. The State Engineer's general regulations can be found at 2 Colo. Code
Regs. § 402 (2007).

17. This is markedly different from riparian and regulated riparianism, which
attempts to manage water to give all a reasonable use of the available supply.

18. *See* Colorado Ground Water Management Act, Colo. Rev. Stat.
§ 37-90-103(21).

19. 205 P.3d 1165 (Colo. 2009).

20. While the facts of the *Vance* case surrounded CBM mining, the decision
applies to all produced water—from CBM mines or otherwise.

21. Tributary groundwater" is water that is hydraulically connected to surface
water. If the SEO finds that pumping groundwater from a well influences a
surface stream within a 100-year period, the SEO will presume the groundwater to be tributary in nature. Conversely, if a water user can show that
pumping from a well does *not* influence a surface stream within a 100-year
period, the well can receive a "non-tributary" designation.

22. *See* 1965 Ground Water Management Act, Colo. Rev. Stat. § 37-90-101
et al.

23. The full text of the COGCC regulations are available at http://cogcc.state
.co.us/ (follow "Rules" hyperlink).

24. Casing and cementing create a barrier between the well shaft and freshwater resources.

25. Pursuant to COGCC regulations that took effect in February 2012, operators must also disclose their chemical information to FracFocus, a public online database that is a joint project of the Ground Water Protection Council and the Interstate Oil and Gas Compact Commission. This website is http://fracfocus.org/.

26. Texas provides 27 percent of the domestic onshore oil production and 36 percent of the domestic onshore gas production.

27. HALLIBURTON, U.S. SHALE GAS WHITE PAPER (2008), *available at* http://www.halliburton.com/public/solutions/contents/shale/related_docs/H063771.pdf.

28. The rule of capture is also applied in the common law treatment of oil and gas. See *supra* chapter 4 for a more detailed explanation of this concept.

29. Historically, the rule of capture governed all groundwater in Texas, and while the rule is still active, in some areas of Texas groundwater conservation districts (GCDs) have replaced, or at least modified, the rule of capture. GCDs regulate water in three ways: they permit wells, develop comprehensive groundwater management plans, and adopt rules governing groundwater extract that implement their management plans. There are 101 GCDs in Texas, covering all or a part of 175 of Texas' 254 counties. Although the GCDs have the authority to set rules that replace the rule of capture, importantly, GCD authority does *not* extend to oil and gas activities. *See* TEX. WATER CODE § 36.117(b)(2)–(3) (stating the oil and gas activities to which the GCD's authority does not extend). Thus GCDs do not have authority over groundwater pumped for use in conjunction with hydraulic fracturing, and the rule of capture still applies to water pumped for oil and gas purposes.

30. The riparian doctrine of water law recognizes that an owner of land, which borders a watercourse, holds an inherent right to use the water by virtue of owning the riparian land. Generally, the riparian owner is entitled to use as much of the water as needed, so long as it does not interfere with any other riparian owners' reasonable use of the water. In contrast to the prior appropriation system, the reasonable use limitation of the riparian system applies irrespective of who first made use of the water. David H. Getches, WATER LAW IN A NUTSHELL 16, 48 (West 4th ed. 2009).

31. *See* TEX. WATER CODE § 26.011.

32. *See* TEX. WATER CODE § 26.131

33. Tex. R.R. Comm'n Statewide Rule 13.

34. Tex. R.R. Comm'n Statewide Rule 9.

35. All states with chemical disclosure regulations have exceptions available for trade secrets, or "proprietary chemicals." Typically, a state allows companies to keep these chemicals out of public disclosures except in cases of emergency and/or water contamination.

36. FORT WORTH, TEXAS, CODE OF ORDINANCES, ch. 15, art. 2 § 15–36 (2010).

37. *Id.* at § 15–42(A)(3). Whereas hydraulic fracturing operators routinely store hydraulic fracturing fluid or produced water in pits before transporting the waste to the disposal site, the Fort Worth regulations require operators to pump waste directly from the well into a truck for transport. This regulation removes open-pit storage from the waste cycle and eliminates the risk of spills from pits.

38. *Oklahoma Water Facts*, OKLA. WATER RES. BD. (last updated May 10, 2013), http://www.owrb.ok.gov/util/waterfact.php. The amount discharged after all uses in Oklahoma is nearly 20 times the current state surface water use. *See* Okla. Water Res. Bd., Oklahoma Comprehensive Water Plan, Physical Water Supply Availability Report, tbl.3-21 (Nov. 2011), *available at* http://www.owrb.ok.gov/supply/ocwp/pdf_ocwp/WaterPlanUpdate/OCWP _PhysicalWaterSupplyAvailabilityReport.pdf (stating that Oklahoma only consumes 1.87 million acre-feet of surface water per year). By comparison, New York City's current service area population of 8 million uses 1.5 million acre feet per year. Thus Oklahoma's average yearly discharge could provide for the annual water needs of New York City nearly twenty-three times.

39. General information on the OWRB available on its website, http://www .owrb.ok.gov/.

40. OKLA. ADMIN. CODE § 785:20-1-2 Beneficial Use, Mining Use; *see also* OKLA. ADMIN. CODE § 785:30-1-2 Beneficial Use.

41. *Groundwater Permitting*, OKLA. WATER RES. BD, http://www.owrb.ok.gov /supply/watuse/gwwateruse.php (last updated Nov. 20, 2007).

42. *Id.*

43. General information on the OCC available on its website, http://www.occ .state.ok.us/.

44. The most recent ten-year plan, which was due in 2005, was released in October 2011. OKLA. WATER RES. BD., OKLAHOMA COMPREHENSIVE WATER PLAN, EXECUTIVE REPORT (Oct. 17, 2011), *available at* http://www.owrb .ok.gov/supply/ocwp/pdf_ocwp/WaterPlanUpdate/draftreports/OCWP%20 Executive%20Rpt%20FINAL.pdf.

45. Okla. Legislature Senate Bill 1627 (2008).

46. OKLA. WATER RES. BD, Oklahoma Comprehensive Water Plan, Executive Report (2011), at 110.

47. *Id.*

48. Vinnie Rigatti, General Manager, QEP Energy Company, Presenter at the University of Wyoming School of Energy Resources' Fracking Forum (Sept. 26, 2011) [hereinafter "UW Fracking Forum"]. All oral and PowerPoint presentations for this forum are available at http://www.uwyo.edu/SER /conferences/hydraulic-fracturing/speaker-presentations.html.

49. For purposes of this chapter, the Wyoming State Engineer's Office is referred to as WSEO to avoid confusion with the Colorado State Engineer's Office. However, within Wyoming, the term SEO is used.

50. Lisa Lindemann, Wyoming State Engineer's Office, Ground Water Division Administrator, Presenter at UW Fracking Forum (Sept. 26, 2011).

51. The statute authorizing these temporary permits explicitly recognizes that the oil and gas industry could utilize these permits.

52. *See generally Wyoming Cleanup Sites*, EPA, http://www.epa.gov/region8 /superfund/wy/pavillion/ (last updated June 3, 2013).

53. *See also Natural Gas Extraction—Hydraulic Fracturing*, EPA, http://www.epa .gov/hydraulicfracture/ (last visited Aug. 30, 2012) (showing that the EPA is examining how hydraulic fracturing could affect the public health).

9

A Riparian Rights Perspective
Regulating Water Withdrawals for Oil and Gas Development in New York State

Adam J. Yagelski

INTRODUCTION

Water becomes a consideration during the lifecycle of a Marcellus Shale gas well in the following three ways: (1) as precipitation that creates stormwater runoff from a pad site, (2) as an integral component of the frac fluid used during hydraulic fracturing, (3) and as wastewater returning to the surface as a consequence of fracturing and during production,[1] which requires treatment for proper disposal.[2] The large volumes of freshwater required to complete each well can be obtained from various sources, such as groundwater, municipal water systems, existing permitted discharges, and surface waters. This chapter focuses on the quantity of water needed, water sources (specifically fresh water withdrawn from surface waters), and regulation of these water withdrawals in New York State.

WATER DEMAND

The process to complete a single well in unconventional tight shale formations may be broken down into at least two discrete stages—drilling and fracturing—each with different water demands that total about 4.2 million gallon (MG). First, drilling typically requires between 80,000 gallons[3] to 1.0 MG[4] of water to lubricate and cool the drill bit and to remove cuttings from the well bore.[5] The amount of water used during the second stage—fracturing—is much greater, with some estimates placing the figure at one million gallons of water per one thousand feet of the horizontal section of the drill hole.[6] Completing a well typically occurs over the course of three to five days, which means that drillers expend these quantities of freshwater in a short amount of time.

Several other factors complicate this picture of water use. First, multiple wells per pad site are likely to be drilled—as many as six to eight discrete wells, each of which would require drilling and hydraulic fracturing.[7] Water consumption, then, could be multiplied by six or eight times per pad site, which, at 4.2 MG per well, puts gross freshwater demand at 33.6 MG per pad site. Moreover, the way in which gas production declines over the lifespan of such unconventional wells means that refracturing may also be employed as each well ages and its production declines.[8] This could make restimulation a significant part of operations in the Marcellus play over time. These and other considerations, such as operator experience, market conditions, and technological advances, suggest that water use will likely be highly contingent and dynamic. The combination of what one commentator has called "natural complexity" and "industry complexity"[9] makes water demand analysis itself a dynamic endeavor, and overall water demand difficult to estimate precisely.

RELIANCE ON SURFACE WATER SOURCES

The Marcellus Shale underlies portions of at least five major U.S. river basins. These include the Susquehanna River, Delaware River, Ohio River, Great Lakes-St. Lawrence, and Potomac River basins; smaller portions underlie the Hudson River basin in New York as well. This region offers a variety of different water sources available for use for gas drilling operations. In addition to surface water and groundwater, freshwater can be obtained from existing permitted discharges, such as public wastewater systems and marginal drainage from mines, as well as withdrawals originally permitted for other purposes, such as municipal water supply and agricultural operations, with excess capacity.[10] Additionally, companies can also recycle or otherwise reuse produced water. Current estimates indicate that recycled water can supply between 10 and 20 percent of the total required.[11] Because onsite treatment (including reuse) is the preferred method for handling produced water,[12] it is likely that wastewater recycling will supply an increasing proportion of total water needed. Major operators in the Marcellus now commonly recycle all or nearly all produced water. Range Resources recycled 96 percent in 2010[13] and Chesapeake Energy recycled "nearly 100%" in 2011.[14]

At any given well site, the preferred source is determined by balancing a variety of factors, including availability, proximity of a source to the well, quantity, reliability, accessibility, quality, "permittability," disposal of resultant wastewater, and cost.[15] These factors result in a dynamic set of considerations for well operators, especially as new technologies evolve, like recycling of produced water. As one consulting group puts it, "Each service company and operation would need to evaluate local conditions to determine the availability of alternate water sources to a particular gas well."[16]

These local conditions produce considerable variability in sourcewater within and between plays. In the Barnett Shale, groundwater made up between 45 percent and 100 percent of sourcewater by county. In the Eagle Ford Shale, water has come primarily from the Carrizo aquifer, except for areas near the Rio Grande River. Sources can also vary over time. In the Hynesville Shale, initial reliance upon groundwater shifted to use of surface water.[17] In the Marcellus region, however, surface water has been the preferred alternative, followed by municipal water supplies, with groundwater sources a distant third alternative.[18] Chesapeake Energy includes high-flow surface water sources in its list of Marcellus Shale sources,[19] and in general, it appears that drilling companies have focused primarily on these "major" sources of water—rivers like the Susquehanna, Chenango, and Chemung—in this region.[20]

ECOLOGICAL AND SOCIAL IMPACTS

For surface water sources, seasonality, periodicity, and frequency of flow, present problems. Even rivers with significant rates of flow are not immune to these cycles. In general, where winter temperatures allow for snow and ice pack, as is the case across the Marcellus Shale region, streams and lakes have higher flows during spring runoff (March–May) and lower flows during late summer and fall months (August–October). The rate and timing of these flows—the flow regime—is directly related to the level of environmental as well as social benefits water flow provides.[21]

There is a tight link between water quantity, quality, and eco-system health and social utility. For example, eliminating peaks in seasonal flow can disrupt cues fish species need for spawning, egg hatching, and migration, while increasing the rapidity of change in water surface elevation can lead to stranding of aquatic species.[22] Significant alteration to the flow regime may disrupt these natural processes and the important ecological and social services flow confers.

Gas industry experts have also recognized seasonal variation as a withdrawal strategy. Water supplies should be stocked during periods of high flow, while water is plentiful.[23] While regulations commonly attempt to mitigate the deleterious effects of severe or prolonged periods of low flow, maintaining minimum water quantity as a management strategy—based on an understanding of the relationship between aquatic ecosystem function and the amount of water in a body of water at any given point in time—is unevenly applied across the Marcellus region. Withdrawals have the potential to disrupt the rate, timing, or amount of water flow and, therefore, to induce changes to riverine ecosystems.

Additionally, withdrawals for hydraulic fracturing can intensify existing water quality problems. In Pennsylvania, permitted gas wells cluster in the north-central and southwest parts of the state. A combination of mine and drilling waste discharges likely resulted in drinking water advisories issued along the Monongahela River (which supplies drinking water to the Pittsburgh area)[24] but were exacerbated, according PADEP and local officials, by hydraulic fracturing-related water withdrawals as drought conditions caused flow rates to be half as high as normal.[25] In the summer of 2009, a similar combination of water withdrawals, water discharges from an area coal mine, and drought conditions resulted in high total dissolved solids and caused a severe aquatic life kill in Dunkard Creek, a tributary of the Monongahela that snakes across the Pennsylvania-West Virginia state line.[26]

Dunkard Creek, in particular, provides evidence that smaller water bodies with lower volumes of flow show heightened sensitivity to disruptions in that flow, and the volumes of water withdrawn for hydraulic fracturing operations can have significant impacts at the stream level—even when, at the overall watershed level, they might be insignificant. Indeed, in the Susquehanna River Basin (SRB), most drilling will take place in the headwaters, which are comprised of smaller, more ecologically sensitive water bodies.[27] The impact of cumulative uses—withdrawals for multiple wells, for instance, or in combination with other uses—can have significant and deleterious impacts if not carefully planned and controlled.[28]

WATER WITHDRAWAL REGULATION IN THE MARCELLUS SHALE REGION

A complex mix of common law, state, and interstate regulations governs water withdrawals in the Marcellus Shale region.[29] Under common law, the right to water is one of use—not ownership—and it is tied to proximity to the water body and subject to the usage rights of other downstream and upstream users.[30] Notably, common law has generally limited the right of water use to those uses taking place within the watershed of origin, creating a hurdle for interbasin water transfers. Two legal doctrines have come to define common law approaches to the allocation of riparian water rights.

The first, the natural flow doctrine, provides that landowners with property adjacent to bodies of water have a right to use that water, provided their use does not affect the use of those downstream or upstream. Domestic uses tend to be favored more than commercial or industrial uses. Thus, "each riparian owner along a water body is entitled to have the water flow across the land in its natural condition, without alteration by others of the rate of flow, or the quantity or quality of the water."[31] However, the maintenance of existing levels of flow caused difficulties when water uses that did in fact disrupt natural flow intensified. The inflexibility inherent in the natural flow doctrine led to the emergence of the "American rule" of reasonable use. Here, withdrawals are evaluated not by disruption of flow *per se* but by unreasonableness of the withdrawal actions considering all relevant aspects of the circumstance of the withdrawal.

Reliance upon pure common law approaches to water rights management can create economic inefficiencies, environmental drawbacks, and conflict among users. Thus, east of the Mississippi River, many states augment the common law with an additional layer of control. Most fundamentally, this "regulated riparianism" employs water withdrawal permit systems to control the amount, rate, timing, and other aspects of withdrawal activities, although use fees, enforcement, and planning are also salient elements.[32] Such regulatory programs are currently found at both the state and interstate levels (e.g., by interstate compact commissions such as the Susquehanna River Basin Commission and Delaware River Basin Commission).[33]

INCONSISTENT REGULATION OF WATER WITHDRAWALS

Due to the fact that water rights are regulated at the state level or basin level and include a mix of statutory and common law, regulation of withdrawals varies considerably across the Marcellus Shale region. However, most existing regimes include reporting requirements, minimum flow requirements, and the application of standards driven by sophisticated aquatic ecosystem models to determine required minimum flows to remain in a stream during a withdrawal. The Susquehanna River Basin Commission (SRBC) is a good example of a very sophisticated water quantity control program operating in the Marcellus Shale region.[34]

The SRB is about 27,510 square miles in size and comprises 43 percent of the Chesapeake Bay watershed. Significantly, 72 percent of the basin is underlain by the Marcellus Shale formation.[35] An interstate compact gives jurisdiction over water use in the basin to the SRBC, which has developed a comprehensive set of rules, standards, and procedures governing water withdrawals, particularly their use for hydraulic fracturing purposes. Given its broad remit, SRBC has developed an advanced set of instream flow regulations, and since October 2008, has required approval for all natural gas projects in the basin.[36] The actions taken by SRBC essentially move water withdrawals for hydraulic fracturing into the heart of its consumptive use regulation.[37]

SRBC uses conservation releases, consumptive use compensation, and passby flows to mitigate impacts of surface water withdrawals.[38] Conservation releases specify an amount of water to be continuously maintained downstream of an impoundment or dam and apply to surface water withdrawals from these structures. Consumptive use compensation consists of discontinuance of withdrawal, provision of water storage, and payment to SRBC for its water storage and flow augmentation efforts. Finally, passby flows, defined as "a prescribed quantity of flow that must be allowed to pass a prescribed point downstream from a water supply intake at any time during which a withdrawal is occurring," are particularly important[39] and are determined in several ways.

In areas of the Commission's jurisdiction in Pennsylvania covered by the *Pennsylvania–Maryland Instream Flow Study*,[40] a method called the Instream Flow Incremental Methodology (IFIM) is used to predict relationships between water withdrawals and habitat loss for target aquatic species. The most basic standard is that flow must not decrease below Q7-10[41] in SRBC jurisdiction waters. The SRBC also applies several other criteria to determine required instream flows and conducts significant planning and monitoring. Ultimately, the ability to withdraw water is tied to these standards, and during dry periods, the SRBC regularly suspends water withdrawals.[42]

While interstate entities like the SRBC may regulate all use of water in a particular river basin, at the state level, regulation is less comprehensive and more variegated. In New York State, the Water Resources Law (WRL) regulates withdrawals for public water supply, withdrawals for agricultural irrigation, and regional water planning initiatives, but industrial development (including oil and gas development) does not fall under its ambit.[43] New York State does, however, regulate water quality in terms of alteration of flow that would "impair the designated best use of a water body" (the narrative water quality standard for flow).[44]

Under recent legislation, "Any person who withdraws or is operating any system or method of withdrawal that has the capacity to withdraw more than 100,000 gallons of groundwater or surface water per day" is subject to annual reporting requirements.[45] This new statute, which has resulted in a new set of water withdrawal regulations,[46] is directly related to and implements the state's obligations under the Great Lakes–St. Lawrence River Basin Water Resources Compact. Signed in 2005 by the eight Great Lakes states, the Compact, inter alia, stipulates the creation of water withdrawal registration and permitting systems, establishes a common standard for water withdrawal review, and prohibits most interbasin diversions.[47] As proposed, the rule includes mitigation measures, such as passby flows and instream flow standards, that attempt to maintain seasonal variation of flow.[48]

In Pennsylvania, withdrawals are controlled by a combination of the Clean Streams Law,[49] the Water Resources Planning Act of 2002 (WRPA),[50] and recent amendments to the Oil and Gas Act (Act

13).[51] The WRPA contained water resource planning requirements, including a timeline for revising the State Water Plan and a process to identify Critical Water Planning Areas (CWPA). Once defined, the WRPA directs the Pennsylvania Department of Environmental Protection (PADEP) to prepare a nonregulatory Critical Area Resource Plan for each CWPA. The WRPA also led to required reporting of withdrawals that exceed 10,000 gallons per day (GPD).[52]

The main source of regulation in Pennsylvania, however, is Act 13, which requires an approved Water Management Plan (WMP) to be filed with PADEP to obtain a drilling permit. With Act 13, PADEP will now require all withdrawals to meet the sophisticated instream flow criteria required by SRBC, even if the withdrawal is located outside these river basins.[53] Some antidrilling observers have questioned whether PADEP approval of a WMP constitutes a right to withdraw water for nonriparian uses, arguing that companies remain bound by established common law precedent despite the fact that PADEP does not require the demonstration of legal right to withdraw water in submissions of WMPs.[54] These concerns foreground how the existence of disparate approaches to water use control in Pennsylvania creates tension, even as, the State Water Plan notes, the relationship among these approaches "remains unsettled."[55]

West Virginia lacks a comprehensive regulatory approach in governing water withdrawals at the state level. However, like Pennsylvania, provisions for water management plans for hydraulic fracturing are including in a regulation specific to oil and gas development activity—in this case, the 2011 Horizontal Well Act.[56] According to this law, withdrawal of 210,000 gallons or more in any 30-day time period requires filing of a water management plan; it also outlines provisions for maintaining instream flows. The law defines "sufficient instream flow" as maintenance of a pass-by flow "protective of the identified use of the stream." However, the law does not establish numerical standards for flow and ultimately leaves this determination to the West Virginia Department of Environmental Protection. This legislation is supplemented by the Water Resources Protection and Management Act of 2008[57] (formerly the Water Resources Protection Act of 2004), which establishes a registration and reporting program designed to inventory existing withdrawals.[58] The state also sets standards for minimum flows in certain rivers. A state-level management plan for water resources in West Virginia is due in 2013.

LACK OF COMPREHENSIVE REGULATION

On the one hand, there seems to be considerable sanguinity on the part of industry and some regulators[59] that, in the words of an SRBC policy statement, existing water sources will be able to "accommodate a new straw in the water."[60] This confidence stems, in part, from evaluation of the fraction of gas industry water use relative to other water uses. For example, in discussing water use in the Marcellus region, Chesapeake Energy argues that "The natural gas industry is expected to increase the amount used by less than 0.1 percent," equating the 5.6 MG it uses to hydraulically fracture each well with "the amount of water consumed by New York City in eight minutes."[61] On the one hand, such statistics are undeniable—and certainly not unique to the water-rich Marcellus play. In Texas, which has a long history of shale gas development and over 20,000 hydraulically fractured wells, a recent study finds that statewide, gas industry water use was minor (<1 percent) compared to irrigation (56 percent) and municipal (26 percent) water use.[62]

On the other hand, this approach to gas industry water demand has been criticized by environmental groups as well as regulators[63] because it discounts the unevenness of gas drilling developments in the Marcellus Shale region and the localized impacts of withdrawals. Indeed, the Texas study cited above also found substantial intraplay variation of the percent of total county water used for hydraulic fracturing in 2008 in the Barnett Shale, with gas industry use ranging from a low of 1.4 percent to a high of 29 percent, leading the authors to conclude that "Despite the low overall net water use fraction, impacts of water use can be much greater at smaller spatial scales."[64]

These impacts to water resources can be categorized as either probabilistic or deterministic.[65] Probabilistic events like spills, leaks, and well failure are "highly uncertain over time and space" and can only be estimated or inferred based on past experience. Deterministic events, like water withdrawals, however, can be predicted and "their magnitude is directly related to the extent and pace of gas drilling development."[66] Impacts of both categories of events can be mitigated with careful regulation and planning. Deterrents and emergency response planning can mitigate the former, while pacing of development and intensive reuse of water can mitigate impact of the latter.

Faced with the high probability that gas drilling water withdrawals will impact water quantity, states have strengthened water withdrawal regulation and, concomitantly, the relationship between how flow is measured and whether ecological function is protected. In Pennsylvania, for example, the more sophisticated instream flow measures used by the SRBC, which are designed to leave the seasonal hydrograph intact, are now employed as permit conditions, and companies must submit a detailed water management plan. Similarly, both New York and West Virginia appear to be moving in the same direction, *viz.* away from "standard-setting" measures, like Q7-10, which permit significant alteration of water flows, and toward the protection of environmental flows.

Yet the challenge of instituting a regulatory program capable of mitigating the impact of all withdrawals—hydraulic fracturing among them—on water resources remains. Here, protection of instream flow should be viewed as a necessary, but not a sufficient, component. River basin commissions, including the SRBC and the Delaware River Basin Commission, maintain comprehensive permit systems with regulatory requirements for all withdrawals. But the bespoke drilling permit conditions developed by states like New York, Pennsylvania, and West Virginia currently pertain solely to unconventional drilling operations. At present, Pennsylvania has comprehensive water planning enabled by state legislation, West Virginia is moving toward a state water plan, New York is finalizing an expanded permitting system, and all three states collect water use data with withdrawal reporting mechanisms. But there is, as yet, an unrealized opportunity to implement permit systems based on instream flows and comprehensive water planning statewide.

Most existing permitting requirements are applied unevenly by withdrawal amount, source type, and intended use. In New York, for example, the proposed permitting system would apply to withdrawals of 100,000 GPD or more.[67] State approval is currently required in New York for transfers from (i.e., diversions) the Great Lakes Basin, and New York and Pennsylvania have long regulated withdrawals for public water supply. Yet there are gaps, and many withdrawals are regulated via common law—an approach with demonstrable weaknesses.

In spite of its evolution, the system based on riparian rights "lack[s] clarity, predictability, and administrative efficiency."[68] In addition, it does not provide efficient mechanisms for preventing or resolving disputes among competing consumptive uses, for remedies are "often narrow and limited."[69] Thirty years ago, one observer noted several weaknesses in the water law system found in the eastern U.S., including the problem of exempting certain users, the lack of coordination between water resources planning and water permit administration, and inadequate planning for temporary water shortages.[70] These weaknesses remain today, and water withdrawal regulation has lagged behind water demand in most eastern states. Increased competition for water resources posed by hydraulic fracturing technology has brought to light the weaknesses in existing water use regulation at the state level in the Marcellus Shale region, and is prompting a reevaluation of existing regulatory approaches as hydraulic fracturing places new pressures on water supplies that are already stressed.

RECOMMENDATIONS FOR NEW YORK

Pennsylvania, West Virginia, and New York have made clear progress toward meeting social and ecological goals in the management of instream flow. This is progress demonstrated by the robust, ecologically protective instream flow standards to be used as mitigation measures attached to drilling permits. However, gaps in water resource planning are apparent. The Regulated Riparian Model Water Code provides a structure that, if adopted, could provide effective regulation of New York State's water resources in the face of these new pressures. Pennsylvania's recent State Water Plan included a discussion of how weaknesses associated with common law riparian rights doctrine could be mitigated with a comprehensive, statewide approach to water regulation.[71] This model code, developed largely by the American Society of Civil Engineers, would rationalize and modernize state water regulation by replacing common law riparian rights doctrine with an updated, technically sophisticated set of regulations undergirded by the public trust doctrine. This would provide a robust regulatory framework within which instream flow and water withdrawal data collection might proceed. It would also provide mechanisms for water resources planning as well as an improved permitting system—an important and weighty piece of the regulatory approach used by the SRBC. In addition, built into the model code are procedures for coping with drought and other periods of scarcity. Building a permitting system applicable to all water withdrawals, as opposed to the more limited regulations attached as permit conditions currently contemplated by the 2011 revised draft SGEIS at the time of this writing, would better enable the state to take an active, rather than reactive, stance regarding the clear, deterministic impacts gas drilling will have on New York's streams, lakes, and rivers.[72]

To address gaps in water resources planning, review of the New York State Water Resources Management Strategy (WRMS) (which was written as a state-level water plan in 1989), and resurrection of the 15-member Water Resources Planning Council that has been dormant for several decades, would also be beneficial. A range of issues, from increased conflict over water resources to a demonstrated need to "fit" a new industrial process (i.e., hydraulic fracturing) into existing water management practices, point toward the utility of reinvigorating the 1989 water plan. In New York, like many states, water planning is currently fragmentary—regional and issue-oriented—and the WRMS sets out the rudiments of a comprehensive state water plan. The state-level process the plan prescribes has three specific benefits, which include: (1) mechanisms for conflict resolution, (2) increased water data collection, and (3) integration across both environmental and institutional domains.[73]

The state, therefore, has a role to play in setting the broad policy framework within which a series of nested, regional water plans can be developed. Georgia's recent state water planning process provides a useful model.[74] In Georgia, legislation resulted in a water plan adopted for the state, the creation of 11 regional councils, and a regional planning framework to be used by each council. Each regional plan is required to forecast needs for water supply, wastewater assimilative capacity, and stormwater management to uncover gaps between supply and demand, which are then addressed through the development of management practices. While considerable implementation issues will devolve to the local level, regional plans will also inform decisions taken by state agencies. In New York, a similar, nested process resulted in creation of plans for thirteen subregions, although they have not been updated for several years. And in spite of statutory language requiring the Water Resources Council to meet biannually and to revisit and reevaluate the strategy as needed,[75] it has not met in at least a decade. In its place, biannual meetings of stakeholder groups, including representatives from both DEC and DOH, are held.[76] This process can and should be expanded.

CONCLUSION

Fracking has brought the issue of water withdrawals to the fore, and the demands and stresses widespread gas drilling will likely place on the region's water resources are a reflection and an intensification of a pattern of existing pressures. Climate change, sprawling land development, and commercial water bottling are additional challenges that might impel changes in the management of New York's water resources.[77] As such, the prospect of hydraulic fracturing provides a fresh impetus—an opportunity—to consider developing more ecologically protective and comprehensive standards for water resource use throughout the region.

RECOMMENDED RESOURCES

Tom Annear et al., *Instream Flows for Riverine Resource Stewardship, Revised Edition*, Cheyenne, WY: Instream Flow Council, 2004.
    Authored by environmental managers from agencies across the United States and Canada, this accessible book-length treatment of the topic of instream flows provides an overview of the scientific underpinnings and historical evolution of approaches to stream management based on setting and maintaining ecological flows.

Lee Breckenridge, "Maintaining Instream Flow and Protecting Aquatic Habitat: Promise and Perils on the Path to Regulated Riparianism," *West Virginia Law Review* 106 (2004): 596–628.
    In this article, Breckenridge examines the development of regulated riparianism in Massachusetts. She indicates that there is much progress yet to be made if ecological goals are to be advanced as water law and regulation evolves. Measurable goals, biological targets, and administrative interpretation are some of the tools Breckenridge argues can be used to secure water flows for instream and off-stream users.

Dan Tarlock, "Water Law Reform in West Virginia: The Broader Context," *West Virginia Law Review* 106 (2004): 495–538.
    Tarlock situates this detailed discussion of the development of water law in a Marcellus Shale state, West Virginia, in relation to several broader issues, including technological and philosophical forces auguring water law reform; the difference between eastern and western approaches to water law; and new approaches to water management.

Joseph W. Dellapenna, ed., *The Regulated Riparian Model Water Code*. New York, NY: American Society of Civil Engineers, 1997. The American Society of Civil Engineers with this book outlined what is generally considered the standard replacement for common law riparian rights. The book contains a detailed statutory scheme and includes policy statements, regulatory goals, definitions, procedures for implementing a permit system, and adumbrates the terms, conditions, and authority of the state agency charged with its implementation.

Peter H. Gleick, "The Changing Water Paradigm: A Look at Twenty-first Century Water Resources Development." *International Water Resources Association* 25, no. 1 (March 2000): 127–138. Gleick here provides a concise, widely cited summary of several important shifts in water resource planning. Most broadly, Gleick finds that shifting environmental, financial, and social considerations are supplanting supply-side planning, such as the construction of large new water control projects, with demand management, efficiency gains, and reconsideration of diverse stakeholders.

NOTES

1. This is called "produced water." By contrast, "flowback"—a form of produced water—is generally produced in the first few weeks after the fracturing event (for this distinction, see Matthew E. Mantell, *Produced Water Reuse and Recycling: Challenges and Opportunities Across Major Shale Plays* (2011), *available at* http://www.epa.gov/hfstudy/09_Mantell_-_Reuse_508 .pdf). Estimates of the proportion of water recovered in either form are highly variable. EPA, Plan to Study the Potential Impacts of Hydraulic Fracturing on Drinking Water Resources (2011), *available at* http:// www2.epa.gov/sites/production/files/documents/hf_study_plan_110211 _final_508.pdf, at 42.

2. JOHN A. VEIL, FINAL REPORT: WATER MANAGEMENT TECHNOLOGIES USED BY MARCELLUS SHALE GAS PRODUCERS, ARGONE NATIONAL LABORATORY (July 2010), *available at* http://www.mde.state.md.us/programs/Land /mining/marcellus/Documents/WaterMgmtinMarcellusfull.pdf.

3. MATTEHEW E. MANTELL, CHESAPEAKE ENERGY, DEEP SHALE NATURAL GAS AND WATER USE, PART TWO: ABUNDANT, AFFORDABLE, AND STILL WATER EFFICIENT (2010), *available at* http://marcelluscoalition.org/wp-content

/uploads/2010/05/mmantell_GWPC_Water_Energy_Paper_Final.pdf; PowerPoint: John A. Veil, Society of Petroleum Engineers National Capitol Section, *Water Management Practices in the Marcellus Shale* (Oct. 21, 2010).

4. U.S. Department of Energy, Office of Fossil Energy, National Energy Technology Laboratory, Modern Shale Gas Development in the United States: A Primer, 2009, *available at* http://www.netl.doe.gov/technologies/oil-gas /publications/EPreports/Shale_Gas_Primter_2009.pdf, at 64.

5. David M. Kargbo, Ron G. Wilhelm & David J. Cambell, *Natural Gas Plays in the Marcellus Shale: Challenges and Potential Opportunities*, 44 ENVTL. SCI. & TECH. 5679, 5682 (2010).

6. William M. Kappel, *Hydrogeologist Reviews Marcellus Shale and Natural Gas Production in New York*, CLEAR WATERS, Winter 2010, at 11.

7. N.Y. STATE DEP'T OF ENVTL. CONSERVATION, DRAFT SUPPLEMENTAL GENERIC ENVIRONMENTAL IMPACT STATEMENT ON THE OIL, GAS, AND SOLUTION MINING REGULATORY PROGRAM (2009).

8. Re-fracturing, which can boost the rate of gas production by 50 to 100 percent, is used as the rate of gas produced declines from a completed, fraced well; it can frequently restore gas flow to within 75 to 100 percent of initial rates of production, "greatly extending the economic life of a well" (ICF INTERNATIONAL, TECHNICAL ASSISTANCE FOR THE DRAFT SUPPLEMENTAL GENERIC EIS: OIL, GAS AND SOLUTION MINING REGULATORY PROGRAM WELL PERMIT ISSUANCE FOR HORIZONTAL DRILLING AND HIGH-VOLUME HYDRAULIC FRACTURING TO DEVELOP THE MARCELLUS SHALE AND OTHER LOW PERMEABILITY GAS RESERVOIRS 18 (2009)).

9. As Engelder notes, "There's not a particular set of rules for what one does. It's quite an experimental industry . . . there are a number of companies that do it. . . . The companies have different skillsets and different levels of experience. So there's a natural complexity and an industry complexity." Quoted in Kate Mackenzie, *Terry Engelder On Shale Gas: The Good, the Bad, and the Decline Curves*, ENERGY SOURCE BLOG, (July 12, 2010, 1:44 PM), http://blogs.ft.com/energy-source/2010/07/12/terry-engelder-interview/.

10. MICHELE ROGERS, ET AL., PENNSYLVANIA STATE UNIVERSITY, COLLEGE OF AGRICULTURAL SCIENCES, MARCELLUS SHALE: WHAT LOCAL GOVERNMENT OFFICIALS NEED TO KNOW 12 (2008).

11. N.Y. STATE DEP'T OF ENVTL. CONSERVATION, RDSGEIS 6–10 (2011).

12. *See* URS CORP., WATER-RELATED ISSUES ASSOCIATED WITH GAS PRODUCTION IN THE MARCELLUS SHALE 5-18 (2011), *available at* http://www.nyserda .ny.gov/Publications/Research-and-Development-Technical-Reports /Other-Technical-Reports/-/media/Files/Publications/PPSER/NYSERDA /ng/urs-report-11-3-25.ashx.

13. Stephen Rassenfoss, *From Flowback to Fracturing: Water Recycling Grows in the Marcellus Shale*, J. PETROLEUM TECH., July 2011.

14. Mantell, *Produced Water Reuse and Recycling*, *supra* note 1.

15. URS Corp., Water-Related Issues, *supra* note 12, at 7-2, 7-3. "Disposal" is included as a factor because use of a low water quality source may increase recycling and/or treatment costs.

16. URS Corp., Water-Related Issues, *supra* note 12, at 7-3.

17. These estimates are from Jean-Philippe Nicot & Bridget R. Scanlon, *Water Use for Shale-Gas Production in Texas, U.S.*, 46 Envtl. Sci. & Tech. 3580, 3583 (2012).

18. James Richendorfer, *Water Use Profile of Natural Gas Industry in Susquehanna River Basin*, Clear Waters, Winter 2010, at 28.

19. *See* Mantell, Deep Shale Natural Gas and Water Use, *supra* note 3; J. Satterfield et al., Managing Water Resource Challenges in Select Natural Gas Shale Plays, paper presented at the Ground Water Protection Council Annual Forum, Cincinnati, OH, September 21–24, 2008.

20. Satterfield et al., Managing Water Resource Challenges, *supra* note 19.

21. Ecological because periodicity of flow is deemed a key factor in ecosystem maintenance; Social because different levels of flow confer different amounts of "utility." David M. Gillian, Instream Flow Protection: Seeking a Balance in Western Water Use 106–109 (1997).

22. N. LeRoy Poff et al., *The Natural Flow Regime: A Paradigm for River Conservation and Restoration*, 47 BioScience 769, 776 (1997).

23. J. Daniel Arthur, Mike Uretsky, & Preston Wilson, ALL Consulting, LLC, Water Resources and Use for Hydraulic Fracturing (2010).

24. Ian Urbina, *Regulation Lax as Gas Wells' Tainted Water Hits Rivers*, N.Y. Times, Feb. 26, 2011, *available at* http://www.nytimes.com/2011/02/27/us/27gas.html?pagewanted=all.

25. Tim Puko, *Silty, Salty Monongahela River at Risk from Pollutants*, Pittsburgh Trib-Rev., Aug. 24, 2010, *available at* http://triblive.com/x/pittsburghtrib/news/s_696233.html#axzz2dFDFVQQ4.

26. Don Hopey, *Consol to Pay $6 Million for Dunkard Creek Fish Kill*, Pittsburgh Post-Gazette, Mar. 14, 2011, *available at* http://www.post-gazette.com/pg/11073/1131947-100.stm. According to local activist and geologist Lisa Hollingsworth-Segedy, Associate Director of the River Restoration Program at the conservation organization American Rivers, "Drillers are going to the headwaters, especially during low-flow periods." Anecdotal evidence also suggests that flows in the creek have been lower than normal over the past year. Author's Discussion with Lisa Hollingsworth-Segedy, Associate Director, American Rivers (Apr. 10, 2010). *See also* Don Hopey, *Consol to Pay $6 Million*.

27. Richendorfer, *Water Use Profile*, *supra* note 18, at 28.

28. I.G. Jowett, *Instream Flow Methods: A Comparison of Approaches*, 13 Regulated Rivers: Research & Management 115 (1997). NYSDEC, in the 2009 dSGEIS, noted the possibility of a host of specific cumulative impacts from water withdrawals: "Stream flow and groundwater depletion; loss of aquifer storage capacity; water quality degradation; fish and aquatic organism

impacts; [loss of] significant habitats; endangered, rare or threatened species impacts; existing water users and reliability of their supplies; [and] underground infrastructure." N.Y. State Dep't of Envtl. Conservation, dSGEIS, at 6–7 to 6–8 (2009). For criticism of NYSDEC's treatment, see City of New York, "New York City Comments on: Draft Supplemental Generic Environmental Impact Statement (dSGEIS) on the Oil, Gas and Solution Mining Regulatory Program–Well Permit Issuance for Horizontal Drilling and High-Volume Hydraulic Fracturing to Develop the Marcellus Shale and Other Low-Permeability Gas Reservoirs at 12–13 (Dec. 22, 2009), *available at* http://www.nyc.gov /html/dep/pdf/natural_gas_drilling/nycdep_comments_final_12-22-09.pdf.

29. This section relies heavily on an excellent undated summary of the legal issues raised by water withdrawals in Marcellus Shale development written by former PADEP attorney R. Timothy Weston. R. Timothy Weston, K&L Gates, Development of the Marcellus Shale—Water Resource Challenges (2008), *available at* http://www.wvsoro.org/resources/marcellus/Weston.pdf.

30. *Id.* at 5–6.

31. *Id.* at 5.

32. Joseph Dellapenna, *Adapting Riparian Rights to the Twenty-First Century*, 106 W. Va. L. Rev. 539, 586 (2004).

33. The SRBC was formed by an act of Congress in 1972 as an agreement between the States of Maryland and New York, the Commonwealth of Pennsylvania, and the United States Government to "develop and effectuate plans, policies, and projects relating to the water resources of the basin. *See* Susquehanna River Basin Comm'n, Susquehanna River Basin Compact (1972), *available at* http://www.srbc.net/about/srbc_compact.pdf. The DRBC was created by concurrent legislation in Delaware, New Jersey, Pennsylvania, New York, and the United States government signed in 1961. *See About DRBC*, Del. River Basin Comm'n, http://www.state.nj.us /drbc/about/ (last updated July 3, 2013).

34. SRBC is highlighted here because it currently permits gas drilling in the Marcellus Shale and has the most settled regulations governing it.

35. Richendorfer, *Water Use Profile, supra* note 18, at 28.

36. Susquehanna River Basin Comm'n, Accommodating a New Straw in the Water: Extracting Natural Gas from the Marcellus Shale in the Susquehanna River Basin (Feb. 2009), on file with author.

37. Consumptive uses are defined as water considered lost to or removed from the basin, either through extra-basin transfer, or as in the case of hydraulic fracturing, through degradation of quality.

38. Weston, Development of the Marcellus Shale, *supra* note 29, at 16; Susquehanna River Basin Comm'n, Consumptive Use Mitigation Plan (2008).

39. Susquehanna River Basin Comm'n, Guidelines for Using and Determining Passby Flows and Conservation Releases for Surface-Water and

GROUND-WATER WITHDRAWAL APPROVALS (2002), *available at* http://www
.srbc.net/sitemap/Using&DeterminingPassbyFlows.htm. There are several
exceptions to the SRBC's use of passby flow requirements, including "if
the surface-water withdrawal . . . impact is minimal in comparison to the
natural or continuously augmented flow," and in areas "where a passby flow
has historically not been maintained"; withdrawals from impoundments are
also regulated differently.

40. *See* Plate 2, "Hydrologic Regions," THOMAS L. DENSLINGER ET AL., SUSQUE-
HANNA RIVER BASIN COMM'N, INSTREAM FLOW STUDIES: PENNSYLVANIA
AND MARYLAND (1998), *available at* http://www.fort.usgs.gov/Products
/Publications/3998/3998.pdf.

41. SRBC defines Q7-10 as "the lowest average 7-day flow expected to occur
at a 1-in-10-year frequency." SUSQUEHANNA RIVER BASIN COMM'N, CON-
SUMPTIVE USE MITIGATION PLAN, *supra* note 38.

42. For example, low streamflow levels triggered the suspension of sixty-four
withdrawals on July 16, 2012 pursuant to passby-flow standards. This
occurred after SRBC suspended seventeen withdrawals for two weeks
during April of the same year, forcing at least one company to partially
suspend drilling operations (http://www.reuters.com/article/2012/04/30
/talisman-pa-drought-idUSL1E8FUBP820120430).

43. WESTON, DEVELOPMENT OF THE MARCELLUS SHALE, *supra* note 29, at 10.

44. *See* N.Y. COMP. CODES R. & REGS. tit. 6, § 703.2.

45. N.Y. ENVTL. CONSERV. LAW § 15-3301. *See also* J. DANIEL ARTHUR, MIKE
URETSKY, & PRESTON WILSON, ALL CONSULTING, LLC, WATER RESOURCES
AND USE FOR HYDRAULIC FRACTURING 14–15 (2010), *available at* http://www
.all-llc.com/publicdownloads/WaterResourcePaperALLConsulting.pdf.

46. *Part 601: Water Withdrawal Permitting, Reporting and Registration (Exclusive
of Long Island Wells Regulated under Part 602)*, N.Y. DEP'T OF ENVTL. CON-
SERVATION, http://www.dec.ny.gov/regs/4445.html (last visited Sept. 23,
2013).

47. WESTON, DEVELOPMENT OF THE MARCELLUS SHALE, *supra* note 29, at
17–18. This interstate Compact implements, in the United States, the
Great Lakes-St. Lawrence River Basin Sustainable Water Resources Agreement, to which the provinces of Ontario and Quebec are also parties.

48. N.Y. STATE DEP'T OF ENVTL. CONSERVATION, RDSGEIS 7-22 (2011).

49. The Clean Streams Law, 35 PA. CONS. STAT. § 691.1 (1937).

50. The Water Resources Planning Act, 27 PA. CONS. STAT. § 3118(b) (2002).

51. Oil and Gas, 58 PA. CONS. STAT. §§ 2301-3504 (2012).

52. WESTON, DEVELOPMENT OF THE MARCELLUS SHALE, *supra* note 29, at 11–12.

53. PA. STATE UNIV., WATER'S JOURNEY THROUGH THE SHALE GAS DRILLING
AND PRODUCTION PROCESSES IN THE MID-ATLANTIC REGION (2012), *avail-
able at* http://pubs.cas.psu.edu/freepubs/pdfs/ee0023.pdf.cpedler, *Department
Of Environmental Protection Admits It Has No Authority To Permit Water
Withdrawals For Marcellus Shale Gas Drilling In Western Pennsylvania*,

ALLEGHENY FOREST WATCH (Nov. 23, 2010), http://alleghenydefenseproject
.wordpress.com/.

54. PA. DEP'T OF ENVTL. PROT., STATE WATER PLAN PRINCIPLES (2009), *available
at* http://www.elibrary.dep.state.pa.us/dsweb/Get/Document-76835/3010
-BK-DEP4222.pdf.

55. Natural Gas Horizontal Well Control Act, W. VA. CODE § 22-6A (2011).

56. *Id.*

57. Water Resources Protection and Management Act, W. VA. CODE § 22-26
(2008).

58. J. DANIEL ARTHUR, MIKE URETSKY & PRESTON WILSON, ALL CONSULT-
ING, LLC, WATER RESOURCES AND USE FOR HYDRAULIC FRACTURING 15
(2010); David M. Flannery, Blair D. Gardner & Jeffry R. Vining, *The Water
Resources Protection Act and Its Impact on West Virginia Water Law*, 107 W.
VA. L. REV. 749 (2005).

59. *See* ARTHUR ET AL., WATER RESOURCES AND USE FOR HYDRAULIC FRACTUR-
ING, *supra* note 58, at 15. For industry perspectives, see MANTELL, DEEP
SHALE NATURAL GAS AND WATER USE, *supra* note 3; and VEIL, WATER
MANAGEMENT PRACTICES, *supra* note 2. For various perspectives of regula-
tors, see SUSQUEHANNA RIVER BASIN COMM'N, ACCOMMODATING A NEW
STRAW IN THE WATER, *supra* note 36; and NYSDEX, dSGEIS, *supra* note 7.

60. SUSQUEHANNA RIVER BASIN COMM'N, ACCOMMODATING A NEW STRAW IN
THE WATER, *supra* note 36.

61. CHESAPEAKE ENERGY, WATER USE IN MARCELLUS DEEP SHALE GAS EXPLORA-
TION FACT SHEET (2012), *available at* http://www.chk.com/media/educational
-library/fact-sheets/marcellus/marcellus_water_use_fact_sheet.pdf.

62. Nicot, *Water Use for Shale-Gas Production*, *supra* note 17, at 3584.

63. The environmental perspective is set out in ENVTL. ADVOCATES OF N.Y.,
GREEN MEMOS TO THE GOVERNOR AND THE STATE LEGISLATURE: ADVICE
FROM NEW YORK STATE'S ENVIRONMENTAL ORGANIZATIONS, (2011), *avail-
able at* http://sallan.org/pdf-docs/NYGreenMemo_Jan11.pdf. *See* CITY OF
N.Y., NEW YORK CITY COMMENTS, *supra* note 28; EPA, dSGEIS COMMENTS
(Dec. 30, 2009), *available at* http://www.epa.gov/region2/spmm/pdf/Marcellus
_dSGEIS_Comment_Letter_plus_Enclosure.pdf (for examples of criticism
by other governmental agencies).

64. Nicot, *Water Use for Shale-Gas Production*, *supra* note 17, at 3583, 3585.

65. Susan J. Riha & Brian G. Rahm, *Framework for Assessing Water Resource
Impacts from Shale Gas Drilling*, CLEAR WATERS, Winter 2010, 16–19.

66. *Id.* at 16.

67. *ENB—Statewide Notices 11/21/2012*, N.Y. DEP'T OF ENVTL. PROT., http://
www.dec.ny.gov/enb/20121121_not0.html (last visited Dec. 2, 2012).

68. PA. DEP'T OF ENVTL. PROT., STATE WATER PLAN PRINCIPLES, *supra* note 54,
at 32.

69. Richard Ausness, *Water Rights Legislation in the East: A Program for Reform*,
24 WM. & MARY L. REV. 547, 553 (1983).

70. *Id.* at 589.
71. *See* Pa. Dep't of Envtl. Prot., State Water Plan Principles, *supra* note 54, at 37–39 (*Water Withdrawal and Use Management and Recommendations* section); *See also* Robert E. Beck, *The Regulated Riparian Model Water Code: Blueprint for Twenty First Century Water Management*, 25 Wm. & Mary Envtl. L. & Policy Rev. 113 (2000).
72. A bill outlining a proposed permitting system in New York State was recently passed in New York State. The NYSDEC is now charged with permitting entities capable of withdrawing 100,000 GPD or more. Industrial uses would now fall under the purview of state-level withdraw regulation, and those entities withdrawing less than 100,000—like small municipal water systems—would no longer be subject to permitting, given the bill's stated focus on "significant withdraws." A major weakness of this proposed legislation is the focus on rates of withdraws without addressing the impacts of those withdrawals on the water bodies from which they will be taken. Indeed, Breckenridge cites "the ongoing practical and bureaucratic commitment to ongoing withdrawals" and a lack of definition of instream flow needs as key factors in the failure of the Massachusetts system (612). Lee Beckenridge, *Maintaining Instream Flow and Protecting Aquatic Habitat: Promise and Perils on the Path to Regulated Riparianism*, 106 W. Va. L. Rev. 596, 612 (2004). Yet if placed into the context of water planning and premised in part on the variability of stream hydrology, the model code could lay the groundwork for a more ecologically protective regulatory framework.
73. Adam Yagelski, Toward a State Water Plan in New York (Dec. 2, 2011) (unpublished manuscript) (on file with author).
74. *See* Jeffrey D. Mullen, *Statewide Water Planning: The Georgia Experience*, 43 J. Agric. & Applied Econ. 357, 358 (2011).
75. N.Y. Envtl. Conserv. Law § 15-2913.
76. According to Lloyd Wilson, Ph. D., of the Bureau of Water Supply Protection, New York State Department of Health: "The bottom line is the Water resources management strategy is defunct and has been for many years. DEC does have a stakeholder group called the Water Management Advisory Council (WMAC). This groups has representatives from business, government (including county planners), non profits. . . . It is held twice a year and DEC usually has a series of presentations on 'new' issues with protecting our water resources." Author's Communication with Lloyd Wilson, N.Y. Bureau of Water Supply Prot. (Oct. 17, 2011).
77. Trout Unlimited, Tapped Out: New York's Water Woes, *available at* http://www.catskillstreams.org/pdfs/Tappedoutny.pdf (last visited May 10, 2011).

PART 3

Nongovernmental, Governmental, Community, and Industry Perspectives: Case Studies

10

Fractured
Hydraulic Fracturing and the
Environmental Response in Michigan

Lisa Wozniak, Drew YoungDyke, and Jacque Rose

INTRODUCTION

The national and state-level attention focused on hydraulic fracturing in the last two years has made it a priority issue among environmental organizations, but the responses to it have been varied and contentious. Some organizations have pushed for a moratorium on hydraulic fracturing until its effects can be further studied, some have called for an outright ban, and still others have sought to ensure that laws are put in place that are as protective as possible in terms of regulating water quality, water quantity, waste disposal, air emissions, and the protection of human health. Nonprofit organizations educate the public about the specifics of environmental issues and focus public sentiment into an organized voice to advocate for environmental policies. Given the lack of regulatory infrastructure in place at the federal level, states across the nation are beginning to address the expansion of natural gas drilling, with the not-for-profit environmental community playing a large role in communication, advocacy, and the establishment of sound policy solutions.

Michigan has a long history of hydraulic fracturing, especially with relatively shallow and vertical wells, but the attention thrust on the process by the *Gasland* movie[1] and the exploration of deeper shale formations in northern Michigan has brought it to the forefront of state environmental issues. Environmental organizations are playing an increasingly important role in shaping the debate and influencing state policies and public perception.

In the absence of comprehensive federal hydraulic fracturing legislation, most hydraulic fracturing regulation is promulgated and enforced at the state level. The Michigan League of Conservation Voters (Michigan LCV), a statewide environmental advocacy and political organization founded in 1999, has been on the forefront of this issue as it has found increasing prominence in the legislative and public debate. While sharing a name with the national League of Conservation Voters as well as a dedication to education, advocacy, accountability and elections, Michigan LCV (and counter-parts across the country) focuses primarily on state-level legislation and regulation, where hydraulic fracturing policy has, thus far, been decided.

State LCV's are uniquely suited to play a lead role in this increasingly high-profile hydraulic fracturing debate because, like other nonprofit groups, they have complex organizational structures which guide funding and methods of advocacy. Given the construct of LCV institutions, which include 501(c)(3), 501(c)(4), and 527/political action committees (PACs), they are funded by a variety of different means. Section 501(c)(3) organizations are deemed charitable entities, are allowed unlimited provision of educational opportunities but limited activity influencing legislation, and are eligible to receive tax deductable donations. Section 501(c)(4), organizations are social welfare entities and have the opportunity to engage in unlimited lobbying without jeopardizing their tax-exempt status; however they are not able to receive tax-deductible donations. 527 organizations are U.S. tax-exempt entities organized under Section 527 of the U.S. Internal Revenue Code, and are typically created to influence the election or defeat of candidates running for office at the federal, state, or local level. Political action committees (including "super PACs") registered at the federal or state level are one type of 527 organization. Foundations and individual donors comprise the bulk of support for the 501(c)(3) organizations, while individual donors provide much of the support to the 501(c)(4)/527/PACs.

In the midst of increasing attention and concern about hydraulic fracturing, Michigan LCV—along with the National Wildlife

Federation, the Tip of the Mitt Watershed Council, the Michigan Environmental Council, the Michigan chapter of Trout Unlimited, and the Anglers of the AuSable—understanding the current political climate in Lansing, has chosen to advocate for a pragmatic approach designed to ensure that any hydraulic fracturing done in Michigan is done as safely as possible. With an eye specifically to water, these groups have encouraged regulation of water use, chemical disclosure, and waste water disposal.

In November 2012, Michigan LCV's 501(c)(3) sister organization—the Michigan LCV Education Fund—organized over 30 local, statewide, and regional environmental and conservation groups to collectively agree upon a set of issue areas on which to focus during the 2013–2014 legislative session. The groups participating in this effort, known as Great Michigan,[2] chose the following three priority issue areas: (1) Defense of Michigan's Public Lands, (2) Expansion of Energy Efficiency and Promotion of Renewable Energy (as found in Public Act 295), and (3) Chemical Disclosure, Waste Water Disposal and Water Withdrawal Transparency in Hydraulic Fracturing. Next steps in this effort include: (1) the coordination of legislative strategy and tactics, including message development and communication, and (2) increased usage of the Great Michigan web portal to educate and engage voters, legislators, opinion leaders, media, and donors about the importance and the progress toward this "common agenda."

As such, organizations across the state will speak with one voice to the legislature about the importance of addressing the environmental threats associated with hydraulic fracturing and more fully engage the membership of the organizations to advocate for a stronger regulatory response.

On March 20, 2013, board members, staff, and representative members of over 15 organizations convened in Lansing for a full day of meetings with legislators. To date, two pieces of legislation have been introduced this session to address hydraulic fracturing in Michigan, including: (1) House Bill 4061, which would require that hydraulic fracturing companies publicly disclose all chemicals and additives contained in their hydraulic fracturing fluid and require the companies to provide an evaluation of whether there are alternative hydraulic fracturing treatments available that pose less potential risk to public health, and (2) House Bill 4070, which would require that hydraulic fracturing operations submit to Michigan's Water Withdrawal Assessment Tool and would require disclosure of chemicals contained within the hydraulic fracturing fluid 24 hours prior to drilling beginning. In addition, HB 4122 was introduced, which would regulate noise pollution from oil and gas operations in residential areas.

HISTORY OF HYDRAULIC FRACTURING IN MICHIGAN

More than 12,000 wells have been hydraulically fractured in Michigan, most of them vertical. Hydraulic fracturing became widely used in Michigan during the 1980s and 1990s in the Antrim Shale formation of the northern Lower Peninsula. Antrim Shale wells are typically vertical wells productive between 1,200 and 2,000 feet deep.[3] Vertical wells have created little controversy in comparison to horizontal wells, mainly because they utilize fewer water resources and create less wastewater and truck traffic.

In 2010, the Canadian corporation Encana Oil & Gas (USA), Inc. hydraulically fractured a test well in the Collingwood Shale known as the Pioneer well, which is over 10,000 feet deep.[4] This Collingwood Shale test well sparked a record $178 million in leases at the May 2010 state mineral rights auction. Revenues from the biannual state lease auctions go into the Michigan Natural Resources Trust Fund. This fund, which was created in 1976 and protected in Michigan's Constitution in 1984 to purchase public outdoor recreation land, obtains all its proceeds from the sale of public oil and gas rights. Per the statute, once the Natural Resources Trust Fund reaches its predetermined $500 million cap, subsequent revenues must go into the State Parks Endowment Fund until that fund reaches its own $800 million cap.

The existence of these trust funds means that hydraulically fractured oil and gas wells have the potential to create significant public benefit for the state of Michigan, in addition to promoting economic development in general. However, the deeper horizontal wells have raised substantial concerns for Michigan—both for Michigan citizens in the northern portion of the state and environmental groups—because they require significantly more hydraulic fracturing fluid (water plus chemicals) and, thus, significantly greater water withdrawals, chemical inputs, and waste water disposal options. They also result in larger quantities of flowback water. The Pioneer horizontal test well used approximately 5.5 million gallons of hydraulic fracturing fluid, for example, as compared to 50,000 gallons utilized in a typical Antrim Shale vertical well. After the drilling of the first few horizontal wells, leasing of mineral rights took off in Michigan, but the plummeting price of gas has resulted in little complete drilling to date.

ENVIRONMENTAL ISSUES AND REGULATIONS

Michigan is literally defined by water—its name means "Great Lake" in native Anishinaabemowin—and it is enveloped by the Great Lakes, which form the state boundaries. Taken together, the Great Lakes represent almost 20 percent of the Earth's fresh surface water. In addition, Michigan is home to hundreds of inland lakes, rivers, and streams. So it should be no surprise that water is the biggest area of concern for the environmental and conservation communities with regard to increased exploration for natural gas. According to the Michigan Department of Environmental Quality (MDEQ), there has been no negative environmental damage from vertical hydraulic fracturing in Michigan.[5]

However, this claim applies to the discrete process of vertical hydraulic fracturing itself, not to the impacts of oil and gas drilling defined more broadly. While industry professionals strategically and consistently define hydraulic fracturing to mean only the hydraulic fracturing step in well drilling, most environmental advocates— including Michigan LCV—consider the expanded drilling activity required to facilitate hydraulic fracturing to be part of the process, as the one cannot exist absent the others.

There are three main areas where water quality and quantity could be detrimentally impacted in Michigan by horizontal hydraulic fracturing in the absence of improved and strengthened regulations.

1. *Water quantity can be detrimentally depleted when water is withdrawn for use in the hydraulic fracturing fluid.* If water is withdrawn from a sensitive area at the wrong time or under the wrong conditions—such as during a drought—then the flow of a stream or river could be reduced with downstream impacts to fish habitat, for example. Prior to 2011, hydraulic fracturing was exempt from Michigan's Water Withdrawal statute, which prescribes use of a computer modeling tool to predict withdrawal impacts on water resources. In May 2011, at the urging of environmental and conservation groups (including Michigan LCV), the MDEQ issued an order to require use of the Water Withdrawal Assessment

Tool (WWAT) when evaluating high-volume fracturing permits, which applies to withdrawals that average 100,000 cumulative gallons over a thirty-day period, or a fracturing operation that expects to use 100,000 gallons of hydraulic fracturing fluid.[6] The Water Withdrawal statute exempts use of the WWAT for withdrawals related to activity undertaken under Part 615 (DEQ Oil and Gas regulations), but with this 2011 supervisory order within the MDEQ, that exemption no longer stands.

2. *Disposal of the flowback is another concern, since flowback can contain toxic chemicals and radioactivity.* Anywhere from 30 to 70 percent of the fluid used to fracture a well remains in the earth, while the remaining 30 to 70 percent (flowback) is returned to the surface. Michigan requires that flowback be contained in steel tanks until it can be injected into deep Class II injection wells. This requirement is a means to protect Michigan's water resources from flowback contamination, but necessarily removes the withdrawn water permanently from the water cycle. Michigan companies cannot currently recycle flowback due to this requirement, but as it becomes a more established practice in other states, it may become an area that advocates may push to be amended.

3. *Water quality can be affected by the escape of gas from the well bore into the water table.* This is what is alleged to have happened in western states like Colorado and Wyoming and in Dimock, Pennsylvania. Michigan, however, has casing and testing requirements for cementing the external casing to the well bore and including a secondary casing extending a minimum of 100 feet below the water table. This requirement comes from regulations developed for the historically more common vertical wells, and it remains to be seen whether it is sufficient to protect groundwater from contamination from high-volume horizontal wells.[7]

In addition, there are six other related issues of high concern to the Michigan environmental and conservation community:

1. The Chemical Mixture Used In Hydraulic Fracturing Is a Source of Concern. Hydraulic fracturing fluid can contain about 0.5 percent chemical additives by volume. For the deeper horizontal Collingwood wells, that can mean—using the Pioneer test well as an example—that 27,500 gallons of chemicals are being trucked, stored, handled, and injected into each well. The exact recipe for each well is often a trade secret and is proprietary to the service companies that provide the mixture. As it stands, hydraulic fracturing fluid is exempted from some of the underground injection control provisions of the federal Safe Drinking Water Act.[8] Under the Act, the EPA regulates underground injection of chemicals, but a 2005 revision commonly called "The Halliburton Loophole"—named for the Halliburton Corporation, the nation's largest supplier of hydraulic fracturing fluid—specifically exempts chemicals used for hydraulic fracturing, unless they contain diesel. The EPA revised its permitting guidelines for hydraulic fracturing fluid containing diesel in 2012.[9] This means that, unless the fluid contains diesel, an EPA permit is not required to inject fracturing fluid into a well for completion, and regulation falls to the state. At this point in Michigan, the MDEQ requires only posthydraulic fracturing disclosure of chemicals in quantities high enough to require Material Safety Data Sheets.[10]

2. Surface Contamination. From the surface, spillage of the additives used during the mixing of the fracturing fluid, spillage from a faulty flowback preventer, and/or spillage of collected flowback when transferring it to containers or to trucking tanks could result in seepage of fracturing fluid and/or natural gas into the ground, thus potentially contaminating groundwater. Such contamination could also occur due to leakage from surface pipelines transferring brine, flowback water, or natural gas from the well. At this time, Michigan does not have regulations in place requiring that the hydraulic fracturing pad be entirely fitted with a liner. In 2012, the neighboring Great Lakes state of Pennsylvania adopted regulations requiring such linings to prevent spills.[11] This was at least partially in response to three isolated incidents on one Cabot Oil & Gas well pad in Dimock, Pennsylvania, in 2009. These spills resulted in seepage to a nearby creek where fish kill was confirmed by the Pennsylvania Department of Environmental Protection.

Leakage from a drilling pit, sometimes called the mud pit, can also occur. The drilling pit contains the water needed to cool the drilling apparatus, but also contains the cuttings that come up to the surface on the drill from all of the formations being drilled through. Such cuttings can contain heavy metals, arsenic, and may also contain normally occurring radioactive material (NORM). Current Michigan regulation provides for the depth of the drilling pit to be located at least four vertical feet above the uppermost groundwater level and lined with a 20 mil virgin polyvinyl chloride liner or equivalent. The pit contents are required to be tested for benzene, ethylbenzene, toluene, and xylene, unless the well is drilled with water from a source approved by the Supervisor of Wells and no liquid hydrocarbons are encountered.[12]

Contamination can occur if the liner is compromised or if there is overflow from the pit during operation or storm conditions. Prescribed closure of the pit is to harden the contents, fold the pit liner corners over it, cover with another 20 mil liner and bury not less than four feet below the original ground grade level.[13] These regulations, however, appear to be adjusted arbitrarily, as can be seen in the permit application for the Davids Acre well in Ogemaw County, Michigan, where the mud pit specifications state that the pit is to be 15 feet deep and the highest ground water level is 12 feet.[14] While the pad was elevated, it was not elevated the seven feet that would be required to be in compliance with the DEQ regulation.

3. Aquifer Contamination. Groundwater aquifer contamination can occur as a result of improperly constructed wells, including faulty casing or improper seals between the casing and cement or the cement and bedrock. Gas channeling may also occur as a result of naturally occurring shallow gas or from installing a long string of surface casing that would allow migration of shallow gas along the casing and into the potable water supply.[15]

Contamination can also occur at the coupling of pipe stringers. In Michigan, the Lucas well in Kalkaska County is currently the subject of a multiparty circuit court lawsuit arising from alleged leaking "collar" pipe connections throughout the well. This is a horizontal directional well permitted for utilizing hydraulic fracturing. It has been temporarily abandoned due to these problems.[16]

An additional area of concern is the migration of fracturing fluid via existing faults and fractures already present in rock formations, either as a result of normal fault lines, glacial rock formation, or as a result of pressure exerted from other fractured gas wells or waste disposal wells in proximity.

The water wells constructed at the well site are also a cause for concern and a source of possible aquifer contamination. In Michigan, these wells are exempt from the jurisdiction of the local health department. The Office of Oil, Gas, and Minerals (OOGM) of the Department of Environmental Quality has jurisdiction under its Rule 324.403.[17] While it is required under the rule that the temporary water wells be constructed and grouted in accordance with MCL 333.12701, because the local health department does not issue the permit, these wells are not inspected by health department officials and may not be inspected by OOGM staff.

The water well constructed at the David's Acres well site in Ogemaw County, Michigan is a case in point. It was not constructed, grouted, or plugged in accordance with MCL 333.12701.[18] This water well traversed bedrock to access a sandstone aquifer. Local health department rules require that wells traversing bedrock be grouted completely through the bedrock to insure that a lower sandstone source of water is not contaminated with bedrock constituents, which can contain high levels of chlorides and other undesirable elements. The grouting in this well stopped 20 feet short of the lower margin of bedrock, and the borehole was open from that point through to the sandstone aquifer below. In this case, the health department requested the water well records and, after review, requested the DEQ to drill out this water well completely and cement it from the bottom of the well to the surface. Absent a vigilant local health department officer, however, this would have gone unaddressed.[19]

4. Water Withdrawal Assessment Tool (WWAT). MCL 324.72705 requires that large quantity water withdrawals (100,000 gallons per day average in any consecutive thirty-day period) utilize the water withdrawal assessment tool to determine adverse impact.[20] As noted previously, large quantity water withdrawals for oil or gas wells are exempt from Michigan's water withdrawal statute. While the supervisor's order reversed this exemption and persons applying for a permit to extract gas/oil must now utilize the WWAT, this is a discretionary order and does not serve to amend the statute (MCL 324.32727).[21] Moreover, the supervisor may override the findings of the tool and permit the well regardless of adverse impact indicated by the tool. These problems in the application of the tool notwithstanding, the use of the WWAT to gauge water withdrawal impact is itself insufficient and ultimately of little real value to gauge adverse impact of large water withdrawals for hydraulic fracturing for these reasons:

a. The Water Withdrawal program only evaluates one thing—the probable effect on temperature and flowrate of streams or rivers and whether it will change sufficiently to impact the fish that live there to varying degrees, depending upon the nature of the water system where the withdrawal is proposed.[22]

b. The program creates predictions for the entire State based on extrapolated data derived from 148 actual monitoring stations in the State. The predictions are not checked for accuracy.

c. There is no ongoing or consistent monitoring to determine if the tool is accurate as to the assessed impact on a stream or the fish that live there.

d. Cumulative effect of existing large quantity water withdrawals for public wells, irrigation, or other mining activities is not considered or calculated.

e. The individual characteristics of the groundwater aquifer from which the water will be withdrawn is not a factor in the program.

f. Any existing drought conditions are not considered.

5. Alteration of Land Use. An often over-looked impact of hydraulic fracturing is the alteration of land use. The infrastructure required for oil and gas extraction includes a network of pipelines, central processing facilities, access roads, and the land required for the actual well sites. Depending on where development is placed, it can alter the character of the landscape considerably, especially if it is near or in undeveloped wildlife habitat.

6. Increase in Industrial Infrastructure. Hydraulic fracturing can increase the industrial infrastructure in a region because it allows for more intensive development of the gas resource. Horizontal fracturing actually has a smaller footprint than conventional drilling—per volume of gas extracted—with respect to the network of wells and access roads required, because a single well pad can support multiple wells and thereby allow extraction of gas from a much larger area. Well pad site spacing has grown from one well pad every forty acres to one well pad every eighty acres for Antrim shale wells. One well pad every 640 acres has been proposed for deep Collingwood wells, but not yet adopted. In some cases, the industry has applied for exemption from spacing regulations to allow larger spacing units as drilling technology allows increasingly long laterals.[23] The tradeoff is that each deep-shale horizontal well has a larger individual footprint than a conventional well.[24] Multiple wells are drilled from any given pad site, a larger total number of wells are drilled and a greater total linear feet of pipe laid, thereby necessitating greater numbers of trucks, staging and storage areas for pipes, chemicals, and equipment in areas where drilling is taking place. Environmental concerns for air and water are exacerbated in the multi-well pad scenario: all of the water to complete all of the wells is taken from one site and methane and diesel emissions are concentrated.

POLITICAL CLIMATE AND ADVOCACY

Conservation, from a historical perspective, has been a bipartisan issue, both at the state and federal levels. Most of our nation's hallmark environmental laws were put in place with strong bipartisan support and many under the leadership of republican presidents, most notably under President Nixon. Over the past twenty years, however, this bipartisan support has eroded, with environment and conservation often serving as a favorite battleground for intensely partisan standoffs. This has certainly been the case in Michigan as we look at the years since the strong environmental stewardship of Governor William Milliken (R).

Today, while there are several generally proconservation republicans in the Michigan legislature, the overall trend in the republican-controlled House and Senate has been to roll back environmental regulations rather than to strengthen them.[25] Sometimes this is done on the pretense of "economic development," other times for the purpose of "reducing regulations." While it is not a difficult case to make that some regulations are indeed antiquated, the majority serve vital purposes. Most recently, when reducing regulations for reduction's sake arose in 2012, Governor Snyder (R) did veto a bill that would have prevented MDEQ and the Michigan Department of Natural Resource (MDNR) from promulgating stronger environmental rules than their federal counterparts. Unfortunately, the governor has been reluctant to veto other regulatory roll back bills that have found their way to his desk. This all leads to the fact that legislative initiatives to further regulate hydraulic fracturing—and certainly to limit it in any way—will likely face significant obstacles.

In spring 2012, the House Subcommittee on Natural Gas released a report, which recommended "lease it or lose it" provisions for state-owned mineral rights and also included recommendations to allow drilling on current nondevelopment and protected areas. While no legislation has been introduced in 2013 to implement the recommendations, the author, Aric Nesbitt, won reelection in 2012 and returned to the House Committee on Energy and Technology as the new chairman.[26] However, the governor's proposal for storage of natural gas, articulated prominently in his November 2012 Energy and Environment address, may serve as a key tenet of this philosophy in regard to the state's resources on public lands.

In early 2012, hearing growing concern from citizens across the state, democrats in the state house sponsored a package of bills that would have codified the Water Withdrawal Assessment Tool and chemical disclosure requirements. The bills also included a moratorium on high-volume hydraulic fracturing until the completion of an EPA report studying its impacts, which is due in 2014. The bill package did not move, however, given the partisan sponsorship of the package and make-up of the legislature in the 2011–2012 session.

Michigan LCV, along with sister organizations like it in other states, plays a critical role in the passage of strong laws to protect our air, land, and water. Unlike other not-for-profit organizations, Michigan LCV can do more than simply educate and advocate; it can also hold elected officials accountable for their votes—via a *Legislative Scorecard*—and get directly involved in the politics of the state legislature, working to elect (or defeat) candidates for office. Especially in the wake of the *Citizens United* Supreme Court decision that enabled increased and more varied spending in elections, an organization that can operate with a variety of tools is essential. As oil and gas companies wield their clout via political contributions and candidate support so does the growing voice of the state's natural resources via the Michigan League of Conservation Voters.

As such, Michigan LCV plays an important role in facilitating bipartisan dialogue on issues like hydraulic fracturing that have evolved into highly partisan debates. In the face of the antiregulatory political climate in Michigan, Michigan LCV, in partnership with a plethora of smart, purely 501(c)(3) organizations, initiated a legislative information session in 2012 on hydraulic fracturing for the purpose educating and engaging state decision-makers, many of whom know little about the issue. This coalition took a pragmatic approach to the issue by avoiding calls for a ban or moratorium, which were politically untenable, and utilizing various individuals or communities already trusted by particularly wary legislators. This allowed for new in-roads to be made into an otherwise staunchly anti-environment legislature.

As we move into 2013–2014 after playing a significant role in electing a number of new faces to the state House of Representatives,

Michigan LCV is working with legislators to find bipartisan agreement on three key and necessary improvements to existing state law. The three improvements which are believed to be reasonable to both sides of the aisle are chemical disclosure, waste water disposal, and water withdrawal transparency in hydraulic fracturing.

As in 2012, Michigan LCV will also continue work outside the legislature to educate and engage the public. As only one example, over the past twelve months Michigan LCV gave presentations to organizations, such as the Detroit Chapter of NAACP, and participated in public forums organized by the Oakland County Commission and the League of Women Voters. Other organizations are engaged in complementary efforts. For example, a coalition called For the Love of Water (FLOW) compiled a toolkit for communities to use to regulate hydraulic fracturing on a local—rather than state—level, including model ordinances for adoption at the municipal level.

In 2011, pressure from Michigan LCV and others led to the issuance of new rules that marginally strengthened water protections connected to hydraulic fracturing. The small victory was an acknowledgement that, often, action through the executive branch is most expedient. 2013–14 will bring a combined approach in outreach to both the legislative and executive branches as the various complex legal elements of this issue outlined in this article wind their way through the judicial branch of government.

THE NEXT STEPS IN HYDRAULIC FRACTURING TECHNOLOGY AND POLICY IN MICHIGAN

A new development related to hydraulic fracturing in Michigan was unveiled in Governor Rick Snyder's Special Message on Energy and the Environment in late November 2012. The speech and accompanying document laid out the governor's vision for the future of energy production and environmental protection in Michigan. Governor Snyder said the following in his opening prepared statement:

> Michigan's natural gas production has never once had an incident where groundwater was polluted from hydraulic fracturing, even though we've been doing it for decades. That's in part because Michigan has strict regulations on drilling and wastewater management. Those regulations have been no-regrets decisions. We have many successful companies that have safely produced oil and natural gas in Michigan while protecting Michigan's waters.

This statement not only indicates strong support for what appears to be a growing industry, but suggests that the governor would be unwilling to sign legislation that gets anywhere near a ban or a moratorium on the practice.

Later in his prepared statement, the governor also recommended that Michigan create a Strategic Natural Gas Reserve to take advantage of its storage capacity, so that gas can be stored here to be sold in Michigan when prices are advantageous to the state. Finally, the governor highlighted a relatively new form of production using carbon dioxide and recommended carbon dioxide pipelines be granted the same legal status as gas and oil pipelines in Michigan, although it is unclear what exactly the governor meant by this statement.

Using compressed carbon dioxide to fracture shale rock—rather than high volumes of fracturing fluid—could reduce the volume of water withdrawal necessary for hydraulic fracturing and at the same time sequester carbon dioxide emissions from other sources. Governor Snyder used the example of a Michigan company, Core Energy LLC, which captured carbon dioxide emissions from a local ammonia plant and used them to make unproductive oil wells productive once more. He also claimed that the carbon dioxide stays sequestered deep underground. This proposed new technology may be present a new opportunity that some believe deserves further study for both its potential benefits to water usage and reducing carbon emissions and in relation to any potential negative effects from injecting carbon underground.[27]

As with almost any issue within the realm of environmental advocacy, the ideal may not always be the practical. Hydraulic fracturing has opened up natural gas reserves that provide low-cost energy, employment, and fund the protection of Michigan's natural resources through the Natural Resources and State Parks Endowment Funds. Shallow, vertical hydraulic fracturing has had a relatively safe history over the past few decades, but the increased volume of water withdrawal and chemicals used in deeper shale horizontal wells requires greater scrutiny and protective measures.

Deep shale wells are expensive to fracture and, with historically low natural gas prices, new deep shale drilling has stalled in Michigan. While the May 2010 state minerals auction fetched $178 million, subsequent auctions have failed to reach even $5 million.[28] The two initial Collingwood wells are the only two horizontal hydraulically fractured Collingwood Shale natural gas wells to be completed and producing to date. (There are other high-volume wells in shallower shales that produce oil rather than natural gas, and new permits have been issued for additional Collingwood wells, though none are yet producing).

Conclusion

If groups like Michigan LCV are successful in advocating for codification of sensible and strong water withdrawal, flowback disposal, and chemical disclosure regulations now, they can be implemented in time to ensure that hydraulic fracturing in Michigan is as safe as possible when natural prices increase and it becomes economically feasible to fracture deeper wells. Michigan LCV is working to make sure that Michigan's land, air, and water is protected when that time comes.

Notes

1. Movie: Josh Fox, Gasland (2010), *available at* http://www.gaslandthe movie.com/.
2. Great Michigan, www.greatmichigan.org.
3. Sara Gosman, et. al., National Wildlife Federation, Hydraulic Fracturing in the Great Lakes Basin: The State of Play in Michigan and Ohio (2012), *available at* http://www.watershedcouncil.org/learn /hydraulic-fracturing/files/document%203%20-%20hydraulic_fracturing _great_lakes_basin_report.pdf.
4. Susan Hlywa Topp, *Deep Shale Natural Gas Production in Michigan*, Mich. B.J., Jan. 2011, at 32–33.
5. Mich. Dep't of Envtl. Quality, Questions and Answers About Hydraulic Fracturing in Michigan, *available at* http://www.michigan .gov/documents/deq/deq-FINAL-frack-QA_384089_7.pdf.
6. Mich. Dep't of Envtl. Quality, Supervisor of Wells Instruction 1-2011, High Volume Hydraulic Fracturing Well Completions (2011), *available at* http://www.michigan.gov/documents/deq/SI_1 -2011_353936_7.pdf; Letter from Lyman Welch, Water Quality Program Manager, Alliance for the Great Lakes, et al., to Rebecca Humphries Supervisor of Wells, Mich. Dep't of Envtl. Quality & Harold Fitch, Assistant Supervisor of Wells, Office of Geological Survey (Nov. 27, 2010), *available at* http://www.watershedcouncil.org/files/Sign-on_Letter_Fracking _Regulations%20Final%20Nov%2017%202010.pdf.
7. Mich. Dep't of Envtl. Quality, Michigan's Oil and Gas Regulations, *available at* http://www.michigan.gov/documents/deq/ogs-oilandgas -regs_263032_7.pdf.

8. *Regulation of Hydraulic Fracturing under the Safe Drinking Water Act*, EPA, http://water.epa.gov/type/groundwater/uic/class2/hydraulicfracturing /wells_hydroreg.cfm (last updated May 4, 2012).

9. Permitting Guidance for Oil and Gas Hydraulic Fracturing Activities Using Diesel Fuels—Draft, 77 Fed. Reg. 40,354 (July 9, 2012), *available at* https://www.federalregister.gov/articles/2012/07/09/2012-16694/permitting -guidance-for-oil-and-gas-hydraulic-fracturing-activities-using-diesel-fuels -draft.

10. Mich. Dep't of Envtl. Quality, Supervisor of Wells Instruction 1-2011, *supra* note 5.

11. Pennsylvania Act 13 of 2013, § 3218.2.

12. Mich. Oil and Gas Regulations, Part 615, R 324.407, *available at* http:// www.michigan.gov/documents/deq/ogs-oilandgas-regs_263032_7.pdf.

13. *Id.*

14. Davids Acre Permit No. 60582 Application Page 23.

15. PowerPoint: Southwestern Energy, *Assessment Methods for Well Integrity during the Hydraulic Fracturing Cycle* (Mar. 11, 2011), *available at* http:// water.epa.gov/type/groundwater/uic/class2/hydraulicfracturing/upload /assessmentmethodsforwellintegrityduringthehfcycle.pdf.

16. Application to Mich. Dep't of Envtl. Quality to Change Well Status, Atlas Resources, LLC, Permit No. 60198 (application to temporarily abandon well filed June 15, 2011). A recent review of the court file documents indicates that this is a probable mechanical failure and not a contamination issue because they detected it prior to hydraulic fracturing the well. The water well information is added for the Davids Acres water well, which had to be completely drilled out and cemented.

17. Mich. Oil & Gas Regulations, R 324.403.

18. Water Well Records for Permit No. 60,582 (received pursuant to Freedom of Information Act request).

19. Minutes, Meeting of Groundwater Advisory Board, District 2, Michigan held February 26, 2013.

20. Mich. Comp. Laws § 324.32705 *et seq.*

21. A bill has been introduced in the Michigan House of Representatives, HB 5149, which would remove the exemption for oil and gas industry withdrawals from Mich. Comp. Laws § 324.32727. It was referred to the subcommittee on Energy & Technology on November 3, 2011. At the time of writing of this chapter, no action has been taken.

22. Mich. Comp. Laws § 324.32701.

23. The new applications filed by Encana in Michigan in Excelsior Township, Kalkaska County, request an exception from DEQ Rule 324.303 for a 2240 acre unit. This is due to their desire to locate five wells on a pad and run some horizontal legs north and some south for distances up to two miles. In Oliver Township, Kalkaska County, they have requested exception for a 1920 acre unit for the same reason.

24. *General Spacing Orders*, MICH. DEP'T OF ENVTL. QUALITY, http://www
    .michigan.gov/deq/0,1607,7-135-3311_4111_4231-119972—,00.html.

25. Michigan Senate Republicans enjoy a 26-12 majority, and the 2012
    election left Republicans with a 59-51 advantage in the State House of
    Representatives.

26. MICH. HOUSE OF REPRESENTATIVES, SUBCOMM. ON NATURAL GAS, NATU-
    RAL GAS SUBCOMMITTEE REPORT ON ENERGY AND JOB CREATION (2012),
    available at http://house.michigan.gov/sessiondocs/2011-2012/testimony
    /Committee6-4-24-2012.pdf.

27. MICH. EXECUTIVE OFFICE, A SPECIAL MESSAGE FROM GOVERNOR RICK
    SNYDER: ENSURING OUR FUTURE: ENERGY AND THE ENVIRONMENT (Nov.
    28, 2012), *available at* http://michigan.gov/documents/snyder/EE_Message
    _FINAL_pdf_404563_7.pdf.

28. Per a Reuters Special Report, *Striking it Poor*, dated December 27, 2012,
    Chesapeake Energy and Encana Corp are under investigation by both the
    Department of Justice and the Michigan Attorney General in relation to
    a possible violation of anti-trust laws as documents indicate that the two
    companies may have taken measures to avoid bidding against each other,
    thus pushing land acquisition prices down in Michigan.

11

Man Camps, Boomtowns, and the Boom-and-Bust Cycle
Learning from Rifle, Colorado, and Williams County, North Dakota

Sorell E. Negro

Natural gas activities impact the communities and regions in which they occur in significant and potentially dramatic ways, including job creation or displacement, housing prices and availability, and stresses on local government administration, law enforcement, and other public services. Hydraulic fracturing and horizontal drilling have changed the impacts that natural gas development has on communities. Moreover, while natural gas development has traditionally occurred in rural areas, the technological advances over the last decade and additional discoveries of shale deposits have led to more drilling in more densely populated areas. Finally, in many of these communities, much of the growth is often temporary, and the adjustment to the slowdown in drilling activity can be just as difficult as the adjustment to the increase.

Horizontal drilling also concentrates activities at the well site and therefore reduces the surface footprint that the equivalent number of vertical wells would have had if drilled. This also, however, concentrates surface impacts from drilling at the well sites. In addition to the wellhead, a typical well site will have tanks for storing the fluid used for fracturing (consisting of water mixed with sand and chemical additives), sand storage units, chemical storage trucks, fracturing pumps and blenders, and data monitoring equipment. Fracturing also requires significantly more truck loads for bringing equipment and water to the well site for hydraulic fracturing and for carrying away wastewater following the fracturing of the well. The Geologic Resources Division of the National Parks Service estimates that bringing the average horizontal, hydraulically fractured oil and gas well into production requires between 320 and 1,365 truck trips.[1]

Natural gas operations can present unique opportunities for economic benefits[2] but can also present weighty challenges when economic activity declines postdrilling. While oil and gas development creates jobs, studies conflict as to how many jobs are actually created, and many of the jobs are filled by a large, out-of-state, transient work force. Demands for housing and public services, including applications for building permits and calls to law enforcement or emergency responders, also increase. Local governments will need to expand staff or increase job responsibilities to keep up with fast-paced, and often unsustainable, growth.

Many of the transient workers for the industry will leave the community when their work is completed, reversing the initial increases in housing prices, economic activity, and local tax revenue. The initial development phase, when the well is drilled and hydraulically fractured, is the most labor-intensive, but this generally only lasts for a few weeks per well site. After the development phase ends and the production phase takes over, fewer workers are needed because once online and producing, wells mainly require monitoring, which is significantly less labor-intensive than drilling. However, where a majority of drilling/development jobs were filled by out-of-state transient workers, production jobs have a greater potential to be filled by local workers (who have the skills and education for monitoring well sites) and could last for 20 to 30 years.[3]

The development and production phases tend to create a common cycle or pattern of boom-and-bust.[4] In addition, significant economic events, such as a plunge in natural gas prices or termination of subsidies to the oil and gas industry, can also quickly slow down drilling activity or end it in certain communities. To be well positioned to endure a bust, it is important for communities to plan accordingly for appropriate levels and types of development during the boom. Planning combined with strong local leadership can maximize the benefits while minimizing the negative impacts in communities supporting natural gas activities.

This chapter, which is based on case studies in Rifle, Colorado, (Garfield County) and Williams County, North Dakota, addresses impacts of natural gas activities on jobs, housing, and local government administration that are felt every day by the residents who live near these sizable and highly technical operations. The author would like to thank the following individuals, whose rich stories, experiences, and perspectives shaped this chapter: Keith Lambert, past mayor (2001–2011) and current city councilmember for Rifle; Matt Sturgeon, Assistant City Manager and Planning Director of Rifle; Mike Braaten, Government Affairs Coordinator for Rifle; Fred A. Jarman, Director of Building and Planning for Garfield County, Colorado; Jill Edson, Planning and Zoning Administrator for Williams County, North Dakota; and Meghan Thoreau, former planner for Pinedale, Wyoming, and for the Southern Tier Central Region of New York. Through their experiences, this chapter addresses what communities and local leaders preparing for natural gas activities might expect and how they can best prepare for sudden and potentially drastic increases in population, jobs, housing demands, and public service needs.

JOBS GALORE . . . RIGHT?

Many communities have experienced significant job creation and economic growth from natural gas activities.[5] Some of this job growth is in the industry itself. For example, the Marcellus Shale Education and Training Center estimates that the total number of direct natural gas development jobs in Pennsylvania to be created by wells drilled between 2011 and 2014 is between 18,596 and 30,684, which includes between 9,800 and 15,900 new jobs since 2010.[6] But natural gas development can create jobs beyond those tied directly to the industry. Whether it is constructing pad sites, staffing hotels, hauling materials, or serving warm meals to the gas company's crews, communities often welcome natural gas drilling in the hope that these multiplier effects will alleviate unemployment and put people to work.

This distinction, in turn, makes it difficult to quantify how many jobs have been created in a particular region or community as a result of gas drilling, and studies that have tried to provide estimates for job growth from past or future drilling operations have varied widely.[7] Some studies look to the specific jobs created solely within the industry, while other studies also count jobs that are ancillary to the industry, such as trucking, restaurant, and hotel businesses. Ultimately, the number of workers needed depends on the number of wells that will be drilled. In other words, the number of drilling rigs determines the amount of the development and the size of the workforce.

Despite the number of jobs added, oil and gas companies might not employ many locals, particularly when they come to small communities. They bring in crews of out-of-state workers, with whom the company regularly contracts and sends from one drilling site to another. This makes financial sense for the companies because these crews are already trained, whereas local residents would require extensive training. The companies also need elasticity in their workforce as their demand for workers fluctuates and as the locations where they need workers change. And while a relatively small number of workers stay on for monitoring, maintenance, or other limited purposes, the vast majority of the workers are only needed for the initial development phase of natural gas extraction, which includes drilling and many other subcontractors and support industries. As the development phase winds down and the well site enters the production phase, a large portion of the transient workforce will relocate to other plays, perhaps due to a new boom or to rework an existing play. Local residents may not want to sign up to work for the oil and gas companies directly because they may not want to travel to work on remote drilling sites when the operator leaves the vicinity.

Nevertheless, shale development is typically associated with large spin-off effects, as opportunities for work in ancillary industries increase. Certain boom communities, like in the Bakken region of North Dakota, have actually seen a surplus of jobs—both as part of the natural gas operations and services ancillary to them—that cannot be filled quickly enough.[8] The higher paying jobs with the oil and gas companies have attracted many people from outside the region, as well as locals who have left their former jobs for better paying ones connected to the industry. For instance, the Sheriff's Department in Williams County, North Dakota, recently felt this pinch after two well-regarded deputies quit to work in oil fields to make more money. In Rifle, Colorado, during the boom in the mid-2000s, many people left jobs with the local government to work for the industry, particularly people trained in equipment operation, wastewater operation, and process technologies.

In response, compensation for some local non-industry jobs has increased, including in retail, fast food, gas stations, and convenience stores. Salaries in the public and private sectors increased to retain employees. It can be challenging for local businesses as well as local government to retain employees in the face of budget constraints and pressure to compete with higher wages. In Rifle, Walmart struggled to pay the higher wages that were needed to maintain employees and reduced its staff because salaries were so high, leading to consistently long checkout lines. While the oil and gas companies will not meet all of their employment needs through the local population, some local workers will likely be hired and may be enticed to leave their current employment for higher industry salaries.

The influx of workers into a community for drilling also boosts local businesses. Restaurants and hotels generally enjoy an upsurge in activity and profits and often increase prices to capitalize on the swell in demand. Oil and gas workers will spend money on restaurants, hotels, and entertainment. However, the new customers may also displace some traditional tourism. For example, the hotels and restaurants in Garfield County, Colorado, the second most active county in Colorado in terms of gas drilling, were bustling to such an extent during the most recent boom that tens of thousands of hunters who traditionally flocked to the area in the fall to hunt elk, deer, and birds went elsewhere, where hotel rooms were easier to come by. Making things more challenging in Garfield County, gas wells are now in areas that have historically been prime hunting locations. Both directly and indirectly, drilling has changed the ambience and experience for many hunters there.

These pressures, moreover, can be exacerbated by new linkages between communities and energy markets created by natural gas development. The success of the natural gas industry, and therefore of the number of jobs it provides and supports, depends on a high enough price and robust market for natural gas—as well as numerous other variables that may impact those factors, including prospective shale plays, new technologies, trading agreements, and local, national, and international politics. In the last couple of years as hydraulic fracturing technology became more mainstream, the oil and gas industry added an estimated 36,000 jobs. As natural gas prices have plummeted in 2012, the estimated number of jobs lost as a result could be double that number, as other tangential jobs depend on a healthy, active gas drilling industry, such as hotels, restaurants, and the trucking industry.[9] Still, even if the price of gas is low, drilling may continue if other commodities that are also produced from the shale development remain profitable. The effect of lower gas prices on jobs will not be uniform in all communities, making the impact of the oil and gas industry on jobs and local economies even more difficult to predict.

Housing Demands and Shortages

Keith Lambert, mayor of Rifle, Colorado, from 2001 to 2011 and current city councilmember, moved to Rifle in 1981 in the midst of an oil shale boom. He and his wife looked at a total of seven homes before buying one that was under construction. They looked at seven because there were exactly seven homes available in the entire city. Not surprisingly, the prices of those seven homes were very high. With the housing shortages, but jobs to be had, people were living under bridges and in culverts, tents, and campers.

Many people in Rifle have been forced to such extremes. During the mid-2000s, new teachers flocked to Rifle to fill the available teaching positions. One new middle school teacher could not find housing and was forced to live in a tent in Rifle Mountain Park, north of town, from August through October of the school year. He showered at school each morning and returned to the tent each night. This was not an anomaly. Some people making $60,000–$100,000 per year were homeless due to the housing shortage. And the shortage extended even to hotel rooms. In 2007, Mike Braaten, Rifle's Government Affairs Coordinator, wanted his parents to visit so he tried to book a hotel room for them. He quickly became discouraged after learning that hotel rooms were booked solid for two years.

In 2012, driving in Williams County, North Dakota, on an average Monday morning, one sees cars filled to the brim with clothes and household belongings. People from all over the country have flocked to the Bakken Shale for work. While the jobs are plentiful, many people are living out of their cars, in campers, and in RVs simply because there is not enough housing available. For much of 2012, hotels could only be booked Thursday through Sunday, when out-of-state workers went home. With many newcomers who are not familiar with typical North Dakota winters living in tents or cars, local officials in Williams County were concerned about the winter, when wind chills can send temperatures down to 30 or 40 degrees below zero Fahrenheit.

Of course, behind upheaval in local housing markets are the extraordinary population increases that oil and gas development can cause, which are driven by the influx of out-of-state workers plus employees in ancillary businesses. In 2010, before its boom, Williston, North Dakota, had a population of 12,000. In 2012, it was estimated to be over 20,000 or even 30,000 by some estimates. Demand created by such a population swell tends to push housing prices upward, which can be further exacerbated by the higher wages earned in the gas industry. In 2000, the median household income in Williston was $29,688, and in 2010 it reached $55,000.[10] A 2010 analysis of housing demand in Williston stated that half of Williston's population is unable to afford the minimum monthly rent of approximately $1,375 that is needed to pay for new construction, and older buildings that would typically have lower rents are unavailable because of the population surge.[11] It is anticipated that in the next eight to ten years, 9,000 new households will be added to the Bakken Shale region in North Dakota.[12]

However, negative impacts on the community from the drilling activities, such as noise, traffic, and environmental concerns, might lower housing prices, at least in the areas closer to the well pads.[13] Properties in Garfield County that are immediately adjacent to drilling activities saw a net decrease in property values, and owners of such properties have had a more difficult time selling their properties. However, property owners farther away from the drilling activity saw a significant increase in the value of their housing. In 2005, the average price of a single family home in Rifle was $228,000. In 2008, during the boom, it was $332,300. In 2010, postboom, it was back below $228,000.

There may be noticeable income disparity between the well-paid out-of-state crewmembers and long-term residents of the community, and between those residents who financially benefitted from the energy industry and those that did not. In certain communities, this disparity may be palpable, and some long-term residents may experience resentment. Worse, they may begin to be priced out of their homes and neighborhoods if the surge in demand for housing has increased housing prices too much and too quickly. For example, home prices in Williston on the Bakken Shale doubled in four years,[14] and certain boomtowns in North Dakota saw housing values double in one year.[15]

Often rental units offer affordable housing options in communities, but the prices of rental units also shoot up. Garfield County saw a rental vacancy rate of less than 1 percent, and the rental prices soared. In certain communities in North Dakota, rents resemble rates found in New York City and Washington, D.C.[16] In Williams County, if a hotel or rental room is available, it costs around $100 per night. Apartments are $2,000–$3,000 per month. Displaced residents or employees new to the area who are unable to find housing take to living out of cars or in mobile home parks. It is not uncommon for homelessness to increase considerably.

In a worst case scenario, landlords may increase rents and issue eviction orders deliberately to make space for higher-paying oil and gas workers.[17] Communities in North Dakota saw oil and gas companies buying apartment buildings and immediately increasing rent from $650 per month to over $800 per month, then to $1200 per month a year later. Many tenants could not afford the increase. One apartment complex filled with senior citizens received notice in July 2011 that the rent spiked from $800 to $2000, and the tenants had until August 31 to pay or leave. Those tenants who could not afford the price spike were forced to leave. The oil and gas companies' workers could afford to live there, so they moved in. The Planning and Zoning Administrator for Williams County knew of just one landlord in Williston who refused to raise rent.

In the face of such difficult housing conditions and the concomitant need to house a large nonlocal, mostly male, workforce, many oil and gas companies rely on temporary housing. These companies seek an elastic work force so, while they need to ensure that their workers are housed, the housing also needs to be flexible and economical. Some industry workers and workers in ancillary businesses will stay in hotels or rental units. But these options are not enough. As a result, the oil and gas companies have taken to setting up "man camps," also called temporary employee housing, which are temporary housing communities for oil and gas workers that range dramatically in size, scope, and sophistication.

Man camps range from clusters of mobile homes to prefabricated modular buildings. Man camps of this variety are the most sophisticated and can consist of dozens of stacked prefabricated units connected by narrow hallways and common spaces for cooking, eating, watching television, exercising, or playing cards. A significant benefit to having the temporary housing concentrated on, or close to, the well site is that it minimizes the net land disturbance due to the sudden increase in population in the community. This also limits any nuisances on long-term residents of the community as well as impacts to roads and traffic.

There are generally three tiers of these formal man camps in terms of size. First, every well site, regardless of size, has to have some employees on it at all times. These individuals, usually one to eight people, are the central personnel. These employees, who include engineers, monitor the drilling operations and ensure safety. Second, there are work crews, generally of eight to twenty-four people, who might be on a corner of the well site or close to the well pad, but not actually on it. These crews often live in clusters of mobile homes or stacked units that include a kitchen, showers, and bathrooms. These camps can resemble a small town and need a central water system for wells, wastewater, and municipal services. Third, some communities have larger man camps of hundreds of workers. These are less common and not in every state where drilling occurs. They are much larger and require more extensive infrastructure, and they commonly include recreation rooms or buildings, training centers, security guards, laundromats, and even gas stations.

Thus, man camps vary not only with regard to size, but also with regard to services. Some treat their tenants extremely well—providing Italian and French chefs, three meals a day, and packed lunches. These man camps are filled with oil field workers and hydraulic fracturing crews who can afford to stay there for $125 per night. Workers in business that are ancillary to the industry, such as truck drivers, cannot afford to pay $125 per night. Because they typically enforce strict rules, such as curfews, no drinking or drugs, no firearms, and even no women, these man camps tend to cut down on problems associated with certain social ills.

Whether it is because the prefabricated man camps are not permitted, there are not enough units, or the units are not affordable for everyone, sometimes man camps cannot provide housing for all of the additional workers in a community who work for the oil and gas industry or in businesses ancillary to the industry. This forces the remaining workforce to live in mobile homes, RVs, or tents, or out of their cars. Some mobile home lots have water and sewage hookup and electricity, while other camps do not. In fact, such workers can cluster in campgrounds or other spaces and create "informal man camps." In 2007, at the height of Rifle's gas boom, oil and gas workers swarmed campgrounds, living in trailers, RVs, and tents. Enough man camps simply could not be built to house everyone. In 2012, informal man camps sprouted up around the Bakken Shale in North Dakota. In Williams County, lack of regulation as to permissible heating mechanisms of mobile homes has led to fire hazards, a problem exacerbated by lack of occupancy limits at campgrounds.

These and other issues can make informal man camps more problematic for a local community than the formal, structured man camps, which usually require permits and are run by strict rules. Even though it is often the case that communities will not regulate campgrounds as strictly as housing units, regulation at the local level is important for the community's health, safety, and peace. Examples of such local regulation include imposing occupancy limits and noise restrictions and regulating the types of mobile homes and heating mechanisms that are permissible. It is important that local ordinances be updated to define key terms including "man camps," "temporary employee housing," "campground," "mobile home," and "RV." It is also important to determine the permitting process for temporary housing—i.e., will it be a conditional use, special use, or temporary use, and will a site plan review be required?

Other important considerations for any community accommodating a sudden surge in population include the increase in water use and handling the increase in waste and wastewater. Temporary housing facilities should have a waste hauling agreement in writing. Garfield County has addressed these issues by supporting the "vault and haul" approach, by which the oil and gas companies haul the water that they need for their workers up to their sites and then vault away all of the wastewater. A waste truck goes up to the site periodically and drains the waste vault. There is a small risk, of course, that the truck full of wastewater could leak or flip over, or that the potable water on the well pad could get contaminated. But the county explains that these risks are quite small, and the state of Colorado regulates water use in the man camps. This approach is less expensive than having the oil and gas company drill a well and install a septic system that will be there long after the crew has left and drilling has stopped. Even with such permanent infrastructure, there is still a small risk of contamination from the well. Garfield County prefers the "vault and haul" approach because, according to officials there, it results in a smaller impact to the environment and less of a trace of the oil and gas activities after the company has left the site.

In Williams County, water and sewage treatment plants recently hit their capacity. The problem of dealing with increased sewage and wastewater in that county has been addressed in several ways, none of which provide a silver bullet solution. Tioga, North Dakota, is enlarging its facilities to allow for disposal of sewage and wastewater from new development. Waste hauling companies currently take the sewage from man camps to other cities, but this is not a permanent solution. Some of the larger man camps haul or dispose of their waste on their own. Target Facilities, which builds man camps, built a $3 million sewage facility that is large enough to handle the sewage and wastewater from its own man camps and has enough spare capacity to contract with other temporary housing facilities to take their sewage.

Prior to permitting natural gas drilling operations, it can be helpful to take stock of current housing in the community in order to assess how much additional housing will be required for the influx of workers. When temporary housing will be required, such as mobile homes or man camps, the local government, if it has the relevant zoning power, should consider where the temporary housing should be placed. It could benefit a community to design a hotel, for example, so that it can transition into another use in the future that will be needed in the long-term, such as a nursing home, school, or office building. Local governments should also consider what infrastructure will accompany the temporary housing and whether the community could use the infrastructure after the drilling has been completed and the workers have left the area. If a community anticipates residential growth in a certain area, it may choose to ask the gas company to pay for the road, sewer, and water, and plat the land for single family homes. Finally, leases for land on which man camps will be constructed should include reclamation of the land after the man camps are dismantled and removed.

TRUCKS, TRAFFIC, AND ROADS

As mentioned above, fracturing operations require a significant number of truck loads and, consequently, heavily impact roads. For example, a natural gas well in the Marcellus Shale will require about 5.6 million gallons of water to be fractured, which is delivered by hundreds of truckloads.[18] Communities that do not have an extensive infrastructure for roads, especially roads suitable for trucks, will likely need to expand their road system. The roads will also be used much more intensively and will require more frequent maintenance. The costs of maintaining infrastructure are significant. Sublette County, Wyoming, spent over $60 million on its roads and water and sewage systems in 2009 alone, and it still needed an additional $160 million.[19]

The substantial number trucks needed to bring water, sand, chemicals, and equipment to the well sites and to haul wastewater away from well sites, along with local population surges, also leads to increased traffic and congestion. During Garfield County's most recent gas boom, towns suffered from traffic backups impeding on- and off-ramps of interstate highways starting at 6:00 a.m. The central road running north-south through Rifle was typically backed up all day long for a 30-block stretch. In Williston, average commute times have doubled in the last two years, and it is common for people to sit in traffic for a mile in order to make a left-hand turn during rush hour.

There are alternatives to trucking the needed materials that can cut down on these impacts. Garfield County's traffic problems were ameliorated in 2008 when the oil and gas industry implemented a "closed-loop" system of above-ground pipelines for water. This eliminated the steady stream of hundreds of trucks hauling water to and from the well sites and significantly mitigated problems with dust, traffic, and wear-and-tear on roads. While closed-loop systems cannot be implemented everywhere—for example, it cannot be done at high elevations—it works well on fields controlled by the operator where the operator has a large number of gas wells.

Certain municipalities supporting natural gas development have also implemented regulations to minimize impacts from trucks, such as by regulating the times when trucks are permitted on the roads. For example, Collier Township, Pennsylvania, which is in the Marcellus Shale region, requires that the following information be provided when applying for a gas drilling permit: (1) the proposed routes of all trucks to be used for hauling; (2) the trucks' estimated weights; (3) evidence of compliance with weight limits on its streets, or a bond and an excess maintenance agreement to ensure repair of road damage; and (4) evidence that the intersections on the proposed routes have a sufficient turning radius.[20] Government oversight can be aided by this type of information supplied by operators, including number of truck trips and which routes will be used, as it can help regulators understand how each operator will impact roads.

LOCAL GOVERNMENT ADMINISTRATION AND PUBLIC SERVICES: IN THE PRESSURE COOKER

In early 2011, Jill Edson packed her bags and moved to North Dakota from Michigan. She started her job as the Planning and Zoning Administrator for Williams County, North Dakota, on February 1, 2011. In 2012, the number of land use applications (for zone changes, subdivisions, conditional use permits, etc.) coming through her office increased 65 percent from 2011, and there is no sign that this is slowing down. It is extremely difficult trying to keep up with the workload. Like other local planning departments in the midst of a shale boom, she decided to contract out some of the work. She hired a consulting firm of planners from Montana to help with updating the county's zoning ordinance and developing impact fees and to be on call as needed.

An increase in natural gas operations typically leads to a significant increase in permit requests—for drilling operations as well as for general building permits—because new construction tends to accompany the population increase. Williston, for example, which is growing rapidly from the Bakken Shale's boom, has seen contractor permits double in the last year.[21] There will also be an increase in local government meetings held for planning purposes, and there likely will be a need for new ordinances and, possibly, an updated comprehensive plan. Communities also see more requests for zone changes, variances, and conditional use permits. In addition, it is often important to maintain a GIS database and to accurately map the community's resources to understand where development of the resources will or should occur.

A healthy population increase is about 1 percent per year. In the most recent boom for Rifle about 5 years ago, the city experienced 7 percent growth for two or three years. In the mid-2000s, Rifle added three new hotels. The week that La Quinta hotel (one of the three new ones) opened its doors, it returned to the planning department to request a building permit to double its size, saying they mistakenly built it too small. Additional land use requests and processes like these take time and resources, but there may not be an increase in the local government staff or budget. Understanding the increased need for administrative services is essential to determining whether staffing can or should be increased and how current employees' roles or workloads will change to meet the greater demand. As in Williams County, planning departments might consider contracting out some of the planning work that must be done if the workload is unmanageable.

It is extremely difficult keeping up with this pace of growth in terms of housing, social services, security, and education, and it is very difficult to accurately plan for the amount of development that will be needed. There also may be a greater need for a range of public services due to increased homelessness and a greater need for foster care as a result of housing prices increasing dramatically and affordable housing drying up. Population growth may increase public school enrollments. There is also greater strain on law enforcement and emergency services in boomtowns. This is a result not only of the increase in population from the larger labor force, but also because the nature of the work related to gas drilling can be dangerous, and, at least in certain communities, many of the high-paid industry workers spend a significant amount of their earnings on drinking, drugs, and adult entertainment such as strip clubs.[22]

For these reasons, some communities have seen notable increases in crime. From 2011 to 2012, the number of incident reports (which are filed for crimes that require an investigation, such as a robbery) in Williams County tripled, while the number of police officers doubled. The county jail was recently expanded in 2007 and was projected to be full in 50 years. As of October 2012, it was already full. Due to the lack of jail space, the county is providing a dormitory for people convicted of certain offenses like drunk driving or domestic violence, where the offenders leave in the morning for work, but return to the dorm every night and weekend. The county is currently looking to expand the dormitory. Williams County is also facing a lack of judges, prosecutors, and defense attorneys, so the length of time for waiting to have a case heard has increased from six or seven days to three or four months.

In addition to the stress on law enforcement, emergency personnel may be strained. In many communities, firemen and other emergency responders work on a volunteer basis. They may become burnt out from responding to the surge in emergency calls, on top of working their full-time jobs. As mentioned above, some of these people may have the opportunity to instead work for the oil and gas industry for a much higher salary. This can be problematic as the need for emergency personnel increases. It is important for local governments to account for these increased demands when projecting local budget needs for emergency and public services, including law enforcement.

WHAT HAPPENS WHEN THE DRILLING STOPS?

Rifle, Colorado, rode an oil boom in the 1970s when Congress poured money into the development of synthetic fuels. In 1982, that money abruptly dried up, and the oil companies suddenly stopped drilling. On May 2, 1982, Rifle woke up to a stagnant economy and over 2,000 of its 5,000 residents out of work. The value of homes dropped by 50 percent in one week. Within a year, new homes were selling for $30,000. Over the next two or three years, people left in droves. Some left without any notice, leaving their homes filled with furniture and belongings. The city suffered a localized depression for the next 12 years or so—far worse than what the city experienced in the last five years during the housing crisis. Vacancy rates on any given street were between 60 and 90 percent. For eight years straight during the 1980s, not one building permit was taken out in the city. The first one that was issued after the dry spell made the front page of the local newspaper.

While some communities have enjoyed long-term oil and gas drilling economic activity, such as in parts of Texas, many communities that depend on so-called "extraction" resources are subject to the "boom-bust" cycle. The busts are the periods of economic decline following the slowing down or stopping of drilling in the community. Natural gas may be extracted from a well within a few months, or perhaps within a year or two, after which time the operator(s) may move on to a new well or a new area altogether.

Once wells are no longer drilled and the oil and gas companies leave the community, royalties, profits, retail purchases, and tax revenues decline, and jobs are lost or relocated. If the community expanded during the boom due to greater tax revenues and to support a larger population of workers, it may be stuck with new infrastructure and schools that it doesn't need and perhaps can no longer afford. With significantly lower tax revenues, local governments may struggle to maintain infrastructure and services or to meet their overall budget.

In addition, when drilling stops, housing equities drop quickly and substantially, and rental vacancies shoot up. This happens as the population decreases considerably, as workers move to where the industry moves. While Williston, North Dakota, has had a population surge over the last couple of years, local officials anticipate that about one-third of the people currently there will leave when the drilling leaves.

Booms are exciting and filled with fast-paced economic activity and development. If possible, it is best for local governments to save and invest a significant amount rather than to spend every penny of the enticing increase in tax revenues right away—not only for any unseen environmental calamity, but also to invest in the future. Rifle learned this lesson after suffering the drilling bust that hit in 1982 and lasted for over a decade. When the most recent boom started about 10 years ago, local officials, including then Mayor Keith Lambert, knew that they needed to diversify their economy so that Rifle could weather the boom-bust cycle of natural resource extraction and overcome the next bust. With the Colorado River running through the city, Rifle recast itself as a river community. Lambert and other local officials had the vision and determination to take advantage of Rifle's location at the intersection of two major highways and worked diligently to attract businesses and capture commercial retail growth. As its leaders strived to better position Rifle for the next bust, Rifle also began to invest its high revenues in solar power to diversify its economy.[23]

Now, due to the tenacity and resourcefulness of its leaders, Rifle proudly touts Colorado's second largest combined municipal solar array as well as the country's largest community-owned solar array, through which residents can purchase panels in a centralized location and earn income from the electricity produced (rather than put the panels on their individual homes).[24] Rifle has more solar power per capita than any other municipality in the United States. It continues to be forward thinking and is currently engaged in a study to turn switch grass into butanal.

With about 10 percent of its population still working in the oil and gas industry and many more working in ancillary businesses, Rifle still has a strong connection to the industry. But it now has other economic activities supporting it for the long-term. Lambert explains, "Rifle realized that the extraction industry has a lifespan. When it is not profitable to extract anymore, the energy companies leave." Planning is especially important given the inherent uncertainty in the energy markets and, therefore, the length of any boom or bust period. If it is possible for a community or region to diversify its economy, it should make efforts to do so during periods of economic prosperity in order to stymie the economic stagnation that descends when the drilling stops. This is a way in which local leaders can truly make a difference in positioning the community for enduring a bust.

However, even with economic diversity, it can be extremely difficult to plan for the right amount of infrastructure that will be needed and to find ways to fund new infrastructure and maintain old infrastructure. For example, toward the end of its most recent gas boom, Rifle had to build a new $23 million wastewater treatment facility due to the increase in housing needed for the industry's workers. The city also needed to build a $25 million water treatment facility to meet federal water quality standards. Unfortunately, the wastewater treatment plant was constructed with the expectation of growth continuing for many more years, based on the oil and gas companies' statements and predictions that they would be active in the region, for decades. Instead, the price of natural gas declined and, after only five years, many of the companies are no longer drilling in the region, but are simply monitoring wells that were already drilled. Left with the bill, the city is not collecting sufficient revenue to pay off its debt for the wastewater treatment plant as quickly as it expected.

Planning for the boom and planning for the bust go hand in hand. Specifically with regard to housing, the community should understand its current and projected housing needs, including its affordable housing needs, and ensure that a percentage of new development is affordable. It is important, but challenging, not to over-build the housing stock during the boom. Temporary housing units that are easily dismantled and removed can be an excellent option if properly permitted and adequately regulated. There also may be a need for apartment buildings that could be turned into hotels, or vice versa, to suit the community's changing needs. Local governments must also plan for increased demand for administrative and public services. Garfield County tries to emulate the model of the oil and gas companies and maintain elasticity by contracting out for workers on an as-needed basis. Not all communities necessarily have the population or resources to diversify their economics, but they can still benefit from understanding the scope of the economic risks and saving for periods of economic decline to remain solvent.

CONCLUSION: PLAN, MONITOR, ADAPT, AND REPEAT

Planning and leadership can help communities to accomplish the following tasks: (1) distinguish immediate needs from future needs and determine how to pay for those needs, (2) diversify their economies, if possible, and (3) prepare for and adapt to changing economic realities. It is important for local officials to actively monitor systemic stresses on their communities as well as day-to-day concerns in order to respond in a timely and effective manner. Historically, periods of economic decline, at some point, follow such extreme surges of economic and population growth. But communities today have the ability to learn from past cycles, and high economic growth creates an extraordinary potential to save for and invest in the future.

Notes

1. Nat'l Park Serv., Potential Development of the Natural Gas Resources in the Marcellus Shale 8 (Dec. 2008), *available at* http://www.nps.gov/frhi/parkmgmt/upload/GRD-M-Shale_12-11-2008_high_res.pdf.

2. *See, e.g.,* Secretary of Energy Advisory Board, Shale Gas Production Subcommittee 90-Day Report 1 (Aug. 18, 2011), *available at* http://www.shalegas.energy.gov/resources/081811_90_day_report_final.pdf (Secretary of Energy Advisory Board reported in August 2011 that, "[o]wing to breakthroughs in technology, production from shale formations has gone from a negligible amount just a few years ago to being almost 30 percent of total U.S. natural gas production."); Brian Louis, *Fracking in Ohio Sparks Real Estate Rebound: Mortgages,* Reuters (Jun. 11, 2012, 11:00 PM), http://www.bloomberg.com/news/2012-06-11/fracking-in-ohio-sparks-real-estate-rebound-mortgages.html (explaining that, in Ohio alone, Chesapeake Energy Corp. has recently purchased $2 billion in land leases).

3. Jeffrey Jacquet, *Workforce Development Challenges in the Natural Gas Industry,* CARDI Rep. Sept. 2011, at 10, *available at* http://www.greenchoices.cornell.edu/downloads/development/marcellus/Marcellus_CaRDI.pdf (98 percent of gas drilling jobs are needed for actually developing the gas well and are not needed after drilling, and 2 percent are concerned with long-term production).

4. *See* Susan Christopherson & Ned Rightor, *The Boom-Bust Cycle of Shale Gas Extraction Economies,* CARDI Rep. Sept. 2011, *available at* http://www.greenchoices.cornell.edu/downloads/development/marcellus/Marcellus_CaRDI.pdf.

5. *See* Brian M. Johnson, *U.S. Oil and Gas Industry Could Be Key to Economic Recovery,* Wash. Times (Nov. 12, 2012), http://m.washingtontimes.com/news/2012/nov/12/johnson-us-oil-and-gas-industry-could-be-key-econo/ (senior tax advisor for the American Petroleum Institute explains that "[c]urrently, America's oil and natural gas industry supports 9.2 million jobs in the United States," and "[f]rom 2006 through 2011, the U.S. oil and natural gas industry directly created 119,511 jobs.").

6. Marcellus Shale Education & Training Center, Pennsylvania Statewide Marcellus Shale Workforce Needs Assessment 7 (2011), *available at* http://www.shaletec.org/docs/PennsylvaniaStatewideWorkforceAssessmentv1_Final.pdf#zoom=75 ("Across the state of Pennsylvania, the total number of direct natural gas development jobs (not indirect or induced jobs) created by wells drilled between 2011 and 2014 is currently estimated to range between 18,596 and 30,684 [full-time equivalent] jobs, creating 9,800 to 15,900 new jobs over 2010 levels, depending on the total number of wells drilled.").

7. *See* Joan Gralla, *Economists Clash on Jobs Fracking to Bring to NY*, Reuters (Apr. 30, 2012, 7:05 AM), http://www.reuters.com/article/2012/04/30 /us-natgas-fracking-newyork-idUSBRE83T0EH20120430 (listing differing estimates for job creation in New York as a result of fracking). *Compare* Eliza Griswold, *The Fracturing of Pennsylvania*, N.Y. Times (Nov. 17, 2011) *available at* http://www.nytimes.com/2011/11/20/magazine/fracking -amwell-township.html?pagewanted=all ("According to a recent study by Pennsylvania State University, the [natural gas] industry has created 23,000 jobs" in Pennsylvania), *with* Stephen Herzenberg, Drilling Deeper into Jobs Claims (June 20, 2011), *available at* http://keystoneresearch.org/sites /keystoneresearch.org/files/Drilling-Deeper-into-Jobs-Claims-6-20-2011_0 .pdf (explaining that while the media has claimed that gas drilling in the Marcellus Shale created 48,000 jobs, actually no more than 10,000 have been created), *and Hydraulic Fracturing in Pennsylvania*, PennsylvaniaFracking, http://www.pennsylvaniafracking.com/economic-opportunity/ (last visited Sept. 22, 2013) (stating that research from the PA Department of Labor and Industry indicates that over 214,000 jobs have been created in the state "by industries tied to the Marcellus Shale").

8. Audrey Putz, Alex Finken & Gary A. Goreham, Sustainability in Natural Resource-Dependent Regions that Experienced Boom-Bust-Recovery Cycles: Lessons Learned from a Review of the Literature 21 (July 2011), *available at* http://www.ag.ndsu.edu/ccv/documents /sustainability-report ("While the rest of the nation has been facing high rates of unemployment, the Bakken region ha[d] 14,000 jobs waiting to be filled as of March, 2011.") (citation omitted).

9. Joan Gralla, *Fracking States Losing Jobs and Revenue as Industry Shrinks*, Reuters (May 14, 2012, 4:15 PM), http://www.huffingtonpost.com/2012 /05/14/fracking-states-losing-jobs-revenue_n_1516047.html.

10. James Ondracek, North Dakota Communities Acutely Impacted by Oil and Gas Development: Williston Housing Demand Analysis (2010), *available at* http://www.ndhfa.org/Web_Images/williston.pdf.

11. *Id.*

12. Audrey Putz, Alex Finken & Gary A. Goreham, Sustainability in Natural Resource-Dependent Regions that Experienced Boom-Bust-Recovery Cycles: Lessons Learned from a Review of the Literature 19 (July 2011), *available at* http://www.ag.ndsu.edu/ccv/documents /sustainability-report.

13. *See* Webinar: Cornell Cooperative Extension, *Economic Implications of Marcellus Shale Natural Gas Development: Potential Impacts on Tourism, Agriculture, and Housing* (May 9, 2011), *available at* http://cce.cornell.edu/EnergyClimate Change/NaturalGasDev/Pages/CornellSponsoredWebinars.aspx.

14. Steven Mufson, *In North Dakota, The Gritty Side of an Oil Boom*, Wash. Post (July 18, 2012), *available at* http://www.washingtonpost.com/business

/economy/in-north-dakota-the-gritty-side-of-an-oil-boom/2012/07/18
/gJQAZk5ZuW_story_3.html.

15. Audrey Putz, Alex Finken & Gary A. Goreham, Sustainability in Natural Resource-Dependent Regions that Experienced Boom-Bust-Recovery Cycles: Lessons Learned from a Review of the Literature 19 (July 2011), *available at* http://www.ag.ndsu.edu/ccv/documents /sustainability-report.

16. *Id.*

17. *See* Steven Mufson, *In North Dakota, The Gritty Side of an Oil Boom,* Wash. Post (July 18, 2012), *available at* http://www.washingtonpost.com /business/economy/in-north-dakota-the-gritty-side-of-an-oil-boom/2012 /07/18/gJQAZk5ZuW_story.html (reporting on such an incident in New Town, North Dakota, involving a trailer park).

18. Southern Tier Central Regional Planning and Development Board and the Planning Departments of Chemung, Schuyler, and Steuben Counties, Municipal Guide for Energy Impacted Communities 36 (Aug. 2012), *available at* http://www.stcplanning.org/usr/Program _Areas/Energy/Naturalgas_Resources/Final_Municipal_Guide_for _Energy_Impacted_Communities_November_2011_hyperlinked.pdf.

19. Webinar: Cornell Cooperative Extension, *Municipal Planning and Managing Potential Impacts from Natural Gas Development: Practical Steps Local Governments Can Take, available at* http://cce.cornell.edu/EnergyClimate Change/NaturalGasDev/Pages/CornellSponsoredWebinars.aspx.

20. Collier Township, Pa., Ordinance No. 592 § 1703.29.j (2011).

21. *See* Steven Mufson, *In North Dakota, The Gritty Side of an Oil Boom,* Wash. Post (July 18, 2012), *available at* http://www.washingtonpost.com /business/economy/in-north-dakota-the-gritty-side-of-an-oil-boom/2012 /07/18/gJQAZk5ZuW_story.html.

22. Steven Mufson, *Boomtown of Fort McMurray is Busting at the Seams,* Wash. Post (June 30, 2012), *available at* http://www.washingtonpost.com /business/economy/boomtown-of-fort-mcmurray-is-busting-at-the-seams /2012/06/30/gJQAYZDhEW_story.html.

23. *See* Allen Best, *Bad Gas or Natural Gas?* Planning (Oct. 2009).

24. David West, Thomas Knipe, and Susan Christopherson, *Frack or Bust,* Planning (April 2012).

12

Getting Ahead of Drilling Companies in the Haynesville Shale
The Caddo Parish, Louisiana, Experience

Charles C. Grubb

Caddo Parish comprises the extreme northwest corner of Louisiana. It is bordered on the north by Arkansas and the west by Texas and consists of 568,960 acres or 889 square miles. Its population is approximately 265,000, of which 200,000 reside in its principal municipality, Shreveport. It is separated from Bossier Parish and Bossier City by the Red River. Bossier Parish's population is about 158,000, of which slightly over 68,000 reside in Bossier City.

Anyone studying an aerial photograph of Caddo-Bossier would readily conclude that the area enjoys plentiful water. We are not only blessed with the Red River (which thanks to the U.S. Army Corps of Engineers enjoys constant, plentiful flow), but also significant lakes as well as several bayous that hold water year-round. However, as we shall see, appearances can be deceiving.

For over 100 years, oil and gas exploitation has been an essential element of our economy. Around the turn of the 20th century, the first oil well in the nation drilled over water was drilled in Caddo Lake in the northern part of the parish. Since then, thousands of both oil and gas wells have been drilled. However, until recently, virtually all of the wells have been relatively shallow, exploiting the Cotton Valley and Hosston formations.

Things suddenly changed in 2008. We began hearing rumors of leases being acquired on behalf of unnamed parties. At first the leases were being purchased for bonuses of a few hundred dollars per acre and a modest royalty. Literally within weeks, a frenzy developed. At the zenith of the frenzy lease bonuses in excess of $30,000 per acre were being paid. A significant number of people became multimillionaires. To date, Caddo Parish government has received lease bonuses of approximately $38 million for the mineral interests in its roadbeds and another $10 million for the mineral interests associated with its parks and other properties. Even some fortunate urban homeowners negotiated leases with huge bonus provisions. On top of that, royalty payments will keep the money flowing for years to come.

At the same time the leasing frenzy was underway, parish and municipal governments within the Haynesville Shale area realized that if the leasing was followed by uncontrolled drilling and associated activities, the quality of life for our citizens would be severely compromised. This would be especially true with people living in our urban areas. At the time the only other example in the country of urban shale drilling was the Barnett Shale in the vicinity of Fort Worth, Texas. Rather than reinvent the wheel, we contacted Sarah Fullenwider, who is now the City Attorney for Fort Worth but was then an assistant city attorney responsible for advising the city on natural gas drilling and production issues. She graciously arranged for Caddo Parish representatives to meet with a number of Fort Worth officials including the mayor. We came back from those meetings with an appreciation of the daunting task ahead of us if we were going to get out in front of regulating what was about to happen rather than get run over by it.

We began by assessing the powers Louisiana local governments have concerning the regulation of oil and gas drilling. That assessment produced sobering conclusions. Of course like Caddo Parish, most of the state of Louisiana has enjoyed a rich history as an oil and gas producer for over one hundred years. The oil and gas industry is a powerful political force in the state of Louisiana. Over the years, aspiring populist politicians railed that the state was in the hip pocket of the oil and gas industry. They were rarely elected.

Current state law certainly reflects the political power the industry enjoys in our state. Under state law, the state has sole authority to permit wells. Local government is specifically preempted from regulating the location of wells.[1] The state has promulgated comprehensive regulations on where and how wells are drilled.

What the state had not done prior to the advent of shale drilling is address the types of land use issues that can be expected to arise when an intensive industrial activity such as oil and gas drilling takes place in close proximity to incompatible uses, particularly in urban settings. For all the drilling that had previously occurred in Louisiana, little had been done in urban settings. The parish immediately saw that either it or the state was going to have to identify and urgently address those issues or else things would rapidly get out of hand.

At this point, we frankly had little faith that the state was willing or prepared to adequately address our concerns. That did not stop us from meeting with the appropriate state officials, specifically the secretary of the Louisiana Department of Natural Resources and the Commissioner of Conservation. In conversations they were largely responsive to our concerns, but we felt that they did not share our sense of urgency. We decided we were on our own in doing what we had to do.

At the same time we were building our relationships with state regulators, we also did the same thing with industry representatives. Once they realized we were not going to buy their argument that we had no authority to regulate any of their activities, we were able to engage them in productive dialogue. Although they generally resisted our efforts at regulation, we were able to negotiate constructively with them.

While all this was occurring we devised a definitive list of issues we needed to address. In no particular order the following are the issues we identified and how we addressed them.

GENERAL OPERATION OF WELLS

Although we had determined that state law prohibited us from regulating the location of wells and the technicalities of how they are drilled, we concluded there were of a number of issues we could address.[2] Through the adoption of Ordinance No. 4916 of 2009, codified as Chapter 29 of the Caddo Parish Code of Ordinances, we addressed the following issues:

1. *Site Access.* We prohibited access to well sites across public property, including public roads, without prior consent of the parish.

2. *Floodplain/Floodway.* We provided that any drilling and associated activities within any floodplain or floodway identified by FEMA shall be consistent with the parish's legal responsibilities to FEMA to protect these areas.

3. *Dust, Vibration, Odors.* We established a best practices standard to minimize the generation of dust, vibration and offensive orders and further required operators to incorporate reasonable and feasible technological improvements in industry standards in the future to accomplish these goals.

4. *Lighting.* We prohibited any well site lighting from shining directly on public roads, adjacent property, or property within 300 feet of the site and further provided to the extent practicable site lighting be directed downward and internally so as to avoid glare on public roads, adjacent dwellings and other buildings, and any such dwellings or buildings within 300 feet of the site.

5. *Abatement of Exhaust Fumes.* We required that all internal combustion engines and compressors on drill sites be equipped with exhaust mufflers designed to suppress noise and disruptive vibrations and minimize the escape of gases.

6. *Onsite Electric Generation.* We prohibited onsite electric generation without the specific approval of the Parish.

7. *Signage.* We required signage at each well identifying the well name and number, the name of the operator, and a 24-hour emergency telephone number for the operator.

8. *Incident Reporting.* We required any incident involving fire, smoke, or the release of flammable or hazardous materials to be immediately reported to our local sheriff's office and fire department as well as notice as soon as practicable to the appropriate parish official. This latter requirement is especially helpful in order to enable the parish to adequately respond to citizen concerns concerning such incidents.

9. *Use of Public Water Supplies.* We prohibited operators from accessing public water supplies for drilling and fracturing operations without securing necessary permits from both state and local officials.

10. *Discharges.* We prohibited the discharge of anything generated at a well site into any public facility, any body of water, and onto any private property.

11. *Disposal Wells and Compressor Stations.* We limited the location of salt water disposal wells and compressor stations to industrially zoned locations and prohibited them within 500 feet of a protected use (residence, religious institution, commercial building, public building, hospital, school, or public park).

12. *Esthetics and Screening Requirements.* We required that drill sites be free of high grass, weeds, and trash and imposed fencing and screening requirements. In most urban areas we prohibited the storage of pipe, equipment, or materials on a drill site except during the drilling or servicing of a well and for three days thereafter.

13. *Operating Hours.* We established operating hours for all activities at well sites other than drilling, completion, and reworking operations, where the sites were within a certain distance of a protected use. These activities include but are not limited to road work, site preparation, deliveries, and general well servicing.

14. *Noise Standards.* We adopted the state's noise standards on an interim basis pending completion of a comprehensive noise ordinance.

We took an expansive approach to our legal authority as a Louisiana home-rule parish in imposing some of these requirements. We frankly did not worry much about the industry challenging our authority to do so as long as our regulations were reasonable. We not only have confidence in our legal authority but also think the companies realize that confrontation with communities working with them in good faith is a losing proposition for them. They would be foolish to incur the fallout that would follow their challenge of regulations the public supports.

COMPREHENSIVE NOISE REGULATIONS

Oil and gas wells and their associated activities, particularly gas compression stations, are significant noise generators. We had not

previously adopted an ordinance effectively regulating noise generators, and the one we had was constitutionally suspect. Our sister parish
to the east, Bossier Parish, faced a similar predicament. We decided
to jointly draft a state-of-the art ordinance regulating all noise generators, not just those involved in the oil and gas industry. We did
this notwithstanding that the state adopted its own noise regulations.
Frankly, we had no confidence in the process used by the state in
formulating its regulations. The state's consultant hired to develop its
noise standards was selected and paid by the industry. Of course that
gave rise to an impression that the consultant and therefore the state's
regulations were tainted by bias.

Our first step was to engage an acoustical engineering firm to
assist us with the technical aspects of such an ordinance. This proved
to be invaluable. It was helpful that the firm we selected was not local;
that facilitated the public's perception that their recommendations
were not tainted by bias. Our consultant established ambient sound
levels throughout the two-parish area. We then, through the adoption
of Ordinance No. 5072 of 2011, which is codified as Sections 32-20
through 32-26 of the Caddo Parish Code of Ordinances, established
maximum sound levels at different times of the day/night as measured
from several different types of noise receivers. Although it applies to
every type of noise generator, the ordinance provides for exceptions
such as emergency signals and equipment, permitted parades, outdoor
school activities such as athletic events, and construction and demo-
lition activities during certain times of the day/night. Significant
noise generators, those that may be reasonably expected to generate
noise upon adjacent properties that exceeds the limits set forth in
the ordinance, are required to submit a noise management plan to
the parish for advance approval. It requires oil and gas well operators
to continuously monitor the noise generated by their operations and
prohibits certain activities at night and on weekends. Although we
incurred significant expense in creating our ordinance, we are confident it was money well spent.

Road Usage Restrictions

Shale drilling brings with it a great deal of heavy truck traffic, the kind
of traffic that would destroy typical local roads. The drilling rigs and
associated equipment are obviously moved from site to site by truck,

but that is not the biggest problem. Each Haynesville well requires over 5,000,000 gallons of water, approximately 600,000 gallons used in the drilling process and almost 5,000,000 in the fracturing process. Not only does the water have to reach the drill site, but most of it has to be hauled away, sometimes long distances to reach licensed disposal sites. The state regulates the size and weight of vehicles traveling on state highways but not local roads. Even with its regulations in place, the state's enforcement assets are spread so thin that enforcement of the state's standards is ineffective.

Local roads, at least those in north Louisiana, are not built to withstand the pressure of such heavy truck volume. Through the enactment of Ordinance No. 4967 of 2010, codified as Sections 14-111 through 14-126 of the Code of Ordinances, we enacted regulations designed to protect our roads. These regulations are applicable to all truck traffic, not just that related to the oil and gas industry. They establish weight, height, and length limitations. We established a permitting process for vehicles not meeting these standards. This enables the parish to prescribe particular routes for overweight/oversized trucks to follow and thereby avoid public roads not built to standards sufficient to bear the load.

Overweight permit fees are determined by both the weight of the vehicle and the distance it will be traveling on parish roads. Where necessary, we videotape the condition of applicable roads before they are used by overweight vehicles and hold operators responsible for any damages.

We created a Commercial Vehicle Enforcement Unit to enforce our road usage regulations. Unit personnel are deputized law enforcement officers. They routinely patrol the roadways maintained by Caddo Parish and stop vehicles suspected of not conforming to our regulations. The unit includes portable scales. When violators are identified civil monetary penalties are imposed. These civil penalties can be significant. Their size is determined by the amount the vehicle exceeds the allowable gross weight or allowable axle weight, whichever results in a higher penalty. Penalties for both failure to possess the required overweight permit and for operating a vehicle in violation of the standards are cumulative in nature. Our procedures include a two-step appeal process that is available to aggrieved operators.

Our enforcement personnel are busy, but our experience has been that reputable transport firms want to comply with the regulations. Most of the problems come from independent operators, primarily water haulers. In addition to keeping our personnel busy, the scofflaws have significantly contributed to the parish coffers. We have thus far collected in excess of $250,000 in civil penalties and almost $700,000 in permit fees.

With one major exception, we have generally succeeded in protecting our roads from excessive deterioration by all this truck traffic. That exception occurred early in the process of establishing not only our regulations but, perhaps more importantly, our relationships with the operators. In that instance, because an operator was about to lose leases for failure to drill, he became reckless in drilling his well. Equipment was moved on site with no notice to the parish. In order to access the drill site, the operator had to haul equipment, water—everything needed to complete the well—on residential streets in an otherwise quiet subdivision. By the time the parish was notified, the damage had been done. The residents of the subdivision were rightly outraged. Overnight, their subdivision streets became virtual dirt roads. We immediately contacted the operator, and within several days the operator's representatives were meeting in the neighborhood with parish representatives and the residents of the subdivision. Although the residents remained unhappy until the well was completed, the story had a relatively happy ending in that at the parish's insistence the operator paid to have the subdivision's streets completely rebuilt to standards that exceed that of the old roads.

WATER

Although because of the Red River and our lakes we are blessed with seemingly abundant surface water, that surface water is not usually in close proximity to well sites. As a result, drillers are tempted to access groundwater either through drilling water wells themselves or by acquiring water from nearby private property owners. Selling water in the quantities needed in the fracturing process can be very lucrative.

Many rural property owners in our area maintain ponds or small lakes, largely for fishing. Early in the development of the Haynesville Shale, it was common practice for the owners of these ponds and lakes to sell their water to shale drillers. When the surface water was thereby diminished, it was common for the ponds and lakes to be replenished with groundwater. The problem with this practice is that the aquifer underlying Caddo Parish, the Carrizo-Wilcox, is quite fragile.

In Louisiana water wells are permitted by the state; local government has no legal authority concerning the location and size of water wells. We soon learned that state regulations permitted oil and gas operators to apply for permits retroactively. We could foresee a disaster in the making.

We did two things immediately. Water became the principal topic of nearly constant discussions we were having with state regulators. We funded the establishment of a number of wells spaced throughout the parish whose function is to monitor the levels of the Carrizo-Wilcox aquifer. We agreed to pay Louisiana State University-Shreveport to monitor the wells and provide periodic reports. These wells have proven to be invaluable in establishing our case that the aquifer should not be the source of water used in shale drilling.

Our monitoring of wells document the impact on aquifer water levels of operators' access to groundwater. As a direct result of this evidence, today less than 20 percent of the water used in shale drilling and fracturing comes from groundwater. How did this happen? Fortunately, after reviewing the evidence, both the state regulators and the industry itself agreed with Caddo Parish that the aquifer could not sustain the pressure from withdrawals to support shale drilling and at the same time provide water for residential use, traditional industry, and agriculture. The state now has a state-wide water management plan in effect. The practice of replenishing ponds and lakes with groundwater has stopped.

New state regulations permit oil and gas operators to treat, recycle, and reuse water that is produced at well sites. Operators are utilizing parish road rights-of-way to lay temporary surface waterlines up to five miles in length to access surface water from our river and large lakes. As a result, the Carrizo-Wilcox aquifer has stabilized and its viability no longer threatened by shale drilling.

ENFORCEMENT

Caddo Parish's Department of Public Works is responsible for enforcing all of the regulations the parish has established. Its director constantly monitors the issuance of state permits for drilling and utilizes field personnel to monitor both drilling and its associated activities. It has the equipment required to monitor compliance with our noise regulations. The parish's Commercial Vehicle Enforcement Unit is part of the department. All appeals of actions by enforcement personnel are heard by the department's director or assistant director.

LESSONS LEARNED

Although perhaps not as nimble as the parish, the state of Louisiana, and in particular its Department of Natural Resources (DNR), became a good partner in protecting our citizens, especially concerning the preservation of our aquifer. Under the leadership of then DNR Secretary Scott Angelle and Commissioner of Conservation Jim Welsh, the department has worked well with us and enacted regulations strengthening the state's oversight of shale drilling, as well as access to water and other activities associated with exploitation of oil and gas, for which Caddo Parish is very grateful.

Although Haynesville Shale development has slowed due to the abnormally low price of natural gas, in the roughly four years of that development our citizens have greatly benefitted from the economic impact it has brought to our area. Of course some have benefitted more than others. Many property owners have become multi-millionaires. In 2009, for example, Haynesville Shale development was responsible for the creation of 57,637 new jobs and almost $5.7 billion in household earnings in Louisiana. It brought enough business to our hotels, restaurants, stores, car dealers, and other commercial establishments to virtually insulate our area from the economic downturn suffered in the rest of the country.

Even government has shared in the benefits. As previously stated, Caddo Parish alone has received over $50 million in lease bonuses, and our sister parishes and municipalities have received millions more. We estimate that over the past four years the parish has received an additional $47 million in property tax revenues as a result of Haynesville Shale activity. Additionally, the parish's sales and use tax collections have increased dramatically, almost doubling but now slowly tapering off as a result of the cyclical slowdown in natural gas exploration and production. The parish estimates that its sales and use tax revenues have increased over $24 million over the past four years because of shale drilling and its associated activities. Thanks largely to the Haynesville Shale, Caddo Parish is the only governmental entity in Louisiana that enjoys a AAA bond rating.

That our citizens have enjoyed these benefits without significant harm to our environment is no accident. Had Caddo Parish and our neighboring parishes and municipalities not energetically addressed the challenges Haynesville Shale development brought with it, our citizens would have been plagued by environmental disaster before they realized what was happening to them. However, we have come to realize that with the challenges facing the industry in developing shale deposits of oil and gas in other parts of the country, the industry itself, whether driven by greed or more noble goals (you be the judge), now knows that if it is going to succeed in its efforts to exploit shale oil and gas it has to work with the people's representatives at the local level to insure that citizens can coexist with it and all it brings. Railroads like to say that they were here first so government has to work around them in planning infrastructure. Well, the people were here before the shale drillers, so the same is true for them. Our experience is that although they occasionally need some reminding of that, they get it. The result for our citizens has been economic vitality.

This may not be true everywhere. In some ways we are ideally situated for this activity. Because we were already used to oil and gas drilling and production, at least to a degree we were already sensitized to it. We had oil and gas field services and pipeline infrastructure in place before anyone heard of the Haynesville Shale.

We have enough population to be able to absorb and take advantage of the jobs and other economic activity that exploitation of the Haynesville Shale has brought. We look forward to the day market conditions are such that the pace of drilling recovers.

NOTES

1. La. Rev. Stat. § 30:28 (F) provides as follows:

   The issuance of the permit by the [state] commissioner of conservation shall be sufficient authorization to the holder of the permit to enter upon the property covered by the permit and to drill in search of minerals thereon. No other agency or political subdivision of the state shall have the authority, and they are hereby expressly forbidden, to prohibit or in any way interfere with the drilling of a well or test well in search of minerals by the holder of such a permit.

2. Each of the ordinances described above is accessible through Caddo Parish's website, www.caddo.org.

13

Backyard Drilling
Local Regulation of Gas Drilling in the Barnett Shale of North Central Texas

Terrence S. Welch

For many years, natural gas drilling was a land use issue that most significantly impacted the rural areas of Texas and the nation;[1] however, with the advent of natural gas drilling in the Barnett Shale in North Central Texas[2] and other parts of the United States, natural gas wells and associated production facilities have steadily encroached upon both urban and suburban areas, often leading to highly vocal demands by residents that local governments protect them from the sometimes hazardous effects of natural gas drilling. Indeed, in the last several years there have been serious concerns raised by North Central Texas residents that natural gas drilling is hazardous, with benzene, carbon disulfide, and other hydrocarbons being poured into the air, cancer clusters in residential subdivisions located nearby natural gas well pad sites, truck traffic coursing city streets while carrying toxic chemicals, and unhealthy air quality resulting from such drilling. These public health concerns have been compounded by fears that the state and local governments in the shale areas in North Central Texas and the nation are doing little or nothing to address these issues, often citing constrained government budgets and a lack of manpower to monitor hundreds or thousands of natural gas well sites. As a consequence, regulatory authority often has fallen upon cities and counties, which often lack any relevant experience in addressing the complexities of natural gas production activities.

The experience of many municipalities in North Central Texas with the advent of the Barnett Shale drilling boom was both difficult and problematic—most municipal land use regulations in the area simply failed to address in any meaningful way how and by what processes a municipality should consider an application or other authorization to drill for natural gas. Indeed, since the Dallas/Fort Worth Metroplex had almost no recent or meaningful history of oil drilling activities in the area, most North Central Texas cities had no regulations on the books that addressed (or even could be inferred to address) natural gas drilling. The closest most cities came to confronting the issue was a zoning restriction that mineral extraction or similar mining activities (such as a gravel quarry) required some type of specific/special/conditional use permit, with almost no criteria providing any substantive guidance about the factors to be utilized in considering the approval or denial of a permit for such mineral extraction or mining activities. As a result, most cities in North Central Texas were at a loss about how to address natural gas drilling—suddenly, they were confronted with the issue, and at first, many cities floundered. Now, more than a decade later, many cities in the Barnett Shale in North Central Texas have significant experience in dealing with gas drilling inside a city's corporate limits.

The purpose of this chapter is to address the practical responses of local governments when confronted with demands that those governments "do something" to protect residential areas from the perceived ill effects of natural gas drilling, while offering practical observations whether a municipality should view the siting of gas wells as either a zoning issue or a land use matter not directly associated with traditional zoning concepts. The last portion of this chapter addresses specific issues that cities and other local governments should evaluate and address when contemplating the adoption of a natural gas drilling ordinance or other regulatory scheme.

MORATORIUM OR NO MORATORIUM?

The first issue a municipality may be asked to consider prior to the adoption of a comprehensive natural gas drilling ordinance is whether the adoption of a temporary moratorium is both legal and practical while the municipality is considering such natural gas drilling regulations. In general, a moratorium is a legally authorized period for the delay or abeyance of some activity. While moratoriums traditionally have been adopted when cities are considering amendments to zoning or subdivision ordinances, the adoption of a natural gas drilling moratorium has been utilized by several cities in Texas to temporarily cease natural gas drilling activities (or the filing of applications or permits to start natural gas drilling activities) until new or updated gas drilling regulations are considered and approved by the city. Such moratoriums or similar interim land use controls play an important role in protecting the city's natural gas drilling review process by limiting the ability of gas producers to acquire vested rights or other production rights that may conflict with the city's review process. Simply stated, a short-term moratorium on natural gas drilling while a city considers how to address such drilling in an ordinance is a tried and true way to make sure that gas drillers do not get ahead of the city by filing and receiving drilling permits prior to the city adopting an ordinance on the subject of gas drilling.

It is clear that there may be very serious vested rights problems that may arise if there is no temporary cessation by a municipality of either the acceptance of applications for permits to drill or actual drilling activities during the period when a municipality is considering new or stronger natural gas drilling regulations. The vested rights issue is one that any city must seriously consider, in consultation with its attorney. A "vested right" in everyday language means that some type of legal right has been received because an application was made under the law in effect at the time of the application. For example, if an application is made for a gas drilling permit on January 1, then that application is governed by the municipal ordinances in effect on January 1—the fact that the city adopts new gas drilling regulations on February 1 is not relevant—the applicant "vests," or receives the benefits of, the regulations in place as of the January 1 date of application.

While the determination whether a gas drilling moratorium is authorized by law should be determined on a state-by-state basis, it is clear that the failure to adopt a moratorium may result in a flood of applications for drilling permits that are "under the wire," that is, are subject to the prior, often less stringent (or non-existent) regulations in effect prior to consideration of new regulations. Consequently, a moratorium should be considered by a city during the time period when a city is considering the initial adoption of regulations for natural gas drilling or amending its existing natural gas drilling regulations to strengthen or otherwise update them.

Is Local Regulation of Natural Gas Drilling a Traditional Zoning Matter or an Administrative Approval Issue?

When considering the adoption of an ordinance to regulate natural gas drilling (and particularly variances from the terms of such an ordinance), a city council or other governmental body inevitably questions whether it should (1) consider natural gas drilling activities to be a traditional zoning issue (that is, either rezone property for such a use, or consider a specific/special/conditional use permit[3] to allow such a use in all or certain specific zoning districts), or (2) utilize a board or commission, such as the city's existing zoning board of adjustment, as an oil and gas board of appeals to consider such variances. I believe that traditional zoning review by a city's planning and zoning commission, and thereafter review by the city council, of natural gas drilling permit applications and setback variance requests, utilizing traditional zoning procedures as the mechanism by which to review such permits and variance requests, is not desirable. Indeed, as detailed below, it is strongly recommended that this approach not be utilized because (1) it in all likelihood may lead to litigation against the city for unconstitutional takings of property; (2) the cities in North Central Texas that utilize traditional zoning procedures to review permit applications for natural gas wells and setback variance requests have uniformly approved all applications and setback variances[4] and consequently, the use of traditional zoning procedures is untested and of little or no value when considering a city's legal options and potential liability; and (3) if traditional zoning procedures are adopted, a city council may be required to approve any setback variance request by a supermajority vote in those cases where the city's planning and zoning commission denied a variance, thus requiring the city council to choose between siding with local residents who invariably will oppose the setback variance, or unconstitutionally denying a subsurface landowner his/her rights to mine or otherwise exploit the mineral estate.

Several municipalities in North Central Texas utilize traditional zoning procedures when considering natural gas well drilling applications and well setback variances. By "traditional zoning procedures," I mean that applicants apply for a rezoning of property or for a specific use permit (also called special use or conditional use permits) to allow for the extraction of minerals from the subsurface (often called the mineral) estate.[5] Thus, any drilling application or well setback variance request would be subject to notice provisions similar to standard zoning cases (200-foot rule notification and newspaper notice), with a public hearing before the city's planning and zoning commission followed by a public hearing before the city council. Further, as in all zoning cases, any drilling application or variance request denied by the planning and zoning commission would require a supermajority vote (75 percent) by the city council to be approved.[6]

While municipalities that utilize the traditional zoning model appear to be fairly evenly split whether a well site requires a zoning classification change or simply a specific use permit, in none of those cities has that process been challenged since almost every application for a gas well ultimately has been approved.

The second approach is administrative approval of a gas drilling permit application by a municipal official (usually the city's oil and natural gas inspector or other similar administrative official), with review by a board of adjustment (sometimes called an oil and gas board of appeals) for consideration of any distance setback variances to the provisions of the city's natural gas drilling ordinance. This approach results in the administrative approval of a natural gas drilling permit, assuming that all criteria outlined in the natural gas drilling ordinance are met by the drilling permit applicant. If all criteria indeed are met, there is no planning and zoning commission or city council review of the application to drill. However, in the event a distance setback variance of some sort is required,[7] then a board of adjustment or board of appeals reviews the requested variance and, applying specific, setback-related criteria detailed in the natural gas drilling ordinance, determines whether the variance is merited. If so, the gas drilling permit is approved subject to the variance. If the variance is not approved by the board, then an applicant may resort to judicial review, not unlike that type of judicial review afforded an applicant when a zoning board of adjustment has denied a requested zoning variance.[8] As a practical matter in cities that have adopted the administrative approval model, relatively few provisions contained in a natural gas drilling ordinance are subject to variances other than setback distances (that is, the distance from the wellhead or pad site exterior to another nearby structure or use).

I believe the administrative approval model is the preferable approach. First, an appeal board takes the city council out of the "crosshairs" of the community. In almost every city where natural gas drilling is an issue, there are strong feelings in the community whether gas drilling should even be allowed. Requiring the city council to consider each and every permit or variance request places the city council in an untenable political position. There often are intense lobbying efforts by citizens to approve or reject gas well drilling sites. More often than not, as gas drilling creeps closer to urban areas, the political pressure on most city councils is to deny all gas well drilling permits, in effect outlawing natural gas drilling in the municipality. Second, the issues and factors to be considered by a board of appeals are significantly different than the issues and factors a city council utilizes in traditional zoning/land use cases. The inherent tension between surface and mineral rights is rarely, if ever, an issue in a traditional zoning case, which addresses the concept of separating incompatible land uses through the establishment of fixed rules. Third, traditional zoning techniques authorize uses of property in certain zoning districts while not permitting those same uses in other zoning districts. If that model is utilized in a gas drilling context, there could be serious concerns about an unconstitutional taking of property as a consequence; that is, "zoning" by definition separates certain uses of property from other uses of a property—for example, a single family residence is rarely located next to a large industrial facility. If every gas drilling permit is considered through the lens of zoning, and a permit may be granted on a well-by-well basis, then get ready for every permit being approved. Fourth, if small tracts of land are rezoned for natural gas drilling, then there may be a violation of state law, which requires that all zoning must be in accordance with a comprehensive plan.[9] Comprehensive plans traditionally do not contain provisions for natural gas drilling. As a consequence, if a small tract of land is rezoned for natural gas drilling, there may arise an issue of illegal spot zoning. Fifth, in those municipalities that utilize specific/special/conditional use permits to allow gas drilling on a specific tract of land, there usually is either unbridled discretion or very vague standards by which the city council may judge the drilling permit. Clearly, such unbridled discretion or vagueness may result in state or federal unconstitutional takings challenges, due process challenges, or similar constitutional or legal challenges.

There are inherent advantages of board consideration distinct from a city council's traditional zoning consideration. First, the board looks at well siting issues unrelated to zoning districts and zoning classifications. This approach may be utilized to address adjacent uses of property (regardless of underlying zoning/land use districts or classifications) and land features, such as water wells, habitat, floodplain, existing nearby structures, property/tract lines, nearby parks and roadways. Second, an appeals board, much like a zoning board of adjustment, is a quasi-judicial body (not a legislative body) and as such, is afforded more inclusive quasi-judicial immunity in litigation rather than less broad legislative immunity. Third, the board of appeals, after considering variances and other gas-related issues over time, often develops an expertise and understanding of such issues, and may not be subject to political whims, particularly since members often may only be removed for cause. Last, appeals from the decision of a board of appeals proceed directly to court via a writ of certiorari process which, in the long run, is more expeditious and less costly. Moreover, if there is a serious unconstitutional takings issue at play, the city will have the opportunity to consider settlement without having had incurred significant attorney's fees. It is my belief that where the administrative approach has been utilized in North Central Texas, it appears that it has been very successful and the appeal boards have been diligent in making findings and accommodating both residents and the legal interests of natural gas drilling applicants.

CONTROVERSIAL ISSUES IN THE REGULATION OF MUNICIPAL GAS DRILLING

While many North Central Texas municipal gas drilling ordinances usually contain detailed provisions about insurance coverage, application fees, emergency notification procedures, landscape screening and buffering requirements, on-site signage and fencing, among other technical requirements, several issues are far more controversial and vary greatly from city-to-city. Key natural gas drilling ordinance provisions that should be analyzed in great detail follow.

Natural Gas Well Distance Setbacks

Without a doubt, distance setbacks are the most controversial aspect of natural gas drilling in urban and suburban areas. In the Barnett Shale, early municipal gas drilling ordinances generally contained setbacks in the 300–600 foot range.[10] For example, several cities adopted

600 foot setbacks from a wellhead to a residence or other habitable structure, with distance setback variances down to 300 or 400 feet. With greater public concern about the potential health effects of natural gas drilling, many municipal ordinances across the region underwent substantial revisions during the last several years, for example with distance setback measurements being made not from the wellhead but from the edge of the pad site, and not from the pad site edge to a residence or other habitable structure, but to the property line of the residence or habitable structure. Moreover, in many instances, distance setbacks simply were increased. In one North Central Texas city, the setback from the edge of a pad site to a habitable structure was increased to 1,500 feet, with a variance only down to 25 percent of the setback distance (or 1,125 feet).[11]

Public concern about setbacks often has been critical, with allegations that setbacks are either too close (resulting in concerns about the public health aspects of nearby natural gas drilling) or too far (resulting in concerns about such setbacks depriving mineral estate owners of the ability to realize their investments in their property). Besides unconstitutional takings concerns, scientific studies about the effects of natural gas drilling—studies related to air quality concerns, toxins, groundwater and surface water pollution, among others—enter into the picture and often are the subject of intense public debate. For example, in March 2012 the University of Colorado Denver School of Public Health issued a report that air pollution caused by hydraulic fracturing may contribute to acute and chronic health problems for those individuals who live near gas drilling sites. "Our results show that the noncancer health impacts from air emissions due to natural gas development is greater for residents living closer to wells," the report said. "The greatest health impact corresponds to the relatively short-term, but high emission, well completion period. . . . We also calculated higher cancer risks for residents living nearer to the wells as compared to those residing further [away]," according to the report. "Benzene is the major contributor to lifetime excess cancer risk from both scenarios."[12] The general trend in the Barnett Shale has been to increase setbacks rather than reduce setbacks; nonetheless, no single issue is more controversial.

Another key issue associated with setbacks is the legally permitted variance distance. The experience of at least one Barnett Shale municipality is that whatever the designated well setback distance may be, the overwhelming majority of gas drilling applications request distance setback (and occasionally other) variances. In Flower Mound, Texas, for example, the historical data is as follows:

Total Number of Pad Sites Applied for:	22
Total Number of Pad Sites Approved:	19
Pad Sites Requiring Variances:	15[13]

Thus, almost 80 percent of the pad sites approved in Flower Mound, Texas, since the inception of its gas drilling ordinance in 2003 obtained some sort of variance, the overwhelming majority of which were distance setback variances. Therefore, based upon observations of many Metroplex cities, it is reasonable to anticipate that practically every application to drill for natural gas will contain a distance setback variance request. As the foregoing reflects, the minimum permitted setback variance that is allowed by ordinance in all likelihood will become the standard for operators, thereby ensuring that almost every operator will request a distance setback variance down to (or close to) the minimum distance allowed.

Last, the impact of natural gas drilling on residential property values should also be considered in determining appropriate distance setbacks. Although the data on this issue is scant, several studies in the Barnett Shale have reached opposite conclusions about the residential property value impact, if any, as a result of proximity of residential structures to natural gas well sites.[14] It should be noted, however, that there may be a correlation between natural gas drilling and the impact on nearby residential property values. Additionally, as residential sales data becomes more mature, the effect of natural gas drilling operations on residential property values may become more reliable. Thus, if through the setback variance process gas drilling is permitted closer to residential properties, it appears that there may be greater potential for the reduction of nearby residential property values. A reduction of nearby or neighboring property values clearly is emotionally charged.

Drilling in Floodplains

Cities grapple with the issue whether any natural gas drilling should be permitted in the floodplain. While floodplain may be either FEMA floodplain or floodplain as defined in city ordinances, the issue is controversial for a simple reason—floodplains are subject to flooding, and any gas drilling- or production-related equipment (particularly tanks containing undisclosed, toxic hydraulic fracturing chemicals, produced water, or condensate) that is inundated by floodwaters may create significant health and safety risks, threatening water quality and aquatic life. Numerous cities in the Barnett Shale consequently have prohibited gas drilling and operations in any floodplain areas,[15] while others have authorized drilling in the floodplain, but only by obtaining prior approval from the city council.[16]

Those individuals either residing or owning property downstream of gas drilling facilities located in the floodplain may face serious environmental and other physical damages in the event of a flood inundating gas wells and related equipment. Additionally, due to exemptions from several federal laws relative to the disclosure of hydraulic fracturing chemicals, gas drilling operations in the floodplain are different from other uses of property that may be permitted in floodplain areas. It is my opinion that due to the legal status that allows operators to not disclose the chemicals used in hydraulic fracturing, comparing natural gas drilling to other land uses that are not accorded such legal status is neither appropriate nor justifies location of gas drilling operations in the flood plain.

Drilling in Public Parks

Another controversial issue is whether cities should allow natural gas drilling in public parks. The reasons why this is a matter of intense public debate should not be surprising. First, public parkland is a valuable commodity, regardless how the parkland currently is used or where it is located in a city. The use of parkland for natural gas drilling removes that land from the city's inventory of parkland, thereby permitting an industrial use of park property. Additionally, the cost of acquiring future parkland can be prohibitively expensive and time-consuming, especially if eminent domain (condemnation) procedures are utilized, and to willingly permit such parkland to be utilized for gas drilling purposes may be seen by many residents as short-sighted.

Although there exists park property in many cities that may not resemble traditional park uses, the land's designation as a park is for a purpose—the enjoyment of the park by the public. Passive parks are just as important as traditional parks and public playgrounds. Consequently, the removal of passive park areas results in the loss of public parkland. Passive park areas may become active park areas in the future; however, once a site has gas drilling activities and operations on it, that area effectively is lost as a public park area for years, if not decades. The traditional purpose of public parks, in part, is to allow citizens to escape urban activities and to enjoy open space and nature. Regardless of the designation of park property as either active or passive uses, natural gas drilling activities and operations remove that area (and the area immediately surrounding the location of such gas drilling) from any effective use as a park. It should be noted as well that as a general principle, industrial uses are not permitted in the parks of most cities. Not surprisingly, local regulations addressing drilling in park areas vary widely, from prohibiting drilling in parkland,[17] to allowing drilling in parkland only with city council approval,[18] to allowing drilling in public parkland but also not within 300 feet of a public park.[19]

Subsequent Property Development

When many cities consider the adoption of regulatory standards for gas drilling and production activities, the distance setback issue is usually framed in terms of "how close can a gas well be to some type of land use—a residence, a school, a park or a hospital?" An issue that often is overlooked is the converse. What happens when a gas well is permitted by a city, and after the gas well is in production, a landowner or developer opts to seek permission to build a residential subdivision, an apartment complex, or retail center in close proximity to the existing gas well? If there are concerns, for example, that natural gas wells and production equipment have an adverse impact on the public health, is that not still the case if an apartment complex is built within the setback area? Should the apartment owner or developer be required to seek a variance to do so? Which entity would approve the setback variance since the issue is mixed, with concerns about "traditional" natural gas well distance setbacks, such as public health issues and property values combined with concerns about the right of property owners and developers to recoup their investments in land nearby an existing natural gas well or pad site?

The issue of subsequent property development is a significant one. Most municipal ordinances are silent on the issue,[20] and it is the author's opinion that critical unconstitutional takings issues may be at play. For example, several municipal gas drilling task forces that have considered the issue in North Central Texas have opted to treat this topic of subsequent land development differently than the situation where a natural gas well is sited in an existing developed area.[21] In fact, some members of gas drilling task forces have viewed subsequent developers as "coming to the nuisance," with the implication that an apartment builder (not the future apartment residents), for example, "knows what he or she is getting into," and there should be no municipal interference in such subsequent property development, even if located within the natural gas well setback area. In areas where natural gas drilling and production activities have been undertaken for years, such as in the Barnett Shale in North Central Texas, this issue of subsequent property development will be confronted more frequently since the natural gas "boom" in the area may be past, lease and natural gas prices have fallen significantly in the last several years and demand for property development has increased after the recent recession. Any municipal government addressing natural gas drilling and production would be well advised to consider this topic on the front end of gas drilling activities rather than after natural gas wells have been drilled around the city.

Saltwater Disposal Wells

An issue separate from, but clearly associated with, natural gas drilling activities is whether a municipality should allow the location of any saltwater disposal wells inside its corporate limits. Since natural gas reservoirs are found in porous subsurface rocks, saltwater, also contained in those porous rocks, accompanies natural gas to the surface. Often this saltwater is disposed of by injecting the saltwater into underground porous rock formations not productive of natural gas. When hydraulic fracturing operations occur, small quantities of substances used in the drilling, completion, and production operations of a natural gas well may be mixed in the saltwater waste stream. Such substances include drilling mud, hydraulic fracturing fluids, and well treatment fluids. It also is not unusual to find various amounts of residual hydrocarbons in the saltwater waste.

The impact of saltwater disposal wells inside a city is indeed controversial. Often these disposal wells are regulated by state agencies, not local governments, and more troubling is seismic activity that may be associated with such disposal wells.

A 2010 study of seismic activity near Dallas/Fort Worth International Airport (DFW Airport) by researchers from Southern Methodist University and The University of Texas at Austin concluded that the operation of a saltwater injection disposal well in the area was a "plausible cause" for the series of small earthquakes that occurred in the area between October 30, 2008, and May 16, 2009. The study noted that the earthquakes in the area of DFW Airport did not appear to be directly connected to natural gas drilling, hydraulic fracturing, or natural gas production. However, the injection of waste fluids at a nearby saltwater disposal well began in September 2008, approximately seven weeks before the first DFW earthquakes occurred—and none were recorded in the area after the saltwater injection well ceased operation in August 2009. A state tectonic map prepared by the Texas Bureau of Economic Geology reflected a northeast-trending fault intersected at the location where the DFW Airport quakes occurred. The SMU study concluded that it was "plausible that the fluid injection in the southwest saltwater disposal well could have affected the in-situ tectonic stress regime on the fault, reactivating it and generating the DFW earthquakes."[22]

It is not unusual for municipalities in the Barnett Shale to prohibit saltwater injection wells.[23] Disposal wells are considered an industrial use of property separate from natural gas drilling operations, generating large amounts of truck traffic and noise similar to other industrial activities. Additionally, even when nearby natural gas drilling activities have concluded, disposal wells continue in operation and generally accept saltwater waste from any source, including natural gas wells far away. Consequently, saltwater disposal wells are independent businesses that remain in operation for years or decades. Even when efforts are made to limit saltwater disposal well operators from accepting waste from outside a city, such efforts are legally problematic since few industries are limited to such a small area of operation. It is not unreasonable to expect that pressure will mount to "open up" the disposal well to accept saltwater waste from other well sites outside the city due to disposal well operator concerns about financial viability after in-city natural gas operations have ceased or natural gas wells have experienced limited production and are near depletion.

Regulation of Water Sources Necessary for Natural Gas Drilling

Another area of concern is the vast amount of water used in natural gas drilling, including the use of millions of gallons of water in hydraulic fracturing operations. What is the source of the water used in drilling and fracturing—the nearby municipal water system, surface waters, water wells, or other sources? Some cities have mandated that municipal water be used, often resulting in a financial windfall for those cities. Other cities have desired to limit the source of water to nonmunicipal water suppliers, which may result in truckloads of water being transported along city streets and concomitant damage to roadway infrastructure. Coupled with concerns associated with water sources is the issue of water restrictions in periods of drought—is it legally permissible for a city, for example, to limit the water supply to a drill site while other large industrial users of water are not similarly limited? These issues should be evaluated in great detail by a city council or other governmental body prior to the adoption of any natural gas drilling ordinances or regulations.

Impacts of Natural Gas Drilling Activities on Roadway Infrastructure

It is intuitively obvious that natural gas drilling activities are a technically specialized form of an industrial activity, of necessity requiring the use of heavy equipment, from moving drilling rigs onto a site to private vehicular operations of employees and contractors to commercial vehicles carrying away produced water in large water tanker trucks. For the local government, the impact of such traffic on public roadways can be intense, and the damage to roadways resulting from such operations can be very expensive to repair. As a consequence, cities should strongly consider the adoption of a roadway maintenance fee for any damage to city roadways. The approaches cities have taken in addressing this roadway damage issue vary, from requiring bonds or letters of credit being provided by operators in the event of roadway damage (an "after the fact" approach)[24] to "upfront" fees for roadway damage.[25]

In North Central Texas, most cities require upfront fees in the form of a roadway maintenance agreement or roadway remediation agreement instead of a bond or letter of credit. It is my opinion that bonds are often difficult to rely upon, and letters of credit generally are of limited duration and periodically must be renewed, because disputes often arise about damage that is a result of natural gas drilling heavy equipment on a roadway in proportion to a roadway's normal wear and tear that would have occurred without any natural gas drilling activities. Consequently, the ambiguity about who is or may be responsible for roadway damage after years of drilling-related and non-drilling-related traffic on a roadway may render the bond/letter of credit approach virtually useless. The upfront approach, the preferred approach by many North Central Texas cities, generally requires that a city retain a traffic engineer or engineering firm to conduct a traffic impact study and document the structural and functional condition of a road or multiple roadways. Flower Mound, Texas, for example, provides that the road maintenance fee "shall be determined from the paving coefficient index (PCI) methodology enumerated in the final road maintenance agreement prior to execution by the applicant and the town."[26] Regardless of the method used by a city to recoup roadway repair or reconstruction costs it incurs or may incur in the future as a result of heavy vehicular traffic associated with natural gas drilling activities, the failure to address such damage in advance of natural gas drilling activities ultimately may result in large capital expenditures for a city.

CONCLUSION

With technological improvements in natural gas drilling, operations, and production resulting in more gas drilling activities in Texas and throughout the nation, particularly in more heavily populated areas, local government regulation of natural gas production has become both an important and highly controversial issue for citizens, neighborhoods, natural gas operators, city planning departments, local government attorneys, and developers. When a government first faces the issue of whether a natural gas drilling ordinance is either needed or desired, the experience of other local governments that have dealt with this matter should be evaluated. Those experiences no doubt will provide the government with the opportunity to craft an ordinance or other regulatory scheme based upon the trials and errors of those other cities. Regardless of the decisions made by a local government regarding how and in what manner to address the topic of natural gas drilling, the intensity of the political pressures and public interest in urban and suburban natural gas drilling and production cannot be overstated.

NOTES

1. Note: While this chapter discusses regulations with respect to natural gas wells, most state and local laws apply equally to oil wells.
2. The Barnett Shale is a natural gas formation that is approximately 5,000 square miles in size located in North Central Texas and underlies much of the Dallas/Fort Worth Metroplex.

3. A specific use permit (also called a special use permit or conditional use permit in many city zoning ordinances) allows a landowner to use his property in such a manner that is not authorized by the city's base zoning ordinance. Most cities that have adopted zoning ordinances separate the city into different zoning districts and, in each zoning district, certain uses of property are permitted as a matter of right. Zoning ordinances generally have a "special uses" (or "specific uses" or "conditional uses") section in them that allow for uses that are just outside the intended uses for that zone. For example, an industrial zone may not by right authorize an industrial plant to have a helicopter landing pad at the plant site because often high-voltage electrical lines may be located near the industrial plant; however, if there are no such electrical lines in the vicinity, the city council may grant a specific use permit to allow a helicopter landing pad at the industrial plant site. Even though every industrial plant site in the city may not be safe for a helicopter landing pad, that specific industrial plant is safe for such a landing pad, and is allowed under a permit for that plant site.

4. Several cities in the Barnett Shale have adopted extensive natural gas drilling and production ordinances; however, many of the ordinances of those same cities provide that any provision in the ordinance may be subject to a variance approved by the city council. *See, e.g.,* Southlake, Tex., Code of Ordinances § 9.5-223(a) (variances allowed for any requirement contained in the gas and oil well drilling and production ordinance). Consequently, the city council in many cases is confronted with a drilling permit application with multiple variances requests, from a reduction of insurance requirements, to hours and days of permitted drilling operations, to setback distance variances and allowing gas drilling and operations in or near public parks or in the floodplain. To the author's knowledge, and as noted in the text, because literally all gas drilling permits have been approved in such situations, the "let's make a deal" approach to the consideration of variances has not been tested in the courts.

5. *See, e.g.,* Dallas, Tex., Code of Ordinances § 51A-4.203(b)(3.2)(B) (natural gas drilling requires a specific use permit and is permitted in any zoning district in the city); Southlake Zoning Ordinance § 45.1, item 42 on Specific Use Table (oil and gas drilling may be permitted by specific use permit in any zoning district in the city).

6. *See* Tex. Local Gov't Code § 211.006(d) and (f). A proposed zoning change that is protested by at least twenty percent (20%) of (i) the area of lots or land covered by the proposed change or (ii) the area of the lots or land immediately adjoining the area covered by the proposed change and extending 200 feet from that area requires a three-fourths (super majority) of the city council to approve the zoning change, or if the city has adopted an appropriate ordinance, a decision to deny the proposed zoning change by the city's planning and zoning commission requires a similar three-fourths vote of the city council to approve the zoning change, respectively.

7. In the administrative approval model, it is my experience that overwhelmingly the variances considered by a board of adjustment or board of appeals relate to distance setbacks. In many natural gas drilling ordinances, distance setbacks are mandated from existing residences, schools, hospitals, religious institutions, public parks, floodplains, other buildings designed for human occupancy, property lines, water wells, and environmentally sensitive areas in the city. *See, e.g.*, Flower Mound, Tex., Code of Ordinances, ch. 34 (variances allowed only for well setback distances [§§ 34-422(d)(2) and 34-420(o)], work hours [§ 34-422(g)] and certain technical requirements (*see* § 34-427(a)(8) (drilling fluids), (19) (fresh water wells), (21) (gas well stimulation, (25) (lights), (27) (muffling exhaust), (28) (organic solvents), (30) (pits) and (35) (soil sampling parameters)]. *See also id.* § 34-427(b) (listing those subsections of § 34-427(a) for which variances are allowed).

8. *See, e.g.*, Tex. Local Gov't Code § 211.011. *See also* Town of Flower Mound, Tex., Code of Ordinances, § 34-432 (addressing appeal of determination of oil and gas inspector to oil and gas board of appeals and judicial review of decision of board determination relative to variances).

9. *See* Tex. Local Gov't Code § 211.004. An interesting discussion of several regulatory models around the nation (although not particularly instructive as to Texas legal authority) is found in Robert Freilich & Neil Popowitz, *Oil and Gas Fracking: State and Federal Regulation Does Not Preempt Needed Local Government Regulation—Examining the Santa Fe Oil and Gas Plan and Ordinance as a Model*, 44 URB. LAW. 533 (2012).

10. The City of Dallas at present only requires a 300-foot setback from a well bore to any institutional or community service use, recreation use (except when the operation site is in a public park) or residential use, with lower setbacks for fresh-water wells (200 feet from well bore), right-of-way (75 feet from well bore), and property lines, storage tanks or any source of ignition (25 feet from well bore). *See* Dallas, Tex., Code of Ordinances § 51A-4.203(b)(3.2)(E)(iv)(aa)–(ee).

11. Flower Mound, Tex., Code of Ordinances § 34-422(d).

12. *See* News Release, Univ. of Colo. Denver, Study Shows Air Emissions Near Fracking Sites May Pose Health Risk (Mar. 19, 2012), *available at* http://www.ucdenver.edu/about/newsroom/newsreleases/Pages/health-impacts-of-fracking-emissions.aspx (quoting Lisa McKenzie, lead author). While it was not my purpose to review and critique scientific studies on the topic, at an absolute minimum it is clear and undisputed that scholars and scientists in this area of study often strongly disagree about the human health effects of natural gas drilling and hydraulic fracturing.

13. Information provided by the Town of Flower Mound, Tex., Envtl. Servs. Division.

14. In August 2009, Integra Realty Resources ("Integra") prepared for the Town of Flower Mound a Well Site Impact Study ("Study"). The objective of the Study was "to develop an opinion of the impact, if any, of the proximity of

improved residential properties as a result of their proximity to natural gas well sites." The Study concluded, in general, "that in the Flower Mound area, *when houses are immediately adjacent to well sites* there is a measurable impact of value. As distance from the well site increases, this affect quickly diminishes." (Emphasis in original). The 2009 Integra Study further concluded that residential property with price points over $250,000 and immediately adjacent to well sites can experience an impact from –3% to –14% in value based on the sales comparison method. Any influence on property values on a linear basis was found to dissipate at around 1,000 feet from the wellhead. The range in property value decline found in price-distance relationships was observed to be about –2% to –7%. Impact on housing prices by the price-distance method generally dissipated between 1,000 and 1,500 feet. This data suggests that gas drilling has an impact on nearby residential property values, and consequently, if through the variance process gas drilling is permitted closer to residential properties, the greater the potential for the reduction of property values. A copy of the Integra Study may be obtained from the Town of Flower Mound. A study by Integra conducted for the City of Arlington in 2009–10 concluded that "[t]he preponderance of evidence suggests that there is little or no impact on residential property as a result of near proximity to well sites. Minimal measurable impact was found to residential properties that adjoin well sites. Anecdotal evidence also suggests that high-end housing also may be impacted by the proximity to well sites but insufficient data was available to extract quantifiable affects. Lastly, any damages that may accrue to residential property appear to dissipate over time as drilling activity subsides at a well site."

15. See, *e.g.*, Flower Mound, Tex., Code of Ordinances § 34-420(k) (no well may be drilled within 750 feet of a floodplain).

16. See, *e.g.*, Southlake, Tex., Code of Ordinances § 9.5-242(d) (drilling permitted in floodplain with approval of City and, where applicable, U.S. Army Corps of Engineers).

17. See, *e.g.*, Flower Mound, Tex., Code of Ordinances § 34-422(d)(1)(a) (no well may be drilled within 1,500 feet of a public park); Southlake, Tex., Code of Ordinances § 9.5-232(e) (no permits shall be issued to drill in any public park).

18. See, *e.g.*, North Richland Hills, Tex., Code of Ordinances § 104-6(i)(1) (it is unlawful to drill within 600 feet from any playgrounds, competition athletic fields, swimming pools, water slides and playgrounds, concession stands, pavilions, or picnic areas within a public park unless prior consent is obtained from the city council to drill in a public park).

19. See, *e.g.*, Dallas, Tex., Code of Ordinances § 41A-4.203(b)(3.2)(E)(iv)(aa) (gas wells must be spaced at least 300 feet from a "recreation use except when the operation site is in a public park"). The Dallas Gas Drilling Task Force, which met from mid-2011 through late February 2012, and whose comprehensive gas drilling recommendations to the Dallas City Council

have not yet been reviewed or adopted by the Council, voted 5–3 to recommend that gas drilling in parks be authorized (i) only if the park land is not currently being used as a public park or playground; (ii) is located adjacent to industrial uses; (iii) the pad site is as close as practicable to the perimeter of the park land; (iv) the park land is not an environmentally sensitive area; (v) a portion of the revenue generated will go to a park property fund for the Dallas Park and Recreation Department; and (vi) the specific use permit to drill in a park must be approved by a 3/4 supermajority vote of the City Council. The irony of this requirement is that although the Task Force recommended that no gas drilling and production activities occur within 1,000 feet of a public park, such drilling and production activities may occur within the park itself as long as the suggested criteria are met.

20. One notable exception to this rule is Flower Mound, Texas. Section 34-422(c)(4) of the Code of Ordinances provides that "all new and/or proposed construction of any buildings, habitable structures, streets, roads, and/or applicable improvements to the property upon which any oil and/or gas well is located must be in conformance with all applicable setbacks. . . ."

21. The Dallas Gas Drilling Task Force (*see* note 19, *supra*), for example, did not address the applicability of setbacks to subsequent development near a gas well; rather, the Task Force recommended that once a specific use permit for gas drilling has been granted, the City, on its GIS maps and through appropriate document recording at the county, will establish a notice overlay of the gas drilling use within 1,000 feet of the gas drilling pad site to provide notice for future development and further, the notice must remain for the length of the specific use permit.

22. *Texas Earthquakes: Operation of Saltwater Injection Disposal Well in Area Was a 'Plausible Cause,'* SCIENCEDAILY (Mar. 10, 2010), http://www.sciencedaily .com/releases/2010/03/100310134158.htm.

23. *See, e.g.,* Dallas, Tex., Code of Ordinances § 51A-12.107(a)(5); Flower Mound, Tex., Code of Ordinances § 34-427(a)(32); North Richland Hills, Tex., Code of Ordinances § 104-13(y); Grapevine, Tex., Code of Ordinances § 12-145(c)(12); Southlake, Tex., Code of Ordinances § 9.5-242(v).

24. *See, e.g.,* Dallas, Tex., Code of Ordinances § 51A-12.106(h) ("Before issuance of a gas well permit, the operator shall give the gas inspector a road repair performance bond or an irrevocable letter of credit. . . .").

25. *See, e.g.,* Southlake, Tex., Code of Ordinances § 9.5-231 ("A statement of intent to enter into a road repair agreement shall be submitted in conjunction with the application for specific use permit. . . . The terms of the road repair agreement must be approved by the city council as a condition of the specific use permit and signed by the operator prior to the issuance of any specific use permit. . . ."); Flower Mound, Tex., Code of Ordinances § 34-421(d)(18) (With a drilling permit application, an applicant must provide a "signed road maintenance agreement supplied by the town that provides that the operator shall repair, at his or her own expense, any

damage to public roads, streets, or highways caused by the use of heavy vehicles for any activity associated with the preparation, drilling, production, and operation of oil and/or gas wells"); Grand Prairie, Tex., Code of Ordinances § 13-522 (Exhibits A and B to said section provide road damage assessment fees for new and existing wells, respectively).

26. Flower Mound, Tex., Code of Ordinances, Appendix A, fee specified for Section 43-421(d)(18).

14

An Industry Perspective from Texas
Developing Unconventional Shale Oil and Gas Resources

R. Kinnan Golemon

THE "SHALE GALE"

In a rather brief time period—approximately a decade—the era of unconventional resource development has revolutionized the U.S. oil and gas exploration and production (E&P) industry. In the United States, it inaugurated what the International Energy Agency has called an "energy renaissance."[1] This has driven renewed capital investment, ushered in significant technological advancement, resulted in deployment of innovative and more effective and efficient equipment, and brought increased activity in existing oil and gas fields, expansion of exploration to newly accessible resources, and historic upticks in domestic oil and natural gas production.

The author acknowledges the research assistance of Adam J. Yagelski, MRP.

Fundamentally, the technology associated with this revolution has a long and highly successful history. Hydraulic fracturing as a well completion technology can be traced to the use of liquid nitroglycerin to stimulate shallow rock wells in several Appalachian states in the 1860s. Modern hydraulic fracturing can be traced to an experimental fracturing treatment applied in Kansas' Hugoton gas field in 1947 to a well operated by Stanolind Oil. Working with the Haliburton Oil Well Cementing Company, Stanolind later performed the first two commercial slickwater frac treatments. These took place in March of 1949 in Oklahoma and Texas using crude oil as frac fluid and sand as proppant.[2] Advances in fracturing technology since these early treatments, including vastly improved fluids, proppants, pumping and blending equipment, and fracture treatment design,[3] have increased hydrocarbon recovery rates and are key to understanding the "shale gale."[4]

Still, while well over one million wells in the United States have been hydraulically fractured, like Stanolind's early treatments, the vast majority of these have been in the conventional oil and gas context (i.e. vertical wells that are not in tight reservoirs).[5] Thus, it is also important to understand how the Barnett Shale formation in Texas functioned as a test bed for the specific combination of technologies deployed to unlock vast volumes of gas deposits in tight reservoirs. It was the first shale gas formation to be harvested with hydraulically fractured, long lateral, horizontal wells. Due to these novel methods, it became the nation's largest producing natural gas field in less than a decade after their initial deployment. Indeed, approximately 50 percent of the onshore shale gas and oil rigs deployed in the United States are drilling in Texas.[6]

Essential to development of the Barnett—and, thus, the subsequent increase in unconventional drilling in the U.S. and beyond—was the persistence of businessman George Mitchell, who saw that hydraulic fracturing had the potential to unlock hydrocarbons in low permeability, low porosity rock formations;[7] the horizontal drilling expertise of Devon Energy; and the "slickwater frac" technology developed by Union Pacific Resources Corporation (UPRC).[8] This novel drilling practice, the development of which also enjoyed notable federal support,[9] has spurred recovery of previously untapped unconventional (tight) oil and gas resources.

From the industry perspective, "fracking" is not a drilling process or a reference to the overall life of the well; rather, it is an element of well completion necessary to establish production (thus, a short phase at the tail end of the effort to extract recoverable hydrocarbons). In essence, fluid under pressure is deployed to create artificial porosity (fractures) in the very dense and very deep subsurface hydrocarbon bearing formations. Most often, this fluid is composed of water with sand (or other proppants) and approximately 0.5 percent high viscosity chemical additives that combine to form a gel which promotes flow and enhanced stimulation of the hydrocarbon reserve. The mixture is then injected in a multistage operation with fracture stimulations occurring sequentially in each of the various previously perforated well bore sections.

Stephen A. Holditch, petroleum engineering professor emeritus at Texas A&M University, who has focused his career on oil and natural gas well completion and stimulation, has stated, "The most important time in the life of a well completed in an unconventional reservoir is when the fracture treatments are pumped. You can have perfect geology and drilling, run the perfect casing string and build the perfect pipeline, but if the optimum fracture treatment is not designed and pumped, the operator can leave a lot of money on the table. Many times the operator doesn't even know it."[10] Thus, with hydraulically stimulated wells, proper deployment of optimum treatment technology have long been the key to maximizing return on investment.

Given its history of successful use as a well completion and "stimulation" technology, hydraulic fracturing has long been a part of state and local regulatory programs—most often as a subset of the drilling and completion regulations applicable to vertical wells. Therefore, many of the concerns associated with the shale gale, centering on the combination of high-volume hydraulic fracturing and horizontal drilling, are not without precedent. Similarly, many of the mitigation strategies and other protections historically used by the energy industry remain relevant, useful, and effective. However, several novel issues have occurred with the increased deployment of fracturing to access new hydrocarbon deposits.[11]

Groundwater Contamination

While many have alleged that fracking is a significant threat to useable groundwater, this refers to the broader definition of fracking and not to fracturing technology as described above. Proper installation and testing of well bore casing and cementing is critical to preventing groundwater contamination. These steps are also essential for efficient hydrocarbon recovery and thereby part of normal drilling operations, regardless of whether or not fracturing takes place.[12]

Based on the past 100 years or so of oil and gas drilling activity, many threats to drinking water supplies are known and manageable. Surface spills of fluids, handling of drilling and production related fluids at the surface, and inadequate casing design and construction—some of the principal causes of contamination—can be and, indeed, are addressed by industry best practices. They are also codified in applicable state regulations. For example, Pennsylvania requires that an erosion and sediment control plan be prepared for certain construction activities,[13] and Colorado has a number of well casing regulations that outline, among other things, design, construction, and testing standards.[14]

Other frequently cited threats to groundwater are the result of misunderstandings. For example, groundwater commonly contains many naturally occurring constituents that exceed primary and secondary federal drinking water standards.[15] And in areas where coal and other fossil fuels are present at depth, almost 25 percent of the near surface drinking groundwater has detectable methane. In many instances, very significant concentrations of methane are identified as being present prior to any gas and oil exploration taking place. Further, methane is typically present in zones above the targeted hydrocarbon bearing rock, occasionally resulting in blowouts when drilling.

Consumptive Water Use

Since water is fundamental to all types of energy production and energy is essential for water development (e.g., pumping, treating, and distribution), it becomes necessary to look closely at the energy/water nexus. In recent years, the study of this aspect has drawn considerable attention and has been the focus of a number of researchers and academics.[16]

Interestingly, data developed by the U.S. Department of Energy (DOE) in 2006[17] permit a comparison of the water efficiency of all forms of energy production. The result of this comparison is that the most efficient energy supply in terms of gallons of water used per MMBTU of energy produced are conventional and unconventional shale gas extraction (and the industry has reduced gallons of water used per BTU in the past five years or so).[18] Although some water injected as fracturing fluid remains in the target formation for "geologic time," water permanently removed from the hydrologic cycle in this manner is offset by combustion of the gas produced. This is because combustion of methane produces water vapor as a byproduct.[19]

In addition, water used for oil and shale gas drilling tends to be a small amount of water used relative to other water consuming activities in a given basin. In Texas, for example, even in very active drilling areas such as the Barnett Shale, only about 2–4 percent of total water consumed is used in drilling, and only 1.6 percent of the water used statewide is used for oil and shale gas drilling.[20] This consumption level is quite low when compared to water use by agriculture, municipal, commercial, industrial, and electricity generation (the largest consumer in many areas). All of the latter uses are at least in double digit percentages.

However, sourcing water—even in water-rich regions—can remain a challenge, especially during periods of drought in more heavily regulated river basins,[21] and concerns remain about the cumulative local impacts of permanent removal of water from the hydrologic cycle.[22]

Water Quality Management

Greater public scrutiny and the spread of unconventional shale gas and oil development to new geographies have caused many forward-looking companies to develop aggressive plans for holistic water management, a rapidly changing sector of the oil and gas industry that includes advancements in treatment, recycling, and containment.

Among the novel water management challenges posed by unconventional oil and gas development is identification of chemicals included in fracturing fluids. Recognizing this as a central concern, companies have increasingly moved toward voluntary disclosure. Indeed, industry-backed reporting mechanisms like FracFocus.org have formed the foundation of mandatory disclosure rules.[23] In addition, industry and regulators have made progress with regard to spills, leaks, and other issues relating to surface capture and containment. The use of catchments, stormwater runoff controls, groundwater monitoring, and buffers are regularly used by some operators and increasingly required by regulators.[24]

Treatment and/or disposal of produced water is a more significant water management challenge. The initial flowback water from a well that has been fractured has a constituency very similar to the content of the injected "frac fluid," while the character of later returns, the "produced water" exhibits more natural contaminants—salts, in particular—from the hydrocarbon reserve zone.

In conventional oil and gas drilling, the produced water was most often collected, transported by truck, and injected into deep saline aquifer formations, or deep saline aquifers, due to its high salinity.[25] However, due to the spread of shale gas and oil development—some occurring where there is an absence of deep saline aquifers—and the increased volume of contaminated produced water generated, there has been an urgent need for improvements in the technology for handling and treatment of these waters, both to reduce costs and to protect the environment.

Several options currently exist for management of produced water. Broadly, these have included: discharge, disposal in underground injection wells, underground injection to increase oil recovery, evaporation, offsite commercial disposal, and beneficial reuse.[26] Increasingly, recycling and reuse is a sixth management option, especially for flowback waters.[27] Underground injection has historically been the fate of 95 percent of produced water in the U.S. oil and gas industry,[28] but different management options are used in different parts of the country.

Discharge, for example, is used primarily by the offshore segment. Evaporation requires the use of large impoundments, which pose wildlife and dam failure risks. In addition, the concentrated solids left behind must be disposed of. Closed tanks can be used in place of impoundments and are part of proposed regulations—along with secondary containment—in New York State. Beneficial reuse, such as anti-icing application to roadways, is typically contingent upon the quality of produced water.

Treatment—the most complex and resource-intensive option—is evolving. Offsite options include centralized waste treatment facilities (CWT) and publicly owned treatment works (POTWs). Sending produced water to POTWs can be problematic, as treatment processes at these facilities can be disrupted by produced water and they are typically not designed to accept waste with such high salinity (dissolved solids). While CWTs can be designed to remove more salts, other pollutants, such as bromide as well as naturally occurring radioactive material (NORM), require specialized treatment.[29]

Several aspects of oil and gas production have made developing suitable water treatment technology more challenging, such as the wide variability in the makeup of the contaminated produced water, the erosion potential of proppants used (e.g., sand), and the extreme heat content of the fluid. In addition, the pressure tolerance requirements for the shale oil and gas waste water equipment used to collect flowback at the wellhead are very different from what has been most often seen by the water treatment community.

Even after a decade of shale gas and oil development, the vast majority of the produced water is still handled in the traditional manner of aboveground gathering for trucking and disposal via either underground injection or dewatering and burial. Fortunately, however, there currently are significant changes taking place. Increasingly, new treatment and containment technologies are used to recycle and reuse produced water throughout the United States and Canada. As a result, many companies now use a combination of freshwater and produced water in their operations.

Air Quality Considerations

The air contaminants that arise from shale gas and oil operations resemble those of traditional oil and gas production, such as volatile organic compounds (VOCs), methane, and air toxics, such as benzene, among others. These pollutants are emitted at several points of the oil and gas production process, such as well completion, gas processing, and transmission. Thus, many of the measures and devices deployed to minimize such emissions are the same. In addition, for the most part, these are emissions that are classified as "minor sources," a group of sources that, under the federal Clean Air Act, are regulated primarily by states.[30]

However, there are at least two important differences in air quality considerations when comparing conventional versus unconventional developments. The first concerns the marked increase in emissions (particularly of VOCs and methane) during the flowback stage, when up to 40 percent of the fracturing fluid pumped into the formation returns to the surface over a period of several days. The volume of flowback and how it occurs in the well completion process distinguish it from conventional well completion activities. The oil and gas industry, in view of significant lost revenues (i.e., gas not entering a pipeline) has addressed this issue with technology that cuts down on emissions during flowback (so-called green completions)—technology that is now required by federal rules.[31]

The rapid growth of production from shale oil and gas developments has also brought about an increase in "flaring" of waste gas, which, due to its visibility, draws considerable public attention.

The flaring of waste gas occurs in several circumstances, including: (1) when the gas pressure upon well completion is not sufficient to overcome the existing pressure in available gas transmission lines; (2) when gas associated with the production of NGL (natural gas liquids) and crude oil is in a locale with an absence of natural gas transmission lines; and (3) when low pressure gas is generated from production-related units intermittently (causing such waste gas to be routed to a destruction device). In these instances, most state regulatory programs authorize the flaring of the gas, with standards established as to the emission control device efficiency.

Over the past several years, EPA has been in the process of the development of New Source Performance Standards (NSPS) and National Emission Standards for Hazardous Air Pollutants (NESHAPS) for certain oil and gas sector operations and these were finally signed on April 17, 2012.[32]

Various aspects of the rule—primarily affecting only shale natural gas production—are being challenged due to internal inconsistencies within the rule language, certain pieces of equipment not being widely available by the time such are mandated to be in place, EPA misperception of initial emission quantities associated with bringing new gas wells into production (leading to gross over-estimation of methane emissions),[33] the "source category" being expanded well beyond that established for other sectors in prior NSPS rulemakings, a lack of cost effectiveness consideration, etc. While still controversial, the final rule received wider support than earlier drafts EPA had circulated.

Earthquakes

The number and frequency of seismic activity being measured in relatively close proximity to some of the new shale gas and oil plays has also become a topic for significant public discussion as well as the basis for numerous recent investigations.

Although most technical observers have concluded that fracking, due to the depth of its occurrence and the short duration of the fracture activity, is not associated with this phenomenon, a recent Canadian study takes a contrary position. Using several data sources, including proprietary operator data and an historical investigation of past seismicity, this analysis linked fracturing operations to a series of unusual seismic events in the Horn River Basin.[34]

The majority of those who have investigated and studied many of the recent minor earthquake events and found an association with oil and gas activity point to the injection of waste fluids under high pressure at injection well sites located in close proximity to existing faults as being a cause for the increased seismic activity. This has led to scientists at the U.S. Geological Service and elsewhere to undertake comprehensive studies. The result of these investigative efforts will no doubt form the basis for additional state and, possibly federal, rules to be promulgated in the near future that will impact injection well operations.[35]

Landscape and Community Impacts

Some of the most significant impacts of the shale gale are generally associated with community change. The overwhelming volume of new activity associated with intense drilling activity and processing and transmission of produced hydrocarbons can cause highly disruptive changes very rapidly—especially where drilling has not occurred before. These changes can include: lack of available housing, insufficient existing infrastructure to support large population increases, and lack of available public safety, emergency medical and other services, among other impacts. In addition, because high-volume hydraulic fracturing equipment is highly specialized and expensive, if the price of gas goes down, a well crew and its equipment may be transferred to another state to use the equipment to frac for oil.[36]

The effects of truck traffic have become a central concern. Several states impacted by the shale gale have attempted to quantify the impacts on transportation-related infrastructure due to the drilling and production activity. For example, in 2012, Texas Department of Transportation (TDOT) officials testified that "the volume of truck traffic required to bring a single gas well into production is equivalent to the impact of approximately eight million cars." Specifically, TDOT-supported research has documented the following:

1. bringing a single gas well into production results in 1,184 heavy truck loads (>80,000 lbs.);
2. maintaining production annually results in 353 heavy truck loads; and
3. refracturing results in a total of 975 heavy truck loads.[37]

Another way of expressing the truck traffic impacts is to look at the road consumption that is associated with a given activity. A recent Texas study was able to determine the additional road damage associated with natural gas development, given the design parameters (e.g., traffic volume and type) of the highway infrastructure analyzed. The authors found that, during the well construction phase, drilling 10 natural gas wells on one pad site would generate additional traffic sufficient to reduce road service life by as much as 29 percent.[38] For a road built to last 20 years, this means that maintenance intervention would be required after only 14 years.

Such increases in truck traffic have also caused new safety concerns and exacerbated existing road safety issues, including increases in serious accidents and fatalities. Between 2008 and 2009, for instance,[39] Bradford County, Pennsylvania, experienced a 25 percent increase in traffic fatalities.[40] Probably in view of similar concerns, the TDOT has moved to decrease speed limits in some areas affected by energy development. It has also constructed truck inspection sites to ensure that traffic stops and enforcement efforts do not become additional safety hazards.[41]

SHALE OIL AND GAS INDUSTRY IS RESHAPING THE U.S. ENERGY INDUSTRY AND ECONOMY

At the start of this century, less than 2 percent of U.S. domestic oil and gas was being produced from tight formations. Recent projections suggest that by the year 2040, 50 percent of U.S. domestic gas production will come from shale gas formations,[42] and significant geo-political ramifications are expected.[43] In the United States, these effects include job creation,[44] the potential for increased natural gas exports, the lowest natural gas prices in a decade,[45] lower costs for manufacturers,[46] and massive U.S. domestic investments.[47]

Throughout 2012, the United States average daily production of oil has exceeded 6,000,000 bbls per day (a rate last seen in 1990).[48] It is anticipated that this production level will continue to rise once additional pipelines and processing facilities are brought on line to accommodate NGL and oil production occurring in relatively new fields (e.g., Bakken, Cana Woodford, Eagle Ford, Granite Wash, Mississippian, and Utica Shales).

The aforementioned challenges notwithstanding, the emergence of shale oil and gas production has, and will continue to have, many positive impacts on both the energy industry and the U.S. economy. Positive environmental impacts are also occurring. Increased use of natural gas as a fuel source for electricity is displacing coal at a steadily increasing rate and will continue to do so in the future.[49] Thus, according to the Energy Information Agency (EIA), U.S. energy-related carbon emissions were the lowest in the past 20 years during the first quarter of 2012.[50]

In addition, a robust phase of capital investment is occurring. It is primarily directed at establishment of new supply locations (or enhancement of existing locations), delivery of the product to market, and taking advantage of near term opportunities brought into being by lower energy costs. We are currently seeing billions of dollars of investments being announced for crude oil, natural gas and NGL pipelines, processing, storage and delivery facilities, and new chemical manufacturing plants. In addition, several entities are investigating opportunities for the construction of natural gas-to-diesel plants.[51]

Ultimately, consumers will also benefit. The immediate aspect is the investment in new natural gas-fired power plants to replace aging coal-fired units or to meet new consumer demand (often as a result of the phase one and two capital investments). The greater supply of natural gas will likely lead to new investments in the nation's heavy-duty vehicular fleet—new engine technology and fueling outlets will be needed to run buses and fleet vehicles on natural gas. There is also the possibility that natural gas-powered light-duty vehicles will become attractive for capital investors.

SIGNIFICANT ECONOMIC BENEFITS FOR STATE AND LOCAL GOVERNMENTS

The nature of taxation of mineral resource values and production, as well as state and local government ownership of minerals, varies greatly throughout the 50 states. Nevertheless, depending upon the tax structures in place, the ability of state and local governments in areas experiencing increased shale oil and gas production to raise revenue will likely increase.

The author's decades-long experience within Texas serves as a background for the following industry viewpoint:

1. Taxes and royalties paid to Texas state and local treasuries totaled $9.3 billion from the oil and gas sector in fiscal year 2011 (ending on August 31, 2012);[52]
2. Royalties paid in fiscal year 2011 to State of Texas funds amounted to $1.5 billion and property taxes (paid only to

local treasuries) were $3.2 billion, with some 90 percent of Texas counties receiving some property tax revenues from the oil and gas industry; and

3. Severance taxes paid from the production of oil and gas caused $2.6 billion to be added to the State's Economic Stabilization Fund (i.e., rainy day fund) in fiscal year 2011.

Comparison of the taxes and royalties attributable to oil and gas industry employees versus taxes and royalties attributable to all other private sector jobs within a state provides another indication of the economic impact of the oil and gas industry. In Texas, based upon data compiled by the Texas Comptroller's office and the Texas Workforce Commission, Tax & Fiscal Consulting (an Austin, Texas, firm) determined that the oil and gas sector paid an average of $27,731 per job of taxes and royalties to governmental treasuries as compared to an average of $4,733 per job paid to these entities by all other private sector jobs.

Conclusion

Like every other aspect of mineral extraction, the drilling, completion, and production of hydrocarbon resources contained in shale and other tight formations does not occur without some community impacts, changes to the local landscape, or potential threats to the environment.

However, from the perspective of an operator, the potential environmental threats resulting from shale oil and gas development are not really different from a control or management standpoint than long-established environmental controls for conventional onshore oil and gas exploration projects. Balancing negative impacts with positive impacts, such as increased employment opportunities, greater earning potential and—most often—bolstered state and local treasury coffers, can pose a significant challenge.

Issues that need to be addressed include:

1. Developing proper holistic water quality management;
2. Ensuring adequate regulatory programs, unique to the area of drilling activity, are in place, and that enforcement and compliance are made a priority; and

3. Securing a portion of funds generated by drilling to be used to minimize local adverse impacts and to provide adequate infrastructure to ensure that continued production is sustained to meet future energy needs.

As to the immediate future, determining which level (or levels) of government will regulate these things will be considerably easier in those areas of the United States that have previously experienced significant gas and oil exploration, production, and development. In those areas without recent exposure to oil and gas industry activities, it will most likely be quite some time before the details of various levels of governmental controls will be finally resolved.

NOTES

1. This is the IEA's term. INT'L ENERGY AGENCY, WORLD ENERGY OUTLOOK 2012, at 74 (2012) ("the Global energy map is changing [and] is being redrawn by the resurgence in oil and gas production in the United States").
2. Carl T. Montgomery & Michael B. Smith, *Hydraulic Fracturing: History of an Enduring Technology*, J. PETROLEUM TECH., Dec. 2010, at 26; *available at* http://www.spe.org/jpt/print/archives/2010/12/10Hydraulic.pdf.
3. *See id.*
4. As early as 2007, the phrase "shale gale" signified the wide-ranging effects of natural gas from unconventional sources (D. Yergin & R. Ineson, *America's Natural Gas Revolution*, WALL ST. J. (Nov. 2, 2009). More recently, "shale gale" also includes use of gas as an industrial feedstock for the petrochemical industry. R. Westervel, *Shale Gale*, CHEMICAL WEEK, Oct. 15, 2012, at 24–25.
5. *See also supra* chapter 1.
6. *Rig Count Overview and Summary Count*, BAKER HUGHES, http://www.baker hughes.com/rig-count.
7. *See Gas Works*, ECONOMIST, July 14, 2012.
8. Michael Shellenberger, *Interview with Dan Steward, Former Mitchell Energy Vice President*, THE BREAKTHROUGH (Dec. 12, 2011), http://thebreak through.org/archive/interview_with_dan_steward_for.
9. *See* M. Shellenberger & T. Nordhaus, *A Boom in Shale Gas? Credit the Feds*, WASH. POST., Dec. 16, 2011. In a recent interview, a former Mitchell Energy official stated, "[Department of Energy] started it, and other people took the ball and ran with it. You cannot diminish DOE's involvement," referring to government support that helped Mitchell Energy to, among other things, estimate reservoir size, critical geologic properties, drilling Mitchell's first

horizontal lateral, and "crack mapping" during early exploration of the Barnett Shale. Shellenberger, *supra* note 8.

10. Stephen A. Holditch, *Unconventional Reservoirs: Getting to the Source*, AM. OIL & GAS REP., Jan. 2012, at 59.

11. An excellent resource for understanding the perspective of the shale oil and gas industry is *A Joint Association Education Message from the Texas Oil and Gas Industry*, http://www.oilandnaturalgassintexas.com. Some industry-specific viewpoints are set forth separately below.

12. Well integrity (i.e., properly designed and implemented casing and cementing) is "fundamental to good outcomes in drilling oil and gas wells," including isolation of groundwater. *See generally*, SEC'Y OF ENERGY'S ADVISORY BOARD, SHALE GAS PRODUCTION SUBCOMMITTEE: NINETY-DAY REPORT (Aug. 18, 2011) [hereinafter Subcommittee Report]. Indeed, well construction, including casing and cementing, is the subject of industry guidance, AM. PETROL. INST., GUIDANCE DOCUMENT HF1, HYDRAULIC FRACTURING OPERATIONS-WELL CONSTRUCTION AND INTEGRITY GUIDELINES (1st ed. Oct. 2009), *available at* http://www.shalegas.energy.gov/resources/HF1.pdf, as well as widespread—if variable—state regulatory controls, U.S. DEP'T OF ENERGY, STATE OIL AND NATURAL GAS REGULATIONS DESIGNED TO PROTECT WATER RESOURCES 17–21 (NETL) (May 2009), *available at* http://www.gwpc.org/sites/default/files/state_oil_and_gas_regulations_designed _to_protect_water_resources_0.pdf). (*See also* Hannah Jacobs Wiseman, *Risk and Response in Fracturing Policy*, U. Colo. L. Rev. (forthcoming 2013), SSRN #2017104, at 49–51(discussing the importance of well integrity during drilling, fracturing, production, and abandonment).)

13. Erosion and Sediment Control, 1 PA. CODE § 78.53, *available at* http://www .pacode.com/secure/data/025/chapter78/s78.53.html.

14. Colo. Oil and Gas Comm'n, Rule 317d-j.

15. According to EPA, "National Primary Drinking Water Regulations (NPD-WRs or primary standards) are legally enforceable standards that apply to public water systems. Primary standards protect public health by limiting the levels of contaminants in drinking water." By contrast, "National Secondary Drinking Water Regulations (NSDWRs or secondary standards) are non-enforceable guidelines regulating contaminants that may cause cosmetic effects (such as skin or tooth discoloration) or aesthetic effects (such as taste, odor, or color) in drinking water." *See Drinking Water Contaminants*, EPA, http://water.epa.gov/drink/contaminants/index.cfm.

16. *See, e.g.*, Jean-Philippe Nicot & Bridget R. Scanlon, *Water Use for Shale-Gas Production in Texas*, U.S. 46 ENVTL. SCI. & TECH. 3580 (2012); Brian G. Rham & Susan J. Riha, *Toward Strategic Management of Shale Gas Development: Regional, Collective Impacts on Water Resources*, ENVTL. SCI. & POLICY, Jan. 2011, at 12; J. DANIEL ARTHUR, MIKE URETSKY, & PRESTON WILSON, ALL CONSULTING LLC, WATER RESOURCES AND USE FOR HYDRAULIC FRACTURING

IN THE MARCELLUS SHALE REGION (2010), *available at* http://www.all-llc.com /publicdownloads/WaterResourcePaperALLConsulting.pdf.

17. U.S. DEP'T OF ENERGY, ENERGY DEMAND ON WATER RESOURCES: REPORT TO CONGRESS ON THE INTERDEPENDENCY OF ENERGY AND WATER (2006).

18. *See, e.g.*, Erik Mielke, Laura Diaz Anadon & Venkatesth Narayanamurti, *Water Consumption of Energy Resource Extraction, Processing, and Conversion, A Review of the Literature for Estimates of Water Intensity of Energy-Resource Extraction, Processing to Fuels, and Conversion to Electricity*, at 6, 18 (Energy Technology Innovation Policy Discussion Paper No. 2010-15, Belfer Center for Science and International Affairs, Harvard Kennedy School, Harvard University, Oct. 2010) (citing industry and USGS sources, which put the average "water intensity" (defined as "gallons of water per million British thermal unit of fuel for fuel production and processing") for shale gas production between 1.2 and 1.3 gal/MMBtu and stating that "The increased role of shale gas in the U.S. energy sector could result in reduced water consumption.")

19. The most widely cited supporting analysis is MATTHEW E. MANTELL, DEEP SHALE NATURAL GAS AND WATER USE, PART TWO: ABUNDANT, AFFORDABLE AND STILL WATER EFFICIENT (2010), *available at* http://www.springs gov.com/units/boardscomm/OilGas/GWPC%20-%20Deep%20Shale% 20Natural%20Gas%20and%20Water%20Use.pdf. Mantell calculates that combustion of on MMCF of natural gas will produce some 10,700 gallons of water vapor.

20. JEAN-PHILIPPE NICOT, ET AL., TEX. BUREAU OF ECON. GEOGOLOGY, OIL & GAS WATER USE IN TEXAS: UPDATE TO THE 2011 MINING WATER USE REPORT (2012).

21. *See supra* chapters 8 and 9.

22. *See* Heather Cooley, Kristina Donnelly, Nancy Ross, & Paula Luu, HYDRAULIC FRACTURING AND WATER RESOURCES: SEPARATING THE FRACK FROM THE FICTION (2012), *available at* http://www.pacinst.org/reports/fracking /full_report.pdf at 15–17 (citing a lack of watershed-level information on local impacts of water withdrawals).

23. *See* PowerPoint: Kathryn Mutz & Bruce Kramer, Presentation at Institute for Energy Law, 3d Law of Shale Plays Conference, *Best Management Practices for Oil and Gas Development* (June 6–7, 2012). For example, TEX. NAT. RES. CODE S 91.851 and 16 TEX. ADMIN. CODE S 3.29 set out the Texas Railroad Commission's disclosure requirement and establish the FracFocus website as the public reporting mechanism, respectively. Similarly, the Bureau of Land Management is considering adopting the website for disclosure requirements. While the U.S. Department of Energy helped pay development costs, America's Natural Gas Alliance and the American Petroleum Institute currently pay the site's operating costs. Benjamin Haas et al., *Fracking Hazards Obscured in Failure to Disclose Wells*, BLOOMBERG (Aug. 14, 2012, 5:26 PM),

http://www.bloomberg.com/news/2012-08-14/fracking-hazards-obscured-in
-failure-to-disclose-wells.html.

24. Subcommittee Report, *supra* note 12, at 20.

25. "Saline aquifers" are sedimentary rocks saturated with water having a high
dissolved solids content. Like other aquifers, the flow of water can be open or
confined. The term "*deep* saline aquifer" refers to a sedimentary basin confined
from above and below by shales (or other formations), from which water cannot be produced and through which water flows at a much, much lower rate
(i.e., "on a geological time scale"). *See* INT'L ENERGY AGENCY, CO2 CAPTURE
AND STORAGE: A KEY CARBON ABATEMENT OPTION 103–104 (2008), *available at*
http://www.iea.org/publications/freepublications/publication/CCS_2008.pdf
(discussing the characteristics of deep saline aquifers in relation to their carbon capture and sequestration potential).

26. C.E. CLARK & J.A. VEIL, ARGONNE NATIONAL LABORATORY, REPORT NO.
ANL/EVS/R-09/1, PRODUCED WATER VOLUMES AND MANAGEMENT PRAC-
TICES IN THE UNITED STATES 15–18 (2009), *available at* http://www.ipd.anl
.gov/anlpubs/2009/07/64622.pdf.

27. REBECCA HAMMER & JEANNE VANBRIESEN, NATURAL RES. DEF. COUNCIL
REPORT NO. D:12-05-A, IN FRACKING'S WAKE: NEW RULES ARE NEEDED TO
PROTECT OUR HEALTH AND ENVIRONMENT FROM CONTAMINATED WASTE-
WATER 3 (May 2012), *available at* http://www.nrdc.org/energy/files/Fracking
-Wastewater-FullReport.pdf.

28. This figure is for 2007. CLARK & VEIL, *supra* note 26.

29. HAMMER & VANBRIESEN, *supra* note 27, at 5–7.

30. For additional, brief discussion of the distinction between "major" and
"minor" sources, see Hannah Jacobs Wiseman & Francis Gradijan, *Regulation of Shale Gas Development, Including Hydraulic Fracturing*, at 64–67 (University of Tulsa Legal Studies Research Paper No. 2011-11, Oct. 31, 2011),
available at SSRN: http://ssrn.com/abstract=1953547.

31. EPA, Overview of Final Amendments to Air Regulations For the Oil and
Natural Gas Industry, *available at* http://www.epa.gov/airquality/oilandgas
/pdfs/20120417fs.pdf.

32. 76 Fed. Reg. 52,737–52,843 (Aug. 23, 2011) (proposed); http://www.epa
.gov/airquality/oilandgas/pdfs/20120417finalrule.pdf (signed by EPA Administrator Lisa Jackson).

33. TERRI SHIRES & MIRIAM LEV-ON, CHARACTERIZING PIVOTAL SOURCES OF
METHANE EMISSIONS FROM UNCONVENTIONAL NATURAL GAS PRODUCTION:
SUMMARY AND ANALYSIS OF API AND ANGA RESPONSES (Sept. 21, 2012).

34. BC OIL AND GAS COMM'N, INVESTIGATION OF OBSERVED SEISMICITY IN THE
HORN RIVER BASIN (Aug. 2012).

35. For example, Arkansas Oil & Gas Commission has designated certain
earthquake-prone areas as unsuitable for injection wells. *See* Shane Khoury,
Deputy Director/General Counsel, Arkansas Oil and Gas Commission,

Presentation in *When Fracking Comes to a Community Near You: An Ounce of Land Use Planning Is Worth a Pound of Cure*, a CLE program of the ABA Section of State and Local Government Law, at ABA Midyear Meeting in New Orleans, La. (Feb. 2, 2012).

36. *See also supra* chapter 11.

37. Phil Wilson, Impact of Energy Development Activities on the Texas Transportation Infrastructure, Testimony Before the House Committee on Energy Resources (Jan. 26, 2012), *available at* http://ftp.dot.state.tx.us/pub /txdot-info/energy/testimony_062612.pdf). Re-fracturing was assumed to take place every five years.

38. Ambarish Banerjee, Jolanda Prozzi, & Jorge A. Prozzi, Evaluating the Impact of Natural Gas Developments on Highways: A Texas Case Study (Transp. Research Bd. Report # TRB 12-0800, 2012), *available at* http://docs.trb.org/prp/12-0800.pdf; *see also supra* chapter 6.

39. Simona L. Perry, *Development, Land Use, and Collective Trauma: The Marcellus Shale Gas Boom in Rural Pennsylvania*, 34 Culture, Agric., Food & Env't 81, 84 (2012).

40. This could be related increased driver fatigue. Federal Motor Carrier Safety Administration (FMCSA) hours of service (HOS) regulations (Part 395 of the Federal Motor Carrier Safety Regulations), which limit when and for how long drivers may operate commercial motor vehicles (CMV), contain two exemptions for "oilfield operations" (the so-called "24-hour restart" and "oilfield waiting time" exceptions, found at § 395.1(d)(1) & § 395.1(d)(2), respectively). Provided certain conditions are met, these exceptions generally allow operators to increase work performed in a given period. In June 2012, the FMCSA issued regulatory guidance concerning these exceptions, noting that "A significant increase in oil and gas drilling operations in many States has resulted in a major increase in CMV traffic. 77 Fed. Reg. 33,098-33,100 (June 5, 2012).

41. Wilson, *supra* note 37.

42. U.S. Energy Info. Admin., Annual Energy Outlook 2013, at 79 (2013), *available at* http://www.eia.gov/forecasts/aeo/pdf/0383(2013).pdf.

43. According to the IEA, "the Global energy map is changing [and] is being redrawn by the resurgence in oil and gas production in the United States." Int'l Energy Agency, World Energy Outlook 2012, at 23 (2012). This has also been reflected in the popular press, *See e.g., Shale a New Kingmaker in Energy Geopolitics*, Wall St. J. (Sept. 31, 2012); *U.S. Redraws World Oil Map*, Wall St. J. (Nov. 13, 2012).

44. IHS Inc., America's New Energy Future: The Unconventional Oil and Gas Revolution and the U.S. Economy (2012).

45. Contantine von Hoffman, *US recovery fueled by record low natural gas prices*, CBS News (Feb. 24, 2012), http://www.cbsnews.com/8301-505123_162 -57384014/us-recovery-fueled-by-record-low-natural-gas-prices/.

46. Boston Consulting Group Report (Sept. 2012).

47. Am. Clean Skies Found., Tech Effect: How Innovation in Oil and Gas Exploration Is Spurring the U.S. Economy (Oct. 2012), *available at* http://www.cleanskies.org/wp-content/uploads/2012/11/icfreport_11012012_web.pdf.

48. *December 2012 Monthly Statistical Report*, Am. Petrol. Inst., Jan. 18, 2013, *available at* http://www.api.org/~/media/Files/News/2013/13-January/12-December-MSR.pdf.

49. For example, between 2000 and 2010, natural gas represented 81 percent of total electricity generation capacity added over that period (*Most Electric Generating Capacity Additions in the Last Decade were Natural Gas-Fired*, U.S. Energy Info. Agency (July 5, 2011), http://www.eia.gov/todayinenergy/detail.cfm?id=2070), and in April 2012, energy generation from natural gas virtually equaled that from coal—a first since EIA began to collect these data in 2007 (*Monthly Coal- and Natural Gas-Fired Generation Equal for First Time in April 2012*, U.S. Energy Info. Agency (July 6, 2012), http://www.eia.gov/todayinenergy/detail.cfm?id=6990).

50. *See U.S. Energy-Related CO_2 Emissions in Early 2012 Lowest Since 1992*, U.S. Energy Info. Agency (Aug. 1, 2012), http://www.eia.gov/todayinenergy/detail.cfm?id=7350 (citing "a decline in coal-fired electricity generation, due largely to historically low natural gas prices" as one contributing factor).

51. One gas-to-liquids plant will be constructed in Louisiana by South African energy company Sasol. Clifford Krauss, *South African Company to Build U.S. Plant to Convert Gas to Liquid Fuels*, N.Y. Times (Dec. 3, 2012), http://www.nytimes.com/2012/12/04/business/energy-environment/sasol-plans-first-gas-to-liquids-plant-in-us.html?_r=0.

52. While there is not a breakout of the actual share of this total that was attributable to shale oil and gas development, the rapid growth of this sector, accompanied with a multi-decade decline in conventional oil and gas well production, supports the conclusion that much of the $9.3 billion comes from shale oil and gas extraction.

PART

4

Critical Issues:
Getting Beyond
the "Fracking Wars"

15

Resolving the Fracking Wars through Planning and Stakeholder Engagement

Kenneth J. Warren

Introduction

In recent years, oil and gas exploration and production companies have combined the techniques of horizontal drilling and high-volume hydraulic fracturing to access oil and gas reserves in unconventional formations, such as shale, that were previously uneconomical to develop. Numerous tight shale formations in the United States are for the first time becoming major sources of energy. For example, the Marcellus Shale located in southern New York State, Pennsylvania, Ohio, and West Virginia is estimated to hold approximately 141 trillion cubic feet of natural gas, one of the largest reservoirs of natural gas in the United States.[1] The ability to economically extract hydrocarbons from the Marcellus Shale and other unconventional formations has dramatically improved the nation's ability to rely on domestic sources of energy over the next several decades.[2]

The potential development of new sources of domestic energy has been met with great enthusiasm by some members of the public. Many advocates of enhanced domestic energy production contend that, particularly in a struggling economy with high unemployment and stagnant middle class incomes, environmental protection goals must yield to economic growth.[3] The mantras of "drill baby drill" and "jobs, jobs, jobs" are familiar offerings in a politically charged debate. They also emphasize our long history of respecting private property rights.

Other members of the public, however, take a different position. They see intensive natural gas exploration and production activities occurring in rural areas unaccustomed to industrial development as a threat to the environmental integrity of our landscapes and ecosystems. They note the importance of the natural environment to our quality of life and emphasize the moral responsibility of each generation to preserve the environment for future generations. Increased production of fossil fuels is anathema to their vision of a clean energy economy.[4] On both a national and local level, they have mobilized to halt such development by employing multiple tactics including scheduling protests and events to attract media coverage,[5] creating documentary films,[6] participating in regulatory proceedings,[7] and commencing litigation.[8]

To be sure, supporters of the position that environmental protection and economic progress can go hand in hand also seek to be heard.[9] And there are landowners who signed leases granting energy companies access to their lands and minerals but still worry about the potential environmental impacts on their properties and communities. However, the voices of the advocates for positions in the center of the spectrum are frequently drowned out by the demands from the extremes.

The polarized debate poses a challenge for resolving disputes in a way that will promote consensus. The typical models in our legal system include resolution through legislation or administrative rulemaking, which is often followed by litigation. These models without modification are not well-suited to reaching a permanent resolution of the natural gas debate. Rather, they have produced temporary victories for one side or another, often depending on which way the political pendulum swings. This chapter will discuss the policy debate over expanding hydraulic fracturing activities to new, rural landscapes overlying shale formations, the potential harms from introducing oil and gas activities into these landscapes, and the actions and proposals of government to date to avoid or mitigate potential harms. It concludes with some suggestions on elements of a workable stakeholder model to achieve long-lasting consensus and resolution. A more detailed discussion of many of the subjects in this chapter is contained in other chapters of this book and elsewhere.[10]

POLICY DEBATE

The development of oil and gas reserves in tight formations has fomented a vigorous policy debate with both national and community-specific dimensions.[11] National stakeholder groups frequently acknowledge only the validity of their own positions, making compromise exceptionally difficult.

Stakeholders dispute the effects of natural gas development on greenhouse gas emissions. Industry argues that use of shale gas rather than coal and oil at electric generation and other facilities will lessen greenhouse gas emissions and thereby reduce our nation's contributions to global warming.[12] Some environmental stakeholders, however, note that shale gas is comprised of methane, a potent greenhouse gas, some of which is released during gas well development.[13] They also see the availability of cheap natural gas as delaying the shift to renewable energy sources that they believe to be necessary for long-term reduction of carbon emissions.

Industry argues that shale gas will promote energy independence.[14] Its advocates note the considerable cost in dollars and lives to maintain the Middle East as a viable energy source. Shale gas is seen as one of the few scalable alternatives. Environmental advocates and some commentators, however, emphasize that in a global economy, the shale gas produced domestically will not be confined to domestic use. They point to the rise in applications by energy companies for approval to export shale gas overseas where prices are higher.[15] The environmental stakeholders have found allies among chemical and other manufacturers who use natural gas for feedstocks. These manufacturers have benefited from the recent availability of cheap, plentiful, domestic natural gas and desire to preserve the competitive advantages that inexpensive natural gas creates.[16]

A principal area of disagreement is the likelihood that oil and gas exploration and production will create environmental harm. The oil and gas industry contends that it has been operating safely for approximately 150 years. In their view, existing regulation by state agencies with substantial expertise is adequate. They assert that landscape changes are temporary; well pad sites are restored once drilling is complete.[17]

In contrast, environmental advocates question whether states have the will to enforce their regulations against a politically powerful industry and support imposing a stringent layer of federal regulations to ensure the safety of natural gas development activities. They note that companies may take several years to develop multiple wells on a well pad, thereby prolonging the period of land disturbance. They see landscape changes as long-lasting and believe that the risk of contamination from drilling, chemical handling and wastewater storage, transportation, and disposal is significant.

Stakeholders also hold disparate views of the economic effects of oil and gas development on local communities. Industry points to the economic benefits from natural gas activities including opportunities for employment, landowner royalties, and an increased tax base.[18] Their opponents and some state politicians respond that many jobs are given to out-of-state workers with no local roots.[19] They assert that not all residents can or will benefit, but all must bear the environmental impact and the municipal costs of hosting natural gas activities, including the costs of road repair and other municipal services. They also point to the potential permanent loss of tourist income as landscapes change and water resources are threatened, all for benefits that they view to be short-lived.[20]

Against this national backdrop, contentions that natural gas exploration and production activities may cause environmental degradation and risks to human health resonate loudly with some residents in communities where natural gas activities are occurring or may soon occur. People who have witnessed rural landscapes changed by the construction of drilling sites, roads, freshwater and wastewater impoundments, and the introduction of truck traffic and noise may fear the potential long-term effects on their families.

A primary concern for many homeowners is their fear of harm to drinking water. The *Gasland* film publicized the presence of methane in certain drinking water wells located near natural gas production activities. Drilling may encounter shallow pockets of methane which may be transmitted to aquifers if proper drilling and casing techniques are not followed.[21] This apparently occurred in Dimock, Pennsylvania, where the Pennsylvania Department of Environmental Protection ordered the natural gas exploration and production company to provide water treatment systems to several residences with high concentrations of methane in their well water.[22] Some residents believe that hydraulic fracturing may itself cause contamination of aquifers, although whether that has ever occurred is in dispute.[23] Drilling activity may also increase the turbidity of drinking water on a temporary basis. This physical change, even absent any long-term health risk, raises the level of public concern.

Air emissions including volatile organic compounds (VOCs) from diesel engines, trucks, and other machinery used to develop natural gas wells may also be of concern to residents.[24] Some experts have suggested that VOCs, which are ozone precursors, may cause effects many miles from their source location. For example, experts retained by plaintiffs in one federal lawsuit opined that natural gas production in Wayne County, Pennsylvania, would cause increased morbidity and mortality from ozone exposure among residents of New York City, which is located over 150 miles from Wayne County. Defendants and putative intervenors introduced expert evidence to the contrary.[25]

In some communities, debate rages over whether leasing mineral rights is helpful or harmful to efforts to preserve farms and open space. Industry and lessors have asserted that royalties from natural gas production will enable farmers to preserve their farms. This argument, however, rings hollow to other community members and environmental advocates. They believe that oil and gas activities will leave a legacy of pollution as the coal mining industry has done in some places.[26]

GOVERNMENT RESPONSE

Stakeholder responses to federal and state legislative and administrative actions taken to date demonstrate that such actions alone will not resolve the policy debate. To appreciate why a multistakeholder approach is needed, a review of government actions to date is helpful.

Unlike most other industries, the oil and gas industry has from time to time obtained exemptions from environmental laws. Our national environmental statutes for the most part limit pollution or environmental risks by media (e.g., air, water) across industrial sectors. Congress delegated to the Environmental Protection Agency (EPA) the authority to draft industry-specific regulations where appropriate to implement the statutory protections. EPA has generally used this authority to increase regulation of particular industries, for example, through categorical pretreatment standards under the Clean Water Act or emission standards for electric generating facilities under the Clean Air Act.

The oil and gas industry has employed an industry-specific approach by obtaining exemptions unavailable to other sectors. The Energy Policy Act of 2005 exempts injection of fluids or propping agents into oil and gas wells from the underground injection control requirements of the Safe Drinking Water Act unless diesel fuel is used.[27] Similarly, the Clean Water Act exempts certain stormwater runoff from oil and gas exploration, production, processing, or treatment operations from stormwater permitting requirements.[28] Likewise, oil field wastes, including waste generated by natural gas production activities, are exempt from Subtitle C of the Resource Conservation and Recovery Act.[29] The exemptions in the Comprehensive Environmental Response, Compensation and Liability Act for petroleum are well known.[30] The Energy Policy Act of 2005 also establishes a rebuttable presumption that under the National Environmental Policy Act (NEPA), categorical exclusions apply to certain actions of the Secretary of the Interior or Secretary of Agriculture involving use of public lands or national forest system lands for oil and gas exploration and development.[31]

This favorable treatment no doubt removed some impediments to rapid development of our nation's energy resources. But as an unintended result, the exemptions incentivized environmental activism to achieve their eventual reversal. They also at least temporarily left the states and interstate commissions with primary responsibility for protecting the environment through state or regional regulation of oil and gas development.

Although some state legislatures have amended their oil and gas statutes to address the environmental risks posed by the intense oil and gas development that horizontal drilling and hydraulic fracturing of unconventional formations facilitates, for the most part states have left to their administrative agencies the task of ensuring that oil and gas development proceeds in an environmentally responsible manner. Where state legislatures have not enacted protective requirements, in some instances, municipal governments have interceded to impose their own restrictions on development. At times this has created conflict between state and local authorities. In Pennsylvania, the legislature adopted Act 13 which, among other things, exempted oil and gas exploration and production from local zoning laws.[32] The legislation was challenged and its implementation stayed by the Pennsylvania Commonwealth Court on state constitutional grounds.[33] In New York State, the decisions of two courts, which were upheld on appeal, have recognized the authority of municipalities to enforce their zoning ordinances.[34]

While government agencies exercising environmental jurisdiction and water resource authorities have not resolved the policy disputes, they have assessed environmental risks and taken actions to minimize the environmental footprint of natural gas exploration and production activities. Agencies have focused on three principal areas: (1) impacts from water withdrawals, (2) effects of land development, drilling, and hydraulic fracturing, and (3) risks from storage, transport, and disposal of chemicals, fluids, and wastewater.

Water withdrawals to support natural gas exploration and production may be controversial, even in locations where they comprise a very small percentage of total water withdrawals. For example, projected water withdrawals to stimulate natural gas wells in the Delaware River Basin are expected to be approximately .24 percent of total withdrawals—orders of magnitude less than withdrawals currently undertaken to cool electric generating facilities. The larger industrial withdrawals, however, are located in the Delaware River estuary where water is relatively plentiful.

In contrast, water for natural gas development is often withdrawn from headwater streams situated near well pad sites. These activities raise environmental concern because they may alter aquatic habitat in sensitive headwaters with low flows and may interfere with competing water uses. Drilling a vertical production well in the Marcellus Shale requires approximately 85 thousand gallons of water to facilitate the drilling. If the wells are hydraulically fractured to stimulate production, approximately five million gallons of water are required. Water withdrawals of this magnitude are not uncommon in rivers or streams with large flow. But if made from small, headwater streams preferred by drillers because of their close proximity to well pad sites, the withdrawals have the potential to reduce flows to levels that threaten to adversely affect aquatic life, drinking water safe yields and ecosystems.[35] Lower flows may also adversely impact water quality in streams by reducing their capacity to assimilate pollutants or by creating conditions that result in a rise in stream temperature and alter the mix of aquatic life.

In response, regulatory agencies have imposed limits on groundwater and surface water withdrawals to ensure that they do not exceed
sustainable levels.[36] Regulators establish minimum instream flow
(passby flow) requirements to prohibit the water withdrawer from
depleting flows to levels that will cause unacceptable ecological damage. At times of low flow, conservation releases from water storage
facilities may supplement stream flows to ensure adequate water to
sustain aquatic life.

The Susquehanna River Basin Commission's (SRBC's) low flow
protection policy is an example of efforts to protect instream flows
and the ecological integrity of the waterways. Under its former guidelines,[37] the SRBC first predicted the degree of habitat loss that the
proposed withdrawal was expected to create.[38] It then examined the
existing SRBC classification of the water body to establish an amount
of habitat loss that SRBC will allow. Based on this information, SRBC
imposed a minimum passby flow, ordinarily at a level that will prevent
habitat loss in excess of the amount allowed.

On December 14, 2012, SRBC replaced its 2003 policy with its
new Low Flow Policy. The new policy and associated technical guidance, developed in conjunction with The Nature Conservancy, is
aimed at preserving natural ecosystems as well as ensuring the reliability and quality of water supplies.[39] Passby flow requirements vary
on a seasonal basis to better mimic the variability of natural conditions. Limits are imposed on individual withdrawals and cumulatively on all withdrawals in the drainage area. Withdrawals in
extremely sensitive or exceptional quality waters may be prohibited
entirely.

Regulatory agencies have identified additional risks from unreg-
ulated oil and gas exploration and production activities, including
landscape changes that affect water resources and aquatic and terres-
trial habitat. For example, a well pad encompassing five acres and supported by roads, impoundments, and other infrastructure and ancillary
facilities may cause forest fragmentation and habitat loss. In a recent
analysis of the landscape consequences of natural gas activities in two
Pennsylvania counties, the U.S. Geological Survey (USGS) documented loss of interior forests and gain in edge forest.[40] Landscape
changes of sufficient magnitude may cause diminished groundwater
infiltration, increased runoff, and stream impairment.

Accidents at well pad sites may also pose environmental risks.
For example, loss of well bore integrity from improper well casing

installation or cementing may result in contamination of aquifers and drinking water supplies.[41] Similarly, chemical spills, well blowouts, or leaking or overflowing impoundments may cause contamination. At the conclusion of a natural gas well's lifespan, the well bore may serve as a conduit for pollution if the well is not properly plugged and capped.

State environmental agencies and river basin commissions have responded to these risks by adopting or proposing regulations that are designed to address the potential environmental harms. Various state regulations require oil and gas well operators to disclose the identity of the chemicals in fracturing, to use mandatory casings and blowout preventers, to store chemicals and wastewater in tanks instead of impoundments, to leave minimum setbacks between the well pad and water bodies, wetlands and other sensitive ecological features, and to utilize erosion and sedimentation controls during and following construction.

In an effort to establish common standards that may avoid or shape regulations, industry has developed its own set of best practices and in some instances voluntarily disclosed chemicals used in fracturing on an industry website, www.FracFocus.org. Industry has also developed technologies to recycle flowback and production water to enable wastewater to be reused as a source of water for hydraulic fracturing. This practice has the potential to dramatically reduce the amount of freshwater and wastewater disposed.

Federal agencies have likewise recognized the importance of regulating natural gas activities, notwithstanding the existing federal statutory exemptions discussed above. EPA is currently performing a study of the potential environmental effects of natural gas exploration and production which may result in recommendations for statutory or regulatory changes. In the interim, federal agencies are adopting new protections to limit risks from natural gas development activities.

For example, the Department of Interior Bureau of Land Management (BLM) released draft regulations on May 4, 2012, to be codified at 40 CFR part 3160.[42] These proposed regulations would apply to federal and Indian lands comprising 756 million subsurface acres. They are intended to present a consistent oversight and disclosure model for natural gas drilling activities in accordance with the recommendations of the Secretary of Energy's advisory board in its report dated November 18, 2011. On May 24, 2013, BLM published revised proposed regulations; both the initial and revised drafts offer insight into an approach that may provide a starting point for BLM or other regulators.

An important provision of the proposed BLM regulations is the requirement that the drilling operator disclose to the public the identity of the chemicals used in hydraulic fracturing. The operator must submit a report within 30 days after operations are complete. For each additive, the disclosure must include its chemical trade name and the purpose that the additive serves. Disclosure must also include the CAS registry number and the percentage of the chemical by mass. The revised proposal recognizes the posting of the identity of the chemicals on www.FracFocus.org as an approved method of disclosing chemicals. Under the revised proposal, the operator may withhold information as a trade secret if it submits a supporting affidavit to BLM.

The BLM regulations also emphasize the critical importance of maintaining well bore integrity. For that purpose, the operator must submit a detailed description of well stimulation design before drilling. This description must include the anticipated volume of fluid and the anticipated pressure. The operator must perform mechanical integrity testing of the casing under anticipated maximum pressures and must submit cement evaluation or bond logs to verify that the cementing was properly performed and effective in preventing pathways for gas migration. The operator would be required to continuously monitor and report pressures during well stimulation and to isolate all usable water. At the conclusion of the well stimulation, the operator would be required to certify that wellbore integrity was maintained.

The storage, transport, and disposal of chemicals, fluids, and wastewater have also attracted the attention of environmental regulators. Fracturing fluids stored at the drilling site for use in hydraulic fracturing may be spilled or released into the environment if not properly contained. Flow-back and production waters may contain high concentrations of total dissolved solids (TDS) and other substances that may impact the environment if not properly managed. Municipal wastewater treatment plants (WWTPs) do not ordinarily possess the technology to remove TDS, radioactive elements, and other substances from flow-back and production waters. If wastewater from natural gas activity is sent to these WWTPs, the contaminants will pass through the facilities and into the receiving water body.

The BLM proposed regulations would require the operator to submit an estimate of the volume of fluids to be used and the proposed methods of managing and disposing the recovered fluids. The operator would be required to store recovered fluids in tanks or lined pits,[43] and report the actual total volume used and recovered and the methods of handling and disposal used.

Other approaches to management of wastewater adopted or considered by regulatory agencies include provisions to encourage recycling; track wastewater from the time it flows out of the well until its ultimate disposal, treatment, or reuse; analyze wastewater for TDS, radioactivity, and acute and chronic toxicity; perform treatability studies for WWTPs to determine their ability to treat flowback or production waters; establish discharge limitations; and comply with EPA underground injection well control requirements.[44]

Environmental agencies have also addressed the potential air impacts from natural gas exploration and production. Oil and gas activities produce flowback and utilize equipment that may emit VOCs and other hazardous air pollutants. In April 2012, EPA promulgated final New Source Performance Standards (NSPS) for the oil and gas sector.[45] The final NSPS requires, among other things, deployment of reduced emissions completion technology (i.e., green technology) by January 1, 2015, to capture VOCs. EPA expects this emissions technology to achieve 95 percent control of VOCs and simultaneously to reduce methane emissions. Combustion controls (i.e., flaring) are allowed until January 1, 2015.

One of the principal complaints of environmental stakeholders is that regulating each well or well pad individually overlooks the cumulative effects of all oil and gas activities in a region. Regulations in effect in Colorado and proposed by the Delaware River Basin Commission would require natural gas operators to submit area-wide development plans in advance of performing development activities. The development plan is a form of siting plan covering an operator's entire leasehold, a document analogous to a site plan for a residential or commercial development. It includes mapping of siting restrictions and evaluation of the environmental sensitivity of the area to be disturbed. The plan submission requirement encourages the developer to locate the well pads and other facilities in a manner minimizing environmental impact. It shifts the regulatory focus from a well-by-well analysis to a review of the potential cumulative impacts of the entire anticipated development within the operator's leasehold.

Although in theory administrative agencies may provide an oasis from the politicized legislative debates and a forum to apply dispassionate scientific analysis, administrative agencies have achieved little success in resolving stakeholder conflicts. Whether stringent requirements should be adopted for gas well casings, blow-out controls, predrilling and postdrilling sampling of groundwater, surface water, and drinking water wells, well pad restoration and financial assurance/bonding have remained controversial. In the instance of draft regulations published by one federal-interstate water resources agency (the Delaware River Basin Commission (DRBC)), for notice and comment rulemaking, over 69,000 comments were submitted advocating a broad spectrum of positions.[46] Even before the regulations were finalized, environmental groups and the New York State Attorney General commenced litigation in the U.S. District Court for the Eastern District of New York alleging violations of NEPA.[47] The district court dismissed the action without prejudice on the grounds that the plaintiffs lacked standing to sue at this time and that the case would not be ripe for adjudication unless and until final regulations are adopted.[48] Nevertheless, the premature attack on this agency's ongoing rulemaking demonstrated the commitment of these plaintiffs to challenge the adequacy of the regulatory process.

The outcome of the DRBC litigation reflects, among other things, the reluctance of courts to step into a politically charged, scientifically intense debate, particularly where no existing or imminent harm is shown. The role of courts in our legal system is to resolve cases and controversies between parties, not to design regulatory systems. Courts lack the scientific expertise ordinarily possessed by administrative agencies to assess claims that future oil and gas development will result in detrimental impacts to human health or the environment. Courts also lack the expertise to design environmental studies, operating practices, or equipment finely tuned to addressing the specific risks found. Because none of the classic statutory, regulatory, or judicial models works well in this context, the societal challenge is to design a better model consistent with legal requirements.

WORKING TOWARD A CONSENSUS MODEL

The prior discussion reveals the strengths and limitations of employing traditional models to control the environmental risks posed by natural gas exploration and production activities. Legislation, for the most part, has addressed these risks in only general way, leaving to regulatory agencies the responsibility to develop specific protections and requirements. In some instances, however, Congress has expressly exempted the oil and gas industry from federal statutory requirements. To be sure, some federal protections (such as Clean Air Act emissions requirements and Safe Drinking Water Act UIC restrictions when diesel fuel is used as a component of fracturing fluids) still apply. But for the most part, regulation of oil and gas exploration and production activities on private land is left to state control.

State agencies have substantial experience regulating the oil and gas industry. As some are quick to note, horizontal drilling and hydraulic fracturing have been used successfully for many years with only occasional reports of environmental damage. The intensity of natural gas development in the mid-Atlantic region, however, is of recent vintage. The fast pace of development magnifies risks and public concern and calls for a reexamination of the adequacy of existing rules. Some states have enacted new statutes and agencies have promulgated new regulations to address the increased risks, but in many locations substantial oil and gas development occurs before new regulations come into effect.

This process rarely satisfies both industry and the environmental community. Industry questions the need for new regulations. It asserts the safety of its current procedures and a purported track record of operating without serious environmental impacts. On this basis it contends that increased regulatory control or scrutiny is unwarranted. In contrast, environmental advocates emphasize the regulatory violations and environmental harms discovered to date and the scientific uncertainties in predicting how more intense development of rural landscapes will impact ecosystems and human health. In their view, the precautionary principle counsels against allowing intensive drilling and hydraulic fracturing until the risks are better assessed and controlled. Stakeholders have taken these arguments to courts reluctant to engage in environmental policymaking or scientific analysis. Not surprisingly, the results of litigation have not calmed the debate.

There have been some efforts made to date to bridge the gaps among competing interests. For example, the Center for Sustainable Shale Development (Center), located in Pittsburgh, Pennsylvania, is comprised of industry, environmental, academic, and other members.[49] They have recently proposed a set of 15 initial consensus performance standards for operators that are designed to be protective of air quality, water quality, and climate.[50] The proposed standards contain many of the elements of existing government standards discussed above, but their adoption in all jurisdictions would represent measurable progress toward broad implementation of best practices.

While making a valuable contribution, the efforts of the Center are unlikely to successfully lessen the intensity of debate within specific communities. To accomplish that result, stakeholders within those communities must become engaged. A model suited to resolving local issues consensually would contain the following components:

1. Meeting of stakeholders and regulators to define policy and scientific issues.

An initial step in consensus-building is often stakeholder dialogue. An exchange of views allows stakeholders to better understand each other's concerns. The regulatory agency may be the convening entity for a regional dialogue. Where community members are not sophisticated participants, some capacity building such as education or even assistance from scientific experts may be necessary to afford them the information and resources to fully and meaningfully participate. At times, funding of these efforts by regulatory agencies may be required. In the oil and gas debate, however, quite often environmental stakeholders are both sophisticated and well-funded.

In addition to exchanging views and concerns, the initial meeting or series of meetings can identify the scientific issues that must be resolved to properly inform the dialogue. An inventory of sensitive ecological features, monitoring data showing the condition of surface and groundwater, a mapping of likely locations of oil and gas resources, and other information identified by the regulators or stakeholders may serve as the basis for further scientific analysis and stakeholder discussion.

Stakeholders should also have the advantage of existing analyses. The studies and analyses performed by regulators or academics to date may help focus the information gaps that remain. For example, New York State has issued a draft supplemental generic environmental impact statement (dSGEIS) for high volume hydraulic fracturing to be conducted in New York State.[51] The dSGEIS identifies the risks posed by hydraulic fracturing and the measures that can be taken to minimize these risks.[52] For different geographic areas, additional studies may be needed to determine how local conditions may warrant conclusions or implementation of protective measures different from those set forth in the dSGEIS. Nevertheless, the dSGEIS, the ongoing EPA study of hydraulic fracturing, the draft BLM and draft DRBC regulations, and other studies and regulatory requirements may help establish a foundation for further analysis and for dispelling misconceptions held by stakeholders.

2. Application of science by unbiased scientists to answer questions posed by policymakers.

A consensus-based approach should be supported by a commitment to sound science. Stakeholders come to a problem with both facts and misconceptions colored by their self-interest and experiences. To reach consensus, stakeholders must be prepared to reach agreements supported by sound science. Regulators should ensure that the scientists performing the analysis are properly credentialed and unbiased. The DRBC in other contexts has established expert panels to assist multistakeholder advisory committees in making consensus recommendations to the DRBC in areas such as regulation of polychlorinated biphenyls (PCBs). Experts who have the support and confidence of all stakeholders can be of significant assistance in bridging gaps among the stakeholders.

3. Meeting of stakeholders to define policy options supported by sound science.

Application of sound science may narrow the areas of dispute but cannot substitute for policy choices. For example, scientific studies may identify the services that ecosystems provide and estimate the risk posed to those services by oil and gas activities. Policymakers, however, must determine whether the risks are worth taking in light of the projected benefits and, if so, what measures should be required to mitigate the risks or remediate any harm that occurs.

Once stakeholders are informed, they can exchange views on the policy issues, including whether certain areas should be off-limits to drilling because of the risk posed and what mitigation measures are appropriate where drilling or other oil and gas activities will occur.[53] The negotiated rulemaking (reg-neg) process that EPA has at times used (e.g., in determining "all appropriate inquiry" under the Brownfields regulations) provides precedent for this cooperative process. Although it may be overly optimistic to anticipate that the stakeholders will agree on all aspects of how natural gas development should proceed in their communities, they may reach agreement on components of how the existing regulatory regime should be modified to better accommodate competing interests.

4.   Decisions by regulators based on outcomes of stakeholder meetings.

Ultimately, regulators must make the policy decisions that are supported by sound science. The scientific analysis performed and any agreements of stakeholders should help focus the choices. Judgments designed to balance stakeholder interests rather than to support the narrow interest of a single group are likely to be accepted more universally. Providing full explanation of the choices considered and the decisions made will increase the credibility of the result.

Regulators should also seek innovative solutions that accommodate multiple interests. The natural gas development plan requirement discussed above is an example of a mechanism to view cumulative impacts while addressing the energy company's business needs. At the inception of its development of a large leasehold area, a company ordinarily has some flexibility regarding where to locate its well pads, roads, and other structures. Some configurations will have a greater impact than others on forests, wetlands, streams, steep slopes, and other sensitive features. A natural gas development plan serves as a mechanism to identify opportunities to minimize these impacts. When coupled with administrative incentives such as faster permitting for companies with approved development plans, the planning requirement can encourage companies to conduct oil and gas exploration and production in a way that conserves natural resources.

The mission of the regulatory agency should be to apply sound science, prudent policy decision making, and innovative implementation strategies to protect the environment and ecosystems during shale gas exploration and production. Seeking technological solutions to minimize risks should be part of the agency's role. For example, many natural gas companies are recycling flowback and production waters and reusing them in future fracturing activities rather than transporting the wastewater for disposal. Recycling presents the opportunity to minimize potentially harmful water withdrawals and also reduce the amount of wastewater than must be disposed. Some companies have reported that using recycled wastewater rather than fresh water has reduced their costs. When opportunities such as those presented by recycling technologies arise, agencies have the opportunity to craft regulations and incentives to encourage the practice.

Adaptive implementation is another important component of consensus-building regulation. As energy development occurs, impacts to natural resources and ecosystems should be closely monitored. Permits and regulations can be adjusted based upon actual experience.

The process described above is unlikely to eliminate litigation entirely. An energy company or landowner restricted from fully or quickly exploring its resource, or an environmental advocate viewing any fossil fuel extraction as an impediment to development of renewable resources, may be dissatisfied with any compromise result. The reviewing court, however, is likely to be impressed with a transparent process that narrows issues and obtains a critical mass of approval and support from stakeholders. The scientific work performed, and the explanation for policy choices made, should demonstrate that the agency's actions were not arbitrary and capricious. This record will enable a court to affirm the agency's decision without undertaking an independent scientific analysis or substituting its own judgment for that of the agency. In a politicized environment, reaching a consensus-based solution upheld on judicial review may be a significant achievement.

NOTES

1. *See* U.S. ENERGY DEP'T, ANNUAL ENERGY OUTLOOK (2012), *available at* http://www.eia.gov/forecasts/archive/aeo12/pdf/0383(2012).pdf. The uncertainties inherent in estimating natural gas reserves result in a range of estimates. The U.S. Geological Survey (USGS) has estimated that the Marcellus shale formation contains about 84 trillion cubic feet of undiscovered, technically recoverable natural gas. Press Release, U.S. Geological Survey, USGS Releases New Assessment of Gas Resources in the Marcellus Shale, Appalachian Basin (July 23, 2011), *available at* http://www.usgs .gov/newsroom/article.asp?ID=2893&from=rss_home.

2. The Marcellus shale formation is by no means the only major national gas reserve. The Utica Shale underlies the Marcellus Shale in many locations and is estimated to hold 16 trillion cubic feet of natural gas. The Fayetteville Shale is estimated to hold 13 trillion cubic feet, the Haynesville/ Boosier shale 85.8 trillion cubic feet, and the Eagle Ford shale 50 trillion cubic feet of natural gas. *Id.* The USGS has estimated that the Utica shale formation contains about 38 trillion cubic feet of undiscovered, recoverable natural gas. Press Release, U.S. Geological Survey, USGS Releases First Assessment of Shale Gas Resources in the Utica Shale: 38 trillion cubic feet (Oct. 4, 2012), *available at* http://www.usgs.gov/newsroom/article .asp?ID=3419&from=rss_home.

3. *See, e.g.*, IHS INC., AMERICA'S NEW ENERGY FUTURE: THE UNCONVENTIONAL OIL AND GAS REVOLUTION AND THE ECONOMY (2012), *available at* www.ihs.com/unconventionalsandtheeconomy.

4. *See, e.g., Renewable Alternative,* CATSKILL MOUNTAINKEEPER, http://www.catskillmountainkeeper.org/our-programs/fracking/why-we-need-to-ban-fracking-and-adopt-a-renewable-energy-policy/.

5. *See, e.g.,* Nora Eisenberg, *Anti-Fracking Protesters Confront Pennsylvania Gov During Kayaking PR Trip on Endangered River,* ALTERNET (Aug. 24, 2012), www.alternet.org/fracking/anti-fracking-protesters-confront-Pennsylvania-gov-during-kayaking-pr-trip-endangered-river; http://ecowatch.org/2012/5000-people-unite/.

6. GASLAND, www.gaslandthemovie.com.

7. *See, e.g.,* N.Y. DEP'T ENVTL. CONSERVATION, REVISED DRAFT SGEIS ON THE OIL, GAS AND SOLUTION MINING REGULATORY PROGRAM (SEPTEMBER 2011) (2011), *available at* www.dec.ny.gov/energy/75370.html (see comments on New York State draft Supplemental Environmental Impact Statement).

8. *See, e.g.,* PowerPoint, Arnold & Porter LLP, *Hydraulic Fracturing* (last updated July 11, 2013), *available at* http://www.arnoldporter.com/resources/documents/Hydraulic%20Fracturing%20Case%20Chart.pdf; Archive of litigation-related articles, FRACKING INSIDER, www.frackinginsider.com/litigation.

9. *See, e.g.,* Benjamin Grumbles, *Drill, Maybe, Drill!,* U.S. WATER ALLIANCE, (May 17, 2011), www.uswateralliance.org/2011/05/17/drill-maybe-drill/.

10. *See, e.g.,* Kenneth J. Warren, *Water Supply for Shale Gas Production: Lessons from the River Basin Commission Management in the Mid-Atlantic States,* 58 ROCKY MT. MIN. L. INST. 9-1 (2012).

11. Other societal disruptions include "Man Camps" and the burdens on sewer and water infrastructure and local housing. These are the subject of chapter 11, *Man Camps, Boom Towns, and the Boom and Bust Cycle: Learning from Rifle, Colorado and Williams County, North Dakota.*

12. *See, e.g., The Basics of Natural Gas,* CHESAPEAKE ENERGY, www.chk.com/NaturalGas/Pages/Basics.aspx. One recent study by researchers at the University of Texas suggested that methane well completion emissions may be lower than previously estimated. David T. Allen et al., *Measurements of Methane Emissions at Natural Gas Production Sites in the United States,* 110 PROC. NAT'L ACAD. SCI. no. 38 (Sept. 24, 2013).

13. *See, e.g.,* NATURAL RES. DEF. COUNCIL, LEAKING PROFITS, THE U.S. OIL AND GAS INDUSTRY CAN REDUCE POLLUTION, CONSERVE RESOURCES, AND MAKE MONEY BY PREVENTING METHANE WASTE (2012), *available at* www.nrdc.org/energy/leaking-profits.asp; R. Howarth et al, doc:10.1007/S10584-011-0061-5, METHANE AND THE GREENHOUSE-GAS FOOTPRINT OF NATURAL GAS FROM SHALE FORMATIONS (2011), *available at* www.sustainablefuture.cornell.edu/news/attachments/Howarth-EtAl-2011.pdf.

14. *See, e.g.*, Myra P. Saefong, *Shale Gas Gives Rise to Era of Energy Independence*, Wall St. J. MarketWatch (Dec. 5, 2011, 12:02 AM), http://www.market watch.com/story/shale-gas-gives-rise-to-era-of-energy-independence-2011 -12-02.

15. For a list of natural gas export applications, see www.fe.gov/programs/gas regulation/authorizations/Authorizations.html. *See also*, Peter Kelly-Detwiler, *U.S. Natural Gas Exports Poised for Takeoff* (Nov. 8, 2012, 7:51 AM), www .forbes.com/sites/peterdetwiler/2012/11/08/us-natural-gas-exports-poised -for-take-off/.

16. *See, e.g.*, Dow Chemical Co., Natural Gas: Fueling an American Manufacturing Renaissance (2012), *available at* www.dow.com/energy /pdf/Dow_Nat_Gas_0801121.pdf.

17. Regarding the appropriate time for restoring the landscape, see chapter 3: *Leasing Mineral Rights: A Framework for Understanding the Dominant Estate*. *See also* Nat'l Petrol. Council N. Am., Resource Dev. Study Paper #2-25, Plugging and Abandonment of Oil and Gas Wells (Sept. 15, 2011), *available at* http://www.npc.org/Prudent_Development-Topic _Papers/2-25_Well_Plugging_and_Abandonment_Paper.pdf.

18. *See, e.g.*, *The Economic and Employment Contributions of Shale Gas in the U.S.*, IHS Inc., www.ihs.com/info/ecc/a/shale-gas-jobs-report.aspx.

19. *See, e.g.*, Karen Kasler, *Kasich Blasts Out of State Oil and Gas Workers, But Drillers Fight Back*, WYSO (Dec. 6, 2012, 8:35 AM), http://wyso.org/post /kasich-blasts-out-state-oil-and-gas-workers-drillers-fight-back; Food and Water Watch, Exposing the Oil and Gas Industry's False Jobs Promise for Shale Development (2011), *available at* http://www.foodandwater watch.org/reports/exposing-the-oil-and-gas-industrys-false-jobs-promise/.

20. *See, e.g.*, Andrew Rumbach, Natural Gas Drilling in the Marcellus Shale: Potential Impacts on the Tourism Economy of the Southern Tier (2011), *available at* www.greenchoices.cornell.edu/downloads /development/marcellus/Marcellus_CaRDI.pdf. at p. 8; reports catalogued at *The Economics of Shale Gas Extraction*, Catskill Citizens For Safe Energy, www.catskillcitizens.org/learn_one.cfm?t=2&c=22.

21. *See, e.g.*, Hannah Jacobs Wiseman & Francis Gradijan, *Regulation of Shale Gas Development, Including Hydraulic Fracturing*, at 127 *et seq.* (University of Tulsa Legal Studies Research Paper No. 2011-11, updated June 15, 2012), *available at* SSRN: http://ssrn.com/abstract=1953547.

22. Pa. Dep't of Envtl. Prot., Consent Order and Settlement Agreement (Dec. 15, 2010), *available at* http://files.dep.state.pa.us/OilGas/OilGasLanding PageFiles/FinalCO&A121510.pdf.

23. EPA preliminarily determined that hydraulic fracturing is the cause of elevated concentrations of regulated substances in Pavillion, Wyoming. Industry strongly disagreed. EPA did not change its position after reviewing the results of additional sampling of wells in Pavillion conducted by EPA and the U.S. Geological Survey. EPA has issued a draft groundwater report for

public comment, but on June 20, 2013, announced that it does not plan to finalize or seek peer review of the draft report. *See* EPA, http://www2.epa .gov/region8/pavillion.

24. Air emissions are discussed more fully in chapter 10: "Clearing the Air: Reducing Emissions from Unconventional Oil and Gas Development."

25. See expert reports filed by the Delaware Riverkeeper Network in *State of New York v. U.S. Army Corps of Engineers; Delaware Riverkeeper Network v. U.S. Army Corps of Engineers; Damascus Citizens for Sustainability v. U.S. Army Corps of Engineers,* CV-11-2599, CV-11-3780, CV-11-3857 (E.D.N.Y. Sept. 24, 2012). *See also* T. Colborn et al., Natural Gas Operations from a Public Health Perspective, 17 HUMAN & ECOLOGICAL RISK ASSESSMENT: INT'L J. 1039 (2011).

26. *See, e.g.,* ENV'T OHIO RESEARCH AND POLICY CENTER, THE COSTS OF FRACK-ING: THE PRICE TAG OF DIRTY DRILLING'S ENVIRONMENTAL DAMAGE (2012), *available at* www.mothersagainst fracking.org/wp-content/uploads/2012/09/ The-Costs-of-Fracking-Report.pdf.

27. 42 U.S.C. § 300h(d)(1)(B)(ii). This is frequently referred to as the "Cheney exemption" or "Halliburton Loophole" in recognition of the role of then Vice-President Cheney's Energy Task Force in recommending the exemption.

28. 33 U.S.C. § 1342(l)(2). *But see* 40 C.F.R. § 122.26(e)(8) (permits for small construction activities).

29. *See* 53 Fed. Reg. 25,447 (July 6, 1988).

30. *See* 42 U.S.C. §9601(14) (petroleum exclusion in definition of "hazardous substance").

31. 42 U.S.C. § 15942.

32. Act 13 of 2012, amending the Pennsylvania Oil and Gas Act, 58 PA. CONS. STAT. § 601.101 *et seq.*

33. Robinson Twp. v. Pennsylvania, No. 284 M.D. 2012 (Pa. Commw. Ct. July 26, 2012), *appeal pending,* Docket No. 63 MAP 2012 (Pa. Supreme Ct.).

34. *See, e.g.,* Cooperstown Holstein Corp. v. Town of Middlefield, No. 2011-0930 (N.Y. S. Ct. Feb. 24, 2012); Anschutz Exploration Corp. v. Town of Dryden, No. 2011-0902 (N.Y. Sup. Ct. Feb. 21, 2012), *affirmed sub nom.* Norse Energy Corp. USA v. Town of Dryden, Index No. 515227 (N.Y. App. Div., Third Judicial Dept. May 2, 2013); Cooperstown Holstein Corp. v. Town of Middlefield, Index No. 515498, Slip Op 03148 (N.Y. Sup. Ct. May 2, 2013). The New York State Court of Appeals was granted motions for leave to appeal, Mo. Nos. 2013-603 and 2013-604 (August 29, 2013).

35. *See* N.Y. DEP'T ENVTL. CONSERVATION, REVISED DRAFT SGEIS, *supra* note 7, at 6-21 and 6-3 to 6-4.

36. For a fuller discussion of water supply issues related to oil and gas develop-ment, see Kenneth J. Warren, *Water Supply for Shale Gas Production: Lessons from the River Basin Commission Management in the Mid-Atlantic States,* 58 ROCKY MT. MIN. L. INST. 9-1 (2012).

37. Susquehanna River Basin Comm'n, Policy No. 2003-001, Guidelines for Using and Determining Passby Flows and Conservation Releases for Surface Water and Ground Water Withdrawal Approvals, (Nov. 8, 2002).

38. SRBC uses the Instream Flow Incremental Methodology to predict habitat loss. For a description of that methodology see, e.g., PowerPoint: L. Young, *Instream Flow Protection Efforts in Pennsylvania*, *available at* www.portal.state .pa.us/portal/server.pt (search title); *Instream Flow Incremental Methodology*, USGS, http:/www.fort.usgs.gov/products/software/ifim/ (last modified Aug. 28, 2013).

39. *See Public Participation—Business Meeting*, Susquehanna River Basin Comm'n, http://www.srbc.net/pubinfo/businessmeeting.htm.

40. USGS, Landscape Consequences of Natural Gas Extraction in Bradford and Washington Counties, Pennsylvania, 2004–2010 (2012), *available at* http://pubs.usgs.gov/of/2012/1154/of2012-1154.pdf.

41. *See, e.g.*, Wiseman & Gradijan, *supra* note 21.

42. 77 Fed. Reg. 27,691–27,711 (May 11, 2012). The revised proposed regulations may be found at 78 Fed. Reg. 31,635–31,677 (May 24, 2013).

43. Whether lined pits are sufficiently protective remains controversial. In its draft natural gas regulations, the Delaware River Basin Commission proposed requiring flowback and production waters to be stored in tanks.

44. *See, e.g.*, *State Enforcement of Shale Gas Development Regulations, Including Hydraulic Fracturing* (Jan. 20, 2012, updated June 18, 2012), *available at* http://ssrn.com/abstract=1992064 as of April 6, 2013.

45. 77 Fed. Reg. 49,490 (Aug. 16, 2012).

46. *See Comments on Dec. 2010 Draft Natural Gas Regulations*, Del. River Basin Comm'n www.state.nj.us/drbc/programs/natural/draftregs-dec2010 _comments.html (last modified Jan. 20, 2012).

47. Delaware Riverkeeper Network expert reports, *supra* note 25.

48. Delaware Riverkeeper Network expert reports, *supra* note 25.

49. *About the Center for Sustainable Shale Development*, Ctr. for Sustainable Shale Dev., https://www.sustainableshale.org/about/.

50. *Performance Standards*, Ctr. for Sustainable Shale Dev., https://www .sustainableshale.org/performance-standards/.

51. N.Y. Dep't Envtl. Conservation, Revised Draft SGEIS, *supra* note 7.

52. For example, the dSGEIS would prohibit all high-volume hydraulic fracturing in the New York City and Syracuse watersheds because of the risk that it would jeopardize the filtration avoidance determinations for these drinking water systems.

53. Environmental justice stakeholders have utilized dialogue as a means to resolve disputes. *See, e.g.*, EPA, EPA's Environmental Justice Collaborative Problem-Solving Model (2008), *available at* www.epa.gov /environmentaljustice/resources/publications/grants/cps-manual-12-27-06.pdf.

16

The International Community's Response to Hydraulic Fracturing and a Case for International Oversight

Benjamin E. Griffith

INTRODUCTION

An explosive debate is taking place internationally at the intersection of the human right to safe drinking water and the demands on this resource for the increased development of unconventional deposits of natural gas through hydraulic fracturing of shale reserves.

While many in the United States understand the debate as one that engages our federal, state and local governments, similar negotiations, discussions, and trade-offs are actually taking place in many regions of the world. The issues include whether development of

I gratefully acknowledge the assistance of Professor John H. (Jack) Minan of the University of San Diego School of Law in reviewing, editing, and making helpful structural and thematic suggestions that added clarity to this chapter. Since 2001, Jack has served on the Board of Governors of the Southern California Wetlands Recovery Project and as chairman of the Regional Water Quality Control Board. I also thank Clark Griffith, Associate Scientist with Intera Inc. of Austin, Texas, and Wayne Bossert, Manager of Northwest Kansas Groundwater Management District 4, Colby, Kansas, for their helpful suggestions and additional ideas that were incorporated into the final draft.

unconventional deposits of natural gas, or oil sands, and other types of oil and gas development, can be done responsibly and without serious harm to natural resources, particularly water, and whether the risks to natural resources are warranted by the benefits that development of shale gas will likely bring.

This chapter will examine how many of the major international players and regions are approaching shale gas development, and the extent to which technology, reporting, and monitoring standards can offer practicable solutions to a complex issue in which the United States is but one of the many stakeholders. The debate taking place on the international stage has opened a new chapter in the history of sustainable water supply, control over water resources, and management of environmental risks associated with hydraulic fracturing,[1] with implications for our fundamental goals of energy independence, energy development, and global security.

Shale gas exploitation and production have expanded during the past decade to account for over 30 percent of all natural gas production in the United States, with reliable estimates indicating that shale gas can comprise between 40and 50 percent of the United States' total production over the next 30 years.[2] The World Shale Gas Resources: An Initial Assessment of 14 Regions Outside the United States, EIA, April 5, 2011, reports technologically recoverable global shale gas reserves for the United States at 862 tcf, compared to estimates in Australia (396 tcf), China (1,276 tcf), France (180 tcf), Poland (187 tcf), Brazil (226 tcf), Canada (388 tcf), South Africa (485 tcf), Mexico (681 tcf), and Argentina (774 tcf).

Shale gas will continue to play a significant role in international energy development and can potentially contribute to a significant level of energy security on a global scale. But at what price does the international community achieve diversification of energy supplies and reduced energy dependence in the context of an unstable global oil market?[3] Beyond the United States, how is the international community responding—and how should it respond—to the concerns provoked by hydraulic fracturing over public health, the environment, adequate supplies of quality water, and pollution?

As this chapter is being written, over 270 municipalities in the United States have imposed moratoria or taken other action against hydraulic fracturing. The state of Vermont has banned hydraulic fracturing altogether, despite the fact that no shale gas deposits exist in the Green Mountain State.[4] New York and New Jersey have also implemented moratoria.

The hydraulic fracturing debate has moved from its genesis in the United States to several EU member states and nations on the African continent, Australia, Canada, and the Pacific Rim. Whether it is "No Fracking Ireland," "No Fracking UK," "No" to "le Fracking," or "Ja" to "Gegengasbohren," this debate now has a clearly international component that is exacerbating the political gridlock at the national level. While the American Petroleum Institute launched its intensified "Vote 4 Energy" public relations campaign to promote hydraulic fracturing during the 2012 presidential election,[5] a similar campaign was underway in the European Union where the fossil fuel lobby presented "natural gas, including unconventional gas extraction through hydraulic fracturing, as a cheap 'no regrets option' and painting renewable energy sources as unaffordable."[6] France, Romania, the Czech Republic, Bulgaria, and the German Land (State) of North Rhine Westphalia have banned or declared moratoria on hydraulic fracturing. As Jim Dean, chair of Democracy for America, put it during the kickoff of Global Frackdown, a coordinated international grass-roots protest, "The events taking place around the world as part of the Global Frackdown prove that people are tired of the lies from big oil and gas."[7] According to Dean, "We've learned our lessons from Love Canal and the Horizon oil spill—when money is involved, corporations lie to the people to keep their profits up. It's time to end the lies."[8]

Debates regarding the answers to these questions have resulted in political gridlock, hardening of positions between the energy industry, scientists, environmentalists and national governments, and a fundamental lack of public confidence in governments' ability to protect the public interest. In some instances, hostile debate and/or incomplete or biased information regarding handling and treatment of contaminated water, the risk of depleting dwindling water supplies, adequate provision of meaningful and effective warnings and disclosures, and prevention of collateral harm from trucks, drilling equipment, workers, and waste water from hydraulic fracturing activities has complicated efforts to mitigate these problems.[9]

Successful navigation between the extremes of absolute moratoria, on the one hand, and minimal regulation of the hydraulic fracturing process, on the other, is paramount and will require consideration of several facets of the "fracking" debate:

1. *Escalating controversy.* This is an explosive controversy that has driven several nations to impose or consider imposing moratoria on shale gas development through hydraulic fracturing. Within countries the debate is becoming increasingly polarized.

2. *Growing environmental concerns.* Serious evaluation and scrutiny must be undertaken with respect to claims of potential pollution, overuse of water supplies, and other environmental risks associated with hydraulic fracturing[10] as nations evaluate and quantify what promises to be a potential solution to dependence on foreign natural gas.

3. *Public confidence shaken.* Public confidence in the energy industry and in the ability of the government to protect citizens from harms, including those associated with the hydraulic fracturing process, is at an all-time low and must be restored. The debate over unconventional natural gas development in the United States pits an increasingly organized environmental lobby against the shale gas industry proponents seeking minimal governmental oversight and regulation. The natural gas industry's credibility has been questioned by an increasingly uneasy and distrustful environmental community, state governments, and local governments. Even securities regulators like the S.E.C., the investor-and-markets watchdog for the United States government, have stepped into the heated environmental debate over hydraulic fracturing.[11] Concerns have been raised over the additional demand on water resources attributable to the use of millions of gallons of water at each well site, the potential release of wastewater into the environment at a time when the industry has refused to disclose the chemical composition of hydraulic fracturing fluids used, and lack of transparency concerning the industry's operations, including failure to report methane leaks and lack of baseline water quality data before drilling starts. A workable solution must be devised, that will entail greater governmental oversight at the federal and state regulatory level and greater cooperation from the natural gas industry in identifying, quantifying, and managing the scientifically ascertainable risks associated with this natural gas extraction process in a transparent, proper, and safe manner.[12] This balancing process leading to such a solution must satisfy the demand for public safety through enhanced regulatory over-

sight, common sense disclosure and transparency measures, and meaningful efforts to minimize environmental risk, need for development of shale gas as a predictable, and growing energy resource for decades to come.

Serious, thorough, and coordinated analysis must be undertaken with respect to the relevant legal and governmental developments relating to hydraulic fracturing in the European Union, Eastern Europe, Eurasia, the African continent, the Pacific Rim, South America, and North America. Transparency must be the rule and not the exception, and full access must be provided in order to make publicly available all relevant scientific, technical, and commercial information on shale gas operations and chief environmental concerns associated with hydraulic fracturing. Such an analysis must be proactive and include efforts to restore trust and credibility in response to the many concerns voiced over the hydraulic fracturing process, governmental oversight, identification of best practices, and genuine transparency by the natural gas industry.

4. *Recommendations for International Protocols.* In addition to efforts by local, state, and national governments to maximize benefits and minimize negative impacts of hydraulic fracturing, the international community must be given the challenge to augment these efforts through coordinated efforts and comprehensive recommendations for international oversight, risk management, and international protocols that address:

a. Hydraulic fracturing waste fluid;
b. Identification of chemical ingredients used in hydraulic fracturing fluids injected at well sites;
c. Public input and participation in permitting processes;
d. Monitoring of contaminants;
e. Shared technology and understanding of impacts of hydraulic fracturing process on domestic and transboundary water resources and water quality; and,
f. Remediation protocols by the industry.[13]

Successful development and implementation of these recommendations hinges on coordinated work and commitment at the international level leading to regulatory certainty, sound environmental oversight, and energy security.

Sustainable Energy and Water Resources

Proponents for a sustainable energy policy and proponents for a sustainable water policy are on a collision course in the United States, Europe, and other parts of the world. Sustainable energy resources and sustainable water resources are the underpinnings of survival for the human species. The two are interrelated. Energy is needed to produce, sanitize, and distribute water resources, and water is needed to produce energy, particularly from fossil fuels. Efforts to secure energy have long been supported by state governments and international governing bodies. More recently, shortages of water, and more specifically clean water, have transformed water resources protection and management into a national and international priority. And yet, many developed nations are still reluctant to commit the resources necessary to secure water security for all. Developed countries of the world need a sustainable energy policy, the linchpin of economic stability. At the same time, no one can deny that water is critical for sustainable development and is an essential component of environmental integrity and indispensable for human health.[14]

The nations of the world, acting through the 2000 Millennium Declaration by the U. N. General Assembly, adopted the goal of cutting in half the proportion of the world's population unable to reach or afford safe drinking water by the year 2015, while stopping unsustainable exploitation of water resources.[15] The United Nations' action was barely noticed. While the resolution passed by a vote of 122 to zero, 41 nations abstained, including the United States, which nonetheless supported "the goal of universal access to safe drinking water."[16]

The Changing Role of Natural Gas in the Global Energy Market

Increasing pressures have come to bear on nations to identify and secure domestic energy sources. When world market oil prices skyrocketed in 2005, the development of shale gas extraction through hydraulic fracturing received a major boost as the United States, faced with high gas prices, began investing billions of dollars in what promised to be a means of bringing cheap energy to consumers.[17] Members of the EU also began looking at potential shale gas resources on the European continent as a potentially reliable transitional energy source. As late as 2007, before the impact of the shale gas revolution was as obvious as it is today, it was assumed that the United States would be importing large amounts of liquefied natural gas from the Middle East and other areas. Today, the United States is essentially self-sufficient in natural gas and is expected to remain so for many decades, with the only notable imports being from Canada. Such a source of energy, while ultimately nonrenewable, could nonetheless serve as a critical bridge fuel on a path to energy independence, a common goal shared by the United States, the EU, and other members of the international community.

Reducing EU Dependence on Natural Gas from Russia

As of late 2012, Europe currently depends on Russia for a quarter of its gas.[18] Many are already saying that if shale deposits are found in Europe, Moscow will lose the benefit of selling resources to other countries. The U.S. Department of Energy has noted that the phenomenal increase in the domestic supply of natural gas through shale gas production may have significant, long-lasting effects on energy independence and national security, and may lead to "a lessening of both supply and leverage from countries such as Russia and Iran, in part through the strengthening of European consumer markets."[19]

However, Gazprom is not losing any sleep over this supposedly miraculous fuel,[20] and others have challenged the optimistic hype and predictions about the tremendous size of shale gas reserves in Europe.[21] One commentator has noted the following three key problems with the predicted hydraulic fracturing bonanza in Europe:

1. Even as the United States is beginning to face bottlenecks in locating experienced drilling workforces and equipment, the European Union lacks both the experienced workforces and the pressure pumping equipment. Therefore, he queries, if the United States is already facing such restrictions, how will Europe fare, where shale gas developments are still in their infancy?

2. Major energy companies are already expressing reservations in light of the highly uncertain economics of shale gas in the EU in the context of a current gas glut that has depressed prices.

3. Opposition by environmental groups to hydraulic fracturing expansion in the more densely populated parts of Europe has been expanding through citizen-organized initiatives opposing shale gas development, particularly in Sweden, France, and Germany's most populous state of North Rhine-Westphalia. Industry watchers in Europe already believe that Russia is bankrolling some of those groups since hydraulic fracturing could cut down on Russia's natural gas market. While no hard evidence has emerged to validate these rumors, many critics point to Gazprom's ownership of media companies throughout Russia and Europe that have run stories examining the environmental risks of hydraulic fracturing.[22]

HYDRAULIC FRACTURING COMES TO EUROPE

Shale gas resource potential in Europe has been the subject of studies by Advanced Resources International and the Energy Information Administration, and preliminary estimates are being assessed in Austria, Sweden, Poland, Romania, Germany, Croatia, Denmark, France, Hungary, the Netherlands, Ukraine, and the United Kingdom, among others. A technically recoverable assessment of approximately 220 tcf (6.22970 trillion cubic meters or tcm) between Poland, Sweden, Austria, and Germany has been estimated, with 55 percent of that amount being in Poland.[23] Shale gas drilling practices that began in the United States have spread to Canada,[24] the Czech Republic,[25] and elsewhere on an international scale,[26] and a number of these other nations are having second thoughts about the controversial method of natural gas extraction known as "fracking."

Europe's Shale Gas Reserves

The International Energy Agency estimates that Europe may hold 35 trillion cubic meters (1236.013 tcf)[27] of natural gas dispersed in shale formations, more than enough to meet its foreseeable needs based on current annual demand of about .58 trillion cubic meters.[28] One London-based research firm recently reported that Europe's recoverable reserves of shale gas, would be enough to meet its gas demand "for at least another 60 years."[29] This would radically change the EU's position in the global energy market.

The EU is one of the world's largest importers of natural gas and a major player in the international gas market, with Norway being one of the world's largest suppliers of natural gas as part of the extended European Economic Area, followed by the number two supplier, the Russian Federation. One of the key objectives of the EU is a single European energy market, which should level the prices of gas in all EU member states. According to Energy 2020, A *Strategy for Competitive, Sustainable and Secure Energy*, a common EU energy policy has evolved around the common objective to ensure the uninterrupted physical availability of energy products and services on the market, at a price which is affordable for all consumers (private and industrial), while contributing to the EU's wider social and climate goals. The central goals for energy policy (security of supply, competitiveness, and sustainability) are now laid down in the Lisbon Treaty.[30]

In contrast to the United States, the hydraulic fracturing process is still relatively unknown in Europe. Though reportedly used in Germany for at least 20 years in vertical wells, the combination of slick-water hydraulic fracturing, horizontal drilling, multiple-well pads, and multi-stage hydraulic fracturing is relatively new—even in Germany.

Reactions within the EU and in Other Nations

As in the United States, hydraulic fracturing proponents in the EU say that the risks involved with the process are low, and that the process is necessary to meet Europe's energy needs. Opponents have raised red flags about potential contamination of water supplies, attributable in part to unknown chemical additives used in the process,[31] as well as other environmental ramifications of large-scale shale gas development.[32] For example, in France,[33] the government recently imposed a moratorium halting shale gas exploration because of environmental concerns. Similar debates have arisen in Poland,[34] South Africa,[35] and Nova Scotia.[36]

Poland

Shale gas hydraulic fracturing enjoyed a relatively quiet arrival in Poland. The Polish government is understandably eager to develop domestic gas supplies that could help free the country from reliance on Russian gas, the current source of two-thirds of natural gas used in Poland. Tapping Poland's large shale gas reserves, moreover, could change the regional balance of power. According to Poland's Ministry of the Environment, Polish shale gas is "the gold rush of the 21st century," and Poland is a future "energy super-power" with estimated reserves of 1.4 trillion to 3 trillion cubic meters.[37] Shale gas could help reduce Poland's need for coal-derived electricity (currently 92 percent of production) and serve as a "transition" energy source on the way to a more renewable future.

Critics have noted that shale gas drilling could spoil the landscape and exacerbate water shortages in some areas.[38] The opposition is coming mostly from neighbors of drilling wells, while environmental groups like Greenpeace Poland are reserving judgment.

While there may be no concerted environmental campaign against shale gas in Poland at the present time, there are legal obstacles. Poland already requires every big new project to have an environmental impact assessment, and the government will consider hydraulic fracturing proposals on a case by case basis.[39] According to the Polish Environment ministry, this is sufficient to regulate shale gas drilling.

Echoing shale gas drillers in the United States who reject concerns about ground water contamination, the response of one of the major energy companies in Poland is that there is no risk of water pollution from hydraulic fracturing. "You've got shallow water and deep gas, . . . [and][i]f the groundwater aquifer's at 200 meters or even 1000 meters, the shale gas here in Poland is between 2500 and over 4000 meters."[40] A number of Polish geologists and experts as recently as July 2011, have rejected as unfounded the arguments of scientists in neighboring Germany that hydraulic fracturing poses environmental dangers.[41]

As energy-poor Poland begins to move forward with its plans to use hydraulic fracturing to develop the country's natural gas reserves, little controversy has emerged regarding the controversial nature of the hydraulic fracturing process. The Polish experience to date does not appear to address some of the most problematic environmental concerns associated with massive amounts of water required during the process and the potential for surface water contamination.

A more cautious official stance may be in the works. As Poland's Deputy Environment Minister Jacek Jezierski recently observed, "We will be able to say whether amendments to provisions regulating shale gas extraction are needed once we perform a professional assessment of its environmental impact, not an emotional one. Poland intends to control this process, not to ban it." According to Marek Kryda of the Institute of Civil Affairs, "It is necessary to look after issues related to property expropriation and lease. We can already see irregularities at the stage of test drilling."[42]

Germany: Gegen-Gasbohren

The controversy over hydraulic fracturing came to Germany when ExxonMobile Germany proposed to begin test drilling in northern Germany in October 2010, shortly after which several hundred people organized an anti-fracking organization, Gegen-Gasbohren, Through their website at www.gegen-gasbohren.de and through an effective outreach facilitated by the media, newspapers, and television, the organization provided information about hydraulic fracturing on www.shaleshock.org, including scenes from the indie movie *Gasland*.[43] Gegen Gasbohren was founded in September 2010, with groups in several German towns where shale gas fracking was planned, each drawing up to 300 people. As media coverage increased, after only three months every major party in the state of North Rhine-Westphalia is calling for a moratorium on hydraulic fracturing. Some are even calling for a moratorium on test drillings until it is clear that the drilling technology is safe.[44]

France: No to "le Fracking"

As the hydraulic fracturing fight has gone international, citizen groups and environmental organizations raised the alarm in France, the first country to enact a moratorium. The site of what was to be a mad rush to conduct exploration for shale gas in France is the Paris Basin, which is under France's most fertile farmland. The geology of the Paris Basin shale formation, a saucer-shaped rock formation that extends over 140,000 kilometers, is similar to the Bakken Shale formation in North America, where oil production has surged with the increased use of hydraulic fracturing. It is unclear how much of the Paris Basin's estimated 100 to 300 billion barrels will be recoverable using hydraulic fracturing techniques, but industry executives have noted that "[i]f the geological potential is there, it would be a shame for France to pass up this source of energy."[45]

Opponents to "le Fracking" cited public shock over learning that the French government had pushed though drilling permits without any debate, showing disdain for the population and elected representatives. Hydraulic fracturing opponents have also pushed for modifications of rules that will allow public consultation when awarding permits for natural gas exploration. As energy companies began to ready their rigs outside Paris and started to plan for drilling in southern France, local environmental groups began raising concerns about damage to water tables from the hunt for hydrocarbons locked in shale rock.

The French government became increasingly aware of and worried about the potential impact of hydraulic fracturing on the local environment. Its concerns were the following: (1) excessive use of existing water supply, insofar the average amount of water used for each hydraulic fracturing well was as much as the amount 100,000 French people use in one day; (2) potential contamination of both the soil and groundwater; and (3) the large number of wells needed to extract shale gas is 10 to 20 times as many as are used in conventional drilling.

On January 22, 2011, José Bové, a French environmentalist, farmer, former Presidential candidate, and Green party deputy with the European Parliament, started a petition drive that led to the French government ordering an exploration moratorium. On March 11, 2011, French Prime Minister François Fillon extended the ban until June 2011, when parliamentary and ministry reports on the environmental and economic effects were due.[46] The National Assembly, France's lower chamber, passed the moratorium bill on June 21, 2011, after which the French Parliament voted on June 30, 2011 to impose a moratorium on hydraulic fracturing.

Bové took his antifracking battle to the European Parliament and will seek an EU-side ban on exploration by the producers who have already snapped up drilling permits and are now riding out the political storm and waiting until the French government studies are completed.[47] In a study requested by the European Parliament's Committee on Environment, Public Health, and Food Safety, scientists concluded that, "At a time when sustainability is key to future operations, it can be questioned whether the injection of toxic chemicals in the underground should be allowed, or whether it should be banned as such a practice would restrict or exclude any later use of the contaminated layer . . . and as long-term effects are not investigated."[48]

Environmental groups in France complain that in addition to toxic chemical input from hydraulic fracturing, many other problems of natural gas exploration and production are being minimized by the industry, including such problems as "leaks or failures of steel and cement drill casings, deep-well injection of toxic waste which may also increase seismic activity, the storage of explosives on farms and in communities during seismic surveying, increased greenhouse gas emissions, offshore and onshore oil spills that damage fisheries, and waste product contamination of air, water, and soils."[49] According to French environment minister Nathalie Kosciusko-Morizet, an outspoken opponent of hydraulic fracturing, permits given to gas exploration companies the year before should never have been granted. "We have seen the results in the U.S. There are risks for the water tables and these are risks we don't want to take. It was an error. . . . An environmental evaluation should have been done before giving out the permits and not after. . . . There is only one technology that can be used today to produce shale gas and that's hydraulic fracturing and we don't want it."[50]

One can anticipate that the French government will likely condition relaxation of this moratorium, if ever, on an industry-wide commitment to reduce the amount of water needed for the hydraulic fracturing process, placing strict limits on the number and spacing of wells, and other verifiable measures that will reliably protect the environment.

United Kingdom

In Great Britain, the Energy and Climate Change Secretary gave hydraulic fracturing a clean bill of health and insisted it was subject to robust controls. The House of Commons Energy Select Committee also supported the hydraulic fracturing procedure, arguing that Great Britain could have considerable reserves of shale gas that should be exploited in order to reduce the country's reliance on imported energy. Then two earthquakes were recorded in Lancashire, England, in June 2011, leading members of Parliament to call for an investigation into the safety and environmental impacts of drilling for shale gas, based on concerns that hydraulic fracturing could have triggered the seismic activity, in addition to contaminating local water supplies.[51] Cuadrilla Resources, the British company that was exploring for gas in shale formations deep underground, promptly announced that it was temporarily halting hydraulic fracturing operations near Blackpool, in Lancashire after indications that it might have set off the two earthquakes.[52]

South Africa

In mid-April 2011, South Africa's cabinet placed a moratorium on natural gas exploration licenses in the semiarid Karoo region, a vast and ecologically sensitive region where hydraulic fracturing was about to be deployed. Karoo, which means "land of great thirst," is a region that covers much of the 800 miles between Johannesburg and Cape Town, and according to the U.S. Energy Information Administration (EIA) might hold shale gas reserves of about 485 tcf, making this region's shale gas fields the fifth largest in the world. Protection of the Karoo has been had been high priority for conservationists and Karoo farmers. An April 2011 statement issued by the South African government noted that, "The Cabinet has endorsed the decision by the department of minerals to invoke a moratorium on licenses in the Karoo, where hydraulic fracturing is proposed."[53] The minister of mineral resources placed a moratorium on all applications for prospecting licenses through the end of February 2012 to allow for an investigation into hydraulic fracturing, as well as public consultation.[54]

In light of South Africa's heavy dependence on coal-fired power stations for its electricity and crude oil imports for its fuel, an alternative local energy source would have a major impact on the country's energy security. In September 2012, in a move described as a game changer for the South African economy, the South African cabinet decided to lift the moratorium following receipt of a study by a technical task team that eased safety concerns over the hydraulic fracturing method, recommending that it was clearly safe to have that program of exploration of shale gas.[55] The decision was not without its critics, however, who pledged to seek a ruling from South Africa's highest court against hydraulic fracturing on environmental grounds. Environmental groups criticized the decision as hasty and ill-informed, claiming hydraulic fracturing would cause permanent harm, would use a lot of water with enormous amounts of chemicals in a water scarce area, and could endanger rare species of mountain zebra and riverine rabbit living in the sparsely populated Karoo.[56]

Quebec, Canada

Since March 2011, Quebec has banned further hydraulic fracturing for natural gas. Gas leaks at wells that had been hydraulically fractured in Quebec led government officials to question industry control of drilling operations.[57] On September 27, 2012, shortly after the Parti Quebecois government had been installed, Quebec's natural resources minister, Nathalie Normandeau, made it clear that a long-term ban on hydraulic fracturing by the shale gas industry would likely be imposed, stating that she did not believe hydraulic fracturing could ever be done safely. Normandeau noted, "I don't foresee a day when there will be technology that will allow safe exploitation (of shale gas). Our position is very clear—we want a complete moratorium, not only on exploitation but also on exploration of shale gas. We haven't changed our minds."[58]

Bulgaria, Romania, and Other Eastern European Nations

Chevron was anticipating the "next fossil fuel extraction boom in [Eastern Europe]" as it moved ahead with "quietly acquiring rights to drill for natural gas using hydraulic fracturing technology," but the growing opposition has thwarted its plans thus far.[59] According to Guy Chazan, "For years, [Chevron] has been snapping up exploration acreage along a geological faultline that stretches from the Baltic to the Black Sea. A crucial piece of its jigsaw fell into place in May [2012] when it won the right to negotiate a big shale gas contract in Ukraine. That left it with an almost continuous arc of concessions stretching from Bulgaria in the south-east to Poland in the north. The blocks in Romania alone cover 2,700sq km."[60] Faced with a major protest against Chevron's plans to drill in the most fertile farm region in the country, Bulgaria banned hydraulic fracturing.[61]

Romania, like almost all of the countries in this region, wants affordable energy, but politicians have taken note of the NIMBY (not in my back yard) contingent as well as modern technology and social media through which antifracking petition drives have been publicized. In Romania, Chevron encountered fierce opposition, after it had already acquired licenses in the northeast and southeast Dobrogea region near its southern border with Bulgaria and in the northeastern part of the country near the border with Moldava. According to Nicolae Rotaru of Civic Platform in Romania, "We examined the Chevron contract and . . . encountered suspicious secrecy at all levels. We want a law to be worked out to regulate the drilling for shale gas in Romania . . . It is dangerous for human life."[62]

When the new government came into power in mid-2012 under the leadership of Victor Ponta, the centre-left prime minister, it imposed a moratorium on shale gas exploration and extraction. A campaign was waged against the former government's decision to grant Chevron a license to explore potential shale gas deposits in the Barlad Block, near the border with Moldova, following which the situation was unclear as to whether the moratorium on exploration, extraction, and production was actually in force, and, if it was, what exactly it covered. According to a Romanian analyst, the new Romanian government put all contracts on hold, probably because they were the pet projects of the previous administration, and the new government has closer ties to Russia and local oil-producing companies, which in turn may translate into long delays for hydraulic fracturing projects. The Ponta government has not ruled out developments and says it will lift the hydraulic fracturing moratorium if investigations prove hydraulic fracturing to be environmentally safe.[63]

State-Owned Enterprises (SOEs) Reaching Out for Shale Gas Reserves

Canada has recently confronted the politically sensitive issue of how best to address attempts by state-owned enterprises, primarily businesses owned and operated by China and Malaysia, to purchase Canadian oils sands and other unconventional energy projects. Emphasizing the difference between a resource-rich nation being open for foreign investment and a nation being up for sale to the highest bidder, Canada has now adopted a policy to curtail raiding of its lucrative oil sands by state-owned enterprises with interests that go beyond commercial objectives, warning that SOEs will not be allowed to take a controlling stake in Canada' oil sands companies other than on "an exceptional basis only."[64] Canada's newly announced restrictive policy may provide guidance for the United States, which has recently allowed SOEs from India, Korea, and China to invest in U.S. shale gas projects.[65]

International Treaties and Protocols

Existing treaties, protocols, and international conventions can serve as the foundation for a coordinated, multinational, fair, and totally transparent process to address the tempest over hydraulic fracturing. International oversight, monitoring, and reporting can and should be implemented without further delay.

The following types of issues could be addressed by international treaties and protocols: (1) the development of best practices for monitoring hydraulic fracturing sites and wastewater disposal at or near transboundary locations, (2) the development of standards for reporting and oversight relating to remediation in case of spillage, pollution, or equipment malfunctions or accidents leading to release of hydraulic fracturing fluids, wastewater, or pollutants into water bodies, particularly in geographic regions near national boundaries, and (3) uniform standards and regulatory oversight procedures for reporting, remediation, and oversight, including disclosure of chemicals utilized in the hydraulic fracturing process, that would best be promulgated and applied in a uniform manner under a uniform, internationally sanctioned regime back up by international consensus. The existing international legal landscape offers some structure for development of the necessary framework.

Berlin Rules

The 2004 International Law Association's Berlin Rules apply to all aquifers confined and connected to surface waters, regardless of whether they receive surface recharge. The Berlin Rules adopt the principle of equitable apportionment augmented by the precautionary principle and call for the adoption of sustainable management regimes that are integrated into surface water allocation and management systems.[66]

NAFTA

Greater conservation of border groundwater resources shared by the United States and Mexico may be hastened by the North American Free Trade Agreement. For example, the Integrated Environmental

Plan for the Mexico–United States Border Area makes potential groundwater contamination a more visible issue, and the plan's groundwater quality monitoring proposals should promote the greater exchange of groundwater information. Such international collaborative efforts can lead to a more coherent, mutually beneficial, and enforceable regime for addressing pollution of internationally shared aquifers and transboundary groundwaters.[67]

Montreal Rules and Helsinki Rules

An important objective of international water law is pollution prevention, and that objective has been the focal point of several international treaties and standards. The 1982 Montreal Rules on Water Pollution in an International Drainage Basin declare that the right to equitable utilization includes the correlative duty to prevent new or increased water pollution that causes substantial injury to the territory of another state and to take all reasonable measures to abate the pollution. Under the Montreal Rules, basin states are required to cooperate to ensure an effective system of pollution prevention and abatement. The Helsinki Rules and the 1991 ILC Draft Rules integrate water quantity and quality considerations. This is done by the Helsinki Rules by making states liable for transboundary pollution, while the 1991 Draft ILC Rules extend state liability, making them liable for activities that caused appreciable harm to other states.[68]

The Bellagio Draft Treaty on Transboundary Groundwaters

Professor Albert Utton, a leading international groundwater scholar, has proposed a draft international groundwater treaty[69] that would establish transboundary commissions with power to establish conservation areas and adopt comprehensive management plans based on equitable apportionment. The Bellagio Draft Treaty on Transboundary Groundwaters provides an international mechanism to deal with transboundary groundwater pollution.[70]

CONCLUSION

Stepping back from the emotional frenzy and hyperbole that has characterized much of the debate and controversy over hydraulic fracturing and its impact on the environment, human health, and safety, particularly with respect to water resources, we must consider two issues.

One is the fundamentally national issue of how best to achieve energy independence, in itself a global issue calling for international consensus, by securing alternative sources of energy on a sustainable basis to power the nations and economies of our world. Assuming such energy independence can be achieved for a given nation, natural gas may play a substantial role as an economic driver and critical bridge fuel. The other is the fundamental issue of how best to achieve sustainability of water resources and protect the fundamental human right to safe drinking water.

In the United States, a tension exists between local/state and federal control over water resources. There is a strong legal tradition of deference to state law and local jurisdictions in land use decisions, many of which have significant impacts on water resources. The traditional 10th Amendment presumption that states have the paramount right to establish substantive water law with respect to water resources within their boundaries, is in tension with federal regulation of transboundary waterways and water pollution. The expansive reach of the Clean Water Act following *Rapanos*,[71] the assertion of federal authority over state waters under the Endangered Species Act, and other Federal laws have steadily expanded Federal oversight of water in the United States, especially to the extent that water resources are an integral part of waterways and water supplies that cross state boundaries. However, neither of these approaches addresses the regulatory needs of a global shale gas boom implemented by multinational corporations. A more compelling argument can and should be made for international oversight in a collaborative role with member states under applicable provisions of existing U.N. treaties and protocols.

On an international scale, creation of an international mechanism similar to the FRAC Act of 2011[72] may provide the communication and information network that is an essential element of ensuring that our global water resources are protected, public health is not compromised, and states and communities are not exposed to unknown environmental risks. Such an international mechanism is within reach and could develop international protocols for the following:

1. treatment, disposal, or recycling of hydraulic fracturing waste fluid;
2. a transparent and effective process for disclosing the identity

of all chemical ingredients, components, and additives used in cracking fluids and propping material;

3. expanded public input and participation in the permitting process when dealing with transboundary aquifers and water resources;

4. coordinated, independent monitoring of contaminants utilized in the hydraulic fracturing process by shale gas exploration and drilling enterprises should be undertaken by independent public-private inspection entities with established competence and capabilities (a) with complete transparency at every phase of the monitoring and reporting process; (b) grounded on a reliable, generally accepted, scientifically sound, and consensus-based international mechanism; (c) focusing on contaminants such as radium, barium, strontium and other heavy metals, radioactivity, and other environmental risks associated with hydrofracking fluid waste, backflow, reinjected hydrofracking fluids, and proppants;

5. increased public-private collaboration to increase sharing of technology and understanding of the impacts of drilling and extraction processes on the management and protection of transboundary water resources and water supplies; and

6. remediation standards by the industry-provisions to authorize and facilitate payment of monetary damages to landowners and others determined to have suffered injuries or losses as a result of failures during the hydraulic fracturing process, accidental spills or contamination attributable to spillage, leakage, or other contamination above or below the surface at or near hydraulic fracturing sites.

A monitoring and management mechanism could be crafted using the framework of existing international water law, treaties, and protocols designed to address transboundary groundwater pollution, water quality monitoring, and comprehensive management of internationally shared groundwater and surface water resources, including fundamental tenets of the Bellagio Draft Treaty, the Berlin, Montreal and Helsinki Rules, and NAFTA. Creation of such a monitoring and management mechanism would provide states and the international community as a whole with the means to share critical risk-related information and to develop and implement environmental safeguards while preserving the rights of sovereign states to control their own resources.

A recent report from the Department of Energy's Secretary of Energy Advisory Board (SEAB) Natural Gas subcommittee recommends a coordinated, comprehensive mechanism for oversight and risk management.[73] Such a mechanism based upon the above treaties and protocols can include components that parallel the key recommendations enumerated in the SEAB report. Coordinated work on the national and international levels can help strike a balance between public safety and the development of shale gas as a growing energy resource for the future. This requires commitment at every level—national, international, subnational, and private sector—and will not be a panacea. It can nonetheless lead us away from the political gridlock and acrimonious debate over natural gas development and provide a pathway for states and communities to realize the economic benefits of natural gas as a reliable, transitional energy source and a critical bridge fuel on a path to energy independence for our nation and for the world.

NOTES

1. THE EVOLUTION OF THE LAW AND POLITICS OF WATER 408 (Joseph W. Dellapenna & Joyeeta Gupta eds., 2008).
2. Juliette Kayyem, *Rethinking the Fracking Debate*, BOSTON GLOBE, Aug. 22, 2011, http://www.boston.com/bostonglobe/editorial_opinion/oped/articles/2011/08/22/re_thinking_the_fracking_debate/; KENNETH B. MADLOCK III, AMY MYERS JAFFE & PETER R. HARTLEY, JAMES A. BAKER III INSTITUTE FOR PUBLIC POLICY AND U.S. DEPARTMENT OF ENERGY, SHALE GAS AND U.S. NATIONAL SECURITY at 23 n.14 (July 2011) [hereinafter NAT'L SECURITY], *available at* http://www.bakerinstitute.org/publications/EF-pub-DOEShaleGas-07192011.pdf. IHS Global Insight's study entitled THE ECONOMIC AND EMPLOYMENT CONTRIBUTIONS OF SHALE GAS IN THE UNITED STATES showed that shale gas will represent 60% of total U.S. natural gas production by 2035. INST. FOR ENERGY RESEARCH, EMPLOYMENT IN SHALE GAS INDUSTRY TO GREATLY INCREASE (Aug. 15, 2012), *available at* http://www.instituteforenergyresearch.org/2012/08/15/employment-in-shale-gas-industry-to-greatly-increase/; KPMG LLP, SHALE GAS-A GLOBAL PERSPECTIVE (2011), *available at* at http://www.kpmg.com/Global/en/IssuesAndInsights/ArticlesPublications/Documents/shale-gas-global-perspective.pdf (citing Energy Info. Admin., WORLD SHALE GAS RESOURCES: AN INITIAL ASSESSMENT OF 14 REGIONS OUTSIDE THE UNITED STATES (2011)).
3. NAT'L SECURITY, *supra* note 2.

4. NAT'L SECURITY, *supra* note 2.

5. *Opposition to Fracking Mounts in Europe*, ECOWATCH (Sept. 20, 2012), http://www.occupy.com/article/opposition-fracking-mounts-europe.

6. *Id.*

7. Duane Nichols, *Thousands Rally Around the World to Ban Fracking*, FRACKCHECK WV, September 23, 2012, http://www.frackcheckwv .net/2012/09/23/thousands-rally-around-the-world-to-ban-fracking/.

8. *Id.*

9. Juliette Kayyem, *Rethinking the Fracking Debate*, Boston Globe, Aug. 22, 2011, http://www.boston.com/bostonglobe/editorial_opinion/oped/articles /2011/08/22/re_thinking_the_fracking_debate/.

10. Using decades-old technology from horizontal drilling and high-pressure fracturing, deployment of the fracking process began increasing in the United States about a decade ago when shale gas made up 1% of our nation's natural gas supply. As the world market price for gas skyrocketed in 2005, this form of exploration of unconventional natural gas skyrocketed as well, and today, shale gas accounts for 25% of the United States' natural gas supply. *The Rise of Unconventional Gas*, INDUSTRIAL FUELS AND POWER (Mar. 26, 2010), http://www.energytribune.com/3937/the-rise-of-unconditional -gas#sthash.Cj9dOee0.dpbs. Major energy firms are poised to commence exploratory operations to determine the extent of what many believe to be substantial unconventional deposits of shale beneath the surface of many countries in Europe in what has been compared to the great natural gas rushes of the past, with concessions purchased or applied for in Germany, Poland, Sweden, Ukraine, Denmark, France, the Netherlands and the Czech Republic. Ben Schiller, *'Fracking' Comes to Europe, Sparking Rising Controversy*, ENVIRONMENT 360 (Feb. 28, 2011), http://e360.yale.edu /feature/fracking_comes_to_europe_sparking_rising_controversy/2374/; *Shale Gas in Eastern Europe: Gas or Hot Air*, ECONOMIST, June 14, 2010, *available at* http://www.economist.com/node/21007490 ("Only now, with the shale gas boom in full swing, are environmental concerns mounting in the US. In Europe, by contrast, exploration starts with these concerns already being widely discussed. UG production needs huge amounts of water and, more importantly, uses chemicals that seep into the ground (usually at a depth of several thousand metres but that could store up problems in later years)").

11. Deborah Solomon, *SEC Bears Down on Fracking*, WALL ST. J., Aug. 25, 2011, at B1, (noting that the Tokyo Electric Power Company's Fukushima Daiichi nuclear power plant meltdown in March 2011 and the April 2010 BP Deepwater Horizon oil spill in the Gulf of Mexico are fresh in the minds of securities regulators, and that in both energy-related disasters, "some investors were surprised at the risk to which the companies were exposed, and their share prices fell sharply.").

12. Matt Armstrong, *The Process and Policy Implications of EPA's Hydraulic Fracturing Study*, 42 TRENDS, July/Aug. 2011, at 1 (ABA Section of Environment, Energy, and Resources Newsletter); Fred Krupp, *The Smart Path for the Shale Gas Revolution*, WALL ST. J., Aug. 18, 2011, at A15.

13. SEC'Y OF ENERGY ADVISORY BD., SHALE GAS SUBCOMM., THE SEAB SHALE GAS PRODUCTION SUBCOMMITTEE NINETY-DAY REPORT (Aug. 11, 2011), *available at* http://www.shalegas.energy.gov/resources/081111_90_day_report.pdf.

14. International Decade for Action, "Water for Life," 2005–2015, G.A. Res. 58/217, U.N. Doc. A/Res/58/217 (Dec. 23, 2003).

15. THE EVOLUTION OF LAW AND POLITICS OF WATER 339 (Joseph W. Dellapenna and Joyeeta Gupta eds., 2009).

16. *Id.*

17. RT, *Shale Gas: Cheap, Readily Available, Made In USA*, EURASIA REV. (Apr. 20, 2011), http://www.eurasiareview.com/shale-gas-cheap-readily-available-made-in-usa-20042011/.

18. Jakub Parushinski, *Europe Seeking Alternatives to Russia's Natural Gas*, ALASKA DISPATCH (Dec. 23, 2012), http://www.alaskadispatch.com/article/europe-seeking-alternatives-russias-natural-gas; Jonathan Stern, *Natural Gas In Europe—The Importance of Russia*, *available at* http://www.centrex.at/en/files/study_stern_e.pdf; Kevin Begos, *Natural Gas Boom in the US: Is Russia the Big Loser?*, CHRISTIAN SCI. MONITOR (Oct. 1, 2012), http://www.csmonitor.com/Environment/Latest-News-Wires/2012/1001/Natural-gas-boom-in-US.-Is-Russia-the-big-loser.

19. Derek Weber, *From Drake to the Marcellus Shale Gas Play—Distribution Developments*, 237 PIPELINE & GAS J., no. 4, Apr. 2010, *available at*, http://pipelineandgasjournal.com/drake-marcellus-shale-gas-play-distribution-developments?page=show.

20. William Yeatman, *'Fracking' in Europe: Who's in, Who's Out*, GLOBAL WARMING.ORG (May 12, 2011), http://www.globalwarming.org/2011/05/12/%E2%80%98fracking%E2%80%99-in-europe-who%E2%80%8099s-in-who%E2%80%99s-out/.

21. Roderick Kefferpütz, *Europe's shale gas bonanza? Don't believe the hype*, EURACTIV (May 9, 2011; updated Dec. 23, 2011), http://www.euractiv.com/energy/europe-shale-gas-bonanza-believe-analysis-504640. Kefferpütz is an associate research fellow at the Centre for European Policy Studies (CEPS), political advisor to German Green MEP Reinhard Bütikofer in the European Parliament, and an associate at Berlin-based think-tank 'stiftung neue verantwortung.'

22. *Id.*; Kevin Begos, *Natural Gas Boom in the US: Is Russia the Big Loser?*, CHRISTIAN SCI. MONITOR (Oct. 1, 2012), http://www.csmonitor.com/Environment/Latest-News-Wires/2012/1001/Natural-gas-boom-in-US.-Is-Russia-the-big-loser ("The Kremlin is watching, European nations are rebelling, and some suspect Moscow secretly bankrolling a campaign to derail the West's strategic plans.")

23. Nat'l Security, *supra* note 2.

24. *The Rise of Unconventional Gas, supra* note 10.

25. "Across Europe, a host of energy companies are exploring for unconventional deposits in what some are comparing to the great natural gas rushes of the past. ExxonMobil has bought up concessions in Germany and Poland. Shell is active in Sweden and Ukraine. Chevron is in Poland. Total is in Denmark and France. And Cuadrilla is also exploring in the Netherlands and the Czech Republic." Ben Schiller, *'Fracking' Comes to Europe, Sparking Rising Controversy*, Environment 360 (Feb. 28, 2011), http://e360.yale.edu /feature/fracking_comes_to_europe_sparking_rising_controversy/2374/.

26. *Shale Gas in Eastern Europe, supra* note 10.

27. Conversion from TCM to TCF was calculated based on the online conversion tables at http://www.metric-conversions.org/volume/cubic-meters-to -cubic-feet.htm.

28. U.S. Energy Info. Admin., Technically Recoverable Shale Oil and Shale Gas Resources: An Assessment of 137 Shale Formations in 41 Countries Outside the United States (June 10, 2013), *available at* http://www.eia.gov/analysis/studies/worldshalegas/; *cf.* Int'l Energy Agency, World Energy Outlook 2012 (2012), *available at* http://www .iea.org/publications/freepublications/publication/English.pdf.

29. Maximilian Kuhn & Frank Umbach, European Centre for Energy and Resource Security, Strategic Perspectives of Unconventional Gas: A Game Changer with Implications for the EU's Energy Security (2011), *available at* http://www.kcl.ac.uk/sspp/departments/warstudies /research/groups/eucers/strategy-paper-1.pdf; *cf. Supply and Demand*, The National Academies, http://www.nap.edu/reports/energy/supply.html ("Known world reserves of conventional natural gas total about 6,000 TCF, with perhaps another one-tenth of that amount still undiscovered. At that rate, known reserves will be adequate for about 60 years."); *First Viewpoint: Enough Energy Resources for the Coming Decades*, EGOproject (May 10, 2003), http://www.egoproject.nl/Twoviewp.html (quoting Peter R. Odell, Emeritus Professor International Energy Studies, Erasmus University, Rotterdam, The Netherlands, "the reality of conventional plus nonconventional supplies prospects indicates that the industry could progress in an expansionist way for at least another 60 years to produce a mid-21st century almost three times its present size.").

30. Communication from the Commission to the European Parliament, The Council, The European Economic and Social Committee and the Committee of the Regions, Energy 2020A Strategy for Competitive, Sustainable and Secure Energy, http://www.energy.eu/directives/com-2010-0639.pdf; *Natural Gas*, Wikipedia, http://en.wikipedia.org/wiki/Natural_gas#European _Union (last modified Aug. 23, 2013).

31. *Fracking Arrives in Europe*, Wall St. J., July 28, 2011, at B4.

32. *Id.*

33. Anita Elash, *French Farmland Tapped for Oil*, THE WORLD (Dec. 24, 2010), http://www.theworld.org/2010/12/french-farmland-tapped-for-oil/.
34. David McGuire, *Poles Unfazed by Fracking?*, THE WORLD (Apr. 29, 2011), http://www.theworld.org/2011/04/poles-unfazed-by-fracking/.
35. Geraldine Bennett, *DMR moratorium on fracking endorsed in Parliament*, MONEYWEB (Apr. 21, 2011), http://www.moneyweb.co.za/moneyweb-special -investigations/dmr-moratorium-on-fracking-endorsed-in-parliament ("In a welcome and unexpected move South Africa's cabinet has endorsed a Department of Mineral Resources moratorium on hydraulic fracturing, and drilling of any kind related to onshore gas exploration.").
36. http://www.thepetitionsite.com/1/stop-fracking-in-nova-scotia; Ben Schiller, *'Fracking' Comes to Europe, Sparking Rising Controversy*, YALE ENVIRON- MENT 360 (Feb. 28, 2011), http://e360.yale.edu/feature/fracking_comes_to _europe_sparking_rising_controversy/2374/.
37. Schiller, *supra* note 36.
38. *Id.*
39. *Id.*
40. *Id.*
41. In mid-July 2011, European Union officials received a critical report on the consequences of shale gas exploration and extraction, prepared by a German think tank, Ludwig-Bölkow Systemtechnik, and commissioned by the Environmental Committee of the European Parliament. In the report, scientists demand that the European Commission should not only strictly control the process of exploration, but also that it should prepare regula- tions to govern the extraction of shale gas. The report's authors argue that existing laws are too loose and that the fracking process is dangerous for the environment because it requires the use of toxic substances that are pumped into the ground in a solution with water, and the fracking fluids which eventually rises to the surface are contaminated with heavy metals and radioactive material.
42. Joao Peixe, *Proposed Shale Gas Development Stirs Passions in Poland*, CELSIAS (July 13, 2011), http://www.celsias.com/article/fracking-stirs -passions-poland/.
43. http://www.yidio.com/movie/gasland/31651?utm_source=Google&utm _medium=Search&t_source=64&gclid=CJ2Nv4Gt4LkCFZCd4AodrX8 ANA.
44. *Gegen Gasbohren: A New German Anti-Fracking Initiative*, AVA'S TRANS- ATLANTIC GREEN SALON (Jan. 14, 2011), http://avasgreensalon.wordpress .com/2011/01/24/gegen-gasbohren-a-new-german-anti-fracking-initiative/.
45. Tara Patel, *The French Public Says No to 'Le Fracking,'* BUSINESSWEEK (Mar. 31, 2012), http://www.businessweek.com/magazine/content/11_15 /b4223060759263.html.

46. *Id.*

47. *Id.*

48. *European Union Report Says Ban Fracking*, Voxy (July 27, 2011, 10:57 PM), http://www.voxy.co.nz/national/european-union-report-says-ban-fracking /5/96387.

49. *Id.*

50. Mamta Badkar, *France to Ban Fracking*, Business Insider (May 12, 2011), http://www.businessinsider.com/france-bans-fracking-2011-5#i.

51. Nigel Morris, *MPs call for inquiry into shale gas drilling after earthquakes*, The Independent (June 8, 2011), http://www.independent.co.uk/environment/nature /mps-call-for-inquiry-into-shale-gas-drilling-after-earthquakes-2294389. html.

52. David Jolly, *U.K. Company Suspends Controversial Drilling Procedure*, N.Y. Times (June 1, 2011), http://www.nytimes.com/2011/06/02 /business/global/02fracking.html?_r=1; *U.K. Fracking Halted After Earthquake*, UPI.com (June 3, 2011, 7:41 PM), http://www.upi.com/Science _News/2011/06/03/UK-fracking-halted-after-earthquakes/UPI -21541307144514/.

53. Ruona Agbroko, *S.Africa Imposes "Fracking" Moratorium in Karoo*, Reuters (Apr. 21, 2011), http://af.reuters.com/articlePrint?articleId=AFJOE73K 0LV20110421.

54. *Under Pressure: Exploring the Karoo Basin's Shale Gas Reserves has Created Controversy*, Oxford Business Group, http://www.oxfordbusinessgroup .com/news/under-pressure-exploring-karoo-basin%E2%80%99s-shale-gas -reserves-has-created-controversy.

55. *South Africa Fracking To Proceed After Shale Gas Moratorium Is Lifted*, Huffington Post (Sept. 7, 2012), http://www.huffingtonpost.com/2012/09/07 /south-africa-shale-gas-fracking_n_1864260.html; *Update 3—S.Africa Lifts Moratorium on Shale Gas Exploration*, Reuters (Sept. 7, 2012), http://www .reuters.com/article/2012/09/07/safrica-gas-idUSL6E8K739020120907.

56. *Fracking the Karoo*, Economist (Oct. 18, 2012), http://www.economist .com/blogs/schumpeter/2012/10/shale-gas-south-africa.

57. http://forests.org/shared/reader/welcome.aspx?linkid=213318.

58. *Quebec Fracking Ban? PQ Eyes Banning Shale Gas, Shutting Nuclear Reactor, Ending Asbestos Industry*, Huffington Post (Sept. 20, 2012), http:// www.huffingtonpost.ca/2012/09/20/quebec-fracking-ban_n_1900807 .html.

59. Pratap Chatterjee, *Chevron Faces Opposition Over Eastern Europe Fracking Plans*, CorpWatch, (Aug. 6, 2012), http://www.corpwatch.org/article .php?id=15763.

60. *Id.*

61. *Id.*

62. *Id.*

63. Kester Eddy, *Fracking: Easier Said than Done In Romania*, Finan-
    cial Times BeyondBrics Blog (June 7, 2012), http://blogs.ft.com
    /beyond-brics/2012/06/07/fracking-easier-said-than-done-in-romania
    /#axzz2FAUCXdS2.

64. Heenan Blaikie, *End of a Trend? Canada Approves CNOOC/Nexen and
    Petronas/Progress Acquisitions, but Revises Approach to SOE Investment*,
    JDsupra Law News (Dec. 13, 2012), http://www.jdsupra.com/legalnews
    /end-of-a-trend-canada-approves-cnooc-87874.

65. Kevin Brown, *Malaysia: Petronas strikes $1.1 bn shale gas deal in Canada*, Finan-
    cial Times BeyondBrics Blog (June 3, 2011), http://blogs.ft.com/beyond-
    brics/2011/06/03/petronas-strikes-1bn-shale-gas-deal/#axzz2F0FtzOgd.;
    John Daly, *China's Purchase of U.S. Fracking Company will give it Advanced
    Technology*, Oil Price.com (Nov. 1, 2012), http://oilprice.com/Energy
    /Energy-General/Chinas-Purchase-of-U.S.-Fracking-Company-will-give
    -it-Advanced-Technology.html; Colin Sheck, *Energy-Hungry China Seeks
    Shale Gas Supremacy*, Al Jazeera, (Dec. 13, 2012), http:/www.aljazeera
    .com/indepth/features/2012/12/20121211133750745950.html.

66. Dan Tarlock, Law of Water Rights and Resources §11.10, at 11–18
    (2010) (citing *The Berlin Rules on Water Resources*, 71 I.L.A. 337, 385
    (2004); Joseph Dellapenna, The Berlin Rules on Water Resources: The
    new Paradigm For International Water Law, *available at* http://www.scribd
    .com/doc/11564014/The-Berlin-Rules-on-Water-Resources.

67. *The Berlin Rules on Water Resources*, 71 I.L.A. 337, 385 (2004); M. Diane
    Barber, *The Legal Dilemma of Groundwater Under the Integrated Environmen-
    tal Plan for the Mexican–United States Border Area*, 24 St. Mary's L.J. 639,
    642-43 (1993); Mumme, *Minute 242 and Beyond: Challenges and Opportuni-
    ties for Managing Transboundary Groundwater on the Mexico–U.S. Border*, 40
    Nat. Resources J. 341 (2000).

68. Salman M. A. Salmon, *The Helsinki Rules, the UN Watercourses Conven-
    tion and the Berlin Rules: Perspectives on International Water Law*, 23 Water
    Resources Dev. 625 (2007), *available at* http://www.internationalwaterlaw
    .org/bibliography/articles/general/Salman-BerlinRules.pdf; The Helsinki
    Rules on the Uses of the Waters of International Rivers, adopted by the
    Int'l Law Ass'n Aug. 1966, *available at* http://www.internationalwaterlaw
    .org/documents/intldocs/helsinki_rules.html.

69. R. Hayton & A. Utton, *Transboundary Groundwaters: The Bellagio Draft
    Treaty*, 29 Nat. Resources J. 663 (1989).

70. Dan Tarlock, Law of Water Rights and Resources §11.10, at 11–17
    (2010).

71. Rapanos v. United States, 547 U.S. 715 (2006).

72. *See* Frac Act, S. 587, 112th Congress, *available at* http://thomas.loc.gov /cgi-bin/bdquery/z?d112:s.587.
73. The final report of the SEAB Shale Gas Production Subcommittee, dated November 18, 2011, is available at http://www.shalegas.energy.gov /resources/111811_final_report.pdf.

17

Shareholder Engagement as a Tool for Risk Management and Disclosure

Richard A. Liroff

Since 2009, shareholders in natural gas companies have been asking energy companies to provide fuller disclosure of the environmental risks and community impacts of their shale energy operations and the steps companies are taking to reduce these risks and impacts. These requests have been most visible in 31 shareholder resolutions at 19 companies asking for company boards of directors to report.[1] The requests have also come in letters to companies and in meetings with company management. On the basis of engagements with multiple companies, in December 2011, the Investor Environmental Health Network (IEHN) and the Interfaith Center on Corporate Responsibility published *Extracting the Facts: An Investor Guide to Disclosing Risks from Hydraulic Fracturing Operations*,[2] which provides a detailed outline of investor disclosure expectations.

This chapter describes how investors have engaged companies, the impacts of these engagements, and the larger political/social context within which these engagements have occurred.

The shareholder engagements have been codirected principally by IEHN[3] and Green Century Capital Management.[4] IEHN is a collaboration of sustainability and faith-based investors, organized in 2004, concerned about the financial and public health risks associated with corporate toxic chemicals policies. IEHN, through dialogue and shareholder resolutions, encourages companies to adopt policies to continually and systematically reduce and eliminate the toxic chemicals in their products and supply chains. This concern about toxic chemicals extends to the community and occupational impacts of toxic chemicals, such as those associated with the production of energy from shale formations.

Companies adopting safer chemical policies can anticipate and avoid "toxic lockout" from the marketplace, such as government bans or restrictions on products, and consumer and institutional decisions to seek safer products. They also can reduce their reputational and legal risks and enhance long-term shareholder value. Companies producing and selling safer products can gain market share, grow their top- and bottom-lines, and enhance their brands.

By extension, energy companies can benefit in the market place by reducing the chemical and other environmental risks from their operations and, in so doing, protect their "social license to operate." Put another way, they can avoid "toxic lockout" by reducing their "toxic footprint."

According to the website www.sociallicense.com, "social license" can be explained as follows:

> The social license has been defined as existing when a project has the ongoing approval within the local community and other stakeholders, ongoing approval or broad social acceptance and, most frequently, as ongoing acceptance.

> At the level of an individual project the social license is rooted in the beliefs, perceptions, and opinions held by the local population and other stakeholders about the project. It is therefore granted by the community. It is also intangible, unless effort is made to measure these beliefs, opinions, and perceptions. Finally, it is dynamic and non-permanent because beliefs, opinions and perceptions are subject to change as new information is acquired. Hence the social license has to be earned and then maintained.

The International Energy Agency (IEA), in its 2012 report, *Golden Rules for a Golden Age of Gas*, addressed the need of the energy industry to maintain or earn its social license to operate, stating that "full transparency, measuring and monitoring of environmental impacts and engagement with local communities are critical to addressing public concerns."[5] IEA continued, "Operators need to explain openly and honestly their production practices, the environmental, safety, and health risks and how they are addressed."[6] IEA emphasized quantitative reporting. Following a heading of "measure, disclose, engage," IEA described the need to establish baselines for key environmental indicators—provide operational data on water use, waste water, and air emissions; consider establishing emissions targets; and recognize the case for third party certification of industry performance.[7]

A similar call for enhanced quantitative reporting had been made in 2011 by an advisory panel to the secretary of the U.S. Department of Energy. The panel's August 2011 report addressed public perceptions, adequacy of existing chemical disclosures, emissions of airborne contaminants, and other issues pertinent to practices and indicators.[8] In a November 2011 follow-up report, the panel urged that companies "adopt a more visible commitment to using quantitative measures as a means of achieving best practice and demonstrating to the public that there is continuous improvement in reducing the environmental impact of shale gas production."[9]

The U.S. Securities and Exchange Commission (SEC) has also begun to push for greater disclosure. SEC staff have sought "detailed information about oil and gas companies' hydraulic fracturing operations, including environmental impacts" and are looking for whether companies are disclosing risks associated with the practice.[10] The list of SEC areas of inquiry reportedly has included:

1. Established steps to ensure that drilling, casing, and cementing adhere to known best practices;
2. Real time monitoring of the rate and pressure of the fracturing treatment;
3. Evaluation of the environmental impact of chemical additives; and,
4. Efforts to minimize water use or minimizing the impact of disposal on surface waters.[11]

Natural gas production from shale formations in the United States has grown dramatically since the early 2000s, amidst expanding controversy over the horizontal drilling and hydraulic fracturing used to access the gas. The supplies of newly accessible gas are an energy game changer, and companies are now examining the potential for shale exploitation on nearly every continent both for natural gas and petroleum production.

Many governments and communities around the world are looking to learn from the United States' experience before deciding whether and how to permit exploitation of their shale resources. In the United States, there have been numerous incidents of poorly constructed wells, equipment failures, degraded local and regional air quality, water contamination, strained community relations, and related government enforcement actions and private lawsuits. Moratoria or bans have been proposed in New York State, by the Delaware River Basin Commission, and by local governments in several U.S. states. Outside the United States, France, Bulgaria, and the Province of Quebec, Canada, among other jurisdictions, have acted to delay or ban hydraulic fracturing.

Social License to Operate and Shareholder Advocacy

Bans and moratoria are denials of companies' social license—denials of public consent—to operate arising from concerns about environmental and social risks. Bans and moratoria impose a wide range of costs on companies, ranging from the costs of delays to complete loss of access to valuable resources where sunk costs must be written off.

Companies must be publicly transparent about managing their environmental footprint and social impacts and engage with key community stakeholders to earn and maintain their social license. Transparency requires full disclosure of steps being taken to minimize risks, acknowledgment of challenges and failures, and clearly defined steps to continually improve operations.

Reducing environmental and community impacts requires not only strengthening federal, state, and local regulations, but encouraging the industry to take protective, precautionary steps where stringent regulations have not yet been adopted or where they are not well-implemented. Investors offer a unique voice. Shareholders advocate for reducing environmental and community risks, separate from grassroots activists and regulators. Shareholders also strengthen progressive company voices too often drowned out by trade associations and laggard companies.

INVESTOR INFORMATION NEEDS AND THE BUSINESS CASE FOR BEST PRACTICES

Generally speaking, investors make decisions based on assessments of risks and rewards. Traditionally, these assessments have focused on dollars-and-cents financial numbers, but there has been growing recognition within the investment community that the value of investments can be affected by how well companies manage environmental, social, and governance challenges. In investor parlance, these have come to be known as "ESG" factors.[12] Within this broader context, investors require specific, detailed information about how companies manage natural gas operations' risks and rewards. It is necessary for investors to have assurances that company managers are reducing business risks by addressing operational hazards and are capturing the genuine, measurable business rewards flowing from environmental management practices that have the potential to lower costs, increase profits, and enhance community acceptance. Investors require relevant, reliable, and comparable information about companies' natural gas operations to make investment judgments based on a robust assessment of companies' environmental, social, and governance policies, practices and performance.

From a business management perspective, companies adopting best practices can do the following:

1. drive operational efficiencies (reduced costs yield increased margins and profitability);[13]
2. provide insurance in case of accident or natural disaster (lower toxicities and volumes of chemicals reduce risks from chemical spills);[14]
3. reduce air emissions and fresh water withdrawals that trigger violations of environmental standards (regulators consequently may ban and limit operations); and,[15]
4. protect and enhance companies' social license to operate by increasing the odds of positive community response to the best-managed, most transparent companies addressing community needs and concerns.

Since mid-2009, through dialogues with companies and shareholder resolutions, investors have been seeking increased disclosure by companies of the environmental risks and community (social) impacts associated with natural gas operations in shale formations and the policies and procedures they are adopting to reduce or eliminate these risks (e.g., traffic congestion and housing shortages). Risks are associated with the entire life cycle of operations, although much public discussion focuses on fracturing or "fracking." Fracturing and horizontal drilling combined has made a substantial recovery of gas from shale economically possible and has brought drilling and production to localities on a scale previously not experienced.

The operations include:

1. taking steps to minimize surface footprint—disruption of natural ecosystems and damage to human communities;[16]
2. transporting millions of gallons of water and thousands of gallons of chemicals to each well site;
3. selecting chemical additives for fracturing;
4. placing layers of pipes and protective cement in the bore hole to prevent leaks;
5. breaking apart (fracturing) subsurface shale formations by injecting water, sand,[17] and chemicals under thousands of pounds of pressure;
6. storing the water and chemicals that return to the surface during the fracturing process (including naturally occurring toxic chemicals in the formation that also surface during gas production);
7. moving and treating waste waters; and
8. managing air pollutants.

Extracting the Facts—Investor Disclosure Guidelines

In 2011, IEHN and the Interfaith Center on Corporate Responsibility published *Extracting the Facts: An Investor Guide to Disclosing Risks from Hydraulic Fracturing Operations.* The guidelines identify core management goals, best management practices, and key performance indicators for assessing progress. They have earned support from investment managers and advisors and asset owners responsible for $1.3 trillion in assets under management in North America, Europe, and Australia.[18]

Extracting the Facts emerged from two sets of engagement processes—the traditional shareholder resolutions and dialogues on the one hand, and Chatham House Rule[19] conversations on the other, described in the next section. From both these processes emerged the idea that both companies and investors would be well-served by a published set of guidelines capturing investor reporting expectations of oil and gas companies.

The guide is organized around 12 core management goals, recommended practices to implement them, and indicators for reporting progress.

Twelve core management goals for natural gas operations include:

1. *Manage risks transparently and at the Board level.* Ensure environmental, health, safety, and social risks are core elements of corporate risk management strategy.
2. *Reduce surface footprint.* Minimize surface disruption from natural gas exploration and production activities.
3. *Assure well integrity.* Achieve zero incidences for accidental leaks of hazardous gases and fluids from well sites.
4. *Reduce and disclose all toxic chemicals.* Comprehensively disclose and virtually eliminate toxic chemicals used in fracturing operations.
5. *Protect water quality by rigorous monitoring.* Identify baseline conditions in neighboring water bodies and drinking water sources and routinely monitor quality during natural gas operations.
6. *Minimize fresh water use.* Draw the minimum potable water necessary to conduct fracturing operations, substituting nonpotable sources to the fullest extent practicable.
7. *Prevent contamination from waste water.* Store waste water in secure, closed containers, not in pits open to the atmosphere, and recycle and reuse waste water to the maximum extent practicable.
8. *Minimize and disclose air emissions.* Prevent/minimize emissions of greenhouse gases and toxic chemicals by systematically identifying emission sources of all sizes, implement operational practices to reduce emissions, install emission control equipment, and monitor ambient air quality prior to and during operations.
9. *Prevent contamination from solid waste and sludge residuals.* Minimize risks and impacts by deploying closed loop systems for solid waste and sludge residuals from drilling and

fracturing operations and fully characterizing and tracking toxic substances.

10. *Assure best in class contractor performance.* Systematically assess contractor performance against the company's own BMPs and KPIs across the entire range of environmental, health, safety, and social concerns, with the objective of engaging and retaining best-in-class, continually improving contractors.

11. *Secure community consent.* During the site selection process, identify all communities impacted and address major concerns central to community acceptance of company operations; establish community engagement process and third party conflict resolution mechanisms.

12. *Disclose fines, penalties, and litigation.* Acknowledge performance issues by disclosing infractions, legal controversies, and lessons learned.

Some of the practices are immediately implementable, for example systematic use of "green completions" to minimize air emissions, while some are more aspirational, such as "virtual elimination" of toxic chemicals from fracturing operations. The guide draws on documented examples of 17 different companies' use of best practices.

The guide also addresses a central concern that invariably arises in discussions of best practices—that a one size fits all best practice may in fact not be best in all situations and might even create perverse incentives. To address this sticking point, the guide adopts the approach of "comply or explain." "Comply or explain" provides companies with an off-ramp for not using best practices in all cases. For example, "green completions" to reduce emissions are increasingly used to reduce air emissions, but they are more relevant to development wells than to exploratory wells. So a company could report that its planning process makes "green completions" the default choice for well completion, except where such completions are not technically feasible.

The companies most likely to be trusted by investors and most readily welcomed by local communities will be those that:

1. Have an across-the-board, transparent record of voluntary actions to reduce the quantity and toxicity of chemicals;

2. Develop innovative methods for reducing use of fresh water—for example, recycling fracturing waste waters or using saline or industrial waste waters for fracturing;

3. Systematically inventory and reduce air emissions from operations, including using green completions where appropriate and substituting closed waste storage structures for open pits;
4. Closely oversee their contractors to prevent shoddy well construction and demonstrate rapid emergency response capability;
5. Know what's in their waste and what happens to it;
6. Anticipate and respond to local community noise, road damage, nuisance, and broader social concerns, such as public safety, public health, and community disruption; and,
7. Acknowledge regulatory transgressions and lessons learned from them.

GUIDELINES IN PRACTICE—A CASE STUDY OF PROMOTING CHEMICAL TOXICITY REDUCTION

To help drive the market for safer chemicals, *Extracting the Facts* specifies a core goal to "reduce and disclose all toxic chemicals," elaborating on that as "comprehensively disclose and virtually eliminate toxic chemicals used in fracturing operations."[20] It specifies several best practices to achieve this goal and three key performance indicators for tracking progress. The case study below further describes models of best practice and available tools.

Risks of contamination by toxic chemicals strongly drive public fear of shale gas operations. The public fears known chemicals (such as acids and biocides that are toxic) as well as the unknown chemicals hidden behind claims of confidential business information. These fears, together with a wider array of concerns about the environmental and community impacts of shale energy operations, translate into the potential loss of companies' social license to operate.

Oil and gas producers have made sizeable strides in disclosing many of the chemicals. But three major questions remain substantially unaddressed:

1. Do producers have systems in place to evaluate whether they are using more toxic chemicals than necessary?
2. What are producers doing to encourage their suppliers to provide safer alternatives?

3. What tools can suppliers use to develop and market safer alternatives?

The economic benefits from smarter management of chemicals include lower costs when fewer chemicals are used and reduced environmental damage and litigation risks from operating errors and accidents. Another potential benefit is reduced delay on projects that might arise from community opposition.

The oil and gas industry understandably downplays the hazards from fracturing chemicals. It stresses they are a very small percentage of the fluids going down the bore hole—approximately 1 percent or less—and these chemicals are commonly found in household products. This rationale ignores scale and life cycle.

Millions of gallons of fluid (mainly water) are used for fracturing, so for a single well, thousands of gallons of chemicals will be hauled to the job site, stored on location, and then pumped down the hole. For example, a fracturing operation using three million gallons of water would likely use 15,000–30,000 gallons of chemicals. Multiply this by thousands of wells drilled in major shale plays and you will get the picture. Some of these fluids will return to the surface and require storage, treatment, and disposal. The greatest contamination risks appear to stem from spills on the surface and from poorly constructed wells.

Described below is a five-part prescription the energy industry should follow to lower hydraulic fracturing's chemical impact and address community concerns with more meaningful public disclosure.

1. Develop a chemical reduction program. Relatively few shale energy producers publicly describe their programs for reducing and eliminating worrisome chemicals. For example, Encana has established a Responsible Products Program.[21] Through its Responsible Product Assessment Tool that taps government toxicity databases, Encana assesses chemicals and decides whether to eliminate them or reduce their risks. Encana prohibits the use of any hydraulic fracturing fluid products containing diesel, 2-Butoxyethanol (2-BE) or benzene and has determined that none of its fracturing products contain arsenic, cadmium, chromium, lead, or mercury.

Chesapeake Energy established its Green Frac program[22] in 2009 to systematically review chemical use. Chesapeake states it eliminated 25 percent of the additives used in hydraulic fracturing fluids in most of its shale plays. Chevron has claimed a reduction of 77 percent in the number of chemical additives requiring Material Safety Data Sheets (documents describing hazardous materials as defined under federal occupational safety law).[23] Neither company has provided further details on specific chemicals eliminated.

UK-based BG Group states,[24] "We do not use diesel or benzene, toluene, ethylbenzene, and xylenes (BTEX) chemicals in hydraulic fracturing fluids in any of our unconventional gas operations."

To systematically reduce chemical risks, all energy-producing companies in shale plays should commit to quickly phasing out "the worst of the worst" chemicals. They should dedicate staff or consultants to continually evaluate chemical additive use and, in requests for proposals and other procurements, should ask their contractors to provide reduced toxicity options. Producing companies should routinely report the results of such efforts publicly.

2. Create a chemical scoring system. There's money to be made from safer chemical alternatives. Oilfield services company Baker Hughes has developed a toxicity scoring system[25] and new product lines[26] so that producing companies can select less-toxic additives to meet their needs. Similarly, Halliburton has also developed a toxicity scoring system[27] and new product lines.[28] Halliburton even presents on its website a cumulative tally of gallons of biocide eliminated through use of its CleanStream process that relies on ultraviolet light for bacteria control.

3. Develop safer alternatives. Baker Hughes, one of the primary providers of hydraulic fracturing services to oil and gas producers in the United States, has demonstrated[29] how a scoring system can be used to drive competition among chemical suppliers to provide safer alternatives. It has placed the highest priority on eliminating diesel oil from its fracturing additives. In 2011, it reported successfully forgoing the use of at least 7.5 million gallons of diesel oil per year through product reformulation. By doing so, it has also removed benzene and some other toxic components of diesel oil.

4. Press suppliers for alternatives. Baker Hughes next pursued priority pollutants designated by EPA under the Clean Water Act. Napthalene, one of these, was present in a 100,000-gallon-per-month product used by Baker Hughes. The company encouraged its chemical suppliers to

develop safer alternatives. An initial reformulation dropped the toxicity score by more than 50 percent and displaced 85 percent of the
old product in the marketplace. A second chemical supplier then provided an even safer alternative whose toxicity score is roughly one-
quarter of the initial safer alternative, and that's now been introduced
into the market.

Baker Hughes also targeted a chemical known as 2-BE, a "poster
child" toxic chemical, having figured in a high-profile legal settlement in which health damage from its use in hydraulic fracturing was
alleged (Baker Hughes was not involved in the litigation[30]). Baker
Hughes asked two suppliers to remove 2-BE from a surfactant product. One supplier removed the 2-BE but a second went even farther
and also removed toxic methanol, dropping the toxicity score much
farther. 2-BE has now been eliminated from Baker Hughes' environmentally preferred hydraulic fracturing product line.

5. Increase disclosure. Oil and gas producers point to the website
www.fracfocus.org[31] as their primary means for disclosing chemical
use. Fracfocus is a noteworthy improvement on the virtually nonexistent disclosure of several years ago, but it reveals chemical use only on
a well-by-well basis and provides no readily discernible information
on broader corporate toxicity reduction programs.

Moreover, its disclosures are principally the chemicals listed on
Material Safety Data Sheets (MSDS). The limitations and omissions[32]
of these data sheets have been noted by Baker Hughes and other commentators. Baker Hughes deliberately goes beyond MSDSs, incorpo-
rating evaluation of chemical components not disclosed in MSDSs
in its product toxicity scores. Increasingly, states that are adopting
Fracfocus as a disclosure tool are requiring information on non-MSDS
chemicals to be listed. Regardless of whether states require it, more
companies should be doing such reporting of non-MSDS chemicals.

Most shale energy producers discuss in only the most general
terms[33] their efforts "[to develop] and use . . . more environmentally
benign ingredients." A toxicity scorecard pioneered by the consumer
products company SC Johnson and Son, Inc. (SCJ) provides an
example of how companies might better demonstrate to concerned
communities their commitment to chemical risk reduction. SCJ's
Greenlist[34] process ranks the materials in its products based on their
impact on the environment and human health, rating materials from
a 0 (restricted use) to a 3 (best). The detailed scoring criteria are
elaborated in a superb SC Johnson case study[35] prepared for the Green

Chemistry and Commerce Council. The goal for individual products and the company as a whole is continual innovation away from the poorest-rated materials towards the best.

SCJ's corporate commitment has yielded impressive results. During the first 10 years of the program, beginning in 2000–2001, SCJ increased its use of "best" ingredients from 4 percent to 27 percent. The company's use of chemicals in both the two highest-rated categories—"better" and "best"—increased from 18 percent to 51 percent, while use of the lowest-rated materials decreased from 10 percent to 4 percent.

Shale gas and oil development is a far more diverse and dynamic market than the consumer market served by SCJ, so developing a toxicity reduction tracking system will be a far greater challenge. Notwithstanding this difficulty, if oil and gas producers and their contractors can report such quantitative results, they would clearly demonstrate how they are implementing a toxicity reduction policy. In view of immense public skepticism about the energy industry's environmental concern, their current vague expressions of support for "more environmentally benign ingredients" just don't cut it.

THE FUTURE COURSE OF CORPORATE REPORTING ON SHALE GAS OPERATIONS

Extracting the Facts has found substantial acceptance among key stakeholders beyond the investment community. Four energy companies (Southwestern Energy, Apache, Talisman, and BG Group) have expressed public support for the guidelines as have two national environmental organizations, Environmental Defense Fund and Natural Resources Defense Council.[36] A major New York City bank drew on the guidelines in developing its own portfolio risk assessment process in 2012 and European banks did the same in 2013.

There's a growing trend of individual energy companies developing their own guidelines against which they will report publicly. This began with Royal Dutch Shell[37] in mid-2011. UK-based BG Group[38] and Canada's Talisman Energy[39] have published similar guidelines. Talisman repeatedly emphasizes its focus on quantitative reporting on key performance indicators, though the first such report is not anticipated until 2013. Hess Corporation has indicated publicly[40] that it is working on such guidelines and two additional companies have indicated in dialogues with investors their plans to do so. Chesapeake

Energy has published a list of "focus programs" that also responds to many investor concerns, though the company's numerous regulatory violations and sizeable fines in the Marcellus Shale of Pennsylvania raise questions about how Chesapeake has carried out its espoused policies on the ground.[41]

SHAREHOLDER ADVOCACY—THE LETTER, DIALOGUE, AND RESOLUTION PROCESS

The world of shareholder advocacy is opaque to those not involved with it. So here's a basic overview, based on investors' shale energy engagement experiences.

The shareholder fracking campaign has been one of the most successful environmental shareholder advocacy campaigns in history, as measured by 30 to 40 percent average votes for shareholder fracking resolutions during the campaign's first three years. Most environmental issues raised for the first time at companies often garner supporting votes in the single digits and take several years to rise into double digits if they get there at all. Although there's a common perception outside the world of shareholder advocates and corporate directors of investor relations that resolutions securing less than a 50 percent are losses, within this world there's shared recognition that a double digit supporting vote signals an issue deserving serious response.

When the numbers of "yes" or supporting votes rise into the 30 to 40 percent range, this indicates that resolution proponents have secured support from a sizeable number of large institutional investors and very likely from the proxy voting advisory services, such as Institutional Shareholder Services, on whose voting recommendations many major institutional investors rely. In the case of the shareholder fracking campaign in 2010, its first year, the votes on six resolutions ranged from a low of 21 percent to a high of 42 percent. During the second year, the votes on five resolutions ranged from a low of 28 percent to a high of 49.5 percent. Shareholder resolutions generally are nonbinding, so even if an additional one-half percent vote had been garnered at the company where 49.5 percent support had been gained, the company would not have been under any legal obligation to respond.

During the third year (2012), the votes on three resolutions ranged from 27 percent to 35 percent. Over the course of the three years, a total of 31 resolutions were introduced at 19 companies. Most not voted on were withdrawn when companies and filers reached mutually satisfactory agreements while a very small number failed to satisfy SEC procedural requirements described in part below.

Companies can vary dramatically in the extent of experience dealing with investors inquiring about environmental and social issues and display a wide variety of responses. Investor engagement customarily begins with a letter from investors to senior management requesting answers to questions. These "inquiry letters" may or may not draw a response from the company, either in writing or by phone. A written or phone response may prove satisfactory to investors or may not. Where there's no response or the response is inadequate, this can lead investors to file a formal resolution (also termed a shareholder proposal) for consideration at the company's annual shareholders meeting to provide a more visible public airing for the issue. The resolution must satisfy certain SEC procedural and substantive requirements that have evolved through SEC guidelines and interpretive rulings.[42]

For example, a resolution cannot exceed 500 words. It must be filed by a date established in advance by the company. An appropriate level of stock ownership for a specific period must be demonstrated. Companies may seek SEC permission to exclude a shareholder resolution from the proxy form if, for example, it can successfully argue it has substantially implemented the shareholder request, or if the shareholder request is so detailed that it inappropriately delves into "ordinary business" that the SEC has deemed beyond the reach of shareholder proposals.

Some companies are more aggressive than others in challenging shareholder resolutions at the SEC. When a resolution is challenged by a company, the filers can elect to withdraw the resolution or rebut the company challenge. The SEC then decides the outcome. Both Chesapeake Energy and ExxonMobil mounted extensive challenges to shareholder fracking resolutions contending they had substantially implemented shareholders' disclosure requests, but the SEC rejected these contentions.[43]

Even if a resolution has survived a corporate challenge, it may still be withdrawn prior to a company's annual meeting if the company and the filers reach agreement on how the resolution's requests can be satisfied. In the case of fracking resolutions, agreements have focused on increasing disclosures by companies about the environmental risks and community impacts of their shale gas operations and the management steps they were taking to minimize them.

Some companies are more comfortable than others in entering conversations with shareholders about environmental and social issues. Many experienced companies see shareholder activism as a "canary in a coal mine"—a signal of an emerging issue of potentially great significance that needs to be understood and addressed sooner rather than later. Investors can be a useful antidote to senior management group-think. Group-think can cause senior management to fool both themselves and less engaged investors, to the detriment of both. Investors can also be silo-busters.[44]

A shareholder request for dialogue can raise management issues that cut across departments and supply chains. Investors can prompt senior management to bring together individuals from diverse corporate departments who should be discussing emerging issues with one another but are not. But then there are other companies who are less comfortable with such direct engagements. The management of one company declined to respond to investor inquiries about hydraulic fracturing, even after two years of resolutions receiving votes in the 20 to mid-thirties percent range.

Most shareholder-company engagements about hydraulic fracturing have followed the tried-and-true process just described. Recognizing the limitations and sometimes adversarial character of these bilateral engagements, Boston Common Asset Management and Apache Corporation embarked on a different, innovative approach. Having evolved a high degree of mutual trust after following the more traditional route of shareholder engagement that started initially in 2003 on the topic of climate change, the two organizations convened a series of "Chatham House Rule" meetings of multiple companies and investors for a candid discussion of shale gas development operational issues. Under the Chatham House Rule, a safe space for discussion is created because nothing said inside can be attributed outside by name or organization. Six meetings were held in 2010 and 2011 including a shifting mix of investors and companies. In addition, one company's technical expert offered a half-day well construction course to educate investors on how to distinguish larger from smaller risks and what companies can do about them.

During the course of both sets of engagement processes, companies were in various ways gradually increasing their disclosures about selected facets of their shale gas operations. Some detailed their waste water recycling and reuse efforts. Others described the steps they were taking to minimize air emissions. Still others discussed their sourcing of millions of gallons of water for hydraulic fracturing operations and their efforts to substitute nonpotable water for fresh water. But overall disclosure remained uneven. They were more qualitative than quantitative and overly reliant on anecdotes telling positive stories rather than on systematic data. As noted in the preceding section, this unevenness led to development of *Extracting the Facts*.

THE EVOLVING CONTEXT OF INVESTOR ENGAGEMENT

Since investor engagement began in 2009, some noteworthy developments have underscored the urgency and timeliness of enhanced corporate risk management and disclosure. Foremost among these is increasing regulation at the federal, state, and local levels. These emerging regulations address chemical identification and disclosure concerns, water management, well construction, and other issues, though there remain serious questions about the adequacy of state oversight budgets and the efficacy of state enforcement.[45] State regulators have been moving to catch up with the sizeable growth of natural gas development in shale formations, but state regulation remains uneven. Many companies report implementing risk-management practices better than their state's requirements. Compliance with existing regulations is just a starting point for risk reduction.[46]

Technological innovation in the energy industry continues at breakneck speed. New approaches to waste treatment and water sourcing, more benign chemical additives, and analytical software for comparative assessment of chemical toxicity have emerged at a rapid pace. Companies seeking to reduce their risk profile and lower costs have a broadened array of tools from which to choose. Waste water recycling and reuse practices continue to grow in popularity amidst increasing awareness of the economic benefits of such practices and tightened government regulations on off-site disposal in treatment plants. Increasing numbers of companies have been voluntarily adopting measures—such as green completions—to reduce emissions of airborne contaminants at some of their locations before new mandatory rules by the U.S. EPA become effective in 2015. They have recognized the economic benefits from such practices and the need to reduce emissions to avoid violations of ambient air quality standards now and in the future.

Extracting the Facts makes it easy for senior managers to understand what they need to report to satisfy investors' needs for reliable comparative information on companies' environmental and social performance with respect to shale gas operations, supplementing customary financial reports. Investor disclosure guidelines encourage senior managers to report systematically on how they are positioning their companies in a rapidly changing regulatory and technological environment to minimize their risks and maximize their returns from smart environmental management.

Notes

1. *Full List of Shareholder Resolutions*, Investor Environmental Health Network, http://iehn.org/resolutions.shareholder.php (search "Search" box for "hydraulic fracturing").
2. Richard Liroff, Extracting the Facts: An Investor Guide to Disclosing Risks from Hydraulic Fracturing Operations (Version 1.0), *available at* http://iehn.org/documents/frackguidance.pdf (last visited Aug. 18, 2013).
3. Investor Environmental Health Network, http://www.iehn.org (last visited Aug. 18, 2013).
4. Green Century Capital Mgmt., http://www.greencentury.com/ (last visited Aug. 18, 2013).
5. International Energy Agency, Golden Rules for a Golden Age of Gas: World Energy Outlook Special Report on Unconventional Gas (2012), *available at* http://www.worldenergyoutlook.org/media/weowebsite/2012/goldenrules/WEO2012_GoldenRulesReport.pdf [hereinafter Golden Rules Report], at 9.
6. *Id.* at 43.
7. *Id.* at 43, 48.
8. Sec'ty of Energy's Advisory Board, Shale gas Production Subcommittee: Ninety-day report (Aug.18, 2011), *available at* http://energy.gov/sites/prod/files/Final_90_day_Report.pdf. The DOE shale gas advisory panel, in its November 2011 "second 90 day report draft" urged "leading companies to adopt a more visible commitment to using quantitative measures as a means of achieving best practice and demonstrating to the public that there is continuous improvement in reducing the environmental impact of shale gas production." (Sec'ty of Energy's Advisory Board, Shale gas Production Subcommittee: Second Ninety-day Report (Nov. 18, 2011), *available at* http://energy.gov/sites/prod/files/90day_Report_Second_11.18.11.pdf, at 9.) Detailed recommendations for best practice have also been provided in the July 2011 report from Pennsylvania of the Governor's Marcellus Shale Advisory Commission. (*See* Governer's Marcellus Shale Advisory Commission, Report (Jul. 22, 2011), *available at* http://www.mde.state.md.us/programs/Land/mining/marcellus/Documents/MSAC_Final_Report.pdf.)

Guidelines have also been issued by the American Petroleum Institute (AMERICAN PETROLEUM INSTITUTE, OVERVIEW OF INDUSTRY GUIDANCE/ BEST PRACTICES ON HYDRAULIC FRACTURING (HF) (2011), *available at* http:// www.api.org/policy/exploration/hydraulicfracturing/upload/Hydraulic _Fracturing_InfoSheet.pdf) and by grassroots community activists. (E.g., EARTHWORKS, DRILL-RIGHT TEXAS: BEST OIL & GAS DEVELOPMENT PRACTICES FOR TEXAS, *available at* http://www.earthworksaction.org/files/publications /Drill_Right_Texas_FINAL.pdf (last accessed Aug. 18, 2013.) The University of Colorado's Natural Resources Law Center has developed a free-access, searchable website of BMPs for oil and gas development in five western U.S. states, characterizing BMPs as "mitigation measures . . . to promote energy development in an environmentally sensitive manner." *See Intermountain Oil and Gas BMP Project*, UNIV. COLO. GETCHES-WILKINSON CENTER FOR NAT. RES., ENERGY, AND THE ENV'T, http://www.oilandgas bmps.org/ (last accessed Aug. 18, 2013).

9. SEC'TY OF ENERGY'S ADVISORY BOARD, SHALE GAS PRODUCTION SUBCOM-MITTEE: NINETY-DAY REPORT (Aug.18, 2011), *available at* http://www.shale gas.energy.gov/resources/111811_final_report.pdf.

10. Deborah Solomon, *SEC Bears Down on Fracking*, WALL ST. J., Aug. 25, 2011, *available at* http://online.wsj.com/article/SB1000142405311190400930457652848417 9638702.html.

11. Gislar R. Donnenberg et al., *Oil and Gas Companies Should Expect Increased SEC Scrutiny of Operations and Reserves*, MARTINDALE-HUBBELL (Sept. 21, 2011), *available at* http://www.martindale.com/natural-resources-law /article_Andrews-Kurth-LLP_1345720.htm.

12. *See, e.g.*, Robert Kropp, *Studies Find Positive Link Between ESG Integration and Investment Performance*, SOCIAL FUNDS (Nov. 18, 2009), *available at* http://dev.socialfunds.com/news/article.cgi/article2826.html.

13. This is often the case with 1. "green completions" that reduce air emissions and create marketable products, and 2. wastewater recycling and reuse that reduces transport emissions and lowers the need for sourcing fresh water.

14. In the simplest of terms, if a company's using a food grade additive in its fracturing operations rather than an acute toxicant or known carcinogen, it's running a lower risk if a pipe breaks, a truck turns over, or some other unfortunate accident occurs.

15. For example, portions of sparsely populated regions in western states have bumped up against the National Ambient Air Quality Standard for ozone because of the cumulative impact of energy operations. *See, e.g.*, Press Release, WYO. DEPT. OF ENVTL. QUALITY, *DEQ Plans for the Possible Issuance of Ozone Advisories in the Upper Green River Basin* (Dec. 22, 2010), *available at* http://deq.state.wy.us/out/downloads/Press%20Release%20ozone% 20advisories%202011.pdf. The Susquehanna River Basin Commission, as a result of local drought conditions in both 2011 and 2012, has cut off water supply privileges for companies needing water to conduct fracturing

operations. *See* Press Release, Susquehanna River Basin Comm'n., *64 Water Withdrawals for Natural Gas Drilling and Other Uses Suspended to Protect Streams* (Jul. 16, 2012), *available at* http://www.srbc.net/newsroom /NewsRelease.aspx?NewsReleaseID=90.

16. For a quantitative comparative assessment of risks from natural gas operations in shales, *see* George E. King (Apache Corporation) *Hydraulic Fracturing 101: What Every Representative, Environmentalist, Regulator, Reporter, Investor, University Researcher, Neighbor and Engineer Should Know About Estimating Frac Risk and Improving Frac Performance in Unconventional Gas and Oil Wells*, SPE 152596 that was presented at the SPE Fracturing Conference, The Woodlands, TX, USA, 6–8 February 2012. For another version of this analysis, *see* George E. King, *Estimating Frac Risk and Improving Frac Performance in Unconventional Gas and Oil Wells* (Jan. 23, 2012) (unpublished manuscript), *available at* http://gekengineering.com/Downloads/Free _Downloads/Estimating_and_Explaining_Fracture_Risk_and_Improving _Fracture_Performance_in_Unconventional_Gas_and_Oil_Wells.pdf.

17. Sand is commonly used to prop open fractures in shale, but manufactured ceramic "proppants" can also be used.

18. Press Release, *Groups: IEA "Golden Rules" for Fracking Track Closely with Steps Already Called for by Investors* (May 29, 2012), *available at* http://iehn .org/news.press.pressreleaseIEA5-29-12.php.

19. The Chatham House rule is described as follows at the website of Chatham House in the United Kingdom: "The Chatham House Rule reads as follows:

When a meeting, or part thereof, is held under the Chatham House Rule, participants are free to use the information received, but neither the identity nor the affiliation of the speaker(s), nor that of any other participant, may be revealed.

The world-famous Chatham House Rule may be invoked at meetings to encourage openness and the sharing of information." *See Chatham House Rule*, Chatham House, http://www.chathamhouse.org/about-us/chatham houserule (last visited Aug. 18, 2013).

20. This section was originally published as a blog at greenbiz.com and is reprinted with permission of GreenBiz Group. *See* Richard Liroff, *5 Ways to Clean Up Fracking's Chemical Act*, The Right Chemistry Blog (Sept. 21, 2012), *available at* http://www.greenbiz.com/blog/2012/09/21 /5-ways-clean-frackings-chemical-act.

21. Encana Corp., Responsible Products Program, http://www.encana.com /environment/water/fracturing/products.html (last visited Aug. 18, 2013).

22. Chesapeake Energy Corp., Green Frac Hydraulic Fracturing Process, http://www.askchesapeake.com/Pages/Green-Frac.aspx (last visited Aug. 18, 2013).

23. Chevron Corp., Responsible Gas Development, http://www.chevron .com/deliveringenergy/naturalgas/shalegas/responsibleshalegasdevelop ment/ (last visited Aug. 18, 2013).

24. BG Group plc., BG Group's Public Position, http://www.bg-group.com /OurBusiness/OurBusiness/Pages/UnconventionalGasResources_position .aspx (last visited Aug. 18, 2013).

25. Andy Jordan et al., Quantitative Ranking Measures Oil Field Chemicals Environmental Impact (Soc'y Petrol. Eng'rs 135517, 2010), *available at* http://public.bakerhughes.com/ShaleGas/collateral/Quantitative _Ranking_Measures_Oil%20Field_Chemicals_Environmental_Impact.pdf.

26. Baker Hughes, The BJ SmartCare System (2010), *available at* http:// public.bakerhughes.com/ShaleGas/collateral/31157.SmartCare_PO_1210 .pdf.

27. Halliburton, Chemistry Scoring Index for Production Enhancement (2013), http://www.halliburton.com/public/pe/contents/Data_Sheets/web/H /H09731.pdf (last visited Aug. 20, 2013).

28. Halliburton, Clean Innovations, http://www.halliburton.com/public /projects/pubsdata/Hydraulic_Fracturing/CleanSuite_Technologies.html (last visited Aug. 18, 2013).

29. Harold D. Brannon et al., Progression Toward Implementation of Environmentally Responsible Fracturing Processes (Soc'y Petrol. Eng'rs Ann. Tech. Conf. and Exhibition, 30 Oct.-2 Nov. 2011, Denver, Colo., 147534-MS, 2011).

30. Donna Gray, *EnCana's Denial Doesn't Deter Woman*, Post Indep. (Jul. 20, 2005), http://www.postindependent.com/article/20050720/VALLEY NEWS/50719013.

31. FracFocus Chemical Disclosure Registry, http://fracfocus.org/ (last visited Aug. 18, 2013).

32. Jordan et al., *supra* note 25.

33. Appalachian Shale Recommended Practices Grp., Recommended Standards and Practices (Apr. 2012), *available at* http://www.eqt.com /docs/pdf/ASRPG_Standards_and_Practices.pdf.

34. *Our Greenlist Process*, S. C. Johnson & Son, Inc., http://www.scjohnson .com/en/commitment/focus-on/greener-products/greenlist.aspx (last visited Aug. 18, 2013).

35. Monica Becker, Green Chemistry and Commerce Council, S.C. Johnson is transforming its Supply Chain to Create Products that are Better for the environment Case Study for the Green Chemistry and Commerce Council (GC3), *available at* http://www.greenchemistryandcommerce.org/down loads/SCJ_final.pdf (last visited Aug. 18, 2013).

36. This public support was disclosed by IEHN Executive Director Richard Liroff in public testimony invited by the Energy Resources Committee of the Texas House of Representatives, June 26, 2012.

37. Royal Dutch Shell plc., Shell Onshore Tight Sand or Shale Oil and Gas Operating Principles, (Apr. 10, 2013), http://s04.static-shell .com/content/dam/shell-new/local/corporate/corporate/downloads/pdf /shell-operating-principles-tight-sandstone-shale.pdf.

38. BG Group plc, *supra* note 24.

39. Talisman Energy, Getting It Right: Shale Operating Principles, http://www.talisman-energy.com/upload/media_element/20120910172345/Talisman_ShaleGasPrinciples-English.pdf (last visited Aug. 18, 2013).

40. Hess Corporation, 2011 Corporate Sustainability Report, http://www.hesscorporation.com/downloads/reports/EHS/US/2011/default.pdf (last visited Aug. 18, 2013), at 20.

41. *Pennsylvania Fines Chesapeake Energy $1.1 million*, BusinessWeek.com, May 17, 2011, http://www.businessweek.com/ap/financialnews/D9N9C7981.htm and *Commitment to Environmental Excellence*, Chesapeake Energy Corp., http://www.chk.com/About/Commitment/Pages/default.aspx (last visited Aug. 18, 2013).

42. SEC Rule 14a-8, 17 CFR § 240.14a-8, *available at* http://www.ecfr.gov/cgi-bin/retrieveECFR?gp=1&SID=97c522ab7f56bd2d595a12cb522ac960&h=L&r=SECTION&n=17y3.0.1.1.1.2.88.226.

43. *See Green Century Equity*, SEC No-Action Letter, *available at* http://www.sec.gov/divisions/corpfin/cf-noaction/14a-8/2010/greencentury041310-14a8.pdf (last visited Aug. 20, 2013) and *As You Sow*, SEC No-Action Letter, *available at* http://www.sec.gov/divisions/corpfin/cf-noaction/14a-8/2012/asyousow032212-14a8.pdf (last visited Aug. 20, 2013).

44. "Silo-busting" is an idiomatic business management expression referring to breaking down communication barriers among organizational units that ought to be working collaboratively with one another.

45. Abrahm Lustgarten, *State Oil and Gas Regulators Are Spread Too Thin to Do Their Jobs*, ProPublica, Dec. 30, 2009, *available at* http://www.propublica.org/article/state-oil-and-gas-regulators-are-spread-too-thin-to-do-their-jobs-1230 and David O. Williams, *State Backlogged with Gas Contamination Cases Dating Back Years*, Colo. Indep., May 11, 2010, *available at* http://coloradoindependent.com/53081/state-backlogged-with-gas-contamination-cases-dating-back-years.

46. For example, a March 2011 review by STRONGER, a collaborative effort of state regulators and other stakeholders, found that Louisiana's spill prevention and control plan regulations require development of a Spill Prevention and Control Plan within 180 days *after* a facility becomes operational and to be fully implemented within one year after the facility begins operation. "Consequently, there is a gap in time between the drilling and hydraulic fracturing of a well and the time that the Spill Prevention and Control Plan is required." *See* State Review of Oil & Natural Gas Environmental Regulations [hereinafter STRONGER], *Louisiana Hydraulic Fracturing State Review* (Mar. 2011), *available at* http://www.strongerinc.org/documents/Final%20Louisiana%20HF%20Review%203-2011.pdf. For more information on STRONGER and its state regulatory reviews, *see* STRONGER, http://www.strongerinc.org/ (last visited Aug. 18, 2013).

Index